Sabers and Brown Shirts

The German Students'
Path to National Socialism,
1918–1935

Michael Stephen Steinberg

In May 1933, shortly after the National Socialists gained control of the government, students in German universities joined in book burnings which the world press headlined as a retreat to barbarism and an attack on civilization. Since Nazism is generally regarded as an anti-intellectual movement, this strong student sympathy with its excesses is exceedingly perplexing. In *Sabers and Brown Shirts*, Michael Steinberg examines student movements of the Weimar Republic and concludes that their significant support for the creation of a National Socialist society was affected less by ideas and ideology than by the social climate in Germany between 1918 and 1932.

Drawing on extensive archival research, Steinberg presents the background of student life and politics in the Weimar Republic, focusing particularly on economic hardships, fraternity life, and political and ideological movements. Student reactions to political events such as the revolution of 1919, the free corps activities, and the Hitler-Putsch of November 1923 are recounted, along with the abortive attempt to create a national student union. Noting the students' progressive estrangement from the Weimar Republic, Steinberg analyzes the character and ideology of the Nazi student movement, its varied appeals, and the conditions fostering its success. The account culminates with the book burnings and the Nazis' successful campaign to manipulate and to control university life.

SABERS AND BROWN SHIRTS

The German Students' Path to National Socialism, 1918-1935

Michael Stephen Steinberg

Steinberg persuasively demonstrates that the students' pressing social and economic problems fostered attitudes particularly responsive to antidemocratic ideologies in general and to National Socialism in particular. Furthermore, he argues that student radicalization is a key illustration of the social and psychological crises that confronted the universities, the educated elite, and the German middle classes in the Weimar Republic. A valuable case study of the evolution of a right-wing student movement, this investigation makes unique contributions to the history of education and to the record of the rise of the Third Reich.

who has taught at Northwestern University and Williams College, is program officer with the Institute of European Studies.

The University of Chicago Press · Chicago and London

The University of Chicago Press, Chicago 60637
The University of Chicago Press, Ltd., London

81 80 79 78 77   9 8 7 6 5 4 3 2 1

Michael Stephen Steinberg, who has taught at Northwestern University and Williams College, is program
officer with the Institute of European Studies.

Library of Congress Cataloging in Publication Data

Steinberg, Michael Stephen.
    Sabers and brown shirts.

    Bibliography: p.
    Includes index.
    1. Students' Societies—Germany—History.
2. College Students—Germany—Political activity—
History. 3. National socialism. I. Title.
LA729.S67   378.1'98'10943   77-2638
ISBN 0-226-77188-1

CONTENTS

ACKNOWLEDGMENTS

I have incurred many debts in the completion of this manuscript. I would like to thank the staffs of the University of Würzburg library, the University of Marburg library, the Johns Hopkins University library, the German Federal Archive in Frankfurt, the German State Archive in Merseburg, the National Archives in Washington and the Northwestern University Library for their aid. I am particularly indebted to Herr Peter Johannek of the University of Würzburg library and Dr. Albin Angerer of the *Institut für Hochschulkunde* in Würzburg who gave generously of their time and advice.

My research in Germany was made possible by a grant from the *Deutscher Akademischer Austauschdienst*. I am also indebted to Williams College for two summer grants.

I owe a special debt of gratitude to Professor Hans W. Gatzke, of Yale University, who guided this project from its inception and whose encouragement nourished it to completion. Professor Vernon Lidtke of Johns Hopkins provided invaluable help in the manuscript's early stages and Professor Konrad Jarausch of the University of Missouri made many helpful suggestions for revisions.

Above all, I thank my wife, Salme Harju Steinberg, for her careful critical reading of the manuscript in its many stages, and the priceless gift of her love, patience, and encouragement which has sustained me throughout the many difficult years which I have devoted to the study of German students.

INTRODUCTION

In May 1933, the world press headlined the story that German students were burning books. The bonfires appeared to be a visible sign that newly National Socialist Germany was retreating to barbarism and that the young heirs to the German intellectual tradition were joining an attack on civilization. Student National Socialism did not first arise in the enthusiasm of the Nazi seizure of power in 1933, however. Student support for Nazism preceded widespread electoral support in the population at large.[1] Indeed, anti-democratic action characterized student life from the inception of the Weimar Republic in November 1918.

Large-scale student support for the National Socialist movement and its right-wing bedfellows presents a laboratory test case for the disease which afflicted the German body politic in the interwar period. The reasons for student disenchantment must be sought in the general crisis of Weimar society. Students do not represent a distinct social group. During the Weimar Republic, the sons and daughters of all major income and occupational groups outside of the blue collar and agricultural populations were well represented in university enrollments. Their disaffection for democracy paralleled the disenchantment of the groups from which they came.

Yet while the students represented a cross section of the German middle and upper classes, their experience was also unique. The German student was a self-conscious member of an elite group. His education alone set him apart from his countrymen, indeed from his parents, who in three out of four instances had never attended a university. The division of German schoolchildren at an early age into elite, university-bound groups and those who would enter the economy in their early teens meant that the nature of their educational experience was considerably different from that of the German majority. Their expectations were also different: an academic degree was a carte blanche to social status and potentially, at least, to relative affluence, although the unemployment of the 1920s did not stop at the doors of the educated.

In this century, political activism has been an increasingly common feature of student life. Students are not subject to the day-to-day pressures people face in the working world. They possess a vantage point for viewing society in which vested interests play a lesser role and so are free to approach social action with an eye to moral and intellectual factors rather than self-interested justification. Unlike their elders, they can afford to be constant critics of the status quo. Possessors of an incompletely formed political sense, student activists are often prone to sweeping solutions, root-and-branch social reconstruction, and millennial goals.[2] All these characteristics were present in the German student movement of the 1920s, and they were reinforced by the special elitist traditions of student life.

The student radicalism of the 1960s has, not surprisingly, promoted a growing literature about student activism and a number of attempts to develop a social psychology of generational protest.[3] Perhaps the most suggestive effort in this field is the work of the developmental psychologist Erik Erikson, who argues that young adulthood brings with it the capacity for a more thoroughgoing commitment to others, in more generalized group associations as well as in sexual relations. This commitment is also accompanied by "distantiation," the readiness to isolate and if necessary to destroy those forces and people "whose essence seems dangerous to one's own and whose 'territory' seems to encroach on the extent of one's intimate relations."[4] Erikson's work provides an explanation for common characteristics of many youth groups: the strong sense of group identification, the intolerance for opponents, and the Manichaean attitude toward perceived enemies.

Erikson's theory perhaps most helps our understanding of the German student movement when associated with Peter Loewenberg's group portrait of the psychological background of the Nazi youth cohort.[5] Loewenberg's work convincingly demonstrates the psychological disorientation of German children as a result of World War I, disorientation which may well have intensified the shared need for strong group identification. Nevertheless, the work of psychological theorists has clear limitations. While historians may readily accept the psychological analysis of generational politics, they are still left with the underlying problem of analyzing the direction these politics take.

In analyzing Weimar student politics, scholars have most often rested their cases on ideological explanations. The intellectual atmosphere of the Weimar Republic is said to have influenced the students toward the right.[6] Two factors may be regarded as particularly important here: the general tone of university education and the importance of antidemocratic thought in Weimar Germany.

The university atmosphere of the 1920s has been much criticized; indeed one encounters few survivors without tales to tell of professors preaching authoritarianism or even racism from the lectern. It would be a gross injustice to assert, however, that the overwhelming majority of Weimar professors ever made use of their positions for right-wing propaganda. The fault of the universities was more a matter of omission than of commission. The universities made no effort to prepare their students for a political world.[7] Students were trained in abstract ideas divorced from practical applications. Humanistically educated students proved disturbingly unpragmatic in their approach to political affairs, but they did not in most cases learn their political views from their professors. Indeed, the theoretical nature of university education and the unpolitical professors were targets of student dissidents.[8]

University education did encourage sympathies for antidemocratic ideologies which tried to identify with the German idealistic and romantic traditions. It was not unnatural for students educated in nineteenth century German philosophy to believe, for example, that the nation was more significant than the individuals who made it up. Nor is it surprising, in the light of the continued life of political romanticism in Germany, that so many students believed the ultimate solution to Germany's social crisis was the re-creation of the folk community (*Volksgemeinschaft*) or that the solution to the political crisis was a politics based upon nationalist sentiment rather than upon the creative acceptance of pluralism.

The widespread importance of antidemocratic thought among students in the Weimar Republic, however, should not be misconstrued. As Wolfgang Kreutzberger has noted, antidemocratic ideology is best regarded as a symptom of the student rightward drift rather than as its cause.[9] The significance of *völkisch* thought has too long been overplayed as an essential ingredient in the rise of National Socialism, tending to obscure the similarities between developments in Germany and elsewhere and to minimize the significance of the social and political crisis of the Weimar Republic.[10] Antidemocratic thought gave form to student discontent, but it did not create it.

The tone and atmosphere of student life have also been seen as an important outlining factor in the political makeup of the Weimar students.[11] It is true that the elite university climate tended to promote a high degree of student arrogance. As heirs to truth and knowledge, German students considered themselves highly qualified to lead the nation out of bondage and into the promised land of national and spiritual renewal. They were intensely aware that another generation of German students a century earlier had been in the vanguard of the nationalist movement while conveniently forgetting that the members of the earlier student movement had often been of liberal persuasion. In Weimar, it was enough that students had been leaders before; they could be leaders once again.

The student movement of Metternich's day, in fact, offered an image ambiguous enough to be fully exploitable by the twentieth century students. Early *Burschenschaft* political goals had often been vague or couched in romantically medieval visions of a restored Holy Roman Empire. Many of the early *Burschenschaften* had excluded Jews as un-German. Karl Follen's incorruptibles had pressed an ideology of total self-sacrifice and favored the transcendence of bourgeois morality in the national cause. Karl Sand, the student who assassinated the reactionary playwright August von Kotzebue, was remembered not as the fanatic whose deed provoked Metternich's Karlsbad decrees, but as a hero.

The elite self-consciousness of the student community was reinforced by the hallowed traditions of German student life. When the student left his family and entered the university community, he somehow mysteriously ceased to be a bourgeois and became a member of an autonomous academic order. Many students, to be sure, did not take this transformation seriously, but the widespread acceptance of a special student code of conduct, epitomized by the persistence of dueling, strongly reinforced the image of a separate, semiaristocratic caste, both among the students and among the general population.

The fundamental justification for the unique student traditions was their association with training for leadership. Equipped by his student experience with the virtues of courage, honor, self-sacrifice, and discipline, the young man who accepted the traditional student pattern considered himself eminently qualified to serve the nation unselfishly. Wrenched from their chivalric and humanistic traditions, however, the old student virtues could not survive with integrity. They served only to gird the natural arrogance of young people who already assumed an exclusive patent on the future. The uncritical embrace of outmoded forms eroded the very civilizing standards nurtured by the classical university experience.

After World War II, the student fraternities with long-standing traditions were attacked because of an alleged relationship with Nazism. Fraternities indeed had given form to student unrest, but the system had accommodated the liberal movement of the 1840s and 1850s no less than the right wing in the twentieth century. Traditional fraternities, in fact, served as a brake on the spread of National Socialism among students after 1930, and it is scarcely surprising that the National Socialist student organization at times presented itself as an alternate fraternity in order to attract members. It cannot be gainsaid that the anachronistic quality of the fraternities tended to reinforce the reactionary tone of student life in Weimar. Yet the fraternity revival undoubtedly stemmed from a more general anxiety: the search for an anchor in the past was one solution to the Weimar crisis.

Traditional student life, in spite of its visibility and apparent resurgence, was in fact seriously challenged in the 1920s. While student affairs retained nineteenth century trappings in the provinces, urban universities like Berlin and Leipzig offered a far different environment. There, large numbers of women, worker-students, and foreign students contributed to a cosmopolitan, heterogeneous milieu. The urban university scene, daily exposed to social want and political strife, and in touch with the nonacademic intellectual community, of necessity mirrored the problems and conflicts of Weimar society. And students in the provinces, in spite of outward appearances, did not remain untouched by contemporary pressures; in political and ideological matters especially, they often looked to Berlin, Hamburg, and Munich for leadership.

Since neither ideas nor institutions in themselves were responsible for the crisis, it is necessary to relate the consciousness of the students to their situation and to understand student politics as one section of a larger movement. The authoritarian trend in modern Germany has been linked to the fact that both governmental modernization and industrialization took place in the absence of democratic institutions. Under the Empire, a unique climate of cooperation between the entrenched aristocracy, a status-conscious career civil service, and an expanding entrepreneurial elite fostered the infusion of much of the middle class with aristocratic values and encouraged the acquiescence of the economic leaders to political domination by the aristocracy and the bureaucracy.[12] In the absence of democratic institutions, a semiaristocratic elite, the *Bildungsbürgertum,* from which the bureaucracy was recruited, grew in political influence. The German professionals were rewarded with honorific titles and social deference. Although this elite was once liberal, the privilege and security they won in imperial society, coupled with power on the local level and influence in the administration, reconciled them to a semiauthoritarian government. In the Republic they faced both loss of status and loss of economic security.

The students were potential rather than actual professional elite, although in large part they came from homes of elite or semi-elite status. What is more significant is that they were caught up in a society which offered them conflicting expectations. On the one hand, the university appeared to promise traditional social status; on the other, it in fact promised very little, since employment prospects were limited and the elite status of professionals had been undermined economically by inflation and psychologically by democracy.[13] The Weimar years were therefore marked by a crisis of the *Bildungsbürgertum* and of the universities whose social function had been to educate the elite. Many university graduates and students reacted by rejection of the democratic institutions which appeared to threaten their position. They were attracted to antidemocratic theories and politics which promised to restore security and status.

Jürgen Habermas has suggested that student radicalism is characteristic of societies experiencing the breakdown of traditional homes and institutions.[14] The Weimar pattern was unique for several reasons. The students who rebelled were the children of parents whose own position was undermined. There is a sense of common despair here, which permitted the sons to identify with their families' plight rather than to consciously advance generational rebellion. In addition, the traditional forms retained more strength in the Weimar period. The halcyon days of the Empire were only a decade or two in the past. The international popular culture of affluence that has tended to undermine tradition everywhere was not yet making a strong impact in central Europe.

The rebellion of the Weimar students takes place against a background of social transition. While the universities themselves were little changed by war and revolution, their traditional social role was undermined. University enrollments expanded rapidly in the early 1920s and again in the early 1930s, coinciding with periods of unemployment, but the universities failed to expand the opportunities for academic graduates. Many students lived in poor conditions and held part-time jobs to sustain themselves, jobs which often would have been regarded as unsuitable before the war.

Although the universities shared the hard times of the German nation as a whole, the majority remained elite institutions recruiting primarily from the middle classes, especially from those groups which had been socially secure before the war. The prewar rewards of social mobility and academic prestige still lured students. The traditional universities' faculties, to be sure, viewed scholarship as its own reward. Challenged by Republican politicians to reform, open their portals to the lower classes, and expand their offerings in the social sciences, these universities attempted to reassert their independence and defend their classical approach to scholarship. Afraid that democratic institutions threatened university autonomy and academic freedom, professors and students shared a distrust for a social and political setting allegedly unsympathetic to the idea of the university.

The new urban universities at Hamburg, Frankfurt, and Cologne and the universities of Berlin and Leipzig with their heterogeneous student bodies and their receptivity to new fields, departed from the traditional pattern. In touch with current opinion and receptive to change, the urban universities acted as the cutting edge of modernization throughout the university system. Yet even here reforms were limited in scope; tradition and innovation carefully balanced.

While faculties were too often conservative and complacent, students were restive and open to change. The desire for a unified voice, the political climate, and the increasing need for organization to ameliorate student living conditions combined to promote the formation of student self-governing councils and a national student organization, the *Deutsche Studentenschaft*, in the early years of the Republic. With the heritage of the early nineteenth century *Burschenschaften* in view, the *Deutsche Studentenschaft* adopted a nationalist tone from the outset and in pan-German enthusiasm extended membership to universities in Austria and Czechoslovakia. By the middle 1920s, the student movement had become openly hostile to the Republican system.

Increased enrollment meant larger universities and a period of rapid growth in student social and political groups. The initial beneficiaries were the fraternities, which appealed particularly to the battle-scarred war generation who found there both comradeship and a reminder of prewar student life. Most fraternities had long been nationalistic, and in the prewar period many had adopted anti-Semitic membership clauses. After the 1918 revolution, the fraternities became increasingly political and more or less anti-Weimar. The active Wilhelmine alumni set the early pace, but the students were more radical and sympathetic to the farther reaches of the German right.

The early 1920s were a period of self-examination within the fraternities, and there were serious attempts to adopt a less aristocratic tone. The arrogant social manner of Wilhelmine students was discarded, and dueling fraternities publicly acknowledged the moral worthiness of Catholic and other fraternities opposed to dueling. The decline in snobbishness was, however, not translated into support of democratic institutions; instead, students saw opportunities in mass politics for nationalist agitation.

The fraternities' excursion into politics was channeled through the *Hochschulring* movement that dominated student politics in the 1920s. The *Hochschulring* championed the idea of a *Volk* community both at the universities by uniting fraternity and free students in one nationalist organization and off the campus through cooperation with similarly minded groups and through cultural, political, and social work in the community. While the *Hochschulring* strove to be the student vanguard of a nationalist revolution, it became too broad an umbrella to cover its constituents effectively. The fraternities, too, proved in the long run to be a poor vehicle for sustained political action, since their social goals retained priority.

In the late 1920s, the National Socialist student movement rapidly succeeded the fraternities as the dominant political voice at the universities. It is the National Socialist student movement which represents both an irrevocable break with the past and the characteristic movement of the new era. Superficially, the Nazis attempted to conform to the role expected of a student organization, in order to win adherents. Like other student groups, the Nazis defended the universities' autonomy when state authorities threatened. Like other groups, they sponsored forums and speakers on academic questions. They even encouraged their own followers not in fraternities to accept the fraternity students' code of honor, and in the early 1930s Nazi student leader Baldur von Schirach toyed with the idea of Nazi fraternities. While they accommodated themselves to the university climate, much of the Nazis' appeal was based on their egalitarian image, which was particularly effective at a time when mass democracy was unquestionably the current mood.

Yet Nazi rhetoric at the universities was unique in its thinly veiled anti-intellectualism and its explicit rejection of traditional bourgeois culture. The Nazi students were a clear threat to the university in their demands for changes in curriculum, their introduction of violence into university corridors and attacks on professors' freedom of speech, and their attempts in 1932 to abolish student-government democracy for little dictatorships which in turn would exercise vetoes on professorial appointments. The sweeping nature of Nazi student aims at the universities was therefore clear well before the boycott lists, book burnings, and regimentation of student life which accompanied the Nazi seizure of power in the early months of 1933.

For all this, the Nazi students were popular. Their rise must be read against the background of the declining social and economic value of education. The Nazis promised to solve the Weimar crisis through national revival. They were a mass movement with a chance of success. They appeared to offer the students a leadership role. At the same time they were the archenemies of the Marxist parties who were perceived as a great danger to the university community and the students' position.

The predominant role won by National Socialism by the summer of 1931 did not inexorably develop out of the rightward drift of students noticeable as early as 1919. The students of the early 1930s were in fact quite different from those of the early 1920s, and many of the student leaders of the early Republic who continued their interest in student politics were chagrined about the National Socialist turn of events. But the central issues which had motivated the founders of the *Hochschulring* still influenced the supporters of the National Socialists ten years later. The Republican system failed from the beginning to win support from young intellectuals. The state governments failed to adopt a clear student policy, reacting when there was trouble but not seeking a way to prevent the steady estrangement of students from the Weimar system. The university faculties remained, in large part, unconcerned by student affairs. Employment prospects for university graduates became worse rather than better. Moreover, because of chronic unemployment the universities were attracting many students who were basically uninterested in academic work.

The political issues which interested students were still the same throughout this period: the ineffectiveness of parliamentary government, the weak international position of Germany, the burden of the Treaty of Versailles and reparations, the irrelevance of their academic studies to their lives. What divided the students of the early 1930s from their predecessors was the growth in militancy, the demand for realizable solutions, and the insistence that the student could take an active role in changing society, that endless discussions about an ideal future state were ultimately fruitless. There had always been students who supported this attitude, but by 1931 they were legion. And the National Socialist movement was tailor-made to fit the demand for action rather than talk.

It is in the last third of the Weimar Republic that a generational break becomes easily discernible. The origins of this break were social rather than psychological—the inability of the older generation to deal with the new reality, provoking the younger generation to cast about for radical solutions. By the early 1930s increasing numbers of middle-class youth shared the disorientation that Pearl Buck elicited in her interview with Erna von Pustau:

> The desire to come back to earth, to know what life is, the impossibility of knowing where to grasp it, how to approach it, the desperation of old ways lost without seeing any new way on which I could put my foot brought me to a kind of nervous breakdown.[15]

Nazism provided a solution which represented at once a radical break with the past and a still tenuous tie to traditional values. The left-wing intellectuals, Erna von Pustau noted perceptively,

> ridiculed love. Had they taken it seriously, this yearning of all youth to love and to be loved, had they tried to help them to find a new way, or to fight in order to better the world so that they could really love and be loved and live happily ever after . . . . It was the Nazis who *restored* [my emphasis] the "right to love" in their propaganda slogans.[16]

Unlike the students of the early Republic, the young Nazis were able to reject much of the dross of past custom because it was irrelevant to the privations they had known throughout their lives. They were able to identify with the plight of those less well off because they themselves suffered privations, and in doing so they eagerly associated with the Nazi assault on traditional class divisions. Their decision for National Socialism, however, also reveals their continued inability to make a final break from traditional German middle-class attitudes and political behavior. The authoritarian climate, the acceptance of paternalistic administration, the reluctance to rely on individual decisions, overreliance on the expert, and a general fear of sustained conflict circumscribed the rebellious student movement in its most radical stage, just as it dominated the tone of the society at large. The future professional elite of Weimar, like the elite of Wilhelmine Germany, and like their own parents, valued security and order and had little understanding of Western-style individualism and pluralism. Weimar democracy, with its signal failure to solve the economic crisis, was in any case not the magnet for youthful attraction to democratic political thought and action. National Socialism provided the promising alternative of national reconstruction through order.

The young Nazi by no means came to represent the typical student. He coexisted with the haughty corps-student as well as the playboy, the scholar, and the committed Christian. The Nazi victory at the university must be seen against a background that included the committed, the receptive, the apathetic, and the antagonistic. It is the first two groups that are the chief story, however, and the focus of this book.

In the end these two groups were to conflict. In the last years of the Weimar Republic, a group of fraternity leaders attempted to stem the tide of National Socialism at the universities. But these leaders found they could not really distance themselves from National Socialist rhetoric. After all, they had long used similar slogans. The fraternity leadership was made uncomfortable by the entrance of the political struggle into the halls of the university itself. They failed in their attempt to curb Nazi inroads because the Nazi students correctly judged the mood of the 1930s. A new generation had grown up without any memory of Imperial Germany, and this generation accepted the framework but not the heart and substance of the revolution of 1918. They were partisans of a totalitarian mass politics with nothing but contempt for academic tradition or decorum. It was this generation that would fulfill the National Socialist revolution at the universities.

German student life is unique in that it was totalitarianized from within. This was possible because of the predominant role the Nazi students had won before the seizure of power. It was aided by the ambiguity of the non-Nazi majority in the face of a compelling ideology, the widespread sympathy for such populist programs as work-service, the acceptance of the new ideal of community, and the generalized desire to aid national reconstruction. It was furthered by a self-critical attack upon egotism among traditionalist students.

Unlike the Socialist worker, the student was often prepared for an inner *Gleichschaltung*, to accept a program he half-believed in and therefore to acquiesce in the Nazi direction of his extracurricular self. From the perspective of 1933, the brown-shirted student was often seen as a dedicated, active, hardworking, and supremely enthusiastic young person who was really attempting to live the values which had long been common currency. It was not difficult for the less dedicated to accept such people as leaders.

Youthful rebellion is a contemporary phenomenon which transcends national boundaries. For the student, cut off from his family both physically and psychologically, a radical political movement offers a sense of purpose and identity. The disparity between the ideals of Western society and its realities encourages impatience with the inability of governments to effect reform. Student movements are often progressive forces. The tragedy of the German student movement of the Weimar Republic was its deflection from the path of adjustment to technological society into the mire of fascist repression.

ONE

"Autonomy and Freedom": The German University

The modern German university has several images: the cloistered community of scholars expanding the borders of knowledge, the *Student Prince* world of beer and song, the residence of rebellious students challenging the complacency of the world at large. These images may, on first sight, appear contradictory, but the style and structure of the German university have long promoted student political endeavor, while beer-drinking and politics have frequently gone together. The student image promoted by the university lent itself to political action.

Since the early part of the nineteenth century, the universities have been a unique favored child of national society. The reforms of Wilhelm von Humboldt at the new university in Berlin he established in 1808 laid the basis for the enormous prestige of German higher education in modern times. While the primary function of the early nineteenth century university remained the training of state servants, Humboldt successfully argued that humanistic education served the state's purposes in this regard better than vocational education. An autonomous university dedicated to free inquiry would educate the independent, creative state servants the age demanded.[1]

The reformed universities with their achievements in scholarship and science won international renown and prestige, which reflected upon both university graduates and the student community. The slow growth of the commercial and industrial bourgeoisie in Germany, and its effective exclusion from power until the twentieth century, increased the social and political importance of the educated middle class, the *Bildungsbürgertum*, whose position was reinforced by seminoble treatment, deference, and widespread use of titles. The academic middle class achieved considerable political power through the state bureaucracies and local government. At the same time, endowed with a liberal sense of responsibility which the Humboldtian educational system encouraged, the *Bildungsbürger* assumed the lead of revolutionary and reform movements and

11

spearheaded the political drive toward national unification. As a group, the educated middle classes accepted the premise that intellectual endeavor and free development of ideas were necessary for leadership and the essential ingredients of progress.

The activist students, too, tended to view themselves as a representative leadership group in society and the bearers of the academic mission. Perhaps more than their elders, however, they were aware of the contradictions in their own situation and that of the universities. The free inquiry which the university fostered squared only with the role of the bureaucrat at the highest level; the institutional sphere for creative leadership was ultimately limited. The democratic trends of the modern age conflicted with the elite consciousness which university education encouraged. In the nineteenth century, the disparity between the academic ideal and the reality of periods of repression was one major cause of student activism. In the Weimar period, the challenge to the university's leadership role by the representatives of the working classes antagonized students and professors alike.

The educated German elite suffered perhaps less than other groups in Weimar society. The prewar bureaucracy remained intact along with the educational system. Although the educated forfeited much of their former affluence, their social position was not greatly undermined. But the rise to power of Social Democratic and Center Party politicians unsettled the educated who before the war had not been troubled by noble rule.[2] Democracy, it appeared, meant rule by the ill prepared and ill equipped; the politician replaced the "expert."

The freedom of the university promoted student organization. Students chose their own programs; they attended classes and studied when they wished to. Exams were postponed until the end of studies. "Adulthood" was assumed and the students encouraged to play a responsible, independent role. The universities, therefore, did not provide for the students outside of classes. The student dormitories, cafeterias, and unions offered by American universities were virtually unknown in Germany until the 1920s when such institutions were sponsored by the students themselves.

Since the early nineteenth century university reforms, periods of university expansion were invariably accompanied by the widespread proliferation of student organizations which provided the extracurricular community ignored by the university faculties. The eighteenth century *Landsmannschaften,* fraternities of men from the same region, transformed themselves into the elite *Corps* of the nineteenth century, but they were confronted by new organizations like the *Burschenschaften* with political and social goals. The end result was an amalgam. The *Burschenschaften* adopted fraternal forms of organization and behavior, and so subsequently did the anti-Semitic *Vereine deutscher Studenten* of the 1880s and even the Nazis of the 1920s and 1930s. At the same time, traditional corporative groups dabbled in politics. Student organizations with their independence of the university thus tended to assume two functions: as the social organization of student life not provided for in the university community and as political groups in time of stress. Social organization, for this reason, often provided an entry into political activity.

Moreover the genesis stage of the political student movements ordinarily has coincided with periods of rapid expansion of student numbers: the *Vormärz,* the 1880s and 1890s, the 1920s (and 1960s). The new groups announcing their competition with older fraternal organizations have tended to stress the democraticization of the student community and have linked this stress with the pursuit of democraticization of society as a whole.

Since the expansion of universities bore little relation to the economy's needs, university growth usually engendered a surplus of educated men, unemployment, and fierce competition for jobs, a particularly serious problem in a society that limited the nature of jobs suitable for academic graduates. It was possible for militant students to seek solutions in two spheres: by challenging snobbish and well-connected elements at the university and by demanding overhaul of the political and social setup of the nation. While student militancy recurred frequently, it is not at all surprising that many student firebrands eventually found respectable employment and exchanged their radical leanings for the paternalistic liberalism of the middle-aged *Bildungsbürger.*[3] Indeed the entire history of German student radicalism is characterized by a tension between elite pretensions to leadership and the identification with mass movement politics.

The Weimar universities accentuated the problems which had long led to student protest. While enrollments burgeoned, the universities proved ineffective both in satisfying the students' educational needs and in preparing them for the real world. Fossilized in a model created a century earlier in a totally different, preindustrial society, the universities' structural organization made them extremely resistant to change. They counted their warmest supporters among traditionalist bureaucrats and professionals whom they educated. Big businessmen and labor leaders, whose influence was crucial in state parliaments, were less sympathetic. A growing public indifference made the universities vulnerable to partisan pressures and subject to financial setbacks.

By the late nineteenth century, the Berlin model fulfilled neither the humanistic ideal of philosophical education nor the needs of German society. The symbiotic association of *Wissenschaft* with professional education worked far less well in the positivistic age than it had when science and scholarship were still closely linked with philosophy. Lectures geared to a professor's current research, while justified in the natural sciences, were of questionable value in fields like law and government. Growth and specialization increasingly undermined the unity of the university.

The university system encouraged conservatism. Control remained mainly in the hands of the *ordentliche* professors who were salaried civil servants with tenure and the exclusive right to sit on examination boards. There were no professional administrators until the Weimar reforms. University rectors were professors, elected usually for a period of two years. The professors in effect administered themselves. The inner oligarchy had economic as well as power incentives to maintain their grip. Limits on rivals, on new popular subjects, few younger faculty on examination boards, or other competition, meant more students in one's lecture room and therefore a larger income from lecture fees. The *Privatdozenten,* instructors without professorial rank, who were initially a comparatively small group waiting for civil service status, by the time of the Republic had become a mass of anxious, unsalaried journeymen who had to wait until their forties to become masters, if at all.[4]

By the turn of the century, the universities were training too many students for the traditional academic professions. Private industry and business, however, found the universities to be resistant to their growing needs. The universities opposed the struggle for recognition and status by nonclassical secondary schools and Technical Institutes. They prevented the growth of economics as an academic discipline. Their failure even to satisfy national needs for research in the favored natural sciences promoted the proliferation of independent research foundations before World War I.

The universities' conservatism reflected a Europe-wide pattern in the interwar period. Expanding enrollments were strait-jacketed into conservative curricula. Few countries were able to absorb the new graduates in traditional professions, and academic unemployment often meant unrest among students and the educated alike. In Germany, the proportion of students studying medicine and law remained stable at over 40 percent of all students in spite of the rapid enrollment rise (40.8% in 1914 and 43.8% in 1932).[5]

The much discussed "overenrollment" might therefore have been less wasteful if the universities had reinterpreted their goals. Academic unemployment was in part the result of general hardship but might have been lessened if university graduates were prepared for a greater variety of careers.[6] The university faculties opposed, however, both the expansion of the secondary schools and the academization of other professions, like public school teaching, which might have helped to ameliorate the crisis.[7]

Until World War I, the universities were more or less protected by university-educated bureaucrats who made most of the important financial and administrative decisions and generally accepted the traditional view of university education. After the war, the universities were subject to the political ministries of the state governments in a period of economic want. Although the Weimar politicians for the most part respected education and scholarship, they had other fiscal priorities.

Although it is difficult to compare prewar and Weimar expenditures, there is no doubt that the universities did not hold their own. New construction was delayed by war and inflation. Funds provided in the postinflationary period were insufficient to bring laboratories and libraries up to contemporary standards. Enrollment grew far more rapidly than the teaching staffs, and the standard of living of the professoriate was substantially reduced.[8]

The universities could have done better financially. The poorer, agricultural states of Baden, Hesse, and Mecklenburg-Schwerin managed per capita expenditures of 5.57, 5.83 and 6.73 R.M. on their institutions of higher education in 1929. Prussia, where the majority of universities were located, could (or rather would) muster only 2.78 R.M. Increased funding would have required sufficient changes to convince financial authorities of social need.[9]

The universities also remained inept at persuading industrial and commercial circles of the value of supporting higher education. Private money tended to flow to research institutions which produced visible results. The Emergency Society for German Science (*Notgemeinschaft der deutschen Wissenschaft*), founded in 1920 to support research both within and outside of the university, depended largely upon federal funds.[10] The Reichstag, guided by a "professor's caucus" and concerned about Germany's reputation for *Wissenschaft,* was content to provide 80 percent of the budget to an organization controlled by members of the academic establishment which until the depression distributed scarce research funds evenhandedly to archaeologists, Virgil scholars, and engineering physicists.[11] Support from the business community proved less consistent. The initial campaign in 1922 backed by an entrepreneurial "Who's Who" netted an impressive sum (half of which, to be sure, went directly to the traditional recipients of industrial largesse, the Technical Institutes and the Mining Academies).[12] In subsequent years, business money returned to its favored research institutions, and such private funds continued to provide only 3 to 4 percent of the society's budget.[13]

When private money was available for higher education it flowed most readily to the Technical Institutes, to the Business Colleges, and to the newer universities, notably Frankfurt which grew around the nucleus of a Business College and continued to emphasize economics and sociology. Indeed the three new universities of the Weimar Republic, Frankfurt (1914), Hamburg, and Cologne, found wide support among businessmen, liberals, socialists, and Catholics alike. Community leaders were associated from the start with new university administrations.[14] Frankfurt, which was supported by an endowment as well as municipal and state funds, drew local support by opening many of its courses to townspeople who lacked normal university preparation.[15] Hamburg's international studies program, which developed out of the prewar Colonial Institute, was a welcome antidote to German insularity. The University of Cologne, financed entirely by municipal funds, soon surpassed neighboring Bonn in enrollment. Cologne boasted not only an unusual number of pioneering social scientists but the controversial philosopher-sociologist Max Scheler who until his Cologne call had been reduced to private tutoring in Berlin and Göttingen. At Cologne, Scheler was able to put into practice his call for renewed synthesis in university education by general lectures centered around themes like "the philosophical foundations of democracy and Socialism."[16] Cologne was also the first university to introduce the scholarly study of theater. Martin Spahn, the Nationalist Reichstag deputy, was the first occupant of a chair for history and journalism.[17] But while the new universities' reforms had some impact in the older faculties, they served more as a means of reducing pressure for change than encouraging it elsewhere.

The older universities, in fact, survived the Weimar Republic with little more than formal changes. In spite of the oft stated fears in the university community that the Social Democrats might use their influence to transform the universities from "institutions of a capitalist class-state into workers' academies," the Socialists were far more concerned about public school reform, which affected their constituents directly.[18] To be sure, the Socialists championed democratic university government, more open enrollment, and the appointment of Socialist professors, but Socialist education ministers who had the power of appointment rarely exercised it against the will of the faculties.[19]

In fact the Socialists played only a minor role in university reform. The first postrevolutionary chief of the key Prussian Ministry of Culture, Konrad Haenisch,[20] when queried about his program, promised to improve the position of the *Privatdozenten,* to promote the careers of outstanding Socialists and dissidents, to create new chairs in sociology, to advance democratic government at the Technical Institutes, and to reverse the general trend to overspecialization.[21] Details for reform were left, however, to "experts," especially Carl Heinrich Becker, a non-Party academician who had been in the Ministry since 1916. Becker, later Minister of Culture in his own right, was the dominant figure in German higher education until 1930.[22]

Becker was a modernist seeking restoration rather than revolution in higher education. The participation of *Privatdozenten* and even students in university government would, he hoped, restore the community of scholars. The synthesis which philosophy had once provided could be revived by the widespread introduction of courses in sociology. The civic education which democracy demanded would occur in courses in politics and foreign affairs.[23] Becker also recognized that, in order to modernize professional education, university reform required increased government coordination and eventually the creation of a federal ministry for education, preferably an enlarged Prussian ministry.

Largely in response to Prussian reform pressures, the universities organized the Corporation of German Universities (*Verband der deutschen Hochschulen*). The Corporation rarely innovated; rather it reacted, resisted, and watered down; but it was receptive at least to the extension of university government to the ranks of the lower faculty.[24] Becker's major accomplishment, achieved with Corporation cooperation, was the introduction of new self-governing statutes at the universities between 1928 and 1931.[25]

Becker's own limitations illustrate the inability of government officials to come to grips with the basic need for thoroughgoing reform. Himself an academic, Becker's goals remained within the framework of the traditional university. A liberal humanist in the Humboldtian tradition, he championed a university devoted to both research and education but recognized the need of accommodating the university to modern society's changing demands. A scholar acting in a governmental capacity, he defended the continued independence of the universities from government dictates.

In accord with his basic defense of academic autonomy, Becker hoped that the universities might be goaded forward through greater participation of students and junior faculty in governance, rather than by outside pressure. His reform program met with initial success in two areas. The course of study was made more uniform throughout Prussia by the introduction of state examinations in new fields of study. University constitutions were reformed in the direction of greater corporate independence and democracy. The *ausserordentliche* professors and the *Dozenten* were given a voice in faculty government for the first time.[26] Most important, the students were also granted self-governing powers, a move which Becker hoped would eventually expand to include their participation in university administration, particularly in the realm of discipline.

Student participation in university affairs was central to Becker's program for the renewal and extension of the medieval idea of the community of scholars in a new democratic context. He also hoped that effective student democratic institutions would help educate the students for later service in public life.

The long-run prospects for success of the Becker reform program are obscured by the depression and the Nazi takeover of 1933. The democraticization of the universities coupled with eventual federal coordination in all likelihood would have speeded curricular change. Becker's efforts did serve to protect the universities in a period when they were vulnerable. Internal reform made the universities "democratic." The synthesis created by the introduction of modern subjects was an alternative to pressures for the total separation of teaching and research. To avoid undue ministerial assertiveness in faculty appointments, Becker proposed participation of national professional groups in choosing faculty. He worked to preserve university funding at existing levels. He attempted to transfer control from the states to the Reich where the universities would be less subject to political cross-winds. After Becker's fall in 1930, the weakness of the universities was all too apparent. Educational ministries receded in importance as finance ministries began to cut budgets, veto appointments, and eliminate class fee guarantees.[27] The adversary relationship with government which the professoriate affected during the Becker years now took its toll.

The fears within the university that Weimar democracy threatened their traditional organization and position were not entirely unfounded. Nevertheless, the universities lost the opportunity for limited reforms which would have provided a certain security. The prevailing siege mentality was communicated to the students, who adopted the cause of an academic heritage threatened by parliamentary politics, in spite of the fact that university reform would have benefited them. Becker's hope to use the students as a wedge for reform therefore came to naught.

Becker's efforts on behalf of the students found few supporters. His reforms encountered indifference and frequently hostility from many professors. The Ministry also faced constant attacks from the left because it did not actively press the recruitment of lower class students and because the Ministry was blamed for permitting controversial right-wing political activities of some faculty members.

The enlargement of faculty senates to include the lower ranks did not alter the facts of university control. The prewar professorial establishment which had put "spirit in the service of power" during the war and greeted the revolution with dismay remained firmly in the saddle.[28] The Social Democrats attacked the "reactionary professors" in the state parliaments and the Reichstag, but were rarely able to use their influence in favor of socialist or democratic scholars. Many state ministers of culture hesitated to overrule the nominations of the faculties for vacant chairs even for academic reasons, because they feared their actions might prove a dangerous precedent for the cause of academic freedom. Social Democratic ministers like Conrad Haenisch, Becker's chief in 1919, and Adolf Grimme, who replaced Becker in 1930, were less cautious. The "imposing from above (*Oktroyieren*)" of professors, quite common before the revolution, after 1919 was a major cause of the tensions between university and government.

Carl Becker·used his influence to defend the traditional freedoms of the university in Prussia after the revolution. He defended the right of free speech in the classroom and opposed the public quotation of a professor's lecture.[29] In order to defend this freedom, he called on the professors to exercise self-restraint. He warned that a professor's remarks could be publicized and advised against statements with political repercussions. The right to criticize the state was guaranteed in a democratic society, but the professors as educators employed by the state should exercise discretion.[30]

Many professors ignored this advice. Becker was forced on several occasions to remonstrate with individual professors who published counterrevolutionary articles, reminding them that they were state employees.[31] Such remonstrations were greeted with anger in the faculties and with sharp criticisms of Becker in the right-wing press.

The majority of German professors did not hold well-defined political views. Their opposition to the Republic rarely expressed itself in open political activities. Many supported Gustav Stresemann's German Peoples Party (DVP) which did not welcome the revolution but increasingly accepted the Republic. The majority certainly supported the conservative and anti-Republican German National Peoples Party (DNVP). Theodor Eschenburg, who was a student during the 1920s, has characterized the predominant feeling as one of resentment rather than hatred.[32] He recalled that professors who expressed open opposition to the Republic in the lecture hall were not unusual, and that at Tübingen those professors who were open democrats were often socially ostracized by their colleagues.[33] Eschenburg cited two prominent historians at Tübingen, Johannes Haller and Adalbert Wahl, who used the lectern to attack the Republic. Wahl, for example, justified the "stab in the back" legend (the theory that the war had been lost on the home front) for his students with scholarly arguments.[34] Eschenburg also witnessed a number of anti-Republican lectures at the University of Berlin.

Those professors whose scholarly scruples prevented them from bringing politics into the lecture room ignored the Republic altogether. Law professors would, for example, avoid any classroom discussion of the Weimar constitution.[35]

In 1919, the Prussian Ministry of Culture directed the Prussian universities to sponsor weekly public lectures on the new Republican government in Germany. Even these lectures frequently became forums for insidious attacks on the democratic state and its leaders. When Ernst Lemmer, a student delegate to the German Democratic Party congress in July 1919, criticized the anti-Republican contents of the weekly lectures he had attended at Marburg, he faced disciplinary action when he returned to the university for publicizing the contents of a university lecture and thus injuring faculty-student trust. The University Senate's decision to censure Lemmer, however, was reversed by the Prussian Ministry of Culture.[36]

Anti-Republican statements by professors were more usual outside the classroom than within it. Many prominent faculty members published books and journal articles supporting anti-Republican views. Others contributed to student periodicals hostile to the state or addressed right-wing student conferences. Although the majority avoided political activities, they usually showed an eager understanding of the radicalism of their students in the face of a government they disliked. Professorial speeches and articles indeed repeatedly exhorted the students to take the lead in restoring Germany to greatness.[37] The professors did not create the anti-Republican attitudes of the students nor did they agree with them in detail, but by their skeptical attitude to the Republic they contributed to the growing contempt of a large section of the younger generation for the existing government.

The universities of the Weimar Republic remained curiously out of touch with political reality. Although they were technically state institutions, they guarded their independence from political power jealously, while members of their faculties felt free to criticize not only government policy but the Republican system. It was still much more acceptable for a professor to hold authoritarian or monarchist views than to support the Social Democratic Party. The inability of state governments to alter this circumstance parallels the failure of the 1918 revolution to purge the courts, the army, or the civil service of monarchist sympathizers.

The universities were invulnerable to outside pressure because of their liberal foundations: no republican government could tamper with academic freedom. University faculties too often defended this freedom only to protect their oligarchic control by an entrenched orthodoxy; they robbed academic freedom of its essential liberal content and limited its application to freedom from outside pressure and defense of internal faculty self-government. But freedom also required an internal dialogue too often lacking. By not providing this dialogue or emphasizing a critical approach, the university faculties failed the students and the Republic. Students were rarely trained to question their own basic assumptions. The idealist tradition which still dominated university education helped prevent many from confronting the real world intelligently. The limitations of

university education were manifest in the frequently vague rhetoric which characterized student political statements. Manipulations of poorly defined concepts
such as *Kultur, Civilization, Volk,* or *Gemeinschaft* provided effective polemic,
although they indicated neither serious reflection nor good style.

Germany's academic community, as Fritz Ringer has pointed out, contributed
to the rise of National Socialism by "cultivat[ing] an atmosphere in which any
'national' movement could claim to be the 'spiritual revival.' "[38] It is not surprising that many students, encouraged by their professors to seek panaceas for
Germany's problems in a moral reawakening rather than in pragmatic reform
programs, were attracted to fascism.

TWO

Property and Education:
The German University Student

Enrolling at Heidelberg or Marburg in the early 1920s, a student might almost think that the Kaiser was still reviewing his troops at Potsdam. The universities of the Weimar Republic were still in large part Imperial institutions which had managed to survive war, revolution, and democratic rule with only minor adjustments. Students were still recruited from the upper and middle classes and their educational backgrounds in large part conformed to the classical requirements stressed by Humboldt a century earlier. Student life was dominated, as it had been before the war, by a fraternity system in which caste and class were essential components.

During the first half of the nineteenth century, the universities had been a crucible of the revolutionary nationalist movement. The *Burschenschaften,* organized in the second decade of the century, combined the fraternal principle with the pursuit of a united nation. The *Burschenschaften* encompassed a diversity of political belief ranging from a democratic faith to a romantic nationalism which sought the ideal German state in the medieval Holy Roman Empire. Many students and former students were prominent on the barricades of 1848 and in the revolutionary National Assembly which met in the Paulskirche in Frankfurt am Main.

Rejecting the revolutionary tradition, the students of the later nineteenth century were caught up in the enthusiasm for Bismarck's achievement of German unity. Politics remained a central student interest, but this interest was now couched in bombastic nationalism. Most students, like many professors, were militant and unquestioning defenders of Imperial Germany. The university became a pivot of Imperial society and graduated young men eager to serve state and nation. The fraternities (*Corporationen* or *Verbindungen*) which set the tone of student life after 1870 embodied the aristocratic and military values of the Empire. Student fraternities were never mere recreational groups of companions.

21

They were designed to develop student character; they were integral parts of the university community with an important role to play in academic ceremony; they offered the student essential connections for success in his career.

The classical emphasis in preuniversity education tended to reinforce the elite bias of university studies. The training that the student received was directed at creating cultivated (*gebildete*) adults who would feel at home on the higher plateaus of Imperial society. The fateful decision about who might eventually go to the university and who would either enter the labor market at the age of thirteen or fourteen years or prepare for nonacademic professions such as elementary school teaching, was made for the majority of German children after four years of schooling when children were usually ten years of age. Only a small minority entered the course that was necessary for university study.

The two-class system of education divided both pupils and teachers. Before the 1920s, elementary school teachers who taught most of the German school children were not university educated but attended separate pedagogical academies. Admission to the universities was contingent, for most of the nineteenth century, upon passage of the *Abitur* examination (*Abiturienten-prüfung*) upon completion of the classical *Gymnasium* with its traditional humanistic curriculum.[1] Gradually other secondary schools—the *Realgymnasien* which required Latin but not Greek, and the *Oberrealschulen* which emphasized modern languages and social and natural sciences—succeeded in gaining admission to the universities for their graduates. In Prussia an official order of William II on 26 November 1900 endowed all three types of secondary schools with equal status; however, *Gymnasium* study remained prerequisite for theology, and the *Oberrealschule* graduates were still excluded from state medical examinations.[2] The classical *Gymnasien* continued as the main route to university study during the years of the Weimar Republic.[3]

The German secondary schools, unlike the English public schools, were usually state supported. Theoretically they were open to all Germans, but the lower classes were virtually excluded.[4] The secondary schools all charged tuition, although in many cases free tuition grants were made to a limited number of students. The prolonged costs of nine years of secondary school and four subsequent university years discouraged many parents. In many small towns and in rural areas access to secondary schools was not available without considerable financial sacrifice. It is also probable that the workers just did not venerate the academic professions as highly as did other social groups. The working-class parent was often convinced that his child had little chance of successfully completing university study.[5]

The 1918 revolution had little effect upon the social composition of the student community. After 1918 the number of students rose much more rapidly than the population, but the working classes, who constituted between 50 and 60 percent of all Germans, contributed less than 2 percent of the students in 1928.[6] The percentage of working-class students rose slightly after 1918 because provisions for alternate routes to the universities opened. In the Winter Semester of 1924–25 in Prussia, 1.2 percent of the university students and less than 1 percent of the technical students indicated that their fathers were workers. By 1928, the percentage had risen to 2.07 percent for the Prussian universities and 1.03 percent for the Technical Institutes.[7] Sons and daughters of farmers were somewhat more favored. In 1924, 5 percent of Prussian university students indicated that their fathers were small landowners; 4.42 percent did so in 1928.[8]

The state governments hoped to make the universities reflect the social composition of the country more accurately by eliminating the monopoly of the traditional secondary schools in preparing students for higher education. *Aufbauschulen* were established in some areas which permitted children to begin secondary education after the seventh year of elementary school rather than the standard four. Provisions were also made for highly gifted students to enroll in certain courses after a special examination.[9]

The number of students who were able to take advantage of these changes was small. In the 1928 summer semester over 90 percent of the university students had completed nine-year secondary schools and about 6 percent had reached the university through alternate routes.[10] In the Socialist-led state of Saxony, where large numbers of students were matriculated without having completed secondary education, the percentage of lower-class students was considerably greater than in the other states of Germany.[11]

The state governments also attempted to open their secondary schools to larger sectors of the population. In Prussia, exclusive primary schools associated with secondary schools were largely discarded. All children were enrolled in common primary schools (*Einheitsschulen*) for the first three grades. The secondary schools were greatly expanded. The percentage of children enrolled in these schools grew rapidly.[12]

University teachers generally regarded the students from the newer varieties of secondary schools as poorly prepared. Secondary school expansion often enabled the less able rather than the less affluent to attend the universities. Since the *Abitur* system, in effect, gave the secondary schools the power to set university admission standards, the professoriate was powerless to prevent the onslaught.

Many students would not have attended at all if the employment situation had not been serious. Tragically, students were well aware that for most of them the university would be only a temporary reprieve from unemployment. The unmotivated swamped courses taught by professors on examination boards, ignoring everything else. A minimum of academic effort left more time for outside jobs, for fraternities, and for political involvement.

The pressure of the growth on the secondary school level had its effect at the universities during the final years of the Weimar Republic. The number of students mushroomed after 1928 and accentuated a crisis which had roots in the prewar period. Although the size of student bodies had tripled in the first three decades of the twentieth century, the university faculties did not expand. New universities were founded at Frankfurt in 1914 and in Cologne and Hamburg after World War I. The University of Strassburg, which had attracted students and faculty from all regions of the Reich, was no longer a German university after 1918. The isolation of the individual student within the large universities, particularly in the urban universities, was a growing problem.[13] The diplomat, Rudolf Frahn, who attended the University of Berlin in 1920, later reported that he was made to feel "hopeless and lost." Lectures, like those of Sering, which were attended by 1,000 or 1,500 students were not unusual. "We came to [the lectures] as to a mass feeding and they were like [such a feeding] unsatisfying and dull."[14] Heidelberg, on the other hand, still offered a community of scholars: "Surely, there was scarcely another German university where, as here, [in Heidelberg] teachers and students came together in the forest, in the garden, or in the student apartments for festive and sometimes raucous parties, in order to spend the evening celebrating or even the whole day and night."[15] Contacts between students and professors in most places, however, declined. The fraternities, which grew steadily after 1918, benefited because they offered the student a defined place within the university community.

Any social analysis of the student body of the Weimar Republic is limited by the economic upheaval which threatened the status and position of many middle-class families. The statistics we have about student backgrounds do not, in any event, tell us about the financial positions of their parents. Nevertheless, since class in Germany was often more a question of psychological position than income, the occupational pattern for student fathers is helpful in determining student families' social position and self-conception. In this regard, it should be stressed that prewar conceptions of status tended to prevail in spite of economic upheaval.

The social background of the Weimar students did not differ markedly from the prewar pattern. A majority were the first members of their families to receive higher education (Table 1).

Table 1 Percentage of Fathers of University Students with University Education (Prussia, 1899–1900).

School Year	%	School Year	%
1899/1900	26.98	1927/28	20.00
1905/06	24.18	1931/32	21.47
1911/12	22.07	1932/33	21.47
1926/27	19.99		

SOURCE: *Preussische Statistik* (Amtliches Quellenwerk, 236, Statistik des Landesuniversitäten) Berlin: Verlag des Königlichen Statistischen Landesamts, 1913); *Preussische Hochschulstatistik,* Winter semester 1926/27 and 1927/28; *Deutsche Hochschulstatistik,* 1931/32 and 1932/33.

The percentage of university-educated fathers had declined after the turn of the century and continued at a level reached before the war, around 20 percent. Altogether, a quarter of the Weimar students stemmed from the economic and educated elite: the nobility and the *Besitz und Bildungsbürgertum* (propertied and educated bourgeoisie), the prewar ruling classes. Two-thirds of the students came from the *Mittelstand*, the German middle classes, who by sending their children to the university were pushing them up the social ladder. The majority of these were from the upper ranks of what Theodor Geiger called the new middle class: semiprofessionals, middle-level bureaucrats, managers, school teachers, and white collar workers.[16] A sizable group also stemmed from the old middle class of small tradesmen and shopkeepers. Almost half of students' fathers were state employees: a rather broad category in Germany, since it included not only government workers but teachers and university professors, ministers of the established churches, and government hospital employees including physicians. Few were children of farmers, fewer still of blue collar workers. Overall, the academic professions, the traditional trades, and the bureaucracy predominated. Big businessmen, laborers, nonacademic intellectuals like journalists, artists, and musicians—in short, some of the chief representatives of contemporary civilization—were underrepresented among student fathers (Table 2).

Although the figures are not entirely comparable, the social background of

Table 2   Professions of Fathers of the Students Enrolled in Universities and Technical Institutes during the 1928 Summer Semester.

Profession	Universities	Technical Institutes
Elites		
higher officials	15.03%	12.61
academic free professions	6.96	4.70
Educated elite	*21.99*	*17.31*
large landowners	1.44	1.25
owners and directors of large businesses	5.19	9.28
Propertied elite	*6.63*	*10.53*
Officers and higher military officials	1.30	1.33
Total Elites	*29.92*	*29.17*
New middle class (semiprofessionals) and white collar		
middle officials	28.28	25.81
nonacademic professions	1.50	2.71
managers	4.45	8.97
lower officials	1.62	1.41
other white collar	6.90	7.86
other military	.09	.10
Total new middle class	*42.84*	*46.85*
Old middle class (small business and crafts)		
small business	5.62	5.68
independent craftsmen	13.89	11.67
Total old middle class	*19.51*	*17.35*
Middle and small landowners (Total)	4.26	2.36
Blue collar (Total)	1.99	1.25
Other or unknown	2.02	3.01

SOURCE: *Deutsche Hochschulstatistik*, Summer semester 1928.

NOTE: 1928 is the first semester that statistics were published for all of Germany.

postwar students does not appear to be that different from those of the prewar period (Table 3).

According to the Prussian statistics, published beginning in 1924, the new middle class was the major beneficiary of the rise in enrollments, while the percentage of students from independent middle class homes declined slightly (Table 4).

Table 3 Professions of Fathers of the Students Enrolled at Prussian Universities for the Summer Semester of 1911 and the Winter Semester 1911/1912.

Profession	Percentage
Elites	
higher officials	14.5
professionals	4.8
Educated elite	*19.3*
large landowners	1.4
owners and directors of large businesses	11.0
Propertied elite	*12.4*
Officers	1.1
Total elites	*32.8*
New middle class	
middle and lower officials	26.6
nonacademic professions and managers	0.8
other white collar	3.8
other military	0.1
Total new middle class	*31.3*
small businessmen	15.7
craftsmen and workers	5.9
farmers and peasants	8.8
other and unknown	5.8

SOURCE: *Preussische Statistik,* Amtliches Quellenwerk 236, 1913.

Table 4 Social Origins of Students in Prussia, Universities: 1924–1933.

Social Origins	1924/25	1928	1931/32
Educated elite	21.09	19.98	20.53
Propertied elite	7.83	6.14	4.25
Military elite	1.45	1.45	1.54
Elites	*30.37*	*27.57*	*26.31*
Managers and middle level civil servants	29.11	35.00	35.16
White collar employees	8.71	10.82	11.94
New middle class	*37.82*	*45.82*	*47.10*
Old middle class	21.92	19.33	19.00
Small and middle landowners	5.0	4.4	3.0
Workers	1.3	2.1	4.11
Other or none	3.6	0.8	0.69
Total officials	40.3	46.5	45.9
Total students	30,001	45,036	51,596

SOURCE: *Preussische Hochschulstatistik,* 1924/25 and *Deutsche Hochschulstatistik,* 1928, 1931/32, 1932/33.

The enrollment rise also did not work to the benefit of the Catholic minority who accounted for about a third of the Prussian population but provided little more than a fourth of the Prussian university students (Table 5).

Table 5   Religious Background of Prussian University and Technical students.

Background	1910/1911	1924/25	1928	1930/31	1932/33
Universities					
Lutheran	66.43	59.41	63.79	63.90	63.19
Roman Catholic	27.52	28.72	29.22	27.99	27.35
Jewish	5.60	6.34	4.69	5.41	5.86
Other or none		2.57	1.81	2.51	2.38
Unknown		2.94	0.49	0.63	1.22
Technical Institutes					
Lutheran		64.38	69.86	71.72	69.31
Roman Catholic		23.39	19.79	18.49	19.02
Jewish		3.81	4.07	4.07	4.01
Other or none		5.12	4.58	4.30	4.75
Unknown		3.32	1.71	1.12	2.90

SOURCE: *Preussische Hochschulstatistik*, 1924/25, and *Deutsche Hochschulstatistik*, 1928, 1931/32, 1932/33.

Since admission standards were uniform, the social backgrounds of student bodies did not vary greatly from location to location. The larger urban universities (with the conspicuous exception of Munich) tended to be more democratic. The universities favored by Catholic students were similarly less elite in social composition, reflecting the less privileged position of Catholics in Germany generally (Table 6). Most broadly based of all were the four universities founded in the twentieth century, Münster (1902), Frankfurt (1914), Cologne (1919), and Hamburg (1919), where the "old school tie" had no impact on attendance (Table 7).

Students from home backgrounds of the old middle class were found in greater numbers at the urban universities and at those with a significant number of Catholics. In 1928, urban, 57 percent Catholic Cologne had the highest percentage of independent middle class students (29.0 percent). Rural, 12 percent Catholic Greifswald enrolled only 13.2 percent from this group (Table 8).

While the smaller regional universities attracted relatively few students from the independent middle class, the two southwest German magnet universities, Freiburg and Heidelberg, appealed to both the economic elite and the children of independent businessmen and tradesmen. The democratic political and social climate of Baden, coupled with the academic prestige of the two universities, probably contributed to this result. Heidelberg with 9.4 percent and Freiburg with 5.7 percent in 1929 were respectively first and fifth in Germany in the percentage of Jewish students (see Table 6).

The sons and daughters of the elite were most frequently drawn to heavily

Table 6   Enrollment at German Universities and Technical Institutes, Summer Semester 1929.

Place	Total Students	Lutheran	Catholic	Jewish	Other or None
Prussia					
Berlin	11,278	76.9%	12.2%	7.5%	3.4
Bonn	5,719	41.3	54.8	3.1	0.7
Breslau	3,940	49.2	44.3	6.0	0.4
Frankfurt	3,531	62.7	26.4	8.1	2.8
Göttingen	3,767	88.1	9.8	0.9	1.2
Greifswald	1,726	86.8	12.2	0.3	0.7
Halle	2,144	93.3	5.1	0.8	0.8
Kiel	2,464	84.7	13.2	0.4	1.7
Cologne	5,438	38.0	57.1	3.4	1.6
Königsberg	2,947	85.0	12.0	2.1	0.9
Marburg	3,659	87.8	11.2	0.5	0.5
Münster	3,800	32.2	67.0	0.4	0.4
Aachen T.H.	866	38.9	58.9	0.6	1.6
Berlin T.H.	4,247	81.6	11.6	3.3	3.5
Breslau T.H.	581	68.7	27.0	3.4	0.9
Hanover T.H.	1,673	85.5	13.0	0.5	0.9
Bavaria					
Erlangen	1,697	71.7	25.8	1.2	1.4
Munich	7,922	46.7	49.0	2.4	1.9
Würzburg	2,815	33.7	60.7	3.8	1.7
Munich T.H.	3,411	56.1	41.4	0.6	1.8
Saxony					
Leipzig	5,684	91.1	3.6	1.6	3.7
Dresden T.H.	2,990	93.2	4.4	0.4	1.9
Württemburg					
Tübingen	3,728	79.8	19.1	0.5	0.6
Stuttgart T.H.	2,990	81.0	17.3	0.7	1.0
Baden					
Freiburg	3,728	50.7	42.5	5.7	1.1
Heidelberg	3,479	62.7	26.1	9.4	1.8
Karlsruhe T.H.	1,106	61.3	35.2	0.8	2.7
Hesse					
Giessen	1,621	79.6	17.1	1.9	1.4
Darmstadt T.H.	2,006	75.7	20.3	1.3	2.6
Hamburg U.	3,020	84.0	5.3	3.8	6.9
Mecklenburg-Schwerin					
Rostock	1,588	87.6	9.9	1.1	1.4
Braunschweig					
Braunschweig T.H.	889	88.1	9.9	0.2	1.8

SOURCE: *Deutsche Hochschulstatistik*, 1929.

Table 7   Percentage of Fathers with Higher Education of the Students at German Universities and Technical Institutes during the Summer Semester of 1928.

Universities		Technical Institutes	
Cologne	11.7	Aachen	15.7
Münster	14.3	Hanover	17.1
Frankfurt	15.9	Dresden	17.9
Hamburg	16.8	Stuttgart	19.2
Breslau	17.7	Breslau	19.4
Königsberg	19.6	Berlin	23.1
Bonn	20.4	Braunschweig	23.2
Jena	21.9	Karlsruhe	23.9
Leipzig	22.6	Munich	27.5
Berlin	23.4		
Halle	24.8		
Würzburg	25.1		
Heidelberg	25.9		
Göttingen	26.3		
Greifswald	26.6		
Marburg	26.6		
Freiburg	28.4		
Kiel	29.2		
Rostock	30.0		
Erlangen	31.1		
Tübingen	31.3		
Munich	32.1		
University mean	23.4	Technical Institute mean	21.9

SOURCE: *Deutsche Hochschulstatistik*, 1928.

Protestant schools. Kiel, which attracted students from high civil service families and from the economic elite, was the most upper class, followed by Halle, Tübingen, Marburg, Göttingen, Freiburg, and Greifswald. The smaller regional universities were usually less attractive to the upper classes; their student bodies were dominated by the children of middle-ranking civil servants, independent professionals, and middle-level white collar employees (Table 9).

Businessmen's sons were much more likely to attend Technical Institutes than universities. In 1928, at seven of the twenty-two universities (Giessen's figures were not included), Greifswald, Königsberg, Breslau, Marburg, Göttingen, Tübingen and Halle, at least 50 percent of the students were from civil service homes. The figures are strikingly large even taking into account the broad German definition of civil servant. The "higher" civil service favored Tübingen (many of the Tübingen students were ministers' sons studying theology), Erlangen, Marburg, and Greifswald. Königsberg and Breslau, like Cologne, Münster, and Frankfurt, were more favored by the middle ranks of the civil service, notably by school teachers' sons and daughters (Table 10).

Table 8   Percentage of Students from Old Middle Class and Farm Homes.

	Universities			Technical Institutes	
	Old Middle Class	Old Middle Class and Farm		Old Middle Class	Old Middle Class and Farm
Cologne	29.0	33.5	Munich	20.60	22.83
Frankfurt	24.4	27.6	Dresden	18.37	20.47
Freiburg	24.1	29.4	Aachen	17.69	21.04
Bonn	23.6	27.1	Braunschweig	16.75	21.18
Heidelberg	21.0	23.3	Hanover	16.38	20.45
Würzburg	20.5	27.0	Karlsruhe	15.95	17.97
Münster	20.4	30.7	Berlin	15.95	17.48
Berlin	19.5	21.7	Breslau	15.32	17.90
Rostock	18.8	19.3	Stuttgart	14.81	16.52
Munich	18.7	22.7			
Leipzig	18.5	21.3	Overall	17.35	19.71
Jena	18.4	22.6			
Hamburg	17.47	20.5			
Breslau	16.4	21.6			
Göttingen	16.1	21.4			
Marburg	15.0	18.5			
Halle	14.6	19.9			
Erlangen	14.2	16.5			
Tübingen	13.3	19.7			
Greifswald	13.2	16.4			
Königsberg	12.4	19.7			
Kiel	7.4	13.0			
Overall	19.095	23.4			

SOURCE: *Deutsche Hochschulstatistik,* 1929.

Only one university and one Technical Institute, in Berlin and Munich respectively, counted fewer than one-third of their students from civil-service homes. Even the new universities of Cologne and Frankfurt, with strong economics faculties and close ties to local business communities, had large numbers of civil servants' children. These statistics are significant when one considers the estrangement of the overwhelming majority of students from the Weimar Republic.

The economist, Adolf Wagner, estimated that university graduates in the civil service in the mid-1920s earned the equivalent of one-fifth to one-quarter of their prewar income. The income of blue collar workers did not decline as radically. In addition, officials generally were partially declassed by the substitution of statusless political appointees for the old aristocrats at the upper ranks of government employment.[17] The loss of social position was probably more deeply felt than the loss of income, but both of these concerns were undoubtedly communicated to the younger generation.

Table 9 Elite and New Middle Class Students at German Universities and Technical Institutes during the Summer Semester, 1928.

Place	Educated Elite	Propertied and Military	Total Elite	New Middle Class
Universities				
Berlin	21.98	7.73	29.7	45.8
Bonn	19.29	10.75	30.0	41.9
Breslau	23.5	6.8	30.3	50.1
Frankfurt	14 49	5.6	20.1	49.8
Göttingen	25.49	9.8	35.3	41.44
Greifswald	26.38	8.66	35.0	46.95
Halle	29.35	8.41	37.76	37.43
Kiel	28.4	18.4	46.8	37.9
Cologne	11.33	4.86	16.2	47.8
Königsberg	18.36	5.96	24.32	52.56
Marburg	27.97	7.44	35.4	44.11
Münster	13.74	3.57	17.31	47.77
Erlangen	28.59	5.29	33.88	36 93
Munich	26.15	7.39	33.54	33.09
Würzburg	21.78	5.22	27.0	34 87
Leipzig	22.52	8.50	31.0	44.96
Tübingen	30.60	7.14	37.74	39.80
Freiburg	27.12	8.0	35.17	33.49
Heidelberg	23.97	10.46	34.43	40.11
Jena	22.65	8.07	30.72	42.41
Hamburg	15.01	13.11	28.12	47.86
Rostock	28.66	7.80	36.46	40.83
Technical Institutes				
Aachen	13.64	13.76	27.40	47.51
Berlin	20.25	12.93	33.18	47.34
Breslau	16.13	10.32	26.45	53.55
Hannover	14.02	11.02	25.04	52.74
Munich	16.99	12.72	29.71	36.83
Dresden	16.92	10 43	27.35	49.23
Stuttgart	13.29	12.22	25.51	55.38
Karlsruhe	20.37	9.99	30.36	49.47
Braunschweig	21.18	9.48	30.66	46.06

SOURCE: *Deutsche Hochschulstatistik*, 1928.

The concerns of the civil service were shared by their counterparts in private industry, middle level managers and white collar workers, whose economic situation deteriorated radically during the war and the postwar period. Jürgen Kocka has noted that hard times reoriented the politics of many salaried employees, disenchanted them with the capitalist economic system, and awakened them to the possibilities of economic action similar to that of the blue collar workers.[18]

The deliberalization of the German middle classes was well under way in the

Table 10   Percentage of Fathers Employed by Government.

	Total	Higher Civil Servants
Universities		
Greifswald	58.3	20.6
Königsberg	56.3	12.9
Breslau	54.1	13.0
Marburg	52.3	20.4
Göttingen	50.5	19.5
Tübingen	50.4	24.0
Halle	50.2	18.4
Jena	48.5	16.4
Leipzig	47.1	16.5
Kiel	46.2	19.8
Erlangen	45.8	20.7
Frankfurt	44.4	9.7
Rostock	44.3	17.4
Münster	43.3	9.5
Heidelberg	41.8	15.2
Hamburg	39.9	10.1
Bonn	39.4	12.1
Freiburg	39.2	16.5
Cologne	38.7	7.0
Munich	37.9	16.1
Würzburg	37.8	12.2
Berlin	32.4	14.8
Technical Institutes		
Breslau	49.5	12.7
Dresden	47.7	13.0
Hanover	42.8	10.2
Berlin	42.8	15.0
Karlsruhe	43.6	15.1
Aachen	41.8	9.5
Braunschweig	41.7	14.0
Stuttgart	39.3	9.1
Munich	31.1	11.9

Source: *Deutsche Hochschulstatistik,* 1929.

depression of the late nineteenth century and accelerated during World War I. The antagonism felt by tradesmen and small businessmen for big business and finance capital provided a well of support for extreme nationalist and anti-Semitic groups before the war. In the Weimar Republic salaried government and private employees too turned increasingly against parliamentary democracy and in favor of the programs of the nationalist Right.

   In a sense the deterioration of the economic position of the salaried middle class tended to bear out Karl Marx's prediction that with the growth of monopoly capitalism, the middle class would be absorbed within the proletariat. Their pressed situation increasingly challenged the salaried employees to identify themselves as workers and to become more receptive to labor organization and socialist programs. Countervailing psychological pressures, however, persisted to reinforce their middle class identification in spite of their economic plight. The universities had long been the traditional route for the salaried middle class for social advancement; in the 1920s higher education presented one of the few chances for these families to escape proletarianization.[19] By sending their children to the universities, the parents hoped that they would achieve the economic security and social position they themselves had lost. Germany's economic difficulties encouraged this trend. The young who were unable to find work remained in school. The number of students varied in inverse proportion to the rate of unemployment. In the years following the stabilization of the mark in 1923, the number of students actually decreased, only to rise to new heights in the economic crisis of the early 1930s (Table 11).

The rapid growth of student numbers during the Weimar Republic was due in part to the increased numbers of female students. During the Weimar years, women were tolerated rather than greeted as university students. Women were far more often victims than producers of the academic job crisis of the Weimar Republic, since they were rarely given preference to men on the job market. Still, the increased presence of women was seen by their male competitors as a distinct threat to their own future prospects. This was particularly true for aspiring teachers and doctors, since medicine and the humanities were the favorite subjects for women.[20] Women students remained, perhaps as a result of economic fears, outsiders, excluded from the center of university life, belittled and mocked.[21] Even in the large urban universities, which the women preferred, they were only marginally involved in student affairs.

Women, then, contributed to a growing job crisis among the educated. Before World War I, too many university graduates were already competing for scarce jobs. After the war the extent of this surplus assumed crisis proportions. The migration of intellectuals from the areas lost to the Reich as a result of the Treaty of Versailles increased the competition for positions. Limitations on the size of the German army under the terms of the treaty closed an important avenue of comparable social prestige for many.

Fierce competition for professional positions was apparent as early as 1920. A speaker at the second German student convention (*Studententag*) in the summer of that year warned (with some exaggeration) that prospects for secondary school teachers were already so bad that a philology student who passed his state examination in 1921 might have to wait thirteen years to receive an appointment. The universities were graduating an average of 2,000 applicants each year to fill approximately 675 openings. The job outlook for doctors and librarians was also very bad.[22]

After 1924, when the war veterans who had returned to school began to seek professional positions, the pressure was noticeable in almost all fields of study. Student journals were full of gloomy statistics about the poor prospects graduates faced. The existence of an "academic proletariat" was a commonly acknowledged fact.

Table 11   The Growth of the German Student Population, 1911–35.

School Year	Students	18–25-Year-Olds in Germany	Students as % of 18–25-Year-Olds
1911/12	81,500	9,530,000	0.86
1912/13	83,800	9,720,000	0.86
1919/20	120,300	9,420,000	1.28
1920/21	126,800	9,650,000	1.31
1921/22	127,000	9,915,000	1.28
1922/23	130,700	10,015,000	1.30
1923/24	113,300	10,360,000	1.09
1924/25	97,600	10,610,000	0.92
1925/26	98,900	10,680,000	0.92
1926/27	104,300	10,760,000	0.97
1927/28	111,500	10,760,000	1.04
1928/29	123,000	10,810,000	1.14
1929/30	129,500	10,825,000	1.20
1930/31	133,000	10,790,000	1.23
1931/32	128,000	10,630,000	1.20
1932/33	117,100	10,070,000	1.16
1933/34	99,800	9,390,000	1.06
1934/35	80,700	8,660,000	0.93

SOURCE: Cäcilie Quetsch, *The Numerical Record of University Attendance in Germany in the Last Fifty Years* (Berlin, Göttingen, Heidelberg: Springer Verlag, 1961), Table 12, p. 51.

Government and industry responded by increasing the educational prerequisites for many positions, requiring completion of higher education or at least the *Abitur*. Such actions aroused the wrath of the lower classes who were also facing unemployment and tended at the same time to encourage many who would not formerly have done so to continue studying.[23]

The increased unemployment among academics fed the general disillusionment with the Republican system of government—both among students and among the *alte Herren* (alumni) of the fraternities. Few seemed to remember that Germany had had a large surplus of university graduates before the war.

Germany's economic troubles produced a decisive change in the character of student life. Since family savings were made worthless by inflation, a large number of students were forced to support themselves, a new phenomenon in Germany. Many lived in extremely poor circumstances. Scholarship aid was rare. Students were forced to seek employment both during vacations and in the semester. In 1922, close to half of the enrolled students reported employment either during the summer semester or the summer vacation.[24] Many were doing work that would have been judged beneath the dignity of students before the war, for example factory and agricultural labor.[25] Erich Kästner has graphically recalled the plight of the "work student" during the inflation of the 1920's:

What my parents had taken many years to save became nothing. My native town gave me a scholarship. Soon I could barely buy a pack of cigarettes with the monthly stipend.

I became a work-student, which meant that I worked in an office, received a briefcase full of money at the end of the week, and had to run if I wanted to buy anything to eat with it.

That was 1923. We studied nights. Now (after World War II) there is no coal to heat with. Then, we had no money for coal. . . . When the inflation was over, there was scarcely a respectable person who still had money . . . . During the fair—I prepared for my exams in Leipzig—we hung up placards and earned an additional few Marks by serving as wandering placard posts. Several times a week, poor students could lunch with nice people who made themselves available at the university, at their homes.[26]

Largely through student initiative, placement agencies were organized at the universities in the framework of student aid programs.[27] The idea of self-help through work conformed well with the expressed will of student leaders to reject handouts in favor of cooperative student action.[28] But the cost of work-study was the cloistered university of the past where parent-supported middle class students could devote themselves full-time to scholarship. Studies suffered particularly during the years of inflation when more than half of the students had to find employment during the year.

The possibilities of work-study, to be sure, encouraged the democraticization of student bodies, since lower-class students who had to work were less at a disadvantage. Practically, too, the work experience forced the students to rub shoulders with workers and peasants. The results of this mixing were not always felicitous, since traditional class distrust remained and employers tended to favor the socially equal students over regular workers, often increasing tension.[29] The work experience therefore impressed students with the class struggle without helping to solve it. In addition, work-study, since it scarcely ameliorated student conditions, contributed to a psychological reaction against the Weimar Republic. Before 1924, student earnings, particularly summer earnings, were stolen by inflation, and after 1924, chronic national unemployment made part-time jobs hard to find and poorly compensated.[30]

While the educational authorities repeatedly bemoaned the economic difficulties students faced, government aid for student welfare programs was largely inadequate. In spite of repeated student protests, university fees remained at consistently high levels while funding for scholarships and loans lagged. Private generosity, too, only provided piecemeal and scattered support.[31] It is not surprising that the students, even more than their teachers, resented society's apparent neglect.

The universities of the Weimar Republic, then, continued to recruit largely from the groups that had supplied most prewar students. The number of students from middle class homes, however, expanded both proportionately and in absolute numbers. The greatest number of students were the children of managers and public officials, a group characterized by ambition and bourgeois respectability and a group suffering substantially from the economic conditions of the Republic. Doubtless, the vast majority of these students entered the universities with the hope of achieving the social and economic position traditionally accruing to university graduates. The contraction of the market for academically trained personnel certainly frustrated these goals and contributed greatly to student unrest. Wretched living conditions did not help either. Society and government appeared indifferent if not hostile to the students' plight, while the popular and press image of the student was patently more relevant to the prewar than the postwar student experience. Overall, the students who had been conditioned to expect more than was their due received less. The total university experience, in its turn, with its emphasis on tradition and status, and the subtle antidemocratic bias of the professoriate tended to channel the consequent unrest into right-wing politics.

Although the numerical balance during the Weimar years turned in favor of the lower middle classes, the dominant cultural tone among students remained that of the old elite. This tone was set by the entrenched fraternities which continued to enroll a majority of male students until their demise in 1935 and 1936. The fraternities were at the center of a rich student tradition of time-honored custom, song, and good fellowship. Although the *Student Prince* was a caricature, it captured much of the flavor of student life still present in Weimar.

The German fraternities assumed their modern form in the course of the nineteenth century. *Landsmannschaften,* which corresponded to the Nations of the University of Paris in the middle ages, were the traditional form of student organization before the nineteenth century, but during the Enlightenment more exclusive groups began to develop under the influence of the secret orders. The *Burschenschaften* which were forged in the early struggle for national unification after the end of the Napoleonic wars rejected provincial boundaries in their organization and recognized all "honorable" students as equal—that is, all who subscribed to traditional student concepts of honorable conduct.[32]

The political activities of the *Burschenschaften* quickly incurred the wrath of Prince Metternich who pressured the German states into imposing severe restrictions on all student groups which lasted until the revolution of 1848. With the granting of rights of assembly and organization and the lifting of restrictions on student travel in that year, a renaissance in student societies took place. Local fraternities proliferated, and national unions, known as leagues (*Verbände*), began to unite the locals.

The coming of national leagues encouraged former fraternity members, affectionately called *alte Herren* or "old fellows," to play an increasingly active role in the affairs of the students. The *alte Herren* began to organize their own local groups which in turn created national organizations paralleling those of the students.[33] The financial support of the *alte Herren* enabled the students to build fraternity houses and to carry on a wide range of activities. The *alte Herren* staunchly defended the fraternities and their frequently controversial activities by serving as their spokesmen in the press and in government.[34]

The continued interest of former students in the fraternities proved helpful to members seeking employment. Although the fraternities shamefacedly denied that membership was helpful for career advancement, aid for the "brothers" was openly encouraged in the hard times which followed World War I.[35]

The *Corps* or *Korps*, many of which traced their origins to the eighteenth century *Landsmannschaften*, were the most elite of the fraternities. The prewar *Corps* were proud of their exclusiveness and underlined their separation from the mass of students by their ostentation and social arrogance. Frequently, they refused to participate in official university events. When they did participate, they agreed to march only at the front or the rear of the student processional and kept a noticeable distance from the other marchers.[36] Increasingly their members copied the attitudes of the German Officers Corps, emphasizing the qualities of courage and obedience and dismissing the importance of individual freedom apart from the needs of the group and nation.[37]

The caste spirit of the *Corps* was manifest in the highly charged symbolism surrounding the colors of a member's fraternity. When he wore the *Corps'* colors, he could not do anything which might debase its honor. He could not engage in certain sports like bicycle riding; certainly he could not carry a package.[38] He could not travel fourth class on the train nor could he enter an inn or tavern that was not *colourfähig* (worthy of his colors), such as a place where working people might congregate.[39]

The other fraternities, instead of resenting the social exclusiveness of the *Corps*, accepted them as models. The *Burschenschaften*, whose historical role in the national movement had made them a favorite society for the politically active sons of the liberal middle classes, attempted to divest themselves of their Republican and democratic images after 1870 and to adopt the outward symbols, the principles of honor, the organizational structure, and the customs of the *Corps*. "Reform *Burschenschaften*" who fought these trends and attempted to cleave to the political and social principles of their predecessors proved far less attractive to the students of the era. The newer Catholic and Protestant fraternities which unconditionally rejected the duel nevertheless maintained many traditions of *Corps* life; some even carried the rapier on public occasions. The contempt with which the nondueling fraternities were held by the dueling fraternities was in turn frequently paralleled by a general disdain by both groups towards the nonfraternity students who were more concerned with their studies than with the romantic student tradition.

The students' code of honor was central to their special caste status in German society. The very word *honor* implied a distinction between those members of society who possessed honor to defend and those who did not.[40] Nondueling students were dismissed contemptuously with the phrase: "*Sie sind ja nicht einmal satisfaktionsfähig''* (You are not even capable of ''satisfaction''—that is, defending your honor.)[41] The students' retention of the duel underscored their identification with the officers' corps and the aristocracy and their social superiority to the bourgeoisie.[42]

The student honor code was based essentially upon two virtues: courage and truthfulness.[43] A student's honor was most often attacked by an insult from another student. While the officers in defending their honor defended the honor of the officers' corps, the student defended the honor of his fraternity and to a limited extent the student caste as a whole. The seriousness of the attack and the manner in which honor might be restored was determined by a court of honor (*Ehrengericht*) which might also settle questions of misunderstanding. In practice, duels were few, fatalities rare. The mere possibility of dueling sufficed.

Although dueling was technically illegal and punishable by imprisonment, the laws were poorly enforced even under the Weimar Republic. The influence of the *alte Herren* in government and the courts cushioned any concerted attack against dueling.

Closely related to the duel and frequently confused with it is the *Mensur,* an activity which still exists in the German Federal Republic. The *Mensur* is essentially a fencing match in which the element of danger is not removed. The eyes and bodies of the parties are protected but their faces remain otherwise uncovered. The weapon used is a rapier rather than a sabre or broadsword reserved for affairs of honor.[44]

Originally a series of *Mensuren* between members of two fraternities was organized around a trumped-up insult. After 1870, the *Mensur* was defended as an educational tool to instill the qualities of courage and obedience. In order to win full membership in a fraternity which practiced the *Mensur,* a student usually had to fence successfully three times. If he flinched or if he revealed fear during the contest, he was defeated and had to restore his honor in a second match or face expulsion and ostracism.[45] The facial scars incurred, the *Schmisse,* were the outward sign of a test of courage and consequently a token of honor.

Surviving, indeed expanding, after World War I, the fraternity system epitomized the reactionary ethos that undermined Germany's first experiment in democracy. At their best, the fraternities tended to isolate their members from progressive groups at the universities; at their worst they reinforced snobbery, militaristic values, and the narrowest chauvinistic nationalism. The political excesses of the second Empire in effect formed the political programs of the fraternities in the 1920s. *Alte Herren,* whose university experience had been colored by the pan-German and anti-Semitic mood of the prewar period, helped to transmit the legacy of their own student days to a new generation.

At the same time that the *Corps* were becoming the social arbiters of student life, a new student movement spearheaded a revival and transformation of student political life: the *Kyffhäuser Verband der Vereine deutscher Studenten.*

Organized in a convention in August 1881 in the Harz mountains, the new movement extended across fraternity lines and joined *Corps* students with free students. Unequivocally monarchistic, the students chose the slogan "With God for Kaiser and Reich" pledging to protect Christianity, the monarchy, and German custom and tradition. The movement challenged both an "anaemic bourgeoisie" and "international materialism" and pledged itself to work for the "harnessing of the national powers of the people, serving the Christian *Weltanschauung*, strengthening the social monarchy on behalf of the recovery of the discontented part of the *Volk*."[46]

While retaining its political program, the *Kyffhäuser Verband* soon adopted the form of the traditional fraternities. The program in turn was adopted by many other fraternities. Other groups copied the movement's introduction of the weapons of modern politics to the student scene: effective use of the press, propaganda, and mass meetings and demonstrations. The *Kyffhäuser Verband* counted in its membership numerous political leaders of the Wilhelmian Reich and Weimar Germany ranging from Friedrich Naumann of the moderate Left to Count Kuno von Westarp, leader of the German National Peoples Party on the Right.[47]

The *Kyffhäuser Verband* brought the Jewish question out into the open. The rapid growth of anti-Semitism in Germany in the 1880s and 1890s coincided with an enormous increase in the proportions of Jewish students in the universities of Germany and the Hapsburg Empire at the same time that competition for jobs requiring university study was increasing.[48] The anti-Semitic activities of the *Kyffhäuser Verband* were followed by a growing policy of exclusion of Jewish students by most fraternities, at first on religious and after World War I on racial grounds.

The *Kyffhäuser Verband* also encouraged the revival of the *grossdeutsch* movement which had lain dormant since the Austro-Prussian War. It stimulated renewed contacts between German and Austrian student organizations, and it contributed to a revival of student interest in nationalist politics. It departed from the middle-class consensus of the period even further by wading in the waters of social reform. Like the Nazis after them, the *Kyffhäuser* students linked racism and nationalism with a "social program" in their determination to undercut the Socialists and reestablish national unity.[49]

The broad program of the *Kyffhäuser* movement had marked impact on the fraternities of the 1920s. The sons of the generation of the 1880s and 1890s were to share the nationalist faith of their fathers but with a new ambivalent dimension. The fraternity student of the 1920s did not hope, as many *alte Herren* did, for a restoration of Imperial Germany. But since he could not divest himself of the garments of the past, he could not come to terms with the present. He sought escape in romantic dreams which promised to synthesize contradictions: elitism and egalitarianism, restoration and revolution, authoritarianism and liberty.

The traditional character of the German universities of the Republic was underlined by the efflorescence of the fraternity movement. To the outsider, the fraternities' costumes were a most visible sign of university presence. For the students, fraternity membership remained both a measure of social status and a means of career advancement. The pecking order within the fraternity system reinforced the rigidly stratified character of German society as it was reflected in the universities. The fraternity served as a prime means of integrating thousands of first-generation students into the culture of the elite.

In keeping with their heritage, most German fraternities were nationalist in character. While the elite *Corps* self-confidently proclaimed their apolitical, if patriotic, character, involvement in nationalist action was a means of assertion for the *Burschenschaften* and the other middle-class fraternities. The Weimar climate, too, encouraged politicization of the fraternities, in part because their social character was under attack from outside the university. Politics in the *Burschenschaft* tradition gave the fraternities a *raison d'être*, and permitted them to justify dueling and *Mensur* as part of the national heritage. Nevertheless, the economic plight of the students in the 1920s demanded some reevaluation of fraternity values. While the *Alte Herren* might cling all the more to the symbols of the past, the active students, particularly in the less prestigious fraternities, were more open to the egalitarian currents of the day. The *Burschenschafter* or *Landsmannschafter* who might also be a work-student was less attuned to ideas of status than a student of the prewar generation. The social divisions within the student community fostered by the dueling fraternities were now increasingly bridged. Through the *völkisch* movement too, the fraternities sought links with the masses.

To the outside observer, however, fraternities still appeared an odd and disturbing relic of Wilhelmine society. Their most outstanding features remained bellicose political rhetoric and the worship of an anachronistic cultural tradition. Where they had done so before, fraternity students continued to duel and to practice the *Mensur,* to wear fraternity colors in public and retain the elaborate protocol surrounding them, and to engage in their notorious drinking rituals and pranking, activities which had long offended many of their countrymen. Only the lavish prewar style of life of the *Corps* was a casualty of war, revolution, and hard times.[50]

Dueling and *Mensur* bore the brunt of criticism. On May 15, 1926, the Reich supreme court reaffirmed the prewar judiciary's identification of the *Mensur* with the duel. The liberal Baden state government quickly acted to suppress the *Mensur* and encouraged the other states to follow suit.[51] An inquiry by the Prussian Minister of Culture to the other states revealed that Baden alone had enforced the decision of the court.[52] The Social Democrats, to be sure, who regarded the *Mensur* as a symbol of student arrogance and caste spirit, were outraged by administrators who refused to enforce existing laws.

Nationalist circles supported both the *Mensur* and the duel as essential elements of the German character. To give them up would constitute "a recognition of the contemporary materialistic world view."[53] For strategic reasons the *Mensur* defenders attempted to disassociate it from the duel, as a purely educational exercise; in their own minds, however, the distinction was by no means clear.[54]

Certainly all participants in the *Mensur* accepted the principle of unconditional satisfaction, however rarely put to the test.

The heated defense of dueling was symptomatic of fraternity retrenchment in the Republic. Relics of a bygone era, fraternities were drawn inexorably to political movements which defended the sacred character of the national tradition.

The organized fraternity movement reacted to the 1918 revolution ambiguously. The *Kyffhäuser* convention summed up the mood of many when it voted to retain the motto "With God for Kaiser and Reich" but disavowed support for any "particular form of government."[55] For the most part fraternity spokesmen contented themselves with warnings against radical social upheaval. Fraternity members were encouraged to support the Majority Socialist government against its enemies on the left by participating in temporary military service. In the eyes of many fraternity members, for a brief moment at least, the old regime had been discredited by the loss of the war.[56]

Monarchism had less appeal for student youth than it had for their parents. The *Deutsche Corpszeitung,* the national organ for the elite *Kösener Verband,* published a number of emotional articles in praise of the old regime in the years after the revolution, but as early as the May 1919 issue it included an article which attempted to reinterpret the *Corps'* royalist past in the light of the Republican present. The writer lauded the nonpartisan policy of the prewar *Corps* and praised them as the meeting ground of German princes and other social classes. In the *Corps,* the princes were "anointed with democratic oil."[57] Students appeared once more and for the last time in cap and band at a royal demonstration when the Empress was buried in Berlin in April 1921.[58]

Because of the new importance given to political participation and the lowering of the voting age from twenty-five to twenty-one, many fraternities embarked upon new programs of political education for their members.[59] The content of such programs was defined as nonpartisan and patriotic. Since university professors did not make themselves available to lead political discussions, nationalist-minded *alte Herren* and older students were usually in charge. The fraternity leagues ran study conferences where the instructors were acquainted with the political situation and the ideas of the German Right. Leading nationalist theorists and politicians took a conspicuous interest in fraternity political education and frequented these conferences to lead discussions. Several of the leagues issued handbooks to aid in political education, as well as other nationalist books. The ideas expressed in these handbooks ranged from conservative to National Socialist. They emphasized topics like the national irredenta and the requirements of an effective German foreign policy. One thing they did not do was educate citizens for responsible participation in a democratic state.[60]

After the drafting of the Weimar constitution and the signing of the Versailles Treaty, the leagues began to adopt positions more or less hostile to the new order. The Treaty shocked a generation which had grown up with the bombast of

Wilhelmine "Hurrah patriotism." Middle-class suspicion of internationalist Social Democracy made many eager to accept the infamous delusion that the war
had been lost by a "stab in the back" on the home front.

Former youth movement members entering the fraternities in large numbers
took advantage of the anti-Weimar drift to further a *völkisch Weltanschauung*.
Because of their emphasis on tradition, the fraternities had attracted young men
of the more conservative youth movement groups which emphasized the romantic tradition and the recovery of the German past. But youth movement students
did not adjust easily to the discipline and emphasis on outer form characteristic of
fraternity life. Instead, they attempted to reform the fraternities by making their
activities more meaningful, both by underplaying outmoded social customs and
by encouraging the expenditure of time and energies on cultural, political, and
social questions.[61]

The freewheeling youth-movement activists did stimulate an examination of
the traditional values of the fraternities. But the old ways were not changed, only
given new explanations. The prewar idea of honor no longer sufficed; dueling
needed a *völkisch* justification. The fraternities might defend the student concept
of honor as a necessary part of the national heritage. Or they might state that the
man of honor was somehow in harmony with the principles of a divine moral
order and only such men could lead the German *Volk* to national renewal.[62]
Since the student was a member of the *Volk* community, when he defended his
honor he defended not only the honor of his fraternity but of the nation.[63] By
defending his honor, it was also said, a student demonstrated his willingness to
give his life for the *Volk*.[64]

In spite of new explanations for old practices, youth-movement leaders continued to complain that their students only ended up being seduced by fraternities, that most reform efforts were futile.[65] Many youth-movement members
preferred their own fraternities such as the *Akademische Gilden* who combined
the idea of fraternity with that of *Männerbund:* a mystically united society of
men. Both rambling (*Wandern*) and fencing were regarded as excellent training
for the future leaders of Germany in the *Gilden*. They preached love of the *Volk*,
celebrated pagan festivals such as the harvest and the summer solstice, and
rejected any contact with "alien races." But in a gesture to traditional fraternities, members announced openly before admission whether or not they would
accept a challenge to duel (dueling was not required).[66]

Another spur to *völkisch* influence in the fraternities was renewed contact with
student fraternities beyond the borders.[67] The Austrian fraternities, which now
associated with German leagues, were expert practitioners of the emotional politics of their homeland. The pan-German movement, fathered by Georg von
Schönerer in the 1880s, lacked voters in the general population but counted the
majority of Austrian dueling fraternity students as supporters. The Catholic
fraternities were tied to the clerical authoritarianism of the ruling Christian Social
Party. Pan-German and Catholic students held each other in mutual contempt but
nevertheless united in a shaky alliance founded in their common hatred of Jews

and Socialists. The Austrian fraternities of the post–World-War-I era were well acquainted with metapolitics. Catholic medievalists and mystical anti-Christians were comfortable in the chambers of the Austrian social elite, where they would have been laughed out of the house in Germany.

Within the united fraternity leagues, the Austrians became the spokesmen for radical anti-Semitic goals. It was their self-appointed task to reinforce the anti-Semitic trend in Germany. Ironically, the harbinger of this new wave was the *Allgemeine Deutsche Burschenbund,* the union of reform *Burschenschaften* who in 1883 and again in 1887 resolved to admit German students regardless of religion.[68] In spite of a history of toleration, the *Burschenbund* decided at their October 1919 meeting not to admit new Jewish members. In a statement intended to salve bad consciences, the *Burschenbund* rejected anti-Semitic agitation and called for unity among students regardless of politics, religion, or race.[69]

The anti-Semitic mood spread rapidly to the other fraternity leagues. At the *Deutsche Burschenschaft* convention of August 1920, a motion by three Austrian *Burschenschaften* to exclude all persons with any Jewish blood was accepted with minor changes.[70] In 1920, the always racist *Kyffhäuser Verband* refused to recognize the right of Jewish students to satisfaction with weapons.[71] The same position was adopted by the newly organized General German Dueling Society (*Allgemeiner deutscher Waffenring*) an interleague organization which eventually united almost all Germany's dueling students.[72] In May 1921, the ordinarily cautious university *Corps* came close to excluding all students of Jewish race as well as religion.[73] But many of the *Corps* protested that this constituted undue interference in local affairs.[74] To their credit, it was not the *Corps'* style to follow the lead of others, or to ape every passing vogue. Their strict admission standards sufficed to exclude new blood.

The exclusion of Jews from fraternities was, to be sure, not unique to Germany and Austria. But in Germany, as in Austria, anti-Semitism was not merely a social phenomenon; it was a political issue. The announcement of an anti-Semitic policy by a fraternity in Germany in effect linked that fraternity to the nationalist far right. It was one facet of the politicization of the fraternities after World War I.

In the early years after the 1918 revolution, the fraternities sought increased relevance in a variety of ways. Fraternity values were redefined to give them a "contemporary" *völkisch* cast. Excursions into the political arena satisfied the needs of students to confront the political turmoil of the Republic. The fraternities had not changed fundamentally in character, but they had adopted a new seriousness of purpose which fit the mood of the 1920s. This change in style insured the continued growth of the fraternities during the Weimar Republic, in spite of their anachronistic character.

Politically, the fraternities of the Weimar years can be divided into four groups. On the left, a small minority, which included the Jewish and nonsectarian fraternities, openly favored the Republic. A conservative, but not necessarily anti-Republican, attitude characterized the Roman Catholic fraternities, the religious Protestant fraternities, and the socially elite *Corps*. A third group, which included the *Burschenschaften* and *Landsmannschaften*, adopted many *völkisch* tenets but remained politically close to the German National Peoples Party. On the extreme right a number of fraternity leagues favored a program not unlike that of the National Socialists.

A variety of influences shaped a fraternity's political direction. An Austrian affiliation and influence were often an important factor. Individual students were encouraged to spend a semester or two in Austria where they participated in fraternity activities. Similarly, many Austrian, Sudeten German, and East European German students were active in the German fraternities. Politically concerned students were attracted to organizations with a political tradition such as the *Kyffhäuser* groups. The political traditions of the fraternities were maintained through emphasis on internal education and the active interest of the *alte Herren*.

Since the fraternities of the Weimar Republic tended to underplay social distinctions, it is difficult to document their impact upon recruitment in this period. Certain *Corps* were still known as aristocratic. One, Borussia in Bonn, proudly enrolled the ex-Kaiser's grandson as a "fox" in 1926, the first Hohenzollern to participate in a *Mensur*.[75] Nevertheless, the majority of *Corps* men were undoubtedly of bourgeois origin and members of a bourgeois Corps were not welcomed as transfers in aristocratic *Corps*.

Broadly speaking, older fraternities recruited the sons or nephews of their alte Herren; newer fraternities were more open to the first generation of students. The *Kösener Corps* in 1930 counted almost four alumni to each student member, and one may assume a large percentage of students were relatives of alumni. The *Deutsche Burschenschaft* alumni-student ratio was somewhat smaller. The less prestigious *Landsmannschaften* and *Turnerschaften* and the Catholic *Cartell Verband* fraternities approached ratios of 1:1.[76] Other mechanisms of selection were also sufficiently at work to blur the old social distinctions: friendships, personality, athletic ability, political attitudes all were involved in recruitment.

The old socially prestigious fraternities expanded more slowly in the Weimar years than the less elite ones. The *Kösener Verband* was itself outstripped by the *Landsmannschaften* and *Turnerschaften*. In an effort to maintain exclusivity, expansion of the number of *Kösener Corps* was strictly limited, and new *Corps* usually had to join the less prestigious *Rudolstädter Senioren Convent*.[77] The *Burschenschaften* sustained the greatest growth in numbers but lost ground relatively. Catholic fraternities, now less on the defensive, grew rapidly (Table 12).

Although it is difficult to assemble accurate figures on fraternity membership, it is possible at least to estimate the relative strength of the fraternity movement at the universities (see Table 13). The fraternity movement was weakest at the large urban universities: Frankfurt, Leipzig, Berlin, Hamburg, and Cologne. Munich, a traditional haven for student hijinks, was an exception. The fraternities were strongest at the more popular and prestigious small-town universities, particu-

Table 12 Growth of the Major Fraternity Leagues during the Weimar Republic (Student Members Claimed).

	1913	1919	1925	1927	1929	1930	1933
Deutsche Burschenschaft	6,000	6,000	7,400	7,741	10,270	10,514	12,634
Kösener Verb.	2,900	2,800	3,600	4,871	5,837	5,535	5,544
Landsmannsch.	2,400	2,700	4,100	5,496	6,934	7,603	7,699
Turnerschaft.	2,400	2,400	3,200	2,801	5,396	5,778	6,462
Rudolstädt.	900			2,383	2,704	1,219	1,856
Kyffhäuser	1,500	1,400	1,400	1,400	2,350	2,171	2,362
Sonderhäuser (singing)	1,300			1,260	1,687	1,759	1,868
Sängerschaft.	1,500		2,800	2,600	2,650	3,200	3,486
Weinheimer				2,000	2,885	2,721	2,736
Cartell V. (R.C.)	4,300	4,400	5,800	6,539	9,001	9,901	10,282
KV (R.C.)	2,100	2,000	3,200	3,414	5,000	5,363	5,582
Unitas (R.C.)	700	900	1,500	1,347	2,140	2,251	2,438
Wingolf (Protestant)	800	700	900	891	1,277	1,376	1,384
Schwarzburgbund (Protestant)	600		800	876	1,208	1,350	1,397

SOURCE: Figures compiled from "Die Zahlenmässige Stärke der studentischen Verbände," *Jung-Akademische Pressedienst*, VI (28 January 1927), p. 4; Bleuel and Klinnert, *Deutsche Studenten . . .*, p. 261: *Burschenschaftliche Blätter*, 3 December 1929; *Deutsche Corpszeitung*, September 1924, pp. 128–29; Jürgen Schwarz, *Studenten in der Weimarer Republik* (Berlin: Duncker and Humblot, 1971).

larly Marburg, Tübingen, Freiburg, Halle, Jena, Würzburg, Heidelberg, and Bonn, and at the Technical Institutes. The smaller provincial universities such as Kiel, Erlangen, Greifswald, and Rostock were somewhere in the middle. These variations were influenced more by student self-selection than by differences in the social composition of student bodies. To be sure, the urban universities (but not Munich) included a greater proportion of students from lower middle-class backgrounds who might be expected to avoid fraternity schools for fear of rejection. Commuting students in urban areas were less likely to join fraternities than students who traveled far from home to the popular southwestern universities. Certainly, too, the urban universities attracted students from all classes who were more dedicated to their studies than to student traditions.

With qualification, then, it is still possible to say that socially elite students would be most likely to join the *Corps* where a conservative relatively non-*völkisch* atmosphere prevailed. The *Burschenschaften* attracted the sons of the educated middle classes who had often passed through the *Burschenschaften* themselves. Newer fraternities, like the swastika-wearing *Wehrschaften*, offered their membership a distinctive political program which compensated for lack of status.[78]

In spite of differences in political approach, almost all German fraternities

Table 13   Claimed Fraternity Membership, Winter-Semester 1930/31, as a Percentage of Total Male German Matriculated Full-Time Students at German Universities and Technical Institutes.

	Number of Male Students[a]	Total Claimed %[b]	Mensur[c]	Duel[d]	Catholic[e]	Number of Fraternities[f]
Universities						
Marburg	2,483	134.8	79.8	110.7	11.8	38
Tübingen	2,518	125.8	46.9	72.7	22.5	46
Freiburg	2,541	120.9	41.0	58.5	55.5	52
Hannover T.H.	1,777	123.6	81.5	102.8	16.8	31
Karlsruhe T.H.	1,097	102.5	55.0	69.1	21.6	38
Stuttgart T.H.	1,947	95.1	56.7	76.9	13.7	29
Halle	1,844	85.3	55.3	73.8	4.4	37
Jena	2,298	83.8	57.4	71.9	3.9	31
Würzburg	2,531	83.2	39.3	47.6	33.1	36
Heidelberg	2,378	80.5	35.1	60.6	12.6	37
Bonn	4,301	79.9	24.5	31.7	44.9	99
Königsberg	2,377	77.1	44.6	62.2	7.8	36
Giessen	1,684	74.0	49.4	56.1	8.8	24
Breslau (U & T)	4,107	73.9	21.1	38.8	28.3	67
Darmstadt T.H.	2,161	73.8	39.8	53.8	16.1	38
Münster	3,235	73.4	9.0	16.7	51.5	40
Munich (U & T)	10,526	71.4	34.0	47.8	19.6	106
Göttingen	3,191	72.4	50.5	66.0	6.1	39
Greifswald	1,348	61.1	31.6	50.4	2.5	26
Rostock	1,364	55.9	31.2	46.5	3.4	16
Erlangen	1,754	54.6	26.0	31.9	4.8	22
Kiel	1,973	52.6	27.0	39.4	7.0	23
Leipzig	5,611	49.0	20.1	42.1	2.1	59
Cologne	4,480	49.1	12.9	23.6	23.0	59
Berlin (U & T)	14,929	48.5	21.9	35.6	7.3	144
Frankfurt	2,931	39.1	15.8	21.2	11.8	31
Hamburg	2,742	32.6	13.5	23.1	3.5	16

SOURCE: Compiled from fraternity claims in *Das Akademische Deutschland*, II.

KEY: (a) total male students of German nationality; (b) total number of fraternity members, active and inactive students, claimed by individual fraternities as a percentage of total Reich German male students; (c) members of all fraternities requiring *Mensur*; (d) members of all fraternities who offer unconditional satisfaction in affairs of honor; (e) members of all Catholic fraternities; (f) total number of fraternities of all types.

Deutsche Corpszeitung estimated in 1924 that 9 percent of its membership were members of at least two fraternities (at different universities); see *Deutsche Corpszeitung*, Sept. 1924, pp. 128–29). Because of multiple membership, accurate figures for total on-campus fraternity membership are difficult to arrive at. The figures in the above table are therefore inflated and only approximate. They are provided to indicate relative fraternity strength.

were uncompromisingly nationalist and greater German; few could be characterized as pro-Republican. Political interest rose sharply in all fraternities after the war, but rarely without internal struggles and personal doubts. Traditionalists continued to vie with the politically militant for domination, and the former ordinarily had the advantage of the backing of the *alte Herren*. Political education in most cases took precedence over political action, and social life often preceded both. But if the fraternities were not primarily politically oriented, they were a major medium for the spread of nationalist ideas among students. You might enter a fraternity for social reasons, but you were unlikely to leave it without absorbing some of its values and its nationalistic politics. These politics remained a part of the warp and woof of fraternity life. A nationalist veneer was as socially correct as a dueling scar or a capacity for drinking copious quantities of beer.

THREE

Defenders of a National Faith

In November 1918, working men took up arms and joined the revolution in Germany. Workers paraded in the streets of Berlin, Hamburg, and other large cities. Soldiers and workers organized revolutionary councils, and red flags flew everywhere. The 1918 revolution was made in large part by the members of the well-organized German workers' movement. Its initial successes rested on the power vacuum created by Germany's defeat in World War I. The leaders brought to power in the initial stages of revolution, men risen from the ranks of the Social Democratic Party, sought to remake Germany into a democratic republic similar to that of France rather than into a workers' state.

The middle-class support necessary for the creation of a functioning western-style democracy in Germany was not forthcoming, however. It was not that the middle classes rejected the revolution outright and enrolled in the counter-revolutionary movement. Instead, middle-class sentiment lacked enthusiasm for the Republic while luxuriating in nostalgia for the antebellum age.

In the months after the November revolution, it became apparent that large numbers of students, too, lacked sympathy for Germany's democratic experiment. The pivotal position of the Majority Socialist Party in the formation of the Republic aroused anxieties in middle-class youth brought up to view Social Democracy as a threat to national survival and the representatives of the working masses as unfit for political power. Recurrent left-wing outbreaks kept the fear of radical upheaval alive and brought into question the ability of the new government to maintain law and order.

The unsettled conditions in the years after the war involved the university community in a maelstrom of continued violence. Many student veterans were demobilized only to be recalled as volunteers to help check revolutionary outbreaks. The weakness of the government in the face of disorder permitted the

48

military mobilization of Right as well as Left and involved student volunteers in illegal activities and plots.

In the prevailing atmosphere of confusion and uncertainty, the antidemocratic Right readily regrouped and utilized democratic institutions to attack the Republic. As early as the Reichstag elections of 1920, the Protestant middle classes turned in droves to monarchist parties. In strident election campaigns and in the press, the German Right blamed the Republican leaders for postwar economic disruption and disorder and accused the signers of the Treaty of Versailles of treason. The official contempt for parliamentary politicians assumed by the late Imperial government now bore fruit in bourgeois disillusionment with the democratic process.

In a multitude of little journals and in the salons of Berlin and Munich, nationalist intellectuals discussed "German" alternatives to the "Western" political system introduced by the Weimar constitution. Their arguments and proposals soon found a most significant audience among university students unsettled by prevailing conditions and more open to new solutions than to the old regime's return. One movement in particular, the *Hochschulring,* crystallized both growing student disillusion with Weimar parliamentarianism and the search for an authoritarian alternative which would have a chance of success in an age of mass politics.

The new government, faced with several years of internal rebellion, depended on semisecret irregular forces to fight the revolutionary Left: the freebooting free corps and the community defense groups (*Einwohnerwehren*). In action these groups, often composed of unemployed and disgruntled veterans, proved as much of a danger as bolshevism. Between 1919 and 1923, paramilitary groups were involved in several attempts to overthrow the Republican government, and their members were implicated in the assassination of prominent political figures.

Student veterans, many of whom had been officers during the war, constituted an important pool for paramilitary recruiters. Political authorities, too, encouraged the formation of student companies in university towns to help control local disorders.[1] In the border university towns of Königsberg and Breslau and in Danzig, border protection groups spontaneously organized themselves in January 1919.[2] A month later, Prussian Minister of Culture Konrad Haenisch and Reich Army Minister Gustav Noske joined in an appeal to Prussian students to enter temporary military service and promised state measures to help make up lost study time.[3]

Large-scale participation in the fight against internal rebellion exposed the students as a group to the enmity of many sections of the population. Participation also involved some students in counterrevolutionary plotting at the time of the monarchist Kapp putsch in March 1920.[4] During the putsch students were active in the "Technical Emergency Aid" (*Technische Nothilfe*) which carried on essential utilities abandoned by striking workers.[5] Since the unions had called a general strike to topple Kapp, participation in this program was often tantamount to support of the putsch.

When the Kapp putsch provoked counterinsurgency from the revolutionary Left, students eagerly responded to government and army invitations to aid in putting down rebellions in Thuringia and the Ruhr Valley. When a student contingent shot fifteen alleged "red guard" prisoners near Bad Thal in Thuringia a national furor resulted. The students, who claimed the prisoners were shot in flight, were exonerated in a military trial in spite of ample evidence of deliberate wrongdoing as well as a questionable order to shoot to kill.[6] The verdict was roundly denounced in the Social Democratic press and publicly deplored by the Prussian Minister of Culture who compared the slayings to the brutal murder of Rosa Luxemburg in January 1919.[7] University and student spokesmen in their turn complained that students risked life and limb upon the urging of a Socialist government and their reward was scorn, scorn which extended in fact to all students.[8]

As a result of the Thuringian tragedy, Haenisch forbade student participation in temporary military units in Prussia.[9] Illegal military activities persisted, however. Students played a major role in the free corps during the Upper Silesian disturbances of 1921, and many were involved in the officially condoned Black *Reichswehr* in spite of government prohibitions.[10]

Student paramilitary involvements in Bavaria proved especially persistent. Early in 1919, Reich Army Minister Noske had sent representatives to Würzburg and Erlangen to encourage students to join a free corps under the command of Colonel Franz Xaver Ritter von Epp, later a leading figure in the National Socialist Party.[11] The students in Epp's free corps together with students from Tübingen and Stuttgart were prominent in the military attack upon Munich in late April. They were joined by many Munich students who fought street battles against the revolutionary workers and later linked up with the attacking free corps on the urging of the university Senate.[12] The right-wing Bavarian government which soon took power continued to employ students in local defense units and winked at student participation in other paramilitary groups until 1923.[13]

By this time paramilitary-minded Bavarian students had joined forces with the fledgling National Socialist Party. In 1922, a "national-socialist" student group was founded in Munich as a special section of the Sturmabteilung (SA), the Nazi paramilitary organization.[14] Munich students were involved in significant numbers in the planning and execution of Hitler's Beer Hall putsch in November 1923.[15]

Government authorities had at first turned to students for military aid with the expectation that they would support the government in a more politically neutral manner than the free corps. Those students attracted to paramilitary groups actually proved to be hostile to the Republic, which they associated with the revolutionary Left whom they fought. Large numbers would probably have joined up without official prompting. Indeed, a philosophical leaning to militarism seems to have predisposed many student veterans to paramilitary activities. The literary militarism of Ernst Jünger and Franz Schauwecker who glorified war, praised the spirit of the front as an adventure, and lauded the comradeship of the army as a model for human relations crystallized the attitudes in student circles of the period.[16] The free corps ethic stressed the *bündisch* idea, the belief in the moral and social value of a small, tightly knit group of comrades who sacrificed their own egos to the communal bond, which made them particularly attractive to former youth movement members.

Student military interests did not end with the free corps. The fraternities inculcated essentially military virtues: courage, honor, and discipline. Pacifists were ostracized in the university community. Military solutions to Germany's international problems were mooted at student conferences and in the late 1920s a renaissance in paramilitary training programs took place at universities throughout Germany. The persistence of militarism among students is testimony to the deep roots it had struck in German society before the war.

Early in 1919, a group of students in Berlin who had been active in the youth movement and were associated with the right-wing youth-movement journal, *Jungdeutsche Stimmen,* organized a new society called the *Fichte Hochschulgemeinde,* named for the nineteenth century idealist philosopher and national prophet, Johann Gottlieb Fichte. The *Fichte Hochschulgemeinde* joined with the Berlin *Kyffhäuser Verband* and several members of the Berlin *Burschenschaften* in June in a larger organization called the *Hochschulring Deutscher Art* which soon attracted a large proportion of the students at the university.[17] The *Hochschulring* proclaimed itself to be both nationalist and *völkisch* and strove to become the center of the *völkisch* student movement. The founding students dedicated themselves to the reconstruction of Germany and pledged to defend German character against "internationalism of any coloration."[18] They promised to work within the scope of the new Germany, but only insofar as the new Germany conformed to the historical tradition of the German people.[19]

Contacts among youth-movement members throughout Germany helped the *Hochschulring* idea to spread rapidly. In July 1920, representatives of twenty *Hochschulring* groups and clubs with similar programs met in Göttingen to form a national organization under the leadership of Otto de la Chevallerie, a founder of the *Fichte Hochschulgemeinde* in Berlin.[20] The new group speedily gained the support of most of the important student fraternity associations and of the fraternities on the local level.[21] Fraternities provided necessary financial support for the local groups. In many areas Roman Catholic fraternities also backed the formation of groups in spite of the implied racial anti-Semitism of the movement's statement of principles.[22] Efforts to recruit unaffiliated students were less successful.

The *Hochschulring'*s efforts to define itself as movement rather than party hamstrung its efforts to create real unity on the student right. Like the German National People's Party, the *Ring* encompassed diverse groups and aims and

attempted to fuse conservative and right-wing radical tendencies within one organization. While the movement's founders and continuing leadership envisioned the group's primary goal as the definition and crystallization of a modern nationalist ideology, on the university level the *Ring* tended to operate as a political party as well as a nationalist consciousness-raising group. In order to increase numbers rapidly, local groups encouraged corporate membership of fraternities, sacrificing clarity of purpose for apparent unity of action. The *Ring's* lack of clear relationships to adult political movements and its attempt to preserve a nonpartisan character prevented the adoption of clear stands on concrete political issues or effective programs of action. In the long run, the diverse membership proved unwieldy and unity short-lived.

The *Ring's* somewhat vague ideological program continued the efforts of the prewar *Kyffhäuser Verband* on a broader basis. A minimum consensus was created around such issues as pan-German action, anti-Semitism, and rejection of parliamentary democracy and Marxism. While the national movement sponsored educational programs designed to spread the more specific views of antidemocratic theorists, action programs remained cautious and tentative. Ultimately, the *Ring* was to prove no match for the better organized and ideologically unified Nazi student movement.

During its early years the movement had two general aims: educational and political. The fraternities were the main focus of educational efforts. Those fraternity officials responsible for instructing the "Foxes" (fraternity pledges) were expected to participate in *Ring* activities. In this way the *Ring* reached a far wider circle than is evident by counting attendance at study weeks. In 1920, the *Jungdeutscher* Ring was formed to link the *Hochschulring* with like-minded youth movement groups, and the youth group of the German National Clerks Association (*Deutschnationaler Handlungsgehilfenverband*), a union of conservative white collar workers closely connected to the leadership of the German National Peoples Party.[23] The *Hochschulring's* educational program thus reached beyond the confines of the university.

The *Ring's* chief political aim was to weld nationalist students into an effective force on the university scene. It therefore became a national student political party which contested student government elections, organized parliamentary caucuses on student councils, and attempted to influence the goals and activities of the national student organization, the *Deutsche Studentenschaft*.

The *Ring's* political activities were conspicuously successful. Backed by clear fraternity support, it was able by the spring of 1921 to win majorities on the student councils of a large number of German universities.[24] The electoral victories coincided with a growing involvement of students in political activities. Student government offices, once possessed, became the sites for advocating political programs.

The *Hochschulring* success was by no means limited to fraternity-dominated schools. As the accompanying table reveals, the *Ring* was able to capture a majority of student council seats at the universities in Berlin and Hamburg (Table 14).

Table 14   Percentage of Student Council Seats Won by *Hochschulring* Groups in 1921 (Elections according to Proportional Representation).

Berlin	66	Göttingen	75	Hamburg	90.9
Breslau	80	Greifswald	96	Karlsruhe	95.4
Darmstadt	70.3	Heidelberg	65.2	Kiel	83.3
Erlangen	88				

SOURCE: Mitgau, *Studentische Demokratie; Süddeutsche Akademische Stimmen*, 16 March 1921.

Since the *Hochschulring* was highly decentralized, the politics of the local clubs differed considerably. At some schools, the *Hochschulring* limited itself to political education of all patriotic students and could count on the support of almost all fraternities. At other schools, the leadership drew close to specific political groups. Both the national and local leaderships were selected according to the rules of the "leadership principle" common in the youth movement, rather than by direct election. Outgoing leaders nominated their successors who were approved automatically.[25]

In the national office in Berlin, the reins of leadership remained in the hands of youth-movement graduates with close ties to prominent Young Conservative intellectuals. The Young Conservatives were a diverse group who shared a distaste for parliamentary democracy and favored a political and social revolution which would restore a sense of national community. There was no organized Young Conservative movement. Young Conservative ideas were discussed in small literary circles, influential political clubs, by literary figures, and in newspapers and periodicals, some of which were widely read and others of quite limited circulation. Young Conservative thought was anti-intellectual and elevated irrationalism to a guiding principle. It was often expressed in romantic terminology, contrasting such concepts as organic, universal, dynamic, and soul with mechanical, privatistic, static, and intellect. The Young Conservatives viewed the Weimar Republic as an alien Western import, a mechanical construction which lacked contact with the national spirit. They deplored the alleged weakness of the Republic and championed an aggressive foreign policy. They seldom agreed on the ideal society they wanted Germany to become. Some called for a *Führer* who would express the general will. Others argued for a total reorganization of the nation along the lines of paramilitary *Bünde* like the *Jungdeutsche Orden*. Still others emphasized the need for the rule of small cultural or economic elites. The admirers of Mussolini proposed a corporate state.[26]

The *Hochschulring* leadership maintained close ties with Young Conservative circles in Berlin. For many years, the national office was located at Motzstrasse

22 in Berlin, a beehive of Young Conservative activity. The editorial offices of
Eduard Stadtler's political journal, *Das Gewissen*, were also housed here. The
building was a frequent gathering place for members of Moeller van den Bruck's
circle.[27]

The *Ring*'s advisory council was made up largely of Young Conservative
intellectuals who helped to finance the student groups with the help of political
contacts in the German National People's Party. The most constant friend was
Martin Spahn, a university of Cologne professor, a German National Reichstag
deputy after 1924, a leading spokesman of the Catholic Right, and a tireless
traveler on the university lecture circuit. At Motzstrasse 22, in November 1921,
Spahn founded the Political Seminar for National Political Instruction and
Eduational Work to serve as an intellectual meeting ground for the Young Conservatives and an educational center for *Hochschulring* students.[28] Frequent short-
term lecture series were attended by students from all over Germany. Lecture
series were well publicized in *Ring* newsletters, and several *Ring* leaders were
among Seminar lecturers.[29]

From Berlin, the ideas of the Young Conservatives were spread to student
groups throughout Germany. The national leadership advised local groups to
subscribe to periodicals like *Deutsches Volkstum* and *Jungdeutsche Stimmen* and
to study the writings of Young Conservative thinkers.[30] *Ring* study weeks usually featured Young Conservative speakers.

Although the Young Conservative movement was the dominant intellectual
influence upon *Ring* members in the early 1920s, the organization officially
avoided a clearly defined ideology. The *Ring* advertised itself as a *völkisch*
movement, a purposefully vague description. The term *völkisch*, in its use by the
Ring, defined three areas of endeavor. The *Ring* was anti-Semitic. It favored the
strengthening of the common bond among Germans of all classes and confes-
sions, and the creation of a mystical *Volk* community. Finally, it preached a
struggle for the creation of a *grossdeutsch* Reich with a government responsible
to the will of the *Volk* as a whole, not to warring political parties.

The *Ring*'s anti-Semitism was more a matter of fashion than of considered
political program. In practice, anti-Semitic action was limited to schools where it
was a popular issue. Proposals on the national level for specific guidelines to
prevent the growth of Jewish numbers in university faculties were rejected.[31] The
Ring carefully disassociated itself from "noisy anti-Semitism" (*Radau-
Antisemitismus*). Jews were excluded on the grounds that they were a distinct
nation and could not participate in solving German problems.[32] *Völkisch* education stressed the positive traits of German character while "Jewish influence"
was subtly opposed.[33]

The *völkisch* idea on its positive side emphasized the cultural, political, and
spiritual unity of all Germans. The *Ring* championed the social attitudes characteristic of the prewar *Kyffhäuser Verband*. *Ring* leaders dismissed Marxism as a
materialistic foreign doctrine, void of intellectual content.[34] They believed that

an educated elite should rule and that the students were chosen to be the future leaders of a regenerated Germany.[35]

The *Ring*'s social program was an extraordinary combination of high-minded idealism, shortsightedness, and upper-class arrogance. Its goal was to regain the confidence of the lower classes in a self-appointed national leadership. Since the *Ring* students hoped to wean the workers from Marxism by arousing their nationalist instincts, educational activities were the chief preoccupation of the "social office." The students also sought the confidence of the masses by working in factories and on farms during vacations, acquainting themselves with the everyday problems of the lower classes, and avoiding snobbish airs in personal encounters.[36]

The *Ring*'s political goals were vague and ambiguous. Spokesmen repeatedly announced their "affirmation" of the state, a phrase meant to solace those who opposed revolutionary opposition to the Republic, and those who supported the state in general principle but were only too eager to see its form changed.[37] Criticisms of the state were couched in Young Conservative metaphors.[38] The *Ring* offered no theoretical program for an ideal *völkisch* state; it hoped rather to educate each student and the public morally, ethically, and intellectually so that the spiritual groundwork for a new state might be excavated.[39] The form of the German future would await the founding of a new and greater German Reich.

German expansion was promoted by an extensive program of cultural relations with Germans abroad. The *Ring* cooperated with organizations devoted to the foreign German cause, notably the *Verein für das Deutschtum im Ausland*. Moral and financial encouragement, the students hoped, would strengthen the cultural and political autonomy of German minority groups in Eastern Europe. The *Ring* held lectures and study groups on the problems of German minorities, sponsored student exchanges, organized tours of border areas, and established close contact with foreign German organizations.

The *Ring*'s international activities were soon copied by most fraternity leagues.[40] Indeed if one can believe the panegyrics of undergraduate journals, these efforts became a passion with numerous students. Ties with the German minorities met all the requirements of the "national opposition": they were *völkisch*, nonpartisan, and, best of all, noncontroversial. The preoccupation with the problems of Germans abroad was no doubt at the expense of attempts to understand and solve more pressing problems nearer home. At the same time, it brought students into contact with radical foreign German groups whose ultimate aim was a military revision of the Treaty of Versailles.

The *Ring* ideology and program became the dominant expression of student discontent in the 1920s. The *Ring* offered its membership the common currency of the German Right with an intellectual stamp. The vagueness and superficiality of *Ring* pronouncements exposed the political immaturity of Germany's young educated elite and their unwillingness to come to grips with political, social, and economic realities. The *Ring* sought solutions in the realm of transcendent morality and culture rather than in practical affairs. The political experience of the West, especially democratic elections and parliamentary governments, was rejected *a priori*. Germany's current weakness was seen to be rooted in the imposition of western-style government. It was partisanship founded in parliamentary institutions which divided the country, not the inevitable presence of conflicting social and economic interests in capitalist society. A *German* government based on national institutions would effectively reassert Germany's place in the world.

The *Ring*'s positive program grew out of the neo-Romantic political literature which went back to the 1880s. The complexities of modern society would be overcome by a revived sense of community under an authoritarian political system. German socialism, that is, state-directed capitalism, unlike western capitalism and Russian bolshevism would preserve private property without the devisive and socially disruptive anarchy of untrammeled free enterprise. The development of a true *Volksgemeinschaft* would finish the ugly class conflict and permit Germans of all walks of life to overcome their social differences in the emotional union of nationhood. The unification of German-speaking peoples would make Germany a world power again.

It is not difficult to see the appeal of this program in a Republic faced from its inception with economic chaos and a polarized, militarized politics which verged on civil war. Nor is disillusion with democracy surprising when government economic policies appeared to reward speculators and passively permitted the destruction of the middle class. But the *Ring* program, for all its opacity, clearly implied a fascist-imposed uniformity as the solution to division. The *Volksgemeinschaft* was characteristically defined by the exclusion of Jews, and its practical application demanded a one-party dictatorship. Despairing of the return of authoritarian monarchy, the *Ring* generation quite consciously conceived of fascism as a means of restoring the social and economic status quo antebellum. While the Italian model may have appealed to them, the reality of German-style fascism proved quite different from these romantic musings.

The vagueness of the *Ring* program led inevitably to internal dissension. The movement parasol sheltered reactionaries, conservatives, fascists, and old-style liberals who could not always ignore their underlying differences in a rush of *völkisch* platitudes. By 1922, the organization had developed three divergent groups which contested for leadership. The Berlin office remained under the control of the Young Conservative founders. Although they claimed to be free from political entanglements, they were closely associated with a number of members of the *völkisch* wing of the German National Peoples Party who were unofficial *alte Herren* and financial supporters of the movement. In many local groups where fraternities played the dominant role and free students were largely ignored, the movement was more closely linked with the traditional conservatism of the dominant group of the German National Peoples Party. In Bavaria, an extremist *völkisch* group, associated with the Bavarian free corps and with extreme right-wing parties including the National Socialists, came to the fore. The radical right-wing Bavarians controlled the *Ring*'s official newpaper, the *Deutsche Akademische Stimmen,* which was published and partially subsidized by the *Grossdeutscher Ringverlag* in Munich.[41]

By the fall of 1923, the movement was headed for inevitable rupture. The crisis was provoked by the radicals in Bavaria. Open involvement by the Munich *Ring* in the Beer Hall putsch severely compromised the movement throughout Germany.[42] Kleo Pleyer, who was the chairman of the Munich *Ring* and editor of *Deutsche Akademische Stimmen,* wildly attacked the Catholic Church for its alleged role in thwarting the putsch. He also published inflammatory articles by Nazis and other putsch supporters. One article by a prominent Bohemian National Socialist attacked the Catholic Church, Christianity, and the Old Testament so viciously that the Berlin *Ring* leadership repudiated its contents publicly.[43]

Catholic students in Munich, incensed by Pleyer's attacks upon the Church and upon Munich Cardinal Michael von Faulhaber, angrily denounced his conduct of office. Pleyer, insulted, demanded the right to defend his honor in a duel, a demand which the Catholic students could not meet. The national leadership pleaded with him to withdraw his challenge for the sake of unity.[44] Furthermore, the Bavarian government, finding the *Deutsche Akademische Stimmen* detrimental to public peace, banned the newspaper for four weeks on 4 January, and expelled Pleyer from the state.[45] Under pressure from Berlin, Pleyer finally resigned his editorship.[46]

In the days after 9 November, the *Ring* leadership displayed unusual caution. On 14 November, a nationally circulated memorandum pleaded with the membership to uphold "the united front of all patriotic organisations," to avoid conflict with the army, and to continue to work for the "freeing of the entire Volk."[47] A public announcement on 23 November reiterated the call for unity while gently chastising the Munich *Ring* for involving itself in direct political action. The *Hochschulring,* according to this statement, was a movement dedicated to the "spiritual preparation of all of the German people" and to the principle that "true liberation can only occur after spiritual preparation is actively aspired to."[48] Jürgen Bachmann, the editor of the official *Ring* newsletter who helped write this statement, went on editorially to praise the Munich rebels for their patriotic goals while criticizing their tactics as premature. The putsch was a beginning, not a finale:

> The Munich dead teach us that higher and greater responsibility, and spiritual and physical preparedness will be demanded of us, and that we must not tire in our work among ourselves and among our people with the means of true German idealism.[49]

The national leadership's moderation did not assuage the *Ring*'s Catholic membership. Denunciations of the Church in the wake of the putsch precipitated an open split between Catholic student groups and the *Ring*.[50] A small group of Martin Spahn's followers organized a union of *völkisch* Catholic academics which remained associated with the *Ring*.[51] The Catholic fraternities, however, gravitated to the Center Party. In 1926, the *Görres Ring* was founded as a Catholic alternative to the *Hochschulring* and won the support of the major Catholic student groups.

Although the new association eschewed radicalism, it accepted many of the views associated with the *Hochschulring*. While official statements rejected political beliefs contrary to the "Catholic natural law conception of society," they affirmed a faith in "German nationality . . . because it is something God-given and therefore holy." The Görres Ring stood for the "community of the *Volk*" and emphatically rejected "liberal-humanitarian world citizenship."[52] It "affirmed" the state, yet pledged itself to work for a "Christian organic" reform of the government.[53] Nevertheless, for the period, the Catholic minority represented moderation.

Although the radicals had maneuvered the Catholics into leaving the *Hochschulring,* they failed to gain the cockpit themselves. In February 1924, dissident right-wing *Ring* members founded a German *völkisch* student movement (*Deutschvölkische Studentenbewegung*) which militantly espoused the principles to which, in their view, the *Ring* only gave lip service. General Ludendorff not uncharacteristically accepted the honorary chairmanship of the organization which soon claimed 600 members in Berlin, Munich, Heidelberg, Erlangen, Greifswald, Halle, and Frankfurt.[54] In 1925, a marriage was arranged with the *Völkisch*-Social Student Association of Austria whose newspaper, *Der Student*, became the voice of the united movement.[55] The new group's leaders assured the *Ring* that they would remain within the larger movement as a radical caucus and avoid divisive activities.[56] Its announced program, at least, differed little from the views current in the *Hochschulring*. The first leader announced the group to the public with the usual florid clichés: the goal of an undefined *völkisch* state, the desire for the "renewal of moral-religious spirit," "the will to politics of power" the realization of the "social idea," and "the awakening and deepening of race and *Volk* consciousness."[57]

In reality, the new group represented a root and branch schism from the *Ring*. The *Völkisch* Student Movement was primarily a group of free students who did not always disguise their disdain for fraternities.[58] While the *Ring* had championed nationalist unity and nonpartisanship, the new group had close ties with the Nazis and the related German *völkisch* Freedom Party active in the north. The first meeting of regional leaders in May pledged loyalty to the three political leaders: Ludendorff, Hitler, and Albrecht von Graefe, while avoiding only direct party affiliation.[59] Moreover, these students favored a program of radical political action with the ultimate aim of turning the national student movement as a whole into a political force.[60]

The *Hochschulring*'s checkered career illuminates the course of German student history in the 1920s. Originally organized around a very general set of "national principles," the *Ring* brought together a wide variety of student views under one roof. This broad program proved inadequate to hold the members together. Radical *völkisch* students, middle of the road Catholics, and German Peoples Party supporters soon felt uncomfortable and withdrew support. The conflict between youth-movement oriented free students and fraternity students in the local groups had been more or less resolved by 1928.[61] The fraternities accepted the *Ring*'s ideological leadership with the understanding that the organization would stress education and avoid political action. Although the *Ring* had lost its preeminent place in the university community by the end of the decade, the fraternities had largely succumbed to the Young Conservative ideology emanating from Berlin. The Berlin leadership remained surprisingly stable for a student organization; many of the founders were still active in 1930.

The *Hochschulring* movement harnessed nationalist sentiments among fraternity students and guided them in a Young Conservative direction. Because the fraternities actively supported the *Ring*'s program, right-wing theoreticians were provided with a captive audience. But the *Ring,* like the Young Conservatives, lacked concrete goals. Practical activities were confined to "border work" and, after 1928, military sport. The lackluster social program was gradually abandoned. Furthermore, the *Ring* failed to enlist large numbers of free students. After 1929, it proved unable to compete with more dynamic political groups which espoused action rather than discussion.

For the students of the first decade of the Republic, the *Ring*'s ideology was compelling precisely because of its lack of definition. It offered nostrums for the discontented student whose future was fraught with uncertainties. It promised him the leadership role denied him by the social upheaval which had taken place in the wake of war and revolution. It renewed his pride in his abilities through identification with the *Volk*. It offered him a faith which permitted escape from unpleasant reality by promising future spiritual community.

The *Ring* students' assessment of Germany's problems was not entirely wrong-headed. They recognized the polarization of the political community and the extent to which special interest groups affected Republican policies. But they mistakenly blamed these problems on the defects of the parliamentary system and Germany's territorial losses. Perhaps a renewed sense of national purpose might have provided the social peace which the students so greatly craved, but such a social peace would still have had to be paid for with real rather than romantic concessions to the workers whose needs the *Ring* students never tried to understand. The hierarchical, "organic" government proposed, failing social reform, would by necessity be intellectually and politically repressive. Moreover, the establishment of a greater Germany could only come about through war, a war which promised to be more horrible than the last and might again end in defeat.

The *Ring* students did not foresee or hope for the totalitarian state of the 1930s. Their unwitting aim was to offer past solutions for present problems. Their entire education reinforced an essentially nineteenth century idea: that national strength and unity was the necessary base for a creative, progressive, and prosperous society. They insisted that a paternalistic government like Bismarck's was necessary for national survival. Enchanted by the dichotomy between community and society studied by the sociologist Ferdinand Tönnies, they rejected the complexities of modern society for the psychological security of the preindustrial community.

It is not surprising that the *Ring* flourished in a student community tied to government service either in background or in aspiration. Behind the high-flown phrases lurked the patriarchal civil servant mentality which permeated government, church, and educational system. It was only necessary to dress up the old paternalistic system with new theoretical justifications to combat the seductive theories of democracy and socialism.

The *Ring* ideology was similar to that of the prewar *Kyffhäuser Verband*. The ideas which had been associated once with an activist minority of students now received some support from a large majority. Political anti-Semitism, for example, won respectability and currency with *Hochschulring* support.

Overall, the *Ring* helped prepare for the Third Reich by teaching the greater part of a generation of students to distrust parliamentary government and a foreign policy of compromise and negotiation. It was the principal medium through which antidemocratic thought, so important in undermining the Republic, reached the students. Although the movement avoided direct participation in political struggles, its principles led it into informal relationships with the adult nationalist movement: the paramilitary *Bünde,* the German National Peoples Party, and the Nazis. Its graduates were more comfortable in the "above party" groups of the Right than in the allegedly factious and antinational parties of the Center and Left. Many former Ring members were ultimately won over to National Socialism, notwithstanding its vulgarized version of the *völkisch* creed, because of its demonstrated success in achieving a mass following.

FOUR

German Ancestry and Mother Tongue:
The *Deutsche Studentenschaft*

The ideal of popular sovereignty promised by the 1918 revolution had its impact upon student organization. Student governments were founded at all universities incorporating democratic forms, most copying the Weimar constitution by adopting proportional representation. Individual student governments coalesced into a national student organization, the *Deutsche Studentenschaft*. The formation of student councils was encouraged by state educational authorities in line with their efforts to democratize the university.

Student democratic institutions were never implanted with the seeds of real life. While a lack of clear definition of the prerogatives of student government in a different setting would have permitted students to develop their responsibilities in creative directions, the German faculties were indifferent, if not hostile, to the new phenomenon. Instead, the universities encouraged the traditional fraternities which continued to represent student bodies on ceremonial occasions. The fraternities needed no prompting to use their organized power to dominate most student councils. Proportional representation, instead of creating really representative institutions, tended to favor election campaigns based on political issues and councils consumed by national political quarrels.

Although the development of student welfare programs was the central purpose of the early student councils, the welfare offices ultimately developed separately from student government. With their function undefined, yet clearly limited, student councils by default became sounding boards for political action groups. This development was rather swift, and by 1924, after a series of battles, the *Deutsche Studentenschaft* lost its nonpartisan character and became a right-wing political organization.

In mid-July 1919, while the National Assembly was meeting to write a constitution in Weimar, student representatives met in the baroque city of Würzburg to found an all-encompassing student union along parliamentary democratic lines, but with one important difference. The student founders hoped to fulfill the century-old dream of the *Burschenschaften* by founding a national student movement which would include all German-speaking students in central Europe in a united vanguard of German unity. The sight of fraternity students resplendent in rainbow colors as they wandered from wine cellar to wine cellar or milled in the great courtyard of the eighteenth century bishops' palace where the meetings were held could not help but resurrect images and traditions from other eras. But while fraternity students were the majority voice, free students in somber greys, tans, and blues were heavily represented. Certainly many, both fraternity and free, were still in army dress. Friedrich Georg Jünger reported that in his first postwar semester at Leipzig, fully half the male students still wore uniforms for lack of anything else.[1]

On the whole, a moderate mood prevailed.[2] The representatives of 1919 were active at home filling the lacunae of student life: providing inexpensive housing and eating facilities, inaugurating athletic programs, and giving students a unified voice in areas such as discipline and curricular planning. The constitution passed at Würzburg reflected general support of democratic institutions. The students, like the Weimar National Assembly, adopted the principles of universal and equal suffrage and proportional representation, and made these provisions mandatory for all local councils. They hoped to push university governance in the direction of democracy and involve students in university questions which directly concerned them. Subject committees were proposed on both the local and national levels to enable students to play a role in curricular reform.[3] The assembled students empowered the leaders of their new organization, the *Deutsche Studentenschaft,* to enter into negotiations with state governments with the aim of establishing the local self-governing bodies as legal components of university administration.[4]

The *grossdeutsch* issue which was to occupy the student movement during its first decade first arose at the convention. The problem centered around the relationship to be established with German student councils in Austria and Czechoslovakia. The inclusion of the German universities of the former Habsburg lands was a natural development, since the German intellectual community transcended national boundaries and the universities in the succession states had close ties with those of the Reich. The preservation of German cultural life in East Central Europe had been the special concern of the educated classes who had developed ties with cultural and educational institutions in Germany. The assumption of common bonds was shared by the Left as well as the Right, and the student convention itself was almost unanimously in favor of making their new movement *grossdeutsch*.

The Austrian delegates at Würzburg arrived determined to carry their anti-Semitic principles with them into the *Deutsche Studentenschaft*. The first constitution, in deference to Austrian wishes, included the highly ambiguous provision that membership was open to all students of "German descent and mother tongue." The phrasing was an attempt to confuse as well as defer the issue.[5] It was clear from their statements at the convention that the Austrians and their friends in the Reich would use the phrase to exclude Jews, while Reich German student governments would adopt the "national-cultural" principle which accepted all as German who were culturally German. The door was opened to the union of "Aryan" Austrian and Sudeten student organizations with local student government bodies in the Reich, since the convention, in effect, provided a legal foothold for the exclusion of Austrian Jews. The ambiguous racial clause was therefore bound to become a source of conflict within the organization and a bone of contention with state ministries of education which could only limit the *Deutsche Studentenschaft*'s effectiveness.

The success of student self-government was predicated upon state approval, since state recognition would permit the use of mandatory student fees and would give student institutions official status at the university.[6] When granting recognition, educational officials could ignore neither the problems of the *Deutsche Studentenschaft*'s *grossdeutsch* coalition nor the danger of partisan activities within the student movement. These difficulties were merely tabled by the "Ordinance for the creation of student governments" issued by the Prussian Ministry of Culture in September 1920 and the regulations subsequently issued by the other states in the winter of 1921.[7] Under the model Prussian ordinance, the student governments were permitted to determine which foreign students were eligible for membership. The Prussian student governments were also given the right of coalition with similarly constituted (*entsprechende*) organizations, an ambiguous phrase readily misinterpreted by supporters of the "Aryan" Austrian student councils.

In July 1920, before the announcement of the Prussian ordinance, student representatives convened at Göttingen for a second try at writing a *Deutsche Studentenschaft* constitution. Informed in advance of the Prussian regulations, the delegates, 80 percent of whom were fraternity members, attempted to harmonize the views of Austrian students with those of the state educational authorities.[8] Membership in local student governments was granted to all German citizens and others of German descent and mother tongue. However, the convention recognized the right of the Austrians and Sudeten Germans to exclude Germans of "non-Aryan" ancestry. Jews with German citizenship who attended these universities were allowed to build their own committees which would be represented in the *Deutsche Studentenschaft*. This provision, which did not affect a large number of students, was never tested. No representation provision covered "non-Aryans" with Austrian and Czechoslovakian citizenship, but "Aryan" student governments were permitted to represent "Aryan" students who opposed the racist principle.[9] This compromise, it soon transpired, did not conform to the real wishes of the German educational authorities who could not accept coalitions with the Austrian and Bohemian groups as long as they excluded Jews.

The *Deutsche Studentenschaft* was divided into nine sections called *Kreise*. The Austrian universities constituted *Kreis* VIII and the Sudetenland and Prague,

Kreis IX.[10] The "Aryan" organizations in these countries were given equal rank in the *Deutsche Studentenschaft* and voting strength proportionate to the numbers of German students at their institutions; therefore, these organizations had about 20 percent of all voting delegates.[11] Their representatives were free to vote on all questions including those that did not logically concern them.

The potential influence of these radical foreign Germans upon German student politics frightened many Republican students into renewed efforts against any constitution which permitted "Aryan" student associations. When the Republican minority won temporary control of the organization early in 1922, the right-wing seceded to form a rival association.[12] In the summer of 1922, the schismatic group met in Würzburg to draw up a new constitution which permitted the Austrians and Bohemians full freedom in determining their own membership qualifications.[13]

The leaders of the original *Deutsche Studentenschaft* watched their support melt away to the backers of the Würzburg constitution. Their court struggle to protect their exclusive rights to the name *Deutsche Studentenschaft* was decided in favor of their rivals on a technicality. The state governments whose ordinances they upheld wallowed in indecisiveness. To be sure, a conference of state ministers of culture which met at Stralsund in September 1922 spoke out forcefully against racial membership restrictions and rejected student coalitions with foreign student governments which were not recognized by their states or by the university rectors after 1 October 1923.[14] The Stralsund resolutions, however, were not enforced. The ministers were too split among themselves and too worried about alienating the majority of student leaders to adopt a concerted course of action on this issue.[15]

In January 1924, the leaders of the original *Deutsche Studentenschaft,* their backing now limited to the Rhineland, capitulated and accepted the Würzburg constitution. Their struggle had proved hopeless in the face of student hostility and lukewarm government support. The Würzburg constitution remained the basis of the national student organization until 1933. With the pan-German issue as a basis, the student Right had won elections in most student councils, and local student politics were dominated by the political battle. The Left and Center too ultimately chose to enter the fray, instead of compaigning on local issues. Since only a small minority backed liberal and socialist groups and Catholic students were deeply split on the *grossdeutsch* issue, the Right had a clear field.

With the resolution of the constitutional conflict in favor of the right-wing position, the *Deutsche Studentenschaft* was set upon a nationalist, anti-Weimar course. The *grossdeutsch* coalition played a major role in radicalizing German student politics. The Austrian *Kreis* influenced Reich German opinion directly by their sponsorship of a widely read and frequently racist student journal, the *Deutsche Hochschulzeitung.*[16] In Germany, the *Deutsche Studentenschaft* and the local student governments by 1925 were largely controlled by the fraternities in tandem with the *Hochschulring,* the only organized groups capable of bringing out the vote. Political clubs garnered little support. The minority, pro-Republican

and anti-*völkisch* position remained a factor at the predominantly Catholic Rhineland universities and at the larger city universities. It was almost nonexistent at
the smaller universities, the Technical Institutes, and in Bavaria. Since every
school sent at least one delegate to the national congresses, the smaller schools
were overrepresented. The structure of the *Deutsche Studentenschaft* tended to
buttress the majority's stronghold and to exclude minority representatives from
participation on the national level.

In the mid-1920s, the German student movement defined itself increasingly in
opposition to the state. In conscious recall of the struggle between Metternich
and student radicals of the previous century, twentieth century student spokesmen tended to associate their own cause with the *Burschenschaft* fight for national unity and academic freedom. The university faculties' posture of autonomy under siege provided the backdrop for conflict between student government and state authority.

The nineteenth century radicals had been less than tolerant of antinational
intellectuals, and the students of the 1920s, carried on the tradition by opposing
pacificists and socialists in the professorial ranks. Academic freedom was said to
be in jeopardy from left-wing teachers associated with partisan causes or those
imposed upon the universities by state officials seeking a more balanced academic
community. The tacit support of university faculties for this position is well
illustrated by their actions when unpopular professors were boycotted.

The tide of radicalism among students in the middle 1920s was testified to by a
number of events. The most widely publicized was an organized assault with
anti-Semitic overtones upon an internationally known philosophy professor at the
Hanover Technical Institute, Theodor Lessing.[17] Lessing was guilty of a number
of extracurricular sins in the students' eyes, in particular a controversial series of
essays about the Haarmann sex murder trial (a case which inspired the movie *M*)
and a series of wittily critical articles about Field Marshall von Hindenburg,
penned during Hindenburg's campaign for the presidency. After prolonged and
violent demonstrations, Lessing was relieved of classroom teaching duties, a
compromise applauded by his largely unfriendly colleagues, acceptable to the
Prussian Ministry of Culture, but contrary to generally held principles of
academic freedom.

The Hanover happenings were applauded by an overwhelming majority of
delegates at the National Student Convention meeting in Bonn in 1926. The
assembled students found praise for those riotous Hanover students who coura-
geously and "without fear of the consequences had taken up and carried through
the battle for a high ideal of academic life."[18] The Bonn convention was also the
scene for a childish attack upon the Republican flag.[19] Elections to the *Deutsche
Studentenschaft* executive board confirmed the general impression that the assembly had no more interest in conciliating the increasingly restive Catholic
moderates than they had in listening to the persistent if futile protests of the
Republican stalwarts. The newly elected executive board, made up entirely of

members of dueling fraternities, was headed by Günther Thon, a *völkisch Burschenschafter* from the Sudetenland, a direct challenge to those educational authorities who continued to express annoyance with the *Deutsche Studentenschaft*'s Austrian and Sudeten German connections. The official transcript of the Bonn convention was in fact one sad tale of anti-Weimar petulance and flagrant disregard of the voices of moderation.[20]

Both the Lessing furor and the disturbances over the flag at the Bonn convention were widely publicized and produced a wave of unfriendly criticism. This publicity helped to undermine the already less than cordial relations between the student politicians and left-of-center state governments. The governments of Baden and Hamburg repeatedly attempted to force their students to sever relations with the *Deutsche Studentenschaft*.[21]

The greatest threat to the *Deutsche Studentenschaft* was posed by the government of Prussia. Early in April, a number of delegates in the Prussian Landtag expressed their concern over the political tone of much *Deutsche Studentenschaft* activity, the continued scandal of *Deutsche Studentenschaft* membership provisions, and fiscal irregularities which had been exposed in several local student governments.[22]

On 18 May 1926, the Prussian Landtag formally requested that the Ministry of Culture alter the 1920 student ordinance in order to eliminate the possibility of corruption and to clarify ambiguities in student government membership provisions.[23] On 19 April, Minister of Culture Becker acted independently to reduce the amount of student dues sent by the local groups to the *Deutsche Studentenschaft*.[24] Becker maintained, when questioned later about this action in the Landtag, that the money could be spent for better effect on the local level.[25]

Becker was in fact faced with an embarrassing dilemma. He retained his belief in the ultimate rectitude of meaningful student government as an integral part of the university community and therefore hesitated taking any precipitous action which might endanger the already shaky relations between student leaders and educational authorities. A new conflict might harm the successful cooperation with the students in student welfare programs and in the area of physical education. But he was under continuous pressure from the Landtag to alter the 1920 student ordinance.[26] Democratic students also pressed for action. In Bonn, a liberal-Catholic majority succeeded in December in revising the student government constitution with wording that closely paralleled a Heidelberg constitution which had been overwhelmingly condemned by the national student convention in August.[27]

On 9 December 1926, Becker met with the cultural committee of the Prussian Landtag. A majority expressed opposition to the *völkisch* presence in the *Deutsche Studentenschaft* and the increasing role of right-wing politics symbolized by the events at the Bonn convention in August. Becker replied that the government would insist upon reform and concluded that the Ministry was prepared, in the event of defiance, to discontinue the experiment in student self-government.[28]

Becker addressed the students in a public letter dated 24 December to which the students soon gave the ironic rubric, Becker's "Christmas message." He took care to praise the greater German ideal of the *Deutsche Studentenschaft*'s founders, but insisted that the present association was not *grossdeutsch* but a Reich German association linked with foreign racist groups. He went on to demand that the Prussian student organizations revise their membership provisions in strict accord with the resolutions of the Prussian Landtag and that they unite in future only with groups with the same membership provisions.[29]

The strategy adopted by *Deutsche Studentenschaft* leaders and pursued throughout the ensuing crisis began to assume a recognizable form in a "New Year's reply" to Becker's "Christmas message." Although the Minister's action was prompted by Landtag pressure, the students insisted that their real quarrel was with Becker; that Becker's insidious campaign against student freedom was evident in his demand for financial control over student funds and in his attempt to give the rectors the deciding voice in determining membership in student government. The campaign's anti-Becker focus was capsulized in a poem and a cartoon in *Kladderadatsch*, a conservative journal of satire, which dubbed Becker "student father," because of his allegedly hypocritical concern for student rights.[30]

On 23 September 1927, after the failure of compromise attempts by Prussian student leaders, Becker announced a new student ordinance for Prussia. All students who were members of the German "cultural community" were to be accepted as members of the officially recognized Prussian student organizations. Coalitions with non-Prussian student organizations whose membership provisions differed were strictly forbidden. The financial affairs of the student governments were to be placed under strict controls.[31] Rectors were given until 15 December to hold referendums on the new student ordinance.[32] If a majority of a school's students rejected it, the university would cease to have an officially recognized student government with compulsory dues. The vote would also be counted as negative if a majority of students failed to vote.[33]

The *Deutsche Studentenschaft* leaders reacted by seeking assurances that their flank would not be attacked in other German states. Officials in Bavaria, Württemberg, Hesse, and Thuringia promised not to succumb to Prussian pressures and denied that any change in their policies toward students was imminent. Only Baden and Hamburg were certain to follow Prussia's lead. The students also had an ally in the Reich Minister of the Interior, Walter von Keudell, a member of the German National Peoples Party. Keudell promised to use his influence to garner support for the *Deutsche Studentenschaft* in the other German states.[34] Because Prussia was acting almost unilaterally, the *Deutsche Studentenschaft* leaders apparently hoped that Becker might retreat to a position which would permit a loose association with the foreign German groups.[35] A compromise proposal along these lines was in fact submitted to the Prussian Ministry on behalf of the students by Carl Duisberg, the chairman of the Reich

Association of German Industries.[36] But in a meeting with *Deutsche Student-enschaft* leaders on 14 October Becker rejected any solution which would maintain ties with racist groups.[37]

With the possibility of an acceptable compromise ruled out, the student leaders chose defiance. On 18 October the *Deutsche Studentenschaft* executive board condemned the new ordinance publicly as an attack upon academic freedom and warned that acceptance would destroy the student movement.[38] The following week, the central committee, composed of the ten regional leaders, pronounced the ordinance unacceptable, with only regions V (Rhineland) and X (Brandenburg-Berlin) abstaining.[39] This vote provided the constitutional basis for an organized campaign to defeat the ordinance.[40]

For help in the campaign, the *Deutsche Studentenschaft* turned to the fraternities. With the exception of the Catholics, the major leagues promised all-out aid.[41] "Battle" committees of fraternity members were organized at each university to spearhead the drive. Particular attention was paid to the Rhineland schools and the University of Berlin where the student councils were judged unreliable.[42]

The campaign for a "no" vote culminated in a mammoth demonstration of 4,500 persons in Berlin's *Zirkus Busch* on 27 November. A uniformed *Stahlhelm* contingent was accompanied by a *Stahlhelm* band which played military marches. Professor Martin Spahn addressed the assembled students on academic freedom. The Austrian ambassador, who had also been on the speakers' program, apparently had second thoughts and did not appear.[43]

But opposition to the new student ordinance was not limited to the Right. Many were won over by the argument that financial supervision of student government was insulting and that the ordinance was a serious attack upon student self-determination. An observer in Bonn noted that many free students were planning to vote against the ordinance out of disgust with the existing student government which they resented as a creature of the fraternities.[44] In Cologne, Social Democratic students were reported to be counseling a "no" vote for similar reasons.[45]

In the end, only the students of the small Catholic Theological Academy in Braunsberg accepted the new ordinance. At the University of Münster and the Technical Institute of Aachen it was defeated by an election boycott by antiordinance forces which reduced participation to less than 50 percent.[46] In all of Prussia, 26,315 "no" votes were cast against 7,460 "yes" votes. The ordinance did achieve creditable support in some areas. At the University of Berlin 39 percent and at Bonn 36 percent voted "yes." But at the more nationalistic campuses, the results could only be called a debacle for the government. Typical of the majority was the 6 percent "yes" vote in Halle and the 9 percent in Marburg (Table 15).

The referendum results were a severe defeat for Becker's student policy. The provision for student approval had been a serious miscalculation. Becker had hoped that the desire for state-recognized student organizations would be

Table 15   Vote on New Student Ordinance, 30 November 1927.

	% Voting	No	Yes
Aachen Technical	41	21	360
Berlin Business	65	684	260
Berlin Agriculture	73	343	19
Berlin Technical	87	2,775	541
Berlin Veterinary	88	199	6
Berlin University	ca. 79	4,101	2,570
Bonn University	77	1,702	978
Bonn Agriculture		333	42
Braunsberg Theological	100	1	32
Breslau Technical	79	555	101
Breslau University	76	1,740	691
Clausthal Mining	80	291	3
Düsseldorf Medical	88	46	26
Eberswalde Forestry	85	67	0
Frankfurt University	54	1,101	420
Göttingen	70	1,866	291
Greifswald	73	815	55
Halle	75	1,513	98
Hanover Technical	81	1,337	167
Hanover Veterinary	94	204	4
Hanover-Münden Forestry	88	112	1
Kiel		1,054	187
Cologne	57	2,200	563
Königsberg Business		284	53
Königsberg University		1,255	168
Marburg	78	1,737	179
Münster	30	(automatic rejection—figures not published)	

SOURCE: Leisen, *Die Ausbreitung* ..., p. 146; *Deutsche Akademische Rundschau*, 15 December 1927, p. 8.

stronger than the political demand for a continuation of the Austrian connection. In fact, the *Deutsche Studentenschaft* had been able to persuade many students indifferent to the Austrian question that Becker's real aim had been to undermine student self-government; to restrict severely both the sphere of student government activities and the right of the students to run their own affairs. The coupling of financial controls with the new restrictions upon the right of coalition was a serious tactical error.

Uncertainties about the effects of a negative vote probably contributed to student willingness to vote no. Many student leaders seem to have believed that defeating the ordinance would set the stage for a compromise with the Prussian state. The planning of independent student organizations as successors to the student governments had begun before the referendum, but these governments were most certainly viewed as only temporary solutions.[47] On 11 December representatives of the Prussian student councils meeting in Goslar reaffirmed that their goal remained the creation of officially recognized student organizations governed by the student law of 1920.[48] Probably, if Becker had acted simply by issuing his new ordinance and avoided the referendum campaign, the Prussian student governments would have had no alternative but to submit.

But it was now too late for the Prussian Ministry to retreat. In an emotional speech in the Landtag, punctuated by whistles from the Right, Carl Becker defended his student policy. He deplored the attempts of political groups to capitalize upon the student quarrel with the government, placing particular blame on the hostility of the politically active *alte Herren* of the fraternities and the indifference of the university faculties for the result of the referendum. For Becker, student government in Prussia was now a closed book:

> The beautiful dream of the generation of war participants is over. Student self-government has ceased to exist. What remains is student politics as a part of general politics. Of course, officially guaranteed funds and state buildings will not be provided for these political purposes.[49]

The day before, Becker had sent the Prussian rectors instructions on liquidating student governments. Student participation on university committees was to be terminated. Independent student welfare organizations were to be established where they did not already exist. Student fees would henceforth be distributed by the universities directly to student groups in areas such as athletics and academic clubs. The students were free to set up independent associations, but these were not to be recognized as successors to the official student governments.[50]

The loss of official recognition in Prussia weakened but did not destroy the German student movement. The character of the movement, however, was altered in a direction that might well have given Prussian Ministry officials second thoughts. Robbed of their Republican and left-wing elements and their constructive functions, many of the new independent "free student governments" in Prussia began to concentrate upon political activities which took an increasingly radical form. The *Deutsche Studentenschaft* suffered a severe financial setback with the termination of compulsory dues in Prussia, and the precarious situation increased with the subsequent refusal of most of the other German states to permit student funds to be sent to the central organization. The *Deutsche Studentenschaft* was forced to seek funds from the fraternity leagues which now directly influenced the organization's direction. As in Prussia, political questions increasingly took precedence over student problems in the affairs of the national organization. A weakened *Deutsche Studentenschaft* would be easy prey for a new generation of radical students.

The politicization of the *Deutsche Studentenschaft,* however, had begun before the crisis in Prussia. The real issue of the constitutional struggle was neither the Austrian connection which the Ministry emphasized nor the right of student self-government which the students claimed they were defending. The students were committed to a nationalist movement which by its very nature came into conflict with the Republican government. No Prussian government could justify support to a student organization which had affronted a large part of their constitutency in the Lessing affair and the Bonn student convention. There was good reason to believe that such incidents would multiply in the future. If a crisis had not developed over the *Deutsche Studentenschaft*'s *grossdeutsch* relations, it would certainly have erupted over another issue. The state governments were powerless to arrest the drift of student opinion toward the Right.

FIVE

Students in Brown Shirts:
The Rise of the
National Socialist German Student Union

In the spring of 1926 at twenty universities in Germany, small groups of students could be observed in the motions of feverish organization, distributing leaflets, giving extemporaneous speeches at the gates of the universities, holding open meetings to which the university community was invited, even talking to workers in factories. Their brown shirts identified them as members of the National Socialist movement, a small but growing right-wing political party which heretofore had aroused notice by the abortive beer-hall putsch of November 1923. A *Corps* man gripping his saber on the way to a *Mensur* might well have chuckled at this energetic activity and at the outlandish suggestion that the flotsam and jetsam of the radical Right might gain more than a toehold among students. But his scorn would not have been well placed. Within four years, the brown shirts became ubiquitous at all universities, and their wearers had taken control of student council after student council. Long before the Nazis became a force in national politics, they were to become the dominant political force among students.

The pre-1928 student leadership had combined radical phrases with a largely traditionalist outlook. Their distaste for the politics of the Weimar Republic was rooted in a sincere, if misguided, belief that the Republican leaders were not loyal to the national idea and that the Republic was not capable of restoring Germany to greatness. The *Deutsche Studentenschaft,* from its early days, had adopted as paramount goals the defense of the national ideal and the creation of a greater-German state. The students refused to admit that either of these issues was political. The student leaders believed themselves to be above politics; they insisted that the national movement, as they conceived it, was nonpartisan. The crime of Weimar parliamentarianism was the attempt to inject political questions into areas where they did not apply. The German universities had, at least in theory, traditionally eschewed political questions while remaining faithful to the ideal of a united German nation. Students were heirs to this tradition and to that part of the German liberal heritage which attempted to reconcile the ideal of intellectual freedom with the reality of the authoritarian state forged by Bismarck. The students of the early 1920s also shared with their nationalistic teachers a nostalgia for the world before 1914 in which academic freedom had coexisted with a national state founded in a strong monarchy. The student fraternities in their synthesis of the nationalist tradition, defense of academic freedoms, canonization of Bismarck, and Prussian military values, remained a reflection of the old regime.

The National Socialist movement represented a direct threat to the traditional university. The new movement was anti-intellectual: it praised action and scorned contemplation; it denied the possibility of objectivity and freedom from values. The ideal of intellectual liberty, which had been cherished by generations of German scholars, was mocked by the Nazis as a foreign importation. The nation, they averred, not the individual, was the central social organism, and the national genius would best be grasped intuitively by the simple German peasant or worker, not by corrupted intellectuals. The *völkisch* ideology, shared by many students before the appearance of National Socialism, to be sure, had often stressed similar themes; but such ideas were usually leavened by an elitism which the Nazis rejected. The Nazis alone carried the *völkisch* ideology to its logical populist conclusions, conclusions which should hardly have comforted defenders of the idea of the German university.

The irreconcilable antagonism between the free German university and the totalitarian pretensions of the Nazi movement was to have tragic consequences after 1933. In the 1920s, only a few members of the university community recognized the danger. *Völkisch* ideology, which had made major inroads among university students, made many quite receptive to the Nazi version. The principle that there were no enemies on the Right prompted many more students as well as their nationalistic professors to accept the incongruous presence of Nazis on the university scene and, indeed, to cooperate with them. Before 1930, the Nazis wisely attempted to accommodate their movement to university life. They sought to give their program intellectual content, to emphasize national and academic issues rather than exclusively racial appeals, and to give lip-service to the ideals of academic freedom and university autonomy. Their rapid rise, which culminated in National Socialist dominance of student politics by 1930, proved the success of this strategy.

Radical *völkisch* groups were present at many German universities in the early 1920s, but in most cases they had not seriously challenged the position of the *Hochschulring* movement which found its main strength in the fraternities. In Bavaria, paramilitary activities brought many students into contact with the Nazi movement in its formative years.[1] As early as 1922, a "national socialist" student group was founded in Munich. The Munich group was in effect a special section of the SA, the Nazi paramilitary organization.[2] SA chief, Ernst Röhm in his memoirs had particularly high praise for the students in the SA.[3]

The Bavarian groups in the *Hochschulring* movement also had close contacts with the Nazis in 1923, and the Munich leadership seems to have had some knowledge of putsch plans previous to the Nazi-led rebellion of 9 November 1923, participating in the negotiations for uniting all nationalist groups in a common effort. Student involvement in the November events in Munich, however, did not represent an important trend in student politics. It was several years before the Nazis began to make significant inroads into the student population. At the time of the conflict between the *Deutsche Studentenschaft* and the Prussian government, the fraternities were the unchallenged leaders of student politics. The fraternities were an important factor in the *Hochschulring* organization and dominated most student councils.

Attempts by political groups to organize free students were usually unsuccessful. Socialist and Communist attempts to unite free students around their political programs were repeatedly frustrated in spite of the fact that these groups appealed to the very real resentment provoked by the social pretensions of the fraternities. For the most part, only those students whose backgrounds were working class were attracted to the Marxist groups. Jews, to be sure, were attracted by the Socialist hostility toward bigotry. But the vast majority of free students were upwardly mobile in social outlook and shared the suspicion of Marxism characteristic of the German middle classes.

It was among the free students that the Nazis first began to make headway and until 1933, because of fraternity discouragement, it was free students who provided the hard core of Nazi student support. The Nazis appealed to the anger which many of these students harbored for the social divisions visible at the universities. Their political objectives went beyond mere *völkisch* rhetoric by offering a social program which appealed directly to the large number of students who were in economic difficulties. To be sure, social goals were often expressed in glittering generalities, but from the time of their first contact with the universities the Nazi leaders found it entirely consistent with their own aims to call for a more democratic university, one which admitted a larger percentage of students from the less advantaged classes and provided poorer students with the necessary financial support.[4]

The first official Nazi student group was founded at the University of Leipzig in November 1925. The group's founder, a Party member named Werner Studentkowski, had previously been the leader of the *Völkische Finkenschaft,* a small group of free students organized to contest student government elections.[5] There is no evidence that this new organization was anything but spontaneous or that the Party at this time had any clear plan for entering student politics. The Leipzig group seems to have stimulated activities in Munich where a number of National Socialist students, centering around Wilhelm Tempel and Helmut Pödlich, were apparently given the green light for the organization of a national movement. On 20 February 1926, Tempel and Pödlich announced the foundation of a National Socialist German Student Union (*Nationalsozialistischer Deutscher Studentenbund*) in the pages of the *Völkischer Beobachter,* the official Party paper. By June of that year, twenty groups existed, at least on paper, undoubtedly made up almost exclusively of students who had already been Party members.[6] In July, Joseph Goebbels addressed a national meeting of the Student Union in Weimar. The conference elected Tempel president, pending Hitler's approval, which came the following week.[7]

Under Tempel's leadership, the new organization appealed to students' populist instincts with a two-pronged program: the Student Union sought to bridge the social gap between students and workers and to enroll a greater proportion of working class youth in the universities by increasing financial aid. The first issue of the Student Union journal, the *Nationalsozialistische Hochschulbriefe*, underlined this emphasis by giving over its first page to a call for all students to forsake bourgeois "caste spirit" and fight for "German socialism."[8] A circular sent to all member groups early in 1926 charged them with the basic task of increasing contacts with workers.[9] The strongest local groups during the first year of the organization were at the big city universities of Frankfurt, Breslau, Berlin, Leipzig, and Munich, where lower class youth were enrolled in proportionately greater numbers and where extensive contacts with workers' groups were possible.[10] The Nazi ranks in the earliest years included a high percentage of poorer students, although Tempel's assertion that 90 percent of the Union membership were work-students was probably an exaggeration. Student Union leaders in the Tempel period were all work-students.[11]

To emphasize the populist aim, Wilhelm Tempel's Munich organization held a series of meetings in 1926, to which both students and workers were invited, and which were addressed by National Socialist notables, including Joseph Goebbels and Adolf Hitler. A central theme of these talks was that students and workers were the two most revolutionary groups in German society and that if they were united in national instead of class consciousness, they could lead the way to the national revolution.[12] The worker-student theme was also mentioned in Goebbels's speech to the first national conference of the Student Union in July. The Student Union, moreover, publicized its opposition to the widespread practice of student participation in the Emergency Technical Aid program (*Technische Nothilfe*), which supplied substitutes for striking workers in essential industries. Student members were strictly forbidden from taking part in such strikebreaking activities.[13]

In an open letter to all students, published in the *Völkischer Beobachter* on the eve of the ninth German student convention, Wilhelm Tempel focused attention on the class character of the German universities and condemned the fraternities in particular for antagonizing the workers.[14] The National Socialist German Student Union differed from older *völkisch* student groups such as the *Hochschulring*—Arthur von Behr, the leader of the Berlin National Socialist students, wrote a year later—because of its more militant anti-Semitic stance and its constant emphasis upon "a real community of the *Volk,* that is, extermination of academic class pride [*Standesdünkel*] . . . ." and the opening of the universities to "every gifted German."[15]

The Student Union's initial commitment to the worker-student theme was a cause of recurring controversy within the movement. Wilhelm Tempel, who had hoped to make the new organization one of socially concerned free students, forfeited a great deal of control when he transferred, in the fall of 1927, from the Nazi "capital" of Munich to the University of Leipzig. In September, the Student Union was placed directly under the aegis of the national party leadership and became, at least temporarily, dependent upon the party treasury for funds.[16] The key Munich student group fell to the leadership of Baldur von Schirach, the son of a retired first lieutenant from a guards regiment. Schirach's position was strengthened by his friendship with Adolf Hitler, whom he had first met in Weimar several years before.[17]

Tempel and his friends in Leipzig were increasingly disturbed by the tone of Schirach's Munich organization. Schirach wanted the Student Union to recruit fraternity students, not alienate them.[18] The Leipzig leadership accused Schirach of establishing a lavish clubhouse, a kind of salon for the entertainment of Munich society. Leipzig was suffering, in the meantime, from lack of money; Schirach, it was claimed, had had the effrontery to refuse to subscribe to Tempel's journal, *Junge Revolutionär,* because of clubhouse expenses.[19] Schirach strenuously denied these accusations, claiming he had rented a larger apartment with his own funds in order to provide clubroom space for the Student Union. His "salon" evenings, which in any case were his private affair, had provided a number of Munich poets with a forum they might otherwise not have had, and Nazi speakers such as Alfred Rosenberg had also addressed Schirach's guests. Indeed, Adolf Hitler had occasionally taken part in these gatherings.[20]

This apology could hardly have comforted Tempel, who was incensed by Schirach's social climbing. But when he attempted to exclude Schirach from the Student Union, he only succeeded in earning Hitler's antipathy.[21] Tempel's problems were compounded by a revolt against his leadership in Northern Germany. The local groups in Kiel, Hamburg, and Berlin objected to Tempel's hostility toward the *Hochschulring* and the *Deutsche Studentenschaft* and attempted to pursue an independent course of action. The Kiel group, under the leadership of Joachim Haupt, went so far as to reject the leadership of the central organization, placing itself under the protection of the Schleswig-Holstein party *Gau* officers.[22] Tempel replied first by firing Haupt as Kiel chairman and then dissolving the Kiel organization.[23] Haupt refused to submit and took his case directly to Hitler with the aid of friends in Berlin and Hamburg.[24]

Tempel, who could not win the support of the party in these factional disputes with Haupt and Schirach, finally resigned in disgust in June 1928.[25] After his resignation, Hitler polled the local group leaders for his successor. The majority, according to a memo sent out by Rudolf Hess, supported candidates opposed to the old leadership. From the names suggested, Schirach was chosen the new chairman of the Student Union by the Party leadership.[26] The Schirach-Tempel struggle was one aspect of the conflict between the Nazi Party's Left, led by the Strasser brothers from Berlin, and Adolf Hitler. Tempel's journal, *Der Junge Revolutionär*, had been published by the Strassers' Berlin Kampf-verlag. Schirach's rise was a clear victory for Hitler and insured that the Student Union would remain subordinate to him. His personal fondness for Schirach in this period, however, permitted the latter to provide the basic tone and program of the Union.

The transfer of leadership from Tempel to Schirach marked a decisive break in the development of the Student Union. The class consciousness and social concern of the early members was sacrificed for a program designed to attract the majority of German students. Schirach's struggle with the Student Union's "left-wing" was to continue sporadically, but with Hitler's support he was able, without much effort, to keep the reins of his organization.[27] The upheaval in the Student Union leadership paralleled the end of the attempt by the parent Nazi party to effect major inroads among urban workers.[28] This change in party line could only benefit the Student Union, which in any case did not abandon its efforts to capitalize upon the lower middle class resentment characteristic of its free student constituency. But it did open the way for support from more affluent students, particularly within the fraternities.

A social analysis of the Student Union membership of the Schirach years is not now possible. One study of the group at the University of Freiburg found that membership was recruited from all faculties. The Freiburg group included both free and fraternity students but not all students in the group were identifiable. An unusual number of foreign students of German background played leadership roles also.[29] Statistics relating to the University of Würzburg indicate that the National Socialist group there was much like the general student body in social origin.[30] Those occupational groups most characteristic of students' fathers were all represented significantly in the National Socialist Party before 1933. Of these, white collar workers and the self-employed provided a much higher proportion of party members than civil servants and professionals.[31]

Under Schirach's leadership, the Student Union attempted to win a measure of academic respectability in order to increase its attractiveness among students. The student groups were portrayed as the intellectual "shock troops" of the Nazi movement, and a great deal of effort was devoted to discussion of National Socialist *"Wissenschaft."* In practice the Student Union groups imitated the patterns set by other *völkisch* student associations, particularly the *Hochschulring*. They sponsored lecture series open to the entire student body and also instituted intensive programs for internal education. In June 1929, Schirach described the three principal aims of the Nazi student movement as:

a) scientific (handling special questions of National Socialism)

b) propagandistic (spreading of National Socialist thought in the universities)

c) educational (training of the new leadership generation for the National Socialist Party).[32]

Schirach and Hitler hoped that the students would be a reservoir of talent for the party in areas such as journalism, administration, and party propaganda.[33] Members were encouraged, during their university years, to play an active role in the propaganda activities of the party and to address nonuniversity audiences.[34]

In fulfilling their educational objectives, the Student Union did not limit discussion to the ideas of party theorists. An attempt was made to provide students with a secure grounding in the principles of *völkisch* thought. The *Akademischer Beobachter,* an official Nazi student journal founded in 1929 under Schirach's editorship, sought to include articles by non-Nazi intellectuals like Ernst Jünger, prophet of a militarist ideology; Othmar Spann, a leading Catholic intellectual who proposed a corporate state along fascist lines; and Werner Lass, the leader of the Youth Movement group *Freischar Schill,* as well as party lights like the philosopher Alfred Rosenberg and economic theorist Gottfried Feder.[35]

Party speakers were frequently invited to address university groups in order to provide "expert" knowledge about those subjects which interested students. In April 1931, an extensive list of such speakers and their topics was circulated by the central organization.[36] When outside speakers were not available, group members often gave public addresses.[37] But well-known speakers were preferred because they attracted larger crowds. On one occasion, in 1931, in order to attract a large audience to a speech by Gottfried Feder, the Party's economic expert, in Munich, the posters mentioned that the prominent economist Alfred Weber had been invited to participate in the discussion. Although Weber refused the invitation, the entire hall and stage were crowded with unwitting guests anxious to witness a confrontation between Weber and Feder.[38]

The student groups also sponsored extensive programs of public discussion meetings led by group members. Frequent topics for discussion included criticism of the capitalist system and the liberal Weimar state, the problem of foreign policy, educational reform, and racial anthropology.[39] In addition to the usual Nazi rhetoric, an attempt at a serious scholarly approach to these subjects was necessary in order to convince interested students that the movement had something to offer to intellectuals. Thus, a discussion of racism might emphasize the importance of the racial factor in the understanding of history.[40] A political discussion would concentrate upon a critique of the Weimar constitution.[41] An economic study might trace the growing influence of private capital upon public policy.[42] The works of important non-Party right-wing figures were frequently a subject for discussion, like Othmar Spann and Oswald Spengler.[43] The aim of these studies was not only indoctrination but keeping participants abreast of current politics. In Kiel, in 1931, each member was directed to prepare a paper on a topic chosen from a list drawn up by the group leader, Dr Hempel, and follow this up with a talk at a discussion meeting. The list offers a glimpse of the intellectual interests of members at the time, ranging widely into questions of religion, educational theory, and economic policy. The predictable suggestions, such as "racial hygiene" and "heredity theory and blood group research," were balanced by topics like "presentation and critique of the first (2/15/1919) and the

second (7/31/1920) socialization commission with special regard to the concept
of private property," "state bank politics since 1918 and the relationship of
fascist and bolshevist states to bank capital," "the agricultural policy of the
Soviet Union," "the educational foundations of the new humanist movement:
Werner Jäger, Spranger, Stenzel, and National Socialism," and "the attitude of
modern dialectical theory (Gogarten, Barth, Brunner) to state and *Volk*."[44]

It is certainly no wonder that many students were not entirely sure how the
beliefs of prominent exponents of the *völkisch* view differed from National
Socialism. A letter from the Student Union leadership in 1932 specifically
warned against the infiltration of the student movement by followers of Spann
and Gogarten who supported a Christian universalism.[45] The Party bosses could
hardly have looked with favor upon the ideas of a theological student and Party
member who told a large group in Göttingen in June 1929 that National
Socialism was the natural heir of Christianity. Christianity, like Nazism, he
informed his audience, strengthened the bonds between individual and community; love of one's neighbor was Christianity's greatest gift.[46]

Perhaps to combat such misunderstandings, the Student Union began to coordinate a national educational program in the organization after 1931. A leader for
education (*Schulungsleiter*) was appointed in Munich to organize this program.
Gerd Rühle, who succeeded Schirach in July as Student Union *Führer,* was the
first leader for education. He charged each regional leader with appointing regional education leaders who in turn appointed an educational leader for each
university group. Each local group would begin by studying the twenty-five
points of the Nazi program. Discussion leaders would be indoctrinated at regional study weeks.[47]

In September 1931, Rühle directed the groups to devote major effort to the
slogan, "Every National Socialist student wins a Marxist worker for the National
Socialist Movement! Eight thousand new worker comrades for the brown army!"
Internal education under this theme would be devoted to study of Marxism and
the Nazi social program.[48]

The following year, a new national education leader, Johann von Leers,
chairman of the Berlin region of the Student Union, enjoined a more thorough
concentration upon Nazi thought. All new members were to participate in weekly
discussions of Hitler's *Mein Kampf* and of current political events. Older members were directed to spend two months studying the Nazi economic program and
its challenge to Marxism and Socialism. To insure that no departure from orthodoxy crept in, Leers specifically forbade discussion of Italian Fascist
economic theory unless this theory was treated critically.[49] Leers also continued
Rühle's efforts to extend the student's educational program to the nonuniversity
community. In his capacity as regional leader in Berlin, he set up free courses
taught by students for members of the National Socialist Factory Cell Organization (NSBO) and the SA.[50]

In the years before the Nazi takeover of 1933, the Nazi students treated the
implications of their movement for the university gingerly. A political victory, to

be sure, was expected to democratize the university by recruiting students from the lower classes. But clearly the universities would also be forced to accommodate themselves academically to a *völkisch* state. Because of the "objective bias" of the German faculties, all *völkisch* groups had emphasized extensive extracurricular educational programs to supplement classroom work. The Nazis, however, were the most critical of traditional academic pursuits because they regarded the principle of academic freedom as a liberal invention. However, to say so publicly within the academic community might seriously endanger their standing among students. A Nazi student leaflet, distributed in 1927, clearly illustrates the ambiguity of their position. The leaflet chided the universities for their supposed lack of contact with the German people. The universities "should investigate everything which can be productive for the German people, but not carry on science and scholarship as a goal in itself." It criticized the universities for ignoring the study of relevant subjects like racial studies, while devoting much effort to a dead subject like archaeology. It demanded a more *völkisch* approach to the study of political science. But the leaflet offered no clue as to how such a drastic change might take place; most of the specific proposals it included involved destroying foreign influence, restricting study to students with German blood, and reducing fees for poorer students. The leaflet even contained a plea for the defense of academic freedom and an attack on Carl Becker for allegedly undermining this freedom.[51]

During the early 1930s the Student Union, although it claimed the support of a substantial proportion of the student population, still approached the question of university reform with extreme caution. A statement by three movement leaders on this subject in January 1931 strongly defended the principle of academic freedom. They presented no program for academic reforms, since these supposedly could only take place after a national revolution and the reorganization of society. They suggested that such a reform would entail the establishment of compulsory courses in subjects such as "racial hygiene," folklore, and military politics. State examinations in a Nazi state would emphasize not so much mastery of subject matter as the ability to apply the knowledge gained to the service of the *Volk*.[52]

On the eve of the Nazi seizure of power in January 1933, Andreas Feickert, who had signed an article defending academic freedom two years earlier, and who was to be *Deutsche Studentenschaft* chairman in 1934, wrote a memorandum which summed up the attitude of the Nazi student leadership toward university education in more ominously specific terms. He opposed the attitude of the majority of professors who separated their scholarly interests from the need to educate students for practical careers: scholarship for its own sake was, according to Feickert, inherently liberal in intention. Professors should not be afraid of relevance, he said. Because a large number of faculty members could not be expected to change their ways, a truly reformed university would require massive turnover in teaching personnel. Universities could not retain their autonomy in a

National Socialist state but would have to come under stricter government supervision.[53] Only at this date did the Nazi hostility to Germany's educational heritage become blatant.

The brown-shirted students also encountered difficulty in defining their attitudes toward the student fraternities. The heirs of over a century of academic tradition, the fraternities had proved a fertile field for the sowing of *völkisch* ideology; but they presented certain distinct barriers to the penetration of the Nazi version of the creed. The social exclusiveness of the fraternities contrasted sharply with the National Socialist program. The fraternity heritage, with its emphasis on a strict code of honor, looked backward toward the second Reich, not forward toward a third. While fraternity students were not entirely out of sympathy with National Socialist populism, many *alte Herren* were contemptuous of a movement which they regarded as made up of radical rabble. Nazi demands, too, seemed to threaten the efforts of the fraternities to educate their members in the traditional manner.

These difficulties proved less troublesome to the Nazis than might have been expected. In December 1926, Hans Glauning, a Nazi student who was also a member of a *Burschenschaft,* saw the possibility for recruitment of fraternity students with unusual clarity. It was true, he admitted, that the fraternities were training stations for bourgeois society, and that many students joined because it was good for their careers. But it was also true that these same students were potential rebels who inwardly resented the attitude of their parents. He pointed out the continuing effort of the fraternities since the war to reform themselves and their receptivity to *völkisch* ideals. He also recalled the revolutionary tradition of the *Burschenschaften.* The Nazis might easily affirm many of the fraternities' basic principles—the strict discipline, the community life, and the defense of a concept of honor in an age of moral relativism. If the students could wrest power from the *alte Herren* in their fraternities, they could be put at the service of the national revolution.[54]

Under Schirach's leadership, the Student Union began actively to recruit fraternity students. Invitations to Student Union functions, as well as propagandistic literature, were sent to the fraternities, and in many cases the fraternities responded by attending as a group or by sending official representatives.[55] National Socialist members of fraternities were expected to retain their primary loyalty to the movement, to act as movement "representatives" or "trustworthy men" and to influence the fraternities in a Nazi direction.[56]

Nazi members of fraternities eagerly provided Nazi speakers to address their uncommitted brothers. Prince Hubertus zu Löwenstein, in his memoirs, recalled one such speaker who addressed Löwenstein's Munich fraternity in 1924. The guest, Georg Schott, had recently written a book about Grimm's *Fairy Tales* and offered his audience an allegorical exegesis on "Little Red Riding Hood." In Schott's view, Red Riding Hood represented German innocence, the wolf, a

Jew, and the huntsman, a future leader who would save Germany—to be sure, Adolf Hitler. Allegory in the story had been intentional to avoid the censorship of the allegedly Jewish-controlled medieval Catholic Church.[57]

Other speakers must have had more convincing topics, because the fraternity leadership on its side was often distressed by the Nazi success in attracting fraternity members. They feared that membership in the Student Union was decreasing group loyalty. In 1929, a number of fraternities began to expel Student Union members and to forbid any others from joining.[58] But because of the growing Nazi sympathies among fraternity students, such policies proved almost impossible to implement.

The Student Union was most successful in attracting members from the more radical fraternities, particularly the *Wehrschaften,* who sought to increase their competitive position by identifying with the Nazi cause. As early as June 1928, the *Wehrschaft Markomannia* in Berlin joined the Student Union as a group.[59] But the real spur to close contacts with the Nazis was a split among the *Wehrschaften* at the league convention in May 1929. When the convention voted to forbid membership in Masonic lodges, more moderate local groups left the organization.[60] In July, E. Strömsdörfer, an *alte Herr* and a Nazi party member, proudly informed the Student Union leadership that the *Deutsche Wehrschaft* was entirely free of Masonic influence and proposed that the *Wehrschaften* become official Nazi fraternities, enrolling all Student Union members who wished to belong to a fraternity.[61]

Schirach, at first cool to the idea, began to consider it more seriously in the light of increasing troubles with other fraternity leagues. In January, he and Strömsdörfer drew up a tentative proposal for mutual cooperation, in which the *Deutsche Wehrschaft* would represent the Student Union's interest in dueling student affairs and take part in all Student Union activities. Schirach hoped in this way to gain an official voice in the councils of the General German Society of Dueling Students.[62] For a time, he seriously considered organizing a new bloc of National Socialist fraternities with a *Wehrschaft* nucleus to challenge the older fraternities.[63] In March he drew up plans for a united organization of the Student Union and Nazi fraternities. Student Union members would be permitted to join only member fraternities.[64] But fear that many students, forced to choose between the Student Union and their fraternities, would probably opt for the latter, quickly changed Schirach's mind. He settled, in the end, for informal relations with the *Deutsche Wehrschaft* and a smaller league, the *Hochschulgilde* ''Ernst Wurche,'' both of which promised to follow Student Union political initiatives.[65]

The Nazi message also found many listeners among the other fraternities, particularly among the *Burschenschaften* and in the *Kyffhäuser Verband,* which had long championed right-wing political causes. But interest in National Socialism did not always mean support of the Student Union. The league journals published an increasing number of articles in the early 1930s which expressed general sympathy for the Nazi movement. But the attempts of National Socialist students to monopolize student politics and to put political pressures on the fraternities soon backfired, producing resentment in many quarters. A writer in the *Kyffhäuser Verband*'s *Akademische Blätter* put the matter bluntly: The National Socialist agitators at the universities must recognize, he wrote, that they do not have an exclusive patent on the national cause. The fraternities were not made obsolete by the Nazi movement, nor could the Student Union ever hope to fill their important role. The fraternities had always defended academic freedom, but the Student Union's attempts to politicize the universities, he warned, might well end up by destroying academic freedom and turning the universities into trade schools and schools for training functionaries.[66]

The relationship between the fraternities and the Nazi movement was heatedly debated in the *Deutsche Burschenschaft* journal, *Burschenschaftliche Blätter,* in 1931. But of eleven articles published between January and September on this subject, not one criticized the National Socialist program. Most of the writers agreed about what they saw as the fundamental similarity between the political goals of the *Burschenschaften* and the National Socialists. The debate had been provoked by an article of a Berlin student, Werner Zintarra, disturbed about the activities of the Student Union. He accused the Student Union of undermining *Burschenschaft* loyalties by forcing its members to vote for Nazi candidates in student elections. Student Union members had also violated the principle of fraternity secrecy for political purposes. Zintarra had certain doubts about the Nazi attitude toward student politics. He felt that the National Socialist principles potentially endangered the exclusiveness of the *Burschenschaften,* and perhaps, too, the continued independence of the university itself.[67]

Most of Zintarra's critics argued that the fraternities would have peace with the Nazis if they mutually agreed on which tasks each group could best fulfill. The *Burschenschaften* could stay out of politics and concentrate upon cultural goals, if the Nazis would eschew any interference in fraternity life. Several of the writers defined the Nazi political role as primarily educational: the National Socialists should convert students to their political program but stay out of the politics of the university. One student expressed concern over the tendency among some Nazi students to overemphasize the parallels between the state and universities as if they were also trying to revolutionize the latter. Taken as a group the articles reveal an extraordinary naïvete about the implications of the National Socialist movement and confusion about the aim of the Student Union.[68]

The Student Union's position, stated frankly by Nazi *Burschenschafter* Hans Glauning, illuminates the reasons for the differences more clearly. For Glauning, the *Burschenschaften* had defaulted because they had not allied themselves closely with National Socialism. The *Burschenschaft* program went no further than "bourgeois-intellectual patriotism." Many members were snobbish and had no desire to mix with the people. The Nazi movement could never limit itself to political questions, since its aim was to revolutionize all aspects of German life. If the *Burschenschaften* did not join the Nazi movement, if they did not make German socialism and racism the basis of their educational program, then they would find themselves to be superfluous after the National Socialist revolution.[69]

But in 1931, the situation still demanded that the Student Union soft pedal its ultimate objectives and attempt to reach accommodation with the still very important fraternities. A persistent problem in the attitude of many fraternity members to the Student Union had been the fact that many Student Union members, who were free students, did not accept the dueling fraternities' code of honor. Schirach had faced this problem personally in an incident he recounts in his autobiography. In the spring of 1930, he was challenged to a duel by a Munich *Corps* which he had accused of "blundering" by insulting a National Socialist leader. Schirach wanted to accept the challenge in order not to lose face among the fraternity students. According to Schirach's report, a young secretary in the Student Union office, Henrietta ("Henny") Hoffmann, who overheard Schirach accept the challenge—on condition that the duel be fought with pistols rather than sabers—rushed to Hitler and told him the whole story. Hitler promptly forbade the duel and immediately inserted a notice in the *Völkischer Beobachter* saying that he had done so. Upon hearing of this, Schirach rushed to the typesetting room of the *Völkischer Beobachter* and surreptitiously deleted the notice. Although Hitler gave Schirach a thorough dressing down for this unprecedented insubordination, the story had a happy ending. The *Corps* withdrew the challenge, refusing to permit its members to fight with pistols, and two years later Henny Hoffmann became Frau von Schirach.[70]

In 1930, National Socialist delegates in the *Reichstag* came to the defense of the *Mensur* which had been under attack in the courts. The Student Union hoped to use this action by posing as the best friends of the student dueling tradition.[71] In 1931, it tried to appropriate this custom by adopting its own code of honor. The Student Union henceforth required those of its members who did not belong to dueling fraternities to submit disputes with fraternity members to student honor commissions.[72]

Because of this order, the dueling fraternity leagues expressed their willingness to enter into a wide-ranging agreement with the Student Union in an attempt to settle all outstanding disputes. In April, Student Union representatives met with leaders of the General German Society of Dueling Students in Erfurt to draw up a document which had all the appearance of a peace treaty. All Student Union members, whether free or fraternity, who accepted the duel would henceforth come under the jurisdiction of the Society of Dueling Students' machinery for settling disputes of honor. Those Student Union members who rejected the duel would submit their disputes to the "Erlangen Leagues Agreement," an organization established to handle affairs of honor between students in dueling and nondueling fraternities. Up to four other Student Union members were permitted to be present at all duels which involved Nazi students. The Student Union agreed in turn to avoid any actions that would tend to give it the appearance of a separate fraternity, such as the carrying of swords or participation as a group in official university functions. The Union further agreed to expel any students who had been ostracized from their fraternities.[73]

Both groups agreed to avoid disputes in student politics and student elections and not to exercise pressures on their members to vote for a particular list of candidates. In response to one continuing fraternity complaint, the Student Union also agreed that fraternity members would be excused from Student Union activities when they conflicted with fraternity functions. The Student Union, moreover, agreed not to direct its members to join any particular fraternity.[74]

Although the agreement appeared to incorporate many concessions by the Nazis, the fraternity leadership soon had reason to question their sincerity. The Student Union did not attempt to bridle their drive toward absolute control of student politics. A number of the leagues rejected ratification of the pact at their annual meetings, where seething resentment between Nazis and non-Nazis flared occasionally into the open.[75] Other leagues postponed final agreement, pending further negotiations. The majority of the leagues which had initially accepted the pact withdrew in late summer, in response to an intensified struggle with the Nazis in the *Deutsche Studentenschaft*.[76] Although negotiations continued throughout 1931, the situation rapidly deteriorated. Many leaders in the Student Union now believed that their position was becoming so strong that no agreement was necessary, although they continued to insist that the fraternity leagues had shown bad faith by not ratifying the agreements.[77]

To the dismay of Church authorities, even the Catholic fraternities were not entirely immune to the National Socialist virus. Eyebrows were raised in the spring of 1930 when a Catholic fraternity student was appointed chairman of the Würzburg Student Union.[78] At a number of universities, Catholic students were observed conspicuously wearing party insignia with their fraternity caps and bands.[79]

In July 1930, the spiritual adviser of the *Cartell Verband,* Dr. P. Erhard Schlund, a Franciscan who had criticized the anti-Christian character of the Nazi party as early as 1923, unequivocally asserted that it was not possible to be both a sincere Catholic and a National Socialist. He pointed out that Nazi writings and public statements contradicted Church dogma and that many Nazis had publicly condemned the Old Testament. The totalitarian pretensions of the Nazi movement, he said, clearly endangered the Church.[80] In February of the following year, Schlund recommended that the *Cartell Verband* refuse membership to all students who played active roles in either the Nazi Party or the Student Union. An effort should be made to convince those who sympathized with the movement that such sympathies contradicted their religious beliefs.[81]

When repeatedly, in the course of 1931, the German bishops warned the faithful of the anti-Christian nature of National Socialism, the Catholic fraternities had little choice but to purge themselves of National Socialist militants. The *Cartell Verband* did not entirely exclude Nazis from membership, continuing to respect a degree of freedom of conscience, but forbade its members from playing an active role in the Party or the Student Union and from propagandizing within the fraternities.[82] A National Socialist observer suspected, with justice, that this decision was taken in spite of considerable Nazi sympathies among the student rank and file. Many students, who had spoken out against the decision at the national meeting, ended up voting for it.[83]

The National Socialist German Student Union, in its early years, followed a zigzag course between militance and opportunism. Wilhelm Tempel's small, radical, and socially conscious vanguard was casualty to a program designed to attract mass student support. Under Schirach's leadership, the Student Union attempted to dress itself in intellectual finery as well as profit from the *völkisch* sympathies which were widespread at the time. Seeking to appropriate the university tradition, the Student Union unashamedly portrayed itself as the true heir of the early *Burschenschaften* and the defender of university autonomy and academic freedom. Schirach and his cohorts did not wish to disguise their organization as one more academic club but wanted to persuade students that support for a popular movement with a revolutionary program was not incompatible with their own interests.

For all of its excesses, the Student Union's rapid success rested largely upon the leadership's ability to conform outwardly to the culture of the university community. The bulk of the Union's members continued to be free students or members of the less exclusive fraternities, and a class-conscious critique of the traditional pecking order at the universities remained part of the Student Union's attraction. Yet this critique was strictly balanced both by the attempt to provide intellectual substance and by the effort to attract members and supporters among the socially secure. The penetration of the Nazis into the fraternities, notably among the *Burschenschaften,* illustrates their success in this regard. The very ambiguity of the Student Union position enabled it to capitalize at the same time upon feelings of social resentment, on yearnings for upward mobility, and on egalitarian sentiments. The Nazi students' adoption of a code of honor indeed enhanced the organization's appeal as a kind of quasi-fraternity in its own right.

The Student Union proved highly successful in winning supporters although less successful in winning fully committed members. But many other German students with right-wing views remained suspicious: The Nazi students were, after all, often fanatical. They did not shy away from violence. They preferred to dominate rather than cooperate—in the fraternities as well as in student governments.

The political climate of the early 1930s was, however, more favorable to the militants than the doubters. The economic crisis, the depression, the decline of the political Center, and the uncertainty of the future all combined to produce an atmosphere more conducive to demonstrations than to study. The Student Union could, in fact, become more violent and still continue to grow. The Nazis' success, in the long run, stemmed as much from their ability to excite large numbers of students about the political struggle taking place in the streets as from their success in adjusting to the university setting.

SIX

Years of Struggle:
The National Socialist German Student Union
and the Universities

The efforts of the National Socialist German Student Union were part of the National Socialist struggle for power in Germany. The prize the Student Union sought was the German university; the means, the attraction of the student majority to the Nazi program. To win the students to their banner, the National Socialists applied the methods learned in the political arena: a united, well-disciplined organization, the effective use of propaganda, the exploitation of nationalist causes, temporary alliances with other nationalist groups, and the elaboration of a program which spoke to widespread grievances. Like the parent party, the student leaders soon displayed a sense for political timing and maneuver which enabled them to run circles around the amateurish opposition they faced at the universities.

The Student Union's surge to power was organized and led by students. The student movement remained largely free of the dictates of the Party, although the central student leadership was in close contact with Party offices. The students' regional divisions paralleled the ten regions of the *Deutsche Studentenschaft* rather than the Party districts. Each of the ten regions was led by a regional leader (*Kreisführer*) who was appointed by and directly responsible to the national student leader (*Bundesführer*). The entire organization was governed by the so-called *Führer prinzip* which placed leadership on each level solely in the hands of one man. In 1932, when Baldur von Schirach, previously national leader, was promoted to the office of Reich Youth *Führer,* an attempt was made to coordinate the Student Union with the other Nazi youth organizations, without much practical effect.[1]

Because of the Student Union's independence, the national office and the local groups usually had to fend for themselves financially. Throughout its history, the Union suffered from chronic poverty. Pleas to the Party for aid were almost always ignored. To supplement membership dues, the students often sought

87

contributions from local Party members and other interested people.[2] The Union's ability to win supporters in the face of the superior resources of other student political groups testifies to the dedication of its membership.

Contacts with the Party were cemented in the Union's early years by the requirement that all members join the Party.[3] However, since common membership was accompanied by local Party efforts to control the student groups, this policy was abandoned in many cases by 1929.[4] The relationship between Student Union groups and local Party offices varied from friendly to hostile. In many instances, the natural resentment between the students, who were both educated and middle class, and the Party functionaries, who were neither, could not be contained. Whereas Tempel had attempted to defend the Student Union against Party pressures, Schirach often took the side of the Party offices in quarrels with his subordinates.[5] Schirach's self-serving policy, however, did not mitigate the continuing tension, which was less a matter of organization than of a conflict in style and world-view. Many students who wished to join the Student Union were reluctant to join the Party.[6] Besides, Schirach's program demanded that students devote most of their time and loyalty to the Union organization.[7]

After 1929, students were encouraged to join the SA or become leaders in the Hitler Youth or the Schoolboy's Union (NS-Schülerbund) rather than the Party.[8] In 1929 a memorandum estimated that about 1,000 Student Union members participated in the SA and about 100 in the SS. Of these, 51 were "Shock" troop (Sturmabteilung) Führer in the SA and 21 were "Shock" Führer (Stürmführer) in the SS. There were also 14 students who had risen to the rank of SA troop Führer and 29 group Führer.[9] Käter estimates that at most 40 percent of Student Union members were also enrolled in the SA in the years between 1928 and 1932.[10] In many cases, however, membership did not mean active involvement. In fact, the same social tensions present in student-Party relations were apparent in contacts with the SA also. In practice, the Nazi egalitarian ideology proved insufficient to overcome the class-consciousness of both sides.[11] Nevertheless, Student Union members proved more eager to play an active role in the SA than in the Party.[12]

The Student Union did not aim at a mass membership but attempted to recruit a cadre of active supporters at all German institutions of higher education who in turn might influence the political belief and action of the majority of students. By 1929, the Union could boast active groups at forty-nine schools in Germany, Austria, Czechoslovakia, and Danzig. Many of these groups probably consisted of less than ten members.[13] In spite of a continuous pattern of growth, the Union claimed only 5,500 members in January 1933 and an additional 750 women in the sister "Office for National Socialist women students (ANST)" groups, less than 5 percent of the enrolled student population. In contrast, the four largest faculty leagues all had more than 6,000 student members; the Deutsche Burschenschaft claimed over 12,000.[14] More than one-third of the Union's 1933 membership was concentrated in two of the ten Deutsche Studentenschaft regions: IV (Baden and Württemberg) and VI (Saxony, Upper Silesia, and Thuringia).[15]

The concentration of more than 25 percent of the Student Union membership in the southwestern region is particularly noteworthy (Table 16). Of the 1,699 male members in this region, 472 were enrolled in the so-called career schools (*Fachschulen*) which were low-status schools perhaps most comparable to our community colleges. The Nazis made a special appeal to this group, and in their attempts to fudge over traditional class lines provided this group with status in the movement equal to that of university students. At the Technical Institutes in this area, the Student Union membership was strikingly high—almost 20 percent at Karlsruhe. At the universities, it ranged around 5 percent at Heidelberg, Giessen, and Freiburg but approached 10 percent at Tübingen.

Table 16   Members of National Socialist Student Groups at Institutions of Higher Education in Student Union Region IV (Baden, Württemberg, Hesse).

Institution	Men's Groups	Women's Groups
Darmstadt Technical	175	5
Freiburg	153	21
Heidelberg	124	16
Giessen	90	
Karlsruhe	191	4
Mannheim Business	57	
Stuttgart	166	13
Tübingen	265	19
Hohenheim Agricultural	16	—
	1227	90

Fachschulgruppen:	472
Hochschulgruppen:	1227
Women:	90
	1789

SOURCE: Würzburg, University Library, Records of the NSDStB, 65-alpha 604, 6 January 1933.

NOTE: Membership strength as of 6 January 1933.

In the southwestern region, two groups were strong that were discouraged from entering the Student Union in this period: Catholics and fraternity students. Yet the Nazis had comparatively large groups at Karlsruhe and Tübingen, two of the most socially elite institutions in Germany. Both had high percentages of civil servants' sons enrolled; both were dueling fraternity havens. It is possible of course, that the Nazis were surprisingly successful in recruiting the socially secure students so abundant at Tübingen and Karlsruhe. It is more likely, although difficult to prove, that they capitalized on the resentment of lower middle-class students for the caps and bands of the dueling fraternities. The Student Union provided an alternative fraternity which had the advantage of growing political power. And in spite of the size of the Nazi university group in Tübingen, it proved less successful in student elections than elsewhere.

In region V, which encompassed the Prussian Rhineland and Westphalia, we find similar results. In this area, the Student Union enrolled few members either in the Catholic strongholds of Bonn, Aachen, and Münster or in the big city universities of Frankfurt and Cologne (Table 17). The only place where their recruiting drive achieved moderate success is Marburg, once again a largely Protestant small-town university with a relatively elite student body and a strong fraternity movement. Once again the "counter-fraternity" idea suggests itself.

Table 17   Members of National Socialist Student Groups at Institutions of Higher Education in Region V.

Institution	Men's Groups	Women's Groups
Aachen Technical	40	
Bonn	90	12
Dortmund Teachers Academy	28	10
Frankfurt	45	13
Cologne	54	6
Marburg	132	15
Münster	30	4
	444	60

Fachschulgruppen:	153	
Hochschulgruppen:	444	
Women's Groups:	60	
	657	

SOURCE: Würzburg, University Library, Records of the NSDStB, 65-alpha 604, 6 January 1933.

NOTE: Membership strength as of 6 January 1933.

The Student Union measured its strength less by its membership rolls than by its success in winning student council elections and its control of student electoral posts. Its electoral success can only be described as phenomenal. Few student councils were able to withstand the Nazi thrust.[16] In Prussia, where student governments were not recognized by the state government or the universities after December 1927, large numbers of students continued to vote in elections for "free student governments," and increasingly they chose Nazi candidates. At the University of Berlin, the Student Union, running candidates for the first time in the 1928 summer semester, won fifteen of a hundred seats contested; the following year, with 70 percent of enrolled students voting, the Nazis won an additional five seats, and by winter 1931, the Union had won sixty-five of a hundred seats with 55 percent of the enrolled students voting.[17] In moderate Bonn, the Student Union rose from five of sixty-one seats on the student council, with 63 percent voting in the winter semester of 1929 and 1930, to nineteen of fifty-three seats two years later, with 75 percent voting. At the University of Munich, where student government was still state-recognized and between 80 and 90 percent of the students ordinarily voted, the Student Union rose from three of thirty seats in the winter semester of 1929 and 1930, to eleven of thirty-one seats in the winter semester of 1931–32. Similar gains were made throughout the country.[18]

During the 1929–30 winter semester, the Nazis won electoral majorities in the student councils of the universities of Greifswald and Erlangen. A year later, they could claim majorities at nine additional schools and substantial blocs of votes almost everywhere. Fraternity domination of student affairs, which had characterized the 1920s, was now largely history; indeed, the fraternities were often unable to prevent their members from voting for Nazi candidates.

Even at the height of their pre-1933 success, in the early part of 1932, the Nazis rarely attained a majority of all eligible students. Assuming that almost all Nazi sympathizers would have voted in student elections, the Nazis probably could claim the support of between 30 and 40 percent at most universities and technical institutes. They were strongest in central Germany, Saxony, Thuringia, northern Bavaria, Hesse, the Technical Institutes, and in Munich. The two universities, Jena and Erlangen, where they earned the support of a majority of all students were both in areas where the Nazis also won strong support in national elections. Both universities were largely Protestant, and their social composition approximated the national average. The Nazis did poorly at strongly Catholic universities in the central Rhineland but well in the Catholic southwest and in Bavaria. At some schools where fraternities were strongly entrenched, notably at Tübingen and the Technical Institute at Hanover (earlier the scene of the anti-Lessing riots), the Nazis fared less well. They were also somewhat weaker at the large urban universities than they were in the small towns (See Table 18).

Since nationalist opponents often argue that they supported the Nazi Party but not the Student Union, and since large numbers of students abstained from voting altogether, these figures may not be an entirely accurate gauge of student sentiments. While traditional nationalists and moderates might emphasize local issues as much as national politics, the Nazi students identified themselves clearly as an arm of a national movement and tried to turn student elections into political referenda. Although opponents might still win supporters on specifically student issues, the Nazi voter was usually registering his support for the goals of the movement as a whole.

Nazi conduct of student election campaigns had all the earmarks of professional political action. Handbills were distributed, mass meetings organized, and opponents attacked without regard to truth or gentlemanly ethics. Election issues ran the gamut from purely local problems to attacks on the policies of the Prussian Ministry of Culture and current political controversies such as that surrounding the Young Plan, the international agreement arranged in 1929 for the regulation of Germany's reparations payments. Leading Nazi personalities often came to address the students on the eve of student elections.[19] Occasionally, when their campaigns could be significantly aided, the Student Union entered into temporary electoral alliances with groups of fraternities or with other political groups.[20] But the Nazis preferred to run a separate list of candidates in order to dispel any doubts about their electoral strength, even when other groups were

Table 18   National Socialist Success in Student Elections (Winter Semester 1931/32).

	% Participating	Nazi % of Vote or % of Seats under Proportional Representation	Nazis as a Percentage of Eligible Voters
Aachen		30.76	
Berlin University	55	65	35.75
Berlin Technical	62.2	74.07	46.07
Bonn	75	26.38	19.78
Breslau	35.4	77.84	27.55
Darmstadt Technical	80.0	47.5	38.0
Dresden (summer 1932)		70.0	
Erlangen	82.0	68.0	55.76
Frankfurt (summer 1931)		29.16	
Giessen	80.0	53.84	43.07
Göttingen	52	65.0	33.8
Greifswald	63.7	60.0	38.22
Halle (summer 1932)	76	50.0	38.0
Hamburg	64	45.45	29.09
Hanover	74	22.22	16.44
Heidelberg		45.00	
Jena	79	83.33	65.83
Karlsruhe (winter 1931/32)	76	48.00	36.48
Kiel (winter 1930/31)	34	38.88	13.22
Königsberg	72	48.48	34.90
Leipzig		60.0	
Freiburg (summer 1931)		38.33	
Marburg (summer 1931)	72	51.21	36.87
Munich Technical	92	45.38	41.74
Munich University (with allies)	93	45.41	42.23
Rostock		63.60	
Tübingen	70.0	41.66	29.16
Würzburg	87.0	40.00	34.80

Source: Frankfurt, DSt., Bd. 26, Hochschulpolitische Arbeitsgemeinschaft, Rundschreiben Nr. 7, 22 February 1933; NSDStB A128-alpha 64, Mitteilungen des NSdStB H.S. group Leoben, 17 February 1932; Leise, "Ausbreitung," pp. 171–72, 280–94.

anxious for a coalition.[21] In December 1931, Hitler made this preference into policy, forbidding any Nazi students in future from running on any but Student Union slates.[22] By this time the Party leadership was gleeful about the prestige won in student electoral victories and pressured the students to work hard to maintain the momentum of increasing success.[23]

Election victories brought with them responsibilities in student government, responsibilities which the Nazis quickly turned into political dividends. Nazi student government activities were coordinated by the central Student Union organization, which demanded strict discipline from all representatives. All student officials on local councils and in the *Deutsche Studentenschaft* organization were directly responsible to Student Union leaders at the corresponding organization levels. After September 1931, memos of student representatives required the countersignature of a Student Union official.[24] In 1932, Student Union representatives were actually required to sign a pledge promising to vote according to the directives of the national office of university politics.[25]

Where the Nazis remained a minority in student councils, they were cautioned by the central organization not to retire into fruitless opposition, but to attempt to win important posts through cooperation with other nationalists, which would enable them to draw attention to the work of the Student Union.[26] The editorship of local student newspapers was a particularly coveted post, and as early as 1929 a number of these newspapers were taking on all the hallmarks of the Nazi Party press.[27] In July 1929, Nazi students had won control of the press offices at the University of Kiel, the Business Institute in Mannheim, the Technical Institute in Berlin-Charlottenburg, and the University and Technical Institute in Breslau; they also held key positions on the papers of the University and Technical Institute in Munich, as well as the Universities of Erlangen, Würzburg, and Berlin.[28] Once Nazi students were in secure control of press offices, the newspapers were open not only to local group members but to national Party figures.[29]

Nazi representatives also sought successfully to win other student government posts that might be put to propaganda uses: head of the lecturing office, libraries, offices for political education or border work (*Grenzlandarbeit*). Since the Student Union did not give priority to politically unimportant offices such as secretary, treasurer, or athletic director, its members could concentrate their efforts on winning the politically valuable posts.[30] When such posts did not yet exist, the Nazis made an effort to inaugurate them. In Würzburg, for example, in 1929, the Student Union group successfully sponsored the establishment of an office for political education which would organize lecture series and extracurricular course work on political questions.[31] In Hamburg, in 1931, where a Student Union member, Heinz Haselmayer, had been elected student council chairman, a lecture office was established in the expectation of sponsoring talks by Party members and other right-wing figures. Haselmayer also reorganized the foreign student office, which now offered an extensive program of borderland trips and sought special relationships with right-wing student organizations in Italy, Hungary, Finland, Sweden, and Flemish Belgium. Lectures were held under the auspices of the foreign student office on geopolitical and ethnological questions. Haselmayer also hoped to set up summer work camps devoted to the development of the comradely spirit and instruction in military sport.[32]

An anti-Semitic program was a key part of the baggage that the Nazis brought with them when they entered student government. The movement, from its inception, had pledged to end "Jewish influence" at the universities by severely limiting the number of Jewish students and professors and by excluding Jews from student organizations on the Austrian pattern.[33] In their discussion of the anti-Semitic issue, the Student Union members carefully refrained from the violent tone characteristic of Party gatherings but unsuited to academic audiences. The Bonn Student Union group, for example, suffered extreme embarrassment in May 1929, when a party member from Cologne told an open meeting of students that "he could not harm a mouse, but he could cut the throat of a Jew with a blunt knife without blinking an eyelash."[34] The Student Union hoped to win support for its anti-Semitic program not with bloodthirsty slogans but by subtly implying the professional advantages which would accrue to graduates through the restriction of Jewish competition. At a time when large numbers of students faced unemployment after the receipt of their diplomas, this message was often convincing.

Late in 1928, the Student Union began to introduce resolutions in student councils calling for a quota (*numerus clausus*) on the number of Jewish students at the universities, which would correspond to the percentage of Jews in the general population. Whereas the Jews represented fewer than 1 percent of the population, they made up 4.36 percent of the university students and 2.43 percent of those at the Technical Institutes in 1928 (but only 3 percent of the total number of male students; more than 10 percent of the female students were Jewish). The statistics, as is often the case, were far more striking than the physical presence of Jews. Almost a third of all Jewish university students were concentrated at the university of Berlin; more than half of the Jewish technical students were studying at the Technical Institute in Berlin-Charlottenburg.[35] In Berlin, and a few other universities, the issue fed on existing tensions. Elsewhere, students had to be educated about the "problem."

In December, the Nazis succeeded in carrying a *numerus clausus* resolution at the University of Berlin against the sole opposition of the Communist representatives. However, under pressure from the *Deutsche Studentenschaft* leadership, the dueling fraternities, who had voted for the motion, had second thoughts. The motion was returned to the floor, where it was decided to refer it to the *Deutsche Studentenschaft* court of appeals, to see whether or not it conflicted with the *Deutsche Studentenschaft* constitution. The national student leaders viewed the *numerus clausus* as a political question and therefore not a proper subject for student government discussion. The Berlin Nazi leadership, in turn, warned the *Deutsche Studentenschaft* that rejection of the resolution might force a break between the Student Union and the *Deutsche Studentenschaft* since "he who rejects the fight of the German students against the Judaization of the German universities, cannot be viewed as the representative of the interests of the German students."[36]

Ignoring the dispute over the *numerus clausus* question in the *Deutsche Studentenschaft* organization, the Student Union continued to introduce similar resolutions in the early part of 1929. The resolution was rejected decisively at the Technical Institute in Berlin-Charlottenburg because of the uncertainty surrounding it.[37] In Erlangen, twenty-four of twenty-five student council representatives, only eight of whom were National Socialists, voted for a *numerus clausus* for all non-Germans, "but especially for students of the Jewish race." The Erlangen leadership unequivocally asserted that race, not religion, would be the basis of the quota system.[38] The resolution was sent from Erlangen in an open letter to all student governments asking them to follow the Erlangen example.[39] At the same time, a letter went out from the Student Union central leadership to the local groups ordering them to introduce similar resolutions.[40] This effort proved successful only at the universities of Würzburg and Giessen and the Technical Institute in Munich, although sympathy for the measure was greater than this limited success indicated.[41] In many cases, opposition was stated only on technical grounds.[42]

Early in July, the *Deutsche Studentenschaft*'s court of appeals decided that the student organization could only support a *numerus clausus* if its constitution were changed, since the present constitution made no distinctions among students of German citizenship.[43] The subject was debated later that month at the national student convention in Hanover. A *numerus clausus* resolution, introduced by the Technical Institutes of Munich and Brünn in the Sudetenland, was rejected by a vote of 102 to 72, although it had the strong support of the Austrian and Bohemian representatives.[44] The issue was then left to rest, although local Nazi groups occasionally attempted to put their student councils on record in favor of a quota. In February 1931, the *Deutsche Studentenschaft*'s central committee, which by this date had a substantial Nazi minority, proposed that all student governments organize open discussions about the *numerus clausus* issue; but the issue was not actively pursued at this time.[45] In all likelihood, the Nazi student leaders feared that a renewed campaign would endanger their efforts at respectability.

The National Socialists brought with them a violent style and tone, which, although not new to the universities of the Weimar Republic, greatly contributed to the growing tension. This was not always the intention of the Student Union, since Schirach was initially quite concerned about the possibility that violence and extreme language might alienate otherwise friendly members of the academic community. In an order of January 1929, he forbade the Munich groups from participation in further disturbances at public functions such as theater performances and lectures of political opponents.[46] The following year he angrily lectured the leader of the University of Cologne group, Ferdinand Bohlmann, for permitting a public lecture, which he chaired, to end in a brawl because of intemperate remarks by a National Socialist speaker. The upshot of the meeting had been the prohibition by the university rector of the group, which Schirach regarded as an avoidable disaster. "We are not debating," Schirach argued,

> Whether or not the expressions "criminal, pimp and rag-picker" are correct in relation to the current possessors of power, but the question should be answered whether it is expedient and in the interests of the movement to make such statements in a meeting of the National Socialist German Student Union which must recruit among the student body.[47]

It is doubtful that the part-time SA members, who were a major factor in the

Student Union, liked the cautious tactics Schirach favored. In Hamburg, one student was expelled from the local group for complaining that fraternity students were alienated by inflammatory statements and by the presence of rowdy SA members, who were not students, at school functions. The Student Union leader who expelled the protestor heaped scorn upon "his concept of academic dignity."[48]

The Nazi students were not, of course, solely responsible for the violence which seemed to accompany their activities. Extreme rhetoric or attempts to shout down members of other groups at student meetings often provoked their opponents to the point of physical attack. The very appearance of the Nazi students, with their "jack" boots, brown shirts, and swastikas, was highly provocative. Repeated efforts by university authorities to ban such party uniforms and symbols on university grounds met with open defiance.[49]

Fights between competing student groups may have had questionable propaganda value for the Student Union; provoking the police or the political authorities offered a sure path to the benefits of martyrdom. After 1929, student riots and struggles with the police became a recurrent phenomenon, widely reported in the press.

The Nazis denied responsibility for instigating the disorders which broke out in Berlin in the summer of 1929, and they do not appear to have been a major factor in organizing the disturbances. But the Student Union had become increasingly active in Berlin student affairs during the previous year and openly claimed the sympathies of many students not part of the movement.[50] The success of *numerus clausus* resolutions, temporarily as it proved, at both the university and the Technical Institute is testimony for the penetration of Nazi ideas among Berlin students.

The ostensible cause for the Berlin student riots was the prohibition by the Prussian government of faculty participation in a student demonstration, planned for the anniversary of the signing of the Treaty of Versailles on 28 June 1929. The prohibition was probably the result of an overreaction on the part of the Prussian government to the growing influence of right-wing parties among the students. But the Versailles protest, since it had been planned in conjunction with the faculties of the two institutions, hardly looked like a radical meeting. The announced speaker had been the prominent military historian Hans Delbrück, a political moderate. For these reasons the rectors and senates of the university and the Technical Institute wrote to Minister Becker, strongly protesting what they viewed as an infringement on academic freedom.[51]

The students chose to protest in a less genteel manner. On the morning of 28 June, a crowd estimated by the police at about 1,500 students met at the Hegelplatz to demonstrate against the Versailles Treaty. At the close of the meeting, a cry went up, "To the Ministry of Culture: To Becker!" The police assigned to the demonstration were too few to deflect the students from their chosen goal. They later reported that students had cried out, "On to Becker, even if it will cost blood!" What happened, once the students arrived at the Ministry of Culture Unter den Linden, is unclear. The police claimed that the students tried to storm the Ministry. Students' reports indicated that they had sung patriotic songs and shouted, "Down with Becker," "Germany awake," and other slogans. The police fired several shots in the air to frighten the crowd, and when this did not work, charged with billy clubs. The dispersed demonstrators reassembled at the presidential palace, where they sang the *Deutschlandlied,* before they were once again dispersed by the police. An attempt to renew the demonstration in front of the university met a similar fate.[52] Students attempting to demonstrate at the Ministry of Culture and at the *Reichstag* on 4 July were also clubbed.[53]

Rioting recurred in Berlin shortly after the opening of the winter semester. The "free student government" at the university had scheduled a demonstration for 12 November, commemorating the battle of Langemarck. The rector, fearing trouble, forbade the demonstrating students from entering university grounds and requested that the Berlin police send a force to keep the demonstration within bounds. In defiance, the students marched on the university, according to reports shouting, "Germany awake" and "Death to Jews," and fights with opposing students broke out. The university, unable to prevent the fighting with its own guards, requested that the police enter the traditional sanctuary and expel the students.[54]

Although the events of July had elicited demonstrations of support from student organizations in other parts of Germany, the reaction to the November hostilities was decidedly cool.[55] The fact that the November riots were aimed not only at the police but the university administration was uncomfortable news for the student government organizations which, caught in struggles with state governments, were anxious to maintain cordial relations with university faculties. Shortly after the Berlin rioting in November, the regional organization of the *Deutsche Studentenschaft* in northern Germany wrote to the Berlin student leaders pleading with them to restore order at their universities.[56] The central committee of the *Deutsche Studentenschaft* followed this up with a condemnation of the rioting and a demand that the student governments involved investigate the causes of any future rioting and punish the instigators.[57]

The warnings of more responsible student leaders did little to prevent the sporadic violence which continued to break out during the following years. The Student Union had no wish to provide a brake on violence when it suited its purposes, and its growing support prevented the student governments from taking any disciplinary action against them. The pretexts for disorders in fact became increasingly flimsy. The arrival of the new Social Democratic Prussian Minister of Culture, Adolf Grimme, in Halle in July was enough to produce an unruly crowd of students shouting, "Who has betrayed us? The Social Democrats! Who will make us free? The Hitler Party!" and "We want a *German* [italics mine] Minister of Culture!" The expected arrival of the police to disperse the crowd fulfilled the local Nazi student group's objectives.[58]

Increasingly, after 1929, Nazi student groups began violent disruptions of meetings of political opponents. In Halle, in May, the Student Union narrowly escaped suspension because of disturbances at a Socialist lecture.[59] In November 1930, a meeting of several democratic student groups, assembled to discuss the growing fascist sentiment among students, exploded into violence. The Munich *Post* reported that knives, glasses, and bottles were among the weapons used by the Nazis.[60] In Jena, the following month, Nazi students attempted to disrupt a meeting of a democratic student group by throwing paper around the hall and attacked a group of Social Democrats on the street following the meeting.[61]

In July 1931, Baldur von Schirach, no longer wary of violence, was arrested after disturbances in Cologne. Fighting had broken out at a student demonstration against the Versailles Treaty, and the police had been called to break up the meeting. Schirach appeared the following day at a protest meeting as a key speaker, although further meetings had been forbidden. He was arrested and sentenced to three months' imprisonment, but the decision was reversed after an appeal.[62]

Increasing disturbances instigated by Nazi students posed a dilemma for university administrations. Governmental authorities demanded strict disciplinary action to prevent further outbreaks. The National Socialist actions were closely watched by the left-wing parties concerned over the sometimes lenient attitude of school authorities. The appearance of the Rector of the University of Marburg at a meeting which included uniformed Nazis and *Stahlhelm* members in June 1928 provoked a Social Democratic interpellation in the Prussian Landtag.[63] In Bavaria, authorities were accused of permitting Nazi activities, while strictly controlling actions of the Left. The Bavarian Social Democratic Landtag members pointed out early in 1929 that uniformed Nazi students were a common sight in lecture halls and at public university convocations, and that the Munich rector had permitted SA chief Röhm to address a student meeting at the university, while denying a forum to the mayor of Nüremberg because he was a "politically controversial personality."[64] The Bavarian university authorities also appeared more eager to discipline insignificant left-wing student groups than those on the Right. In 1931, for example, the Senate of the University of Würzburg banned a Socialist student club, reputed to be Communist-dominated, at the request of the Nazi-controlled student council. The grounds cited were that the group sought "a reconstruction of social relations through overthrow of the existing legal and governmental order."[65]

As incidents of violence increased, university administrations became more willing to act against the rebellious students but only reluctantly called upon the aid of government authorities and police. The wearing of Party uniforms in the universities was forbidden, the Student Union was denied use of school bulletin boards if they posted offensive materials, and in extreme cases the groups were banned outright. In 1930, ten schools were forced to take this drastic action, which they did reluctantly, since it appeared to contradict academic freedom.[66] The schools were hesitant to call for police aid, since this offended the traditional practice of academic sanctuary on university territory. However, Prussian Minister of the Interior Severing, at least, insisted that academic sanctuary had no basis in law and that the police might preserve the public peace at the universities even without invitations from the schools.[67]

Whereas governmental authorities were usually convinced that firm police action would put an end to disturbances, the university faculties tended to see the growing pattern of violence in different perspective. The Prussian rectors and prorectors issued a statement in December 1930 which attributed the problems of the university to the social and political ills of the society:

> In the light of events at several universities in recent times, we reject the interpretation that unrest among the students is a unique university phenomenon. The same unrest is apparent in other areas of public life. It is only possible to understand and to heal it from this background.
>
> The introduction of partisan battles among academic youth comes from forces that are outside of the university. The lively feelings of our students for the freedom and worth of the fatherland as well as for the difficult social needs of the present should serve reconstruction, not disunity.
>
> Together with our senates and backed by the unanimous will of all university instructors, we will employ all of our authority to insure that academic youth can direct themselves undisturbed to their proper task: study and self-education."[68]

The vague tone of this statement illustrates the indecisiveness of university faculties when pressed to deal with disorders. Caught between a government they disliked and students whose confidence they feared to forfeit, the academic authorities were largely unable to deal with the crisis. The Nazis, in turn, had only contempt for the timidity of their professors. For the brown-shirted students, "White hair and gestures more helpless than dignified . . . . and monotonously-issued appeals to 'academic morality' . . . ." no longer fulfilled the students' demands for academic leadership.[69] Only full support of the national revolution could preserve the university from student attacks.

Because of university hesitancy, the state governments saw fit to take the initiative in reestablishing academic discipline. In 1930, the Bavarian State Ministry for Education and Culture attempted to decrease tension by banning the wearing of Party uniforms and insignia on university grounds.[70] In Prussia, in response to continued refusal by university authorities to take concerted action against the National Socialist students, Prussian Minister of Culture Grimme demanded that disciplinary action against students who disrupted academic order should take no longer than a week and that students convicted be suspended and their state scholarships be withdrawn. Full reports of disciplinary proceedings were to be sent to the Ministry. In addition, stricter controls were to be instituted to keep university buildings free of disruptive nonstudents.[71]

The most serious threat to academic order occurred in a series of Nazi-initiated attacks upon university professors who, like Theodor Lessing, were said to have offended national honor. The inability of the universities to prevent or curb such outbreaks demonstrated their extreme vulnerability to attacks from the Right. The German professors proved to be insufficiently united to protect their own colleagues, even when the men in trouble lacked Lessing's abrasiveness.

The first major assault on a professor after the Lessing affair occurred at the University of Munich in June 1931, with a series of disturbances at the lectures of Hans Nawiasky, a prominent professor of Law and Political Science.[72] Nawiasky was by no means an obvious target. A veteran of the Austrian army who had seen service in World War I, he had close ties with the conservative Bavarian state government, which he had recently served as Bavarian representative on the Constitutional Committee of the Federal Conference of States.

On 23 June 1931, in his regularly scheduled lecture, Nawiasky injudiciously compared the Treaty of Versailles to the Treaties of Brest-Litovsk and Bucharest, imposed by the Germans on the Russians and Roumanians early in 1918. A number of Nazi students attending the lecture apparently decided that this reference made some action necessary. Nawiasky, informed confidentially the following day that he might expect disorders in his lectures, asked the rector for aid.[73] The 26 June issue of the National Socialist newspaper *Völkischer Beobachter,* actually published on 25 June, contained an article facetiously entitled: "A distinguished Munich university professor: Nawiasky defends the Versailles *Diktat.*" The article accused Nawiasky of defending, by implication, the Ruhr invasion, the execution of Leo Schlageter by the French occupying forces, the Polish annexations of German territory, indeed all postwar German diplomatic defeats. The quotations which the *Völkischer Beobachter* attributed to Nawiasky in the article scarcely merited the viciousness of the attack upon him.[74]

On 26 June, Nawiasky's lecture was moved to a smaller lecture hall to avoid disturbance. Demonstrating students, unaware of the change, appeared at his regular lecture hall, where National Socialist songs were sung and a series of speakers attacked Nawiasky. When a student attempted to defend the professor, the Nazis turned on the Republicans and Socialists in the hall. The rector appeared, pleading with the students to leave. The demonstration resumed in front of the room where Nawiasky was lecturing. The rector escorted him from his lecture through a throng of shouting, whistling students.[75]

The flimsiness of the charges against Nawiasky did not at first prevent wide student support for the demonstrators. The Munich student council, meeting on 26 June, expressed its concern about Nawiasky's alleged defense of Versailles and requested an investigation by the university Senate. In their statement they "stressed their concern that their professors are one with them on the question of the German nation and [that they] do not work against the interests of the German people, which is apparently the case in the statement of Professor Nawiasky."[76] Nawiasky protested that students had no right to pass judgment on his lectures, but at the rector's urging agreed to meet with the student council the following day to discuss the charges against him.[77] In this meeting, he was able to convince the student representatives that he had not meant to defend the Treaty of Versailles.[78]

On 29 June, the *Völkischer Beobachter* published the original student council resolution of 26 June, without mentioning the meeting with Nawiasky on 27 June. The paper also included a long article entitled "Nawiasky, a propagandist for a German policy of weakness."[79] In the face of new demonstrations, Nawiasky appeared at the two lectures scheduled for 30 June. His courageous demeanor before large numbers of threatening students now appeared to be winning him support from many quarters. In his lectures, he defended academic freedom and warned that classroom demonstrations and publication of lecture quotations without permission and out of context threatened the necessary trust between students and faculty. The second lecture was repeatedly disturbed by a small group of students, and the rector called in the police to clear the hall. At noon, the rector closed the university pending the restoration of order.[80]

Order was restored to the University of Munich because of the lack of sympathy of the majority of students for Nazi violence. The student council agreed, on the urging of the rector, to establish a student security force to prevent further outbreaks. Entrance to the university was henceforth strictly controlled, and only registered students were admitted to Nawiasky's lectures.[81] After the opening of classes, the student council voted unanimously, with Nazi representatives hypocritically concurring, to condemn the violence.[82] Three hundred students independently signed a resolution praising Nawiasky for his courage and his defense of academic freedom.[83] On 25 July, the university senate reported that Nazi leaders had been threatened with expulsion if demonstrations recurred and that the Student Union had been issued a "sharp warning." While condemning the disorders, the senate reported that there was no evidence that they had been anything but spontaneous and that the ultimate cause was the unfortunate "politicization" of German youth.[84] The relationship between the demonstrations and the articles in the *Völkischer Beobachter* apparently failed to arouse faculty suspicions. However, the flimsy pretext for the attack on Nawiasky does suggest that the Student Union had been seeking an opportunity for action.

Other targets of National Socialist rage were not so lucky as Nawiasky. A Protestant theologian, Günther Dehn, was hounded out of the University of Halle in 1932 after two years of demonstrations because of his defense of conscientious objection and his opposition to all but clearly defensive wars.[85] E. J. Gumbel, a lecturer at the University of Heidelberg and the author of a well-documented expose of the so-called "Fehme" murders of the early 1920s, "Four Years of Political Murder" (*Vier Jahre Politischer Mord*), was subjected to prolonged Nazi-led demonstrations in 1930 and 1931 which eventually cost him his license to teach.[86]

By late 1932 the excuse for disruption of faculty lectures was often little more than a formality. In Breslau, in the fall of 1932, the appointment of a new professor of Law, Professor Cohn, stimulated a series of noisy demonstrations primarily because of his Jewish background. Although the faculty, with a few notable and vocal exceptions, defended Cohn's right to teach, his lectures were suspended in December because he had told a *Berliner Montagblatt* reporter, conducting a survey, that he did not unequivocally oppose political asylum in Germany for Leon Trotsky. The Senate regretfully noted that Cohn lacked the necessary reserve in a delicate situation.[87] In December 1932, in Leipzig, Professor Gerhard Kessler was prevented from lecturing because of an article he had written in the *Neue Leipziger Zeitung* critical of Hitler and the Nazi movement.[88]

With the major exception of the campaign against Nawiasky in Munich, professors attacked were usually those who could not expect much support from their colleagues. Gumbel and Dehn, like Lessing, owed their appointments to political pressures. Cohn held a new chair created by the outspoken Social Democratic Prussian Minister of Culture Grimme. It was possible to attack these men while defending the right of university autonomy and assume at least partial support from some faculty members. The Nazi students failed adequately to exploit this issue, although it was often the key factor in winning the support of the non-Nazi student body. Differences between the Student Union and other nationalist groups arose over the Dehn affair primarily because the latter groups considered the fight against Grimme and the issue of academic autonomy the core of the protest. The Student Union's statements and actions were directed primarily against Dehn himself, and it was in fact only incidental to them that he had been chosen by the Ministry of Culture rather than the faculty.[89] For this reason, the Nazi militants, to the dismay of their allies, did not hesitate to challenge the university administrations and professors who stood in the way of the student campaign.

The alliance between Nazi students and older nationalist groups also showed its weak side in the controversy surrounding the appointment of the racist anthropologist H. F. K. Günther to a new chair for racial studies, established at the University of Jena by the National Socialist Thuringian Minister of Culture, Wilhelm Frick. In Jena, a Nazi-dominated student council provided rear-guard support for Frick in his dispute with the Jena faculty, which had strongly opposed the nomination.[90] The appointment, however, was the subject of critical comments in the student press and in circles high in the *Deutsche Studentenschaft*, who objected to government-inspired faculty appointments, whether they came from the Right or the Left.[91] The issue was debated at the thirteenth national student convention, meeting in Breslau in July 1930. The *Deutsche Studentenschaft* leadership managed to prevent passage of a resolution supporting Frick which they regarded as a dangerous precedent.[92] Mention of this issue was conspicuously absent from official reports of the convention.[93]

By the 1930s, the Nazis were an unavoidable spectre on the student scene. Although a relative minority of students were active participants in the National Socialist student movement, a much greater number could be relied on to support their candidates in student elections, to attend their political meetings and demonstrations, and to provide manpower for individual actions. Alone among the inhabitants of the academic world of the 1930s, the Nazis seemed to have a clear idea of where they and the universities were going. The universities were not equipped to deal with violence, disorder, or serious attacks on the professors' right to teach freely. They were confronted by a student generation that had little use for past tradition, and they found themselves unable to deal with them. There were few voices courageous enough to warn, as Dehn had in his own defense, that if the enemies of liberty were permitted to operate without challenge their appetites would only grow until the inevitable disaster.

National Socialism represented a fundamental assault upon the ideal of the free university. A Nazi regime could hardly have been imagined to be congenial either to the professors or their more serious students. The National Socialist students' sometimes cautious tactics might have tranquilized many to the real extent of the threat. However, by 1931 and 1932 violent demonstrations had become commonplace at many universities. The fact that neither the majority of professors nor that of non–National Socialist students was able to draw the obvious conclusions and forthrightly condemn the Nazi terror can only be explained by the common belief that the Nazis could be controlled and that they offered mass popular support for the programs of the German nationalist Right. Eduard Spranger, Weimar Germany's leading scholar of education, has attempted to explain the general tolerance of the radical students in the early 1930s, which he shared. At the University Corporation (*Hochschulverband*) conference in October 1932, Theodor Litt, the rector of the University of Leipzig, had proposed a joint declaration condemning the Nazi students. Spranger, writing in 1955, explained his opposition to the declaration:

> I held the movement of the national students to be undisciplined in form, but genuine at the core. It would also have had a very damaging effect on the university, if I had expressed my opinion in such a school-masterish way about the national movement, which at that time still had many healthy elements and was generally greeted with warm expectations."[94]

The Nazi students flourished in an environment that was critical of their style, not their message. They were accepted as part of the larger nationalist movement at the university. This situation not only encouraged the support of wavering students but reinforced the Nazi students' own sense of rectitude and association with the nationalist tradition.

SEVEN

Toward a National Socialist
Student Dictatorship:
The National Socialist German Student Union
and the *Deutsche Studentenschaft*

The Nazi students' struggle to control student councils was not an end in itself but a part of the Party's drive for power. Students won to the Nazi cause provided a reservoir of agitators and militant activists. The surge of the student movement, since it preceded the Party's stunning electoral successes in the 1930s, represented a significant propaganda achievement for a group that billed itself a party of youth.

The student movement was indeed a vulnerable target. Politicization of student politics had provoked the withdrawal of many students, placing the center of interested voters to the far Right. University faculties and state governments now had little use for or interest in student political affairs. Against their competitors at the university, the Nazis could offer more effective organization and a militant group of agitators uninvolved in studies or fraternity activities. Unlike most of their competitors, the Nazi student leaders viewed student politics as a field for their personal ambitions. They benefited, too, from a growing student interest in the parent movement, netting many voters who had no interest in joining but generally supported Party goals.

The fraternity leaders, who alone were in a position to offer opposition, lacked program, organization, or clear goals. Their defensive posture limited them at first to responsive reactions to Nazi initiatives. Nevertheless, the rise in Nazi strength ultimately did permit the crystallization of a non-Nazi Right with the tacit backing of university administrations. And when the Nazis, emboldened by power, began to trample on academic order and threaten academic freedom, the momentum moved to their opponents.

The National Socialist German Student Union's growing control of student councils was a stepping stone to the capture of the ultimate prize, the *Deutsche Studentenschaft*. Victory in the *Deutsche Studentenschaft* would permit the National Socialists to pose as spokesmen for Germany's students as a whole. When the Student Union first became a significant force, in 1928, the *Deutsche Studentenschaft* was in disarray in the aftermath of its constitutional struggle with the Prussian government. But with the backing of most fraternities and continued official recognition, if not warm support, outside of Prussia, the *Deutsche Studentenschaft* could still claim with justice that it represented a substantial majority of the student population. The disappearance of a left-of-center opposition within the organization permitted the pendulum to swing decisively to the Right, a situation which made Nazi prospects that much brighter. And the vacillating nationalist leadership, when confronted with a right-wing opposition whose support sometimes extended to members of their own fraternities, had difficulty seeing the handwriting on the wall. Only an agreement with the Prussian government could preserve the *Deutsche Studentenschaft* as a representative organization and prevent it from stumbling into the Nazi bog, and any workable compromise in this direction had few student defenders.

Early in 1928, with mixed success, many of the Prussian student governments were reconstituted as independent student organizations, which claimed to represent a majority of students. Robbed of many of their important functions, such as student welfare programs and athletics, and dependent upon voluntary contributions, the so-called free student governments (*Freistudentenschaften*) faced an uphill battle for survival. In the west, in particular, very little sentiment remained for continued relations with the *Deutsche Studentenschaft*, and only a small group of students in Frankfurt provided the movement with representation on Prussia's western frontier.[1]

The attitude of the Prussian Ministry of Culture bordered on the vindictive. The students, by casting their votes against the proposed student ordinance, had administered a slap in the face to the Ministry with political repercussions; Ministry officials, under Becker's leadership, now regarded the attempts of the *Deutsche Studentenschaft* to retain a foothold in Prussia with decreasing patience. It could hardly have been otherwise, since while the leaders of the student organization continued to seek compromise, much of the local Prussian leadership, as well as the student press, continuously referred to Becker as an archvillain and the enemy of student self-government.

The Ministry of Culture sought actively to insure that the free student governments not be treated as successor organizations of the old official student governments. Student leaders were given a limited amount of time to vacate their offices and to turn over their records to the school administrations.[2] School authorities were requested to avoid official relations with the successor groups. The Prussian Ministry's apparent hope that the other state governments would follow its example and pose their students with the choice of loss of recognition or *Deutsche Studentenschaft* membership proved illusory. With the notable exceptions of Bavaria and Württemberg, however, the state governments speedily acted to suspend all student government dues to the *Deutsche Studentenschaft* organization.[3]

Continued financial support for the *Deutsche Studentenschaft* with funds collected from the compulsory dues of Bavarian and Württemberg students was crucial for the survival of the organization during the following years. Outside of these two states, the *Deutsche Studentenschaft* was dependent upon voluntary contributions and support from the fraternities. Compulsory dues in the southern German states was a source of severe antagonism with the Prussian government.[4] Many Bavarian students resented the fact that they were subsidizing an organization they could not support. In May 1929, a group of Republican student organizations asserted, in a petition to the Ministry, what the budget committee had in effect denied, that the *Deutsche Studentenschaft* was fast becoming an instrument of right-wing political groups. The students protested that Bavarian funds, which included money collected from Jewish students, were directly subsidizing the anti-Semitic Austrian *Deutsche Studentenschaft,* through so-called sponsorships (*Patenschaften*).[5] In spite of the growing Nazi influence in Erlangen and Würzburg, however, the Ministry continued to accept the view which the student government of the University of Munich offered in its own defense: that continued state recognition and membership in the *Deutsche Studentenschaft* was the best way to avoid the radicalization of student organizations and the growth of political party groups.[6]

At the national conference of officials for higher education in September 1929, the Bavarian and Württemberg representatives, faced with pressure from the other states, agreed to review the question of *Deutsche Studentenschaft* dues.[7] In November, the Bavarian Ministry temporarily suspended funds going to the *Deutsche Studentenschaft,* on the grounds that the Bavarian students were paying a disproportionate amount to support the organization.[8] The Württemberg authorities followed suit shortly afterward.[9] In February of the following year, the two governments released a reduced amount to the *Deutsche Studentenschaft* with the proviso that the funds be used only for athletics and border work.[10] Bavarian Education Minister Goldenberger, who had acted only under political pressure, continued to maintain cordial relations with student leaders. In private, he encouraged the other state governments to renew relations with the *Deutsche Studentenschaft.*[11]

National Socialist leadership of the *Deutsche Studentenschaft*'s Bavarian region after 1930 did not produce a change in policy. When the Theological School at Passau withdrew from the *Deutsche Studentenschaft* late in 1931, a ministry official privately warned the regional leaders that further withdrawals would intensify pressure for cutting off funds.[12] Bavarian funds were withheld entirely in April 1932, because of the *Deutsche Studentenschaft*'s plan for a tuition strike and the resignation of several non–National Socialist students from the *Deutsche Studentenschaft*'s executive board.

The attitudes of the smaller German states towards their students' relations with the *Deutsche Studentenschaft* varied with the political climate. In Hamburg, where a left-of-center government faced an increasingly antidemocratic student body, the student organization was openly defiant. Before 1928, a Left minority had managed to block actual membership in the *Deutsche Studentenschaft*, because of a constitutional provision requiring a two-thirds majority. Nevertheless, *Deutsche Studentenschaft* dues were appropriated in the budget after 1927, although the government prevented their collection in 1928. After *Deutsche Studentenschaft* dues were sent early in 1929, the Hamburg City Senate altered the university law to prevent any coalition between the Hamburg University student government and any outside groups not similarly constituted.[13] The Hamburg students, who would have liked a referendum in order to force a break with the city government, denied that the City Senate had any authority to regulate student organization affairs.[14] The authorities refused, however, to stage a repeat of the Prussian debacle, countering that the student government was subject to city law and could not belong to the *Deutsche Studentenschaft*. The Student Council, in its turn, publicly reaffirmed membership in the *Deutsche Studentenschaft* with obstinate frequency, and continued to send representatives to regional and national meetings.[15] But no funds taken from compulsory student fees were sent to the *Deutsche Studentenschaft* after 1929.

In Saxony, the government believed that conditions were more favorable for student referendums on membership in the *Deutsche Studentenschaft*. Presented with the choice of continued state recognition or remaining in the national student organization, Saxon students in Dresden and Leipzig opted for recognition.[16]

The *Deutsche Studentenschaft*'s efforts to regain government support did achieve a few minor successes. The conservative government in Mecklenburg released a reduced amount of student dues to the central organization after 1930.[17] And in Thuringia, after the election of a nationalist government and appointment of the National Socialist Wilhelm Frick to the post of Educational Minister, the students at Jena were permitted not only to resume their payments to the *Deutsche Studentenschaft* but to release funds which had been collected during the two years that payments had been suspended.[18]

In his efforts to undermine *Deutsche Studentenschaft* support, Carl Becker took an active interest in the Republican groups which were attempting to provide a counterweight. Early in 1928, he encouraged the organization of the *Deutscher Studentenverband* which hoped to unite all German, Sudeten, Austrian, and Danzig students who supported Republican principles.[19] The local *Studentenverband* organizations sometimes acted as watchdogs for the Prussian Ministry, informing them when the university administrations were too friendly to the local *Deutsche Studentenschaft*.[20]

The Prussian Ministry of Culture rendered considerable financial assistance to other moderate and left-of-center student groups, including the Roman Catholic *Görres Ring*, the Union of Socialist Student Groups of Germany and Austria, and the nonsectarian liberal fraternity league, the *Burschenbundskonvent*. This assistance enabled these groups to hold "study weeks" and extracurricular courses, where presumably a moderate political climate prevailed.[21] Becker's successor, Adolf Grimme, also sought to develop contacts between

Republican-minded professors and student groups and to encourage such professors to give public lectures on topics such as the responsibilities of citizenship, the Weimar constitution, and the League of Nations.[22]

But the Ministry's belated attempts to encourage democratic activities among students had little effect. After the rupture between the Prussian ministry and the *Deutsche Studentenschaft,* the Ministry had in fact forfeited any effective powers it had over student political affairs. Becker's efforts to undermine the *Deutsche Studentenschaft* and support competing groups now only tended to solidify *Deutsche Studentenschaft* support and to further estrange students from the government.

The *Deutsche Studentenschaft*'s survival as an organization which could claim the allegiance of a student majority was made possible by continued support from the fraternities. On 12 February 1928, after a meeting with the *Deutsche Studentenschaft* leadership, representatives of most of the fraternity leagues promised their aid to the organization, in spite of the loss of Prussian recognition.[23] Subsequently, several organizations of *alte Herren* pledged financial aid to the students.[24] In Prussia, many students who showed nominal interest by voting in elections for the free student governments were markedly reluctant to pay their dues; only the fraternities were able to enforce collection among their members. In November 1928, the *Deutsche Studentenschaft* found it necessary to request additional direct subsidies from the fraternity leagues.[25] These subsidies, which continued until 1933 and included large amounts from *alte Herren,* provided for about half of the *Deutsche Studentenschaft*'s budget.[26] The fraternities also aided the *Deutsche Studentenschaft* by seeking grants-in-aid through their connections in industrial circles.[27]

While funds from the fraternities and the officially recognized student governments in Bavaria and Württemberg permitted the *Deutsche Studentenschaft* to remain solvent, it could scarcely prevent the eclipse of the principles of student self-government, which had motivated the postwar generation. The rapid politicization of the *Deutsche Studentenschaft* after the struggle with the Prussian government disturbed even the staunchest of anti-Becker partisans. Walter Schmadel, the *Deutsche Studentenschaft* national chairman who had led the fight against the proposed student ordinance in 1927, had become a lonely voice of moderation in 1928. Alarmed at the change in the *Deutsche Studentenschaft,* Schmadel now maintained that state-recognized student governments were perhaps in the end of more worth than an uncompromising defense of the racist and politically militant student groups in Austria.[28]

In spite of Schmadel's belated efforts, the *Deutsche Studentenschaft* and its member organizations continued to put increasing emphasis upon partisan questions at the expense of issues dealing specifically with student life.

After 1927, an Office for Political Education extended the *Deutsche Studentenschaft*'s propaganda program to the local level. Each local student government was encouraged to establish a similar office. The central office suggested topics for discussion: most commonly, the border and foreign German communities, the Versailles Treaty, the "war-guilt lie," and suggested media for programs: demonstrations, lectures, film programs, or periodical libraries.[29] After 1929, a separate office for borderland work shared some of these tasks. National coordination of educational programs was increasingly centered around particular themes. During the 1929–1930 school year, political education programs stressed the problem of the eastern German frontier. Each student government was mailed a list of possible speakers expert in this field.[30] In the spring of 1931, the borderland office sponsored a nationwide discussion of the colonial issue and Germany's lost colonies.[31]

Highlights of the student year were two mass assemblies sponsored by the local student councils on 28 June and 11 November, the anniversaries of the signing of the Treaty of Versailles and the battle of Langemarck. The Versailles assemblies were devoted to emotional demonstrations against the "war-guilt lie" and implicitly those Germans who had accepted the lie by signing the treaty. The Langemarck memorial assemblies often amounted to antistate demonstrations because they followed closely upon the anniversary of the revolution of 9 November 1918. "When on November 9," the *Deutsche Studentenschaft*'s 1928 Langemarck announcement read:

> the ten-year effects of the revolution of egotism, which sprang forth from the darkest depths of human error and bestiality, are celebrated, the *Deutsche Studentenschaft* should renew the revolution of self-sacrifice and loyalty of the students of 1914. Against the glorification of the [November revolution's] decay and lack of principle, [the *Deutsche Studentenschaft*] will contrast the [moral] duty which after Thermopylae was never more heroically and greatly fulfilled than at Langemarck.[32]

Every effort was made to include representatives of the universities in these assemblies in order to give them an official academic character.[33] Although the Prussian Ministry of Culture had warned the Prussian rectors to avoid official contacts with the free student governments, rectors and senates were often enthusiastic participants in Langemarck festivities.[34]

By 1929, the *Deutsche Studentenschaft* had clearly become a right-wing political organization. In spite of this, many students and university officials continued to cherish the illusion that it remained an all-embracing nonpartisan student interest organization. When challenged about the political activities of a supposedly nonpartisan association claiming to represent most, if not all, of Germany's students, the *Deutsche Studentenschaft* leaders repeated the mythical distinction between "national politics" and partisan politics. The increasing influence of the Student Union within the organization therefore proved to be a source of embarrassment for the *Deutsche Studentenschaft* leadership. By early 1929, the National Socialist influence in several student councils had already manifested itself in a rash of *numerus clausus* resolutions. The *Deutsche Student-*

enschaft leaders rightly feared that increased National Socialist activities would alienate that part of the moderate student constituency that was still loyal.

The Nazi students were content to support the *Deutsche Studentenschaft* as long as it suited their political purposes. The *Deutsche Studentenschaft* organization and the local student councils were tailor-made to fit the Nazis' aggressive propaganda program. The Student Union always reserved the right in its relationship with the larger organization to challenge the leadership and to press what they trumpeted as a more consistently nationalist program.

Belatedly, the *Deutsche Studentenschaft* leadership attempted to take action against the growing Student Union influence in the student councils. In a letter sent out before the Hanover student convention of 1929, the executive board asserted that "the creation of partisan groups within the work of student self-government contradicts the basic principle of the comradely union of the student body."[35] In order to prevent further Nazi inroads, they proposed that the convention formally request that the university rectors forbid the formation of political student groups and that student governments in future prevent political party lists in their elections.[36]

The occasion of the Hanover student convention did not prove propitious for the suggested maneuver. In July 1929, the Nazi Party joined with the German National Peoples Party, the *Stahlhelm,* and other right-wing organizations, to sponsor a national referendum opposing the Young Plan. The alliance of nationalist forces on this issue probably prevented a rupture within the *Deutsche Studentenschaft*. Schirach, indeed, cautioned Nazi delegates to the convention to adopt a conciliatory attitude.[37] The convention limited itself to a pledge to retain the *Deutsche Studentenschaft*'s nonpartisan character and to continue to seek support from students of all political persuasions.[38]

The Young Plan affair proved to be one of the chief topics of discussion at the Hanover Convention. National Socialist students, as well as those close to the *Stahlhelm,* were anxious to bring the *Deutsche Studentenschaft* into the front supporting the referendum. The *Deutsche Studentenschaft* leadership, although agreeing with the opponents of the Young Plan, feared that an open alliance with frankly partisan groups would destroy the movement's nonpartisan claims. Such an alliance would jeopardize remaining government contacts. The convention, therefore, voted to issue an independent condemnation of the Young Plan negotiations and a plea to the government to reject the new arrangement for war reparations. Prior to the convention, the *Deutsche Studentenschaft* leadership had independently circulated an anti–Young Plan petition, which was signed by thirty-five youth organizations, twenty fraternity leagues, and the *Hochschulring*.[39] Now, in unusually strong language, the *Deutsche Studentenschaft,* claiming to speak for Germany's younger generation, announced:

> Open and free before the entire world: Our generation will never recognize as binding and obligatory law, that which those presently responsible for international negotiations have conceded to the demands of our enemies. If the signatures of German men lay new chains upon our people, let the world listen: German youth remains free!"[40]

This statement, approved by a substantial majority at a convention attended by students representing sixty-six of the seventy-seven institutions of higher education in Germany, Austria, and the Sudetenland, might well have given pause to the negotiators at London.

The forthright stand on the Young Plan was not enough to solve the *Deutsche Studentenschaft*'s internal difficulties. The Student Union could be satisfied with nothing less than full support of the anti–Young Plan coalition. Schirach had gone so far as to refuse to sign the *Deutsche Studentenschaft*'s Young Plan petition on the grounds that Jewish groups had also been invited to sign.[41] The Student Union's strategy was to embarrass the *Deutsche Studentenschaft* leadership by instigating action in the local student governments. In October, the student councils at the universities of Kiel and Greifswald announced their participation in the committee for a referendum to overturn the Young Plan, the so-called Referendum for the freedom law.[42] The *Deutsche Studentenschaft* protested, but this did not prevent subsequent adherence of the student governments at Halle and Frankfurt to the referendum bloc.[43]

The trouble over the Young Plan was quickly forgotten. The requirements of a display of unity to retain the organization's external image prevented any open confrontation between the leadership and the Student Union. The Student Union's strength continued to grow. In May 1930, a Nazi, Walter Lienau, was elected leader of the *Deutsche Studentenschaft*'s Bavarian region, giving the Nazis representation for the first time on the national central committee.[44] The conciliatory attitude he adopted proved calming.[45] The *Deutsche Studentenschaft* leadership turned its interest to other pressing problems: outbreaks of violence at a number of universities and new attempts by Prussian educational authorities to reestablish student governments outside of the *Deutsche Studentenschaft*.[46]

In March 1931, the *Deutsche Studentenschaft* burned its last bridges to the Prussian government by supporting a *Stahlhelm*-initiated referendum for the dissolution of the Prussian Landtag. The lame apology for this frankly political action was that the Ministry of Culture would never change its position on recognition until the present composition of the Landtag was altered.[47] In fact, the *Deutsche Studentenschaft* leadership was attempting to counter growing Nazi support by associating itself with the *Stahlhelm*. The student government at the University of Halle, adhering to the referendum bloc, candidly stated that they were opposing a government which had made Prussia into a "stronghold of Marxism."[48] But Halle's student government, in process of switching gears from the abortive "League against the Peace Treaties" to the campaign against Dehn, was not given to nonpartisan euphemism.

The Student Union's takeover of the *Deutsche Studentenschaft* was timed for the national German student convention in Graz in the summer of 1931. To insure a Nazi majority at the convention, the Student Union had ignored, in many cases, the traditional gentlemen's agreement which provided for proportional representation of all groups among the delegates selected. These tactics, coupled with their increasing electoral victories, had enabled the Student Union to gain two additional regional chairmanships by the summer of 1931.[49] The executive board made a last-ditch attempt to cancel the convention on the grounds that student unrest in Graz and in Germany made the meeting unpropitious; however, they were overruled in the central committee where the Nazi regional leaders each had a vote.[50]

The Nazi takeover of the *Deutsche Studentenschaft* was carefully prepared beforehand. Only the regional leaders of the Student Union were given exact instructions for fear of a security leak. Times and locations for meetings and caucuses were arranged prior to arrival in Graz.[51] Schirach was in jail in Cologne during the convention but remained in close postal contact with the Nazi leaders on the scene.[52] In vain the outgoing chairman, Schulz, pleaded that the *Deutsche Studentenschaft* would fall apart if it were taken over by one party.[53] The Student Union insisted upon the majority of executive board seats as well as the national chairmanship.[54] The opposition was only partially appeased by the election of Walter Lienau, a man considered to be one of the more moderate Nazis, as chairman.[55]

The Nazi takeover of the *Deutsche Studentenschaft* was the inevitable result of the break with the Prussian government and the subsequent politicization of the organization. To be sure, the Nazi supporters would have expanded rapidly in any case. But official status before 1927 was at least a partial defense of the nonpartisan character of student government. The Nazi takeover of the *Deutsche Studentenschaft* was made possible by its nonofficial character; the psychological gain, however, for the Nazis, stemmed from the commonly held understanding that the *Deutsche Studentenschaft* was *the Official* national student organization.

The new *Deutsche Studentenschaft* leadership completed the evolution of the German student movement to the far Right. Political education and propaganda became the paramount objectives of the organization. The Nazi head of the *Deutsche Studentenschaft* Office of Political Education, Gerhard Krüger, was from the start the guiding spirit of the Nazi leadership in the *Deutsche Studentenschaft*. Beginning with Krüger's tenure, the Office of Political Education became a center of propaganda for the Nazi movement. Relations with local offices were tightened in order to coordinate national education campaigns. All efforts during the first year of Nazi control were centered around discussions of two problems: German rearmament and the politics of "living space" (*Lebensraum*). Local student governments were instructed to plan lecture series and demonstrations dramatizing the issues and to devote their school newspapers to similar discussions.[56] Party position papers were prominent among the "educational" materials distributed by the Office. Krüger, to be sure, denied partisan goals: "The Office for Political Education," he told his critics, "views the consignment of party materials merely as the fulfillment of a part of the task assigned to it at the Graz student convention."[57]

The *Deutsche Studentenschaft*'s rearmament campaign was directed at influencing the course of the disarmament negotiations taking place in Geneva.

Each student government was instructed to summon a mass demonstration which would pass a resolution demanding that Germany be given arms parity with the other major European nations. The students were told to express particular concern that under the Treaty of Versailles they did not have the opportunity to do "that which is among other nations the highest national duty and honor, namely preparation for the defense of the homeland . . . ."[58]

Arms discussions were also the theme of a number of study weeks. Ex-officers joined Nazi speakers to discuss questions such as the "historical development of the disarmament question from Wilson to the disarmament conference of 1932," the arms situation and arms technology, and "the psychological and ethical side of the arms ideal."[59] The arms discussions also stimulated demands for the establishment of chairs in military science, demands which often won the support of numerous faculty members.[60]

Since the mass disarmament demonstrations had a public character, an attempt was made to emphasize their nonpartisan purpose. Krüger was moved to apologize to *Stahlhelm* and German National Peoples Party students at the University of Königsberg who complained that an assembly there, on the occasion of the commemoration of the founding of the German Empire in 1870, took a form appropriate to a mass Party rally. The featured speaker, who had been greeted by the Nazi students present with the Party salute, proceeded to insult the Catholic students and to criticize all parties but the Nazis.[61] A meeting in *Zirkus Busch* in Berlin on 31 January 1932, at which Krüger was the featured speaker, was judiciously planned for greater effect. Prior to the meeting, the resolution to be adopted was brought to the Foreign Office. The music corps of the military garrison in Berlin was engaged. The invited guests included representatives of the Ministry of the Army; many World War I veterans; several rectors from the University of Berlin, the Technical Institute, and other Berlin schools; and a large number of professors. The only sign of the Nazi presence was the central position of five party banners on the stage in the midst of the traditional fraternity flag display.[62]

The "living space" campaign, held outside the public gaze, was more characteristically Nazi in tone. Four regional study weeks were planned to provide a central focus under the theme "The battle of German youth for its living space." This theme permitted the campaign to stress not only the need for more territory for Germans to settle in the East but the supposedly related problem of unemployment for academic graduates.[63] To procure Nazi speakers for this program, Krüger enlisted the aid of Joseph Goebbels, *Gauleiter* of Berlin and party propaganda expert.[64]

The National Socialists in their leadership of the *Deutsche Studentenschaft* attempted in part to preserve the illusion of nonpartisanship in the organization. The *Deutsche Studentenschaft*, under Nazi control, did not cleave religiously to the Party line but continued many of the activities associated with the organization of former years. The strident excesses of the years after 1933 were not yet visible. Instead, the academic respectability which the Student Union craved was reflected in the relative moderation of the *Deutsche Studentenschaft* in this period.

Opposition to the Nazi leadership within the *Deutsche Studentenschaft* became apparent as early as the Graz convention. An opposition crystallized around a number of fraternity leaders, including several men who held or had held high offices in the *Deutsche Studentenschaft*. The issues which divided the opposition from the Nazis were never sharply defined. Like many of the quarrels on Germany's extreme Right, the differences often centered around tone, emphasis, and personalities rather than diametrically opposed political views. Like the Nazis, the *Deutsche Studentenschaft* opposition was, or considered itself to be, *völkisch*, greater-German, and antidemocratic.[65] Its major public dispute with the Nazis was that the Nazis were injecting partisan activities into student affairs where they did not belong. Non-Nazi members of the *Deutsche Studentenschaft* of course strongly resented the one-sided leadership of the organization. But the opposition leadership carefully avoided criticism of the Nazi movement itself.[66] They merely objected to partisan politics in the student movement.[67] Handicapped by their refusal to condemn Nazism outright, the opposition was unable to present a clearly defined alternative around which non–National Socialist students might congregate.

Tension between the Nazis and the *Deutsche Studentenschaft* had, for example, erupted over the the Dehn affair in Halle. The opposition was well aware of the dangers for academic freedom implicit in the attack on Dehn and the resentment that the violence was producing in the academic profession. They repeatedly urged that the campaign be directed at the Prussian Minister of Culture's alleged abuse of his power of appointment, not at Dehn himself, who had unimpeachable academic credentials.[68] But they lacked the courage to separate themselves from the campaign, fearing to forfeit their nationalist image. Indeed, they placed emphasis on their greater ability to wage battle in the national cause, greater even than the National Socialists.

The opposition also complained that the Nazis failed consistently to act decisively in student affairs. Walter Lienau proved to be a special scapegoat because of his opposition to a tuition strike proposed late in 1931 when the state governments had jointly raised student fees. But when in February 1932, goaded by the fraternity leaders, the *Deutsche Studentenschaft* executive board decided in favor of a tuition strike, many of the local fraternities got cold feet.[69] In the end, the strike was called off because of the opposition within both the fraternity leagues and the Student Union, although each accused the other of responsibility. Fear of loss of recognition in Bavaria and forfeiture of good relations with university authorities elsewhere was the most important factor in calling off the strike.[70]

Lienau's relations with the fraternity leadership reached their nadir in November 1931, when he published an article, "The Thorn in the Flesh," in the

Sturmfahne, a regional Student Union newspaper. The article denounced fraternity critics of National Socialists in the *Deutsche Studentenschaft*, labeled them tools of the Free Masons, and called upon the fraternity students to turn these leaders out.[71]

The opposition leaders were enraged, considering this article a challenge to their honor and to the good name of their fraternities. Although the article had been published under a pseudonym, the author made no effort to hide his responsibility. A number of fraternity leaders demanded his resignation as *Deutsche Studentenschaft* chairman.[72] Schirach, disenchanted with Lienau, permitted him to be sacrificed, although he saved face by arranging Lienau's election as a *Deutsche Studentenschaft* elder.[73] Gerhard Krüger replaced Lienau as *Deutsche Studentenschaft* chairman.

Early in January 1932, at the annual meeting of fraternity leagues in Goslar, a full-scale rebellion seemed to be in the offing. Demands for Krüger's and Lienau's resignations were coupled with threats that the fraternities would leave the *Deutsche Studentenschaft* to found a new national student association. But the Nazi leaders present were able to divide the leagues and win support from a number of smaller ones, thus forestalling any action. The leagues agreed to accept a peace with a formal statement by Krüger that Lienau's election as elder was not intended to insult the fraternities and that his resignation would be forthcoming.[74] The latter was not really a concession, since Schirach had already asked Lienau to resign for other reasons.[75]

The Goslar truce proved short-lived. The Nazis refused to elect Schulz, a former *Deutsche Studentenschaft* president, to the position of elder vacated by Lienau. In addition, they accused Schulz of undermining the organization and of misappropriating funds in his capacity as head of the Offices for Economic Questions and the Langemarck War Graves Fund.[76] The exaggerated charges against Schulz were intended to produce a final break between the National Socialists and the opposition, while attempting to force the opposition to bear public responsibility for the crisis. In March, the four chief opposition leaders, Fritz Hilgenstock, Konrad Welte, Hans Gierlichs, and Walter Kraak, resigned their *Deutsche Studentenschaft* offices, pledging to organize a movement to restore nonpartisan control.[77] Their positions were quickly filled by fraternity leaders friendly to the Student Union, but this move, and a widely circulated statement signed by seven fraternity leagues, did not dispel the general impression that a formal break had developed between the fraternity leagues and the *Deutsche Studentenschaft*.[78] The opposition organized a group of leagues under the name "Student Fraternity League Service (*Studentischer Verbändedienst*)" to develop strategy and serve as a communications center.[79] During the following months, Fritz Hilgenstock, a *Deutsche Burschenschaft* leader, traveled throughout Germany and Austria exhorting local student assemblies to vote the National Socialists out of office and promoting the establishment of anti-Nazi slates.

In response, the National Socialists moved to undermine the opposition within its own bailiwicks. National Socialist delegates to the unfriendly fraternity league conventions were given careful instructions to oppose the politics of their league's leadership or face expulsion from the Student Union.[80] The Student Union also turned directly to the fraternity membership with a letter defending its policies and attacking the opposition. But these attempts to influence fraternity members only produced resentment. The opposition leadership had little trouble maintaining the support of the fraternity membership.[81] Failing in their attempt to influence fraternity politics, the Nazis moved to consolidate their control of the *Deutsche Studentenschaft* before the opposition gained enough support to vote them out of office. In a display of apparent tactical brilliance, Krüger conceived the plan of revolutionizing the *Deutsche Studentenschaft* by replacing the parliamentary system within the organization by the so-called *Führer* principle. Success in this venture not only would eliminate the danger of Nazi loss of office but would be an ideological victory of major importance. The cleverness of the strategy was that the opposition had unknowingly been playing their cards into the Nazis' hands by talking up their own plan, which would have replaced the existing electoral system by one of fraternity representation. Indeed it would be difficult to find many students in an organization which had long criticized the workings of parliamentary democracy in the federal and state governments who were prepared to defend it as a principle of student government. The chief drawback of the Nazi plan was that it could not be immediately implemented because of the hostility of most state governments. But at least a start could be made in those states where the Nazi party was represented in the governments.

At the Königsberg national student convention, which met in the summer of 1932, the new era in student affairs was launched. Brown shirts had replaced student caps and chest bands as the characteristic dress. Swastika flags stood where once had waved fraternity banners. Partying and drinking gave way to mass accommodations in austere barracks.[82] Several months of parliamentary maneuvering had enabled the Nazis to secure an overwhelming delegate majority.[83]

In his address to the convention, Gerhard Krüger eloquently defended his conduct of the *Deutsche Studentenschaft* chairmanship and sketched his vision for the future of the organization. "University politics," he told his audience,

> can not be viewed in isolation; it is a component part of general politics. Within general politics it has its own distinct and peculiar tasks to fulfill without becoming partisan politics . . . . The students are the youthful legion of the *Volk* . . . . To mold these young troops, to put them into the battle for the nation . . ., that is the task of university politics.[84]

Since the days of the *Burschenschaften,* Krüger noted, students had been the ideological vanguard of the nation. Now once again they were called upon to mark the trail that the nation would follow.[85]

The task the leadership had conceived for the *Deutsche Studentenschaft* would make it the first major national organization to replace the parliamentary system with the *Führer* principle. When the reform was completed, the *Deutsche Studentenschaft*'s central committee and the local student councils would become advisory, not legislative, bodies. Ultimate authority would reside in the will of a national student *Führer* who would appoint national officers, the ten regional chairmen, and his own successor. Local student *Führer* at each university would in their turn appoint the local office holders as well as their own successors. The national student convention, without its legislative function, would devote its meetings to political demonstrations and educational programs for student leaders. The convention in Königsberg voted its support 155 to 3 with 24 abstentions for this program which would, if carried through, rob the members of their right to vote.[86]

Krüger's speech included two additional reform proposals which proved as controversial as the Führer principle. The new student constitutions would include the "citizen of the Volk" membership rules according to the Austrian and Sudeten German models. Only racial Germans would be admitted. The student governments would also seek a greater role in university affairs, including a veto over the appointment of new instructors. This reform, Krüger insisted, would insure that the Gumbels, Dehns, Nawiaskys, and their ilk would no longer be permitted to teach German students.[87]

Between the July meeting of the Königsberg convention and the Nazi takeover of power at the end of January 1933, the Student Union became engaged in a frantic attempt to reorganize the *Deutsche Studentenschaft* according to the principles announced by Krüger. They could only count upon the support of the Nazi government in Mecklenburg and the Nazi-led coalition in Thuringia. The university faculties were suspicious and hostile. The fraternity leaders in opposition rejected the proposals unequivocally, and they were joined by men who had formerly been neutral in the *Deutsche Studentenschaft* quarrel. To be sure, the opposition publicly favored the introduction of stronger leadership within the *Deutsche Studentenschaft*, a "modified *Führer* principle," but with clear safeguards against the eternal perpetuation of Nazi rule. Their trump card was the nationalist government of Franz von Papen, which had taken control of the Prussian state in July. If agreement could be reached with the Prussian authorities for the reestablishment of state-recognized student governments, the Nazis would in all likelihood lose their majorities in the Prussian student councils. In October, the *Deutsche Studentenschaft* found it necessary to meet with the fraternity leaders who had considerably extended their following and changed the name of their organization from the "Student Fraternity League Service" to the no-more-aggressive-sounding "University-political study group" (*Hochschulpolitische Arbeitsgemeinschaft*). Because of the dangerous Prussian situation, the National Socialists made a number of paper concessions to the Study Group's concept of a reformed *Deutsche Studentenschaft*. They also agreed to enter into joint negotiations with the Prussian government, with the expectation that agreement in

Prussia could be delayed while events took their course in Mecklenburg and Thuringia.[88]

Ignoring a promise to the Study Group that they would delay action in the National Socialist–led states, pendihg Prussian developments, the Nazi student governments in Jena (Thuringia) and Rostock (Mecklenburg) went ahead with plans for new constitutions. In Rostock, a model constitution had been drawn up with the cooperation of the local Nazi Party and a Nazi Professor of Medicine, Hans Reiter, who agreed to act as a liaison between the Ministry and the students.[89] The *Deutsche Studentenschaft* leadership also kept in close contact with national Party figures in an attempt to enlist their aid for the proposal. The new constitution was accepted by the student council on 6 October, but the vote was rejected by Rector Poppe on procedural grounds. Poppe subsequently raised legal questions about the constitution which much of the faculty found offensive; however, the student council accepted it once more in November and sent it to the Ministry with the proviso that the Ministry delay approval pending the outcome of the negotiations between the *Deutsche Studentenschaft* and the fraternity leagues.[90] The delay did not satisfy the misgivings of the Rostock fraternities who joined with the German National Peoples Party and German Peoples Party students in a petition calling for a recall election to dissolve the student council. On the eve of the vote to recall, both Gerhard Krüger and Fritz Hilgenstock traveled to Rostock to present their cases.[91] The referendum failed by seventy votes to achieve the necessary amount for dissolution. Nevertheless, the rector strongly recommended new elections because of the importance of the constitutional issue.[92] Early in December, the university council and Rector Poppe appealed to the Ministry to reject the constitution, because it conflicted with both the state constitution and the charter of the university and because its spirit contradicted that of the traditional academic community.[93] To the surprise of the Nazi students, the Ministry stepped back from defying the University faculty and ordered new elections and further negotiations.[94]

The Rostock elections, scheduled for 30 January 1933, were regarded as crucial by both sides in the student struggle. Hilgenstock arrived early in January to organize a bloc of fraternities on a slate opposing the constitution.[95] The Hilgenstock forces campaigned with the slogan that the Rostock constitution was an attempt "to make eternal the dictatorship of the Student Union in the *Deutsche Studentenschaft* and local student governments."[96] The Student Union pulled out all stops in what appeared to be a crucial turning-point campaign. They appealed emotionally to the students' anti-Semitism, distributing a list of distorted statistics, demonstrating that the high percentage of Jews in the professions was the cause of widespread academic unemployment.[97] Hitler was scheduled to speak several days before the election, but because he was tied up in the negotiations to form a new cabinet, Goebbels appeared in his stead.[98] The election proved a decisive victory for the anti–*Führer* principle forces. The Nazi vote declined from a high of 685 the year before to 469, and they lost four of their nine seats on the student council. The opposition won nine seats and a clear majority. A slate of neutral fraternities won one seat.[99] Several days later, the new council requested that the Ministry return the constitution for revisions.[100]

In Jena, on 18 February, a coalition fighting a similar proposed constitution was able to reduce the previous Nazi majority to a standoff of six votes to six in the student council.[101] But political events outside the university would now play the decisive role in the fate of the reform proposals.

The elections in Rostock and Jena proved what the Student Union leaders feared, that the tide among the students had begun to turn against National Socialism. In November and December 1932, the University political Study Group had already been able to report significant declines in Nazi strength in student elections.[102] By February, in spite of Hitler's appointment as Chancellor, the trend was accelerating.[103] The Student Union as a result attempted to postpone student elections or, if possible, cancel them altogether.[104]

Negotiations with Prussian Ministry officials had not gone favorably. The Ministry continued to press for a student law which essentially conformed to the wishes of the fraternity opposition. The Prussian rectors, on their own initiative, had proposed a new student law with similar provisions.[105] The Nazis feared that a new Prussian student ordinance, with a continuation of the proportional representation system, would mean electoral disaster.[106] While feigning interest, the *Deutsche Studentenschaft* executive board did their best to sabotage the negotiations. They insisted on provisions such as the citizen-of-the-*Volk* principle which the Prussian government could not possibly accept.[107] At the same time, they used the Ministry's failure to produce a student law for propaganda advantage.[108] In December, all cooperation between the *Deutsche Studentenschaft* executive board and the University political Study Group had broken down. Charges and counter charges of a trivial nature were traded during the following two months.[109] Many fraternity leagues began to withhold funds from the *Deutsche Studentenschaft*[110].

When the National Socialists assumed power in Germany early in 1933, time had been running against the Student Union. A well-organized national opposition had put a brake on the movement's growth. A conservative government in the Reich and in Prussia supported the fight for a return to a nonpolitical student association. The German academic establishment, aroused by repeated attacks on professors, had thrown much of its support to the student opposition within the *Deutsche Studentenschaft*.[111] The appointment of Adolf Hitler as Chancellor saved the student movement for the Nazis. With ill-concealed glee, the *Deutsche Studentenschaft* executive board told the opposition fraternity leaders in February that the need for compromise had passed. Bernard Rust, the new Prussian Minister of Culture, fully supported the introduction of the *Führer* principle.[112]

The opposition did not readily accept defeat. On 22 February, Hilgenstock warned his followers that the German student might be called upon to

defend academic freedom even under a nationalist government. We must also reckon with the danger that it could be necessary to continue a battle that was begun under Becker, if a nationalist government should decide on a student law, which we must reject from [the depths] of our most inner conviction and our conception of the essence of the *Deutsche Studentenschaft*.[113]

But the hour for protest had passed. For too many of Germany's students the bell of victory was tolling, and the new government proved to have much more effective means of silencing student opposition than did Carl Becker six years earlier.

The student policy of the Prussian Ministry of Culture did not succeed; perhaps it could not have succeeded under any circumstances. Loss of official recognition for Prussian student self-government bodies failed to stem the trend of the students into the radical camp. The *Deutsche Studentenschaft* was weakened but not destroyed and continued to be recognized as the primary spokesman for Germany's students. The loss of official status in Prussia spurred the politicization of the *Deutsche Studentenschaft* and made Nazi penetration that much easier. An alternative Prussian policy might have slowed this trend, but it is doubtful whether it could have prevented it altogether. Continued student government recognition outside Prussia also failed to prevent student radicalization. In Bavaria, where the educational authorities did not interfere with student self-government, the Nazis were as successful as they were in Prussia, Saxony, Baden, and Hamburg, where the authorities did interfere.

Whereas government officials could do little to prevent the rise of student radicalism, the teaching staff might have been able to quench the fire of the Nazi student movement. But the reaction of the professors to growing National Socialist support was delayed too long to have serious effect. In the fall of 1932, in the struggle over student government constitutional reform, many professors, fearing their own freedoms were at stake, lent aid and comfort to those students who were attempting to ward off a Nazi student dictatorship. Even at this late date most professorial opposition to the National Socialist students was expressed in private behind-the-scenes negotiations attempting to prevent the implementation of the so-called Rostock model constitution.

The fraternity leaders, who attempted to depose the Nazis from the chairs of power in the *Deutsche Studentenschaft* and the student councils, had certain severe handicaps in their struggle. Unlike the National Socialists, they lacked clear goals or a well-defined ideology, calculated to attract wide support. They had neither the will nor the desire to attack Nazism head on; they continued to adhere to the principle that there were no enemies on the Right. Their goals were in many respects similar to those of the Nazis. They were men with a high standard of honor who fought a rival braced with brass knuckles, not gloves, who was prepared to use character assassination and violence, who broke promises without compunction, who had nothing but contempt for student ideals of fraternal loyalty. They appealed to a gentlemanly ethic in an age of mass politics, to a reverence for the past against a movement which promised a better future. They shared the fatal misunderstanding of the old Right for the new: the new Right which demanded total submission, which did not understand compromise, which would brook no rivals, which made only tactical concessions. By late 1932, the students of the non-Nazi Right had begun to shed their illusions and, benefiting from a growing annoyance with Nazi student activities, began to achieve some success. Unfortunately, national developments cut short their attempt to win back control of student offices. The future belonged to those with clearer vision.

In the final years of the Weimar Republic, the Nazi students clearly exhibited those qualities which enabled them to ride herd over all comers after the Nazi takeover in 1933. Dedicated, fanatical, possessed of a belief in their own infallibility, the Nazis alone were professional practitioners of student politics. Student politics for the hard core indeed was far from an extracurricular activity—it was a sure road to future success in Nazi Party and state. It is scarcely a wonder that non-Nazi groups had difficulty competing with full-time politicians.

A keystone of Nazi success was the plight of the lower middle class student at the universities. Large numbers of students from lower middle class homes attended universities in order to circumvent the economic crisis. But a country in the midst of depression scarcely could absorb hosts of academic graduates, and this new social class of students usually lacked the contacts which made professional success possible. Students otherwise unreceptive to racial mythologizing were only too happy to protest Jewish competition for professional position. Many students who were frightened by the lack of employment prospects, bored by their studies, and discriminated against by fraternities were available for full-time commitment to the National Socialist movement. The movement offered renewed self-esteem and good career prospects should the Nazis achieve power. The ambitions of Nazi student leaders, frustrated in traditional channels, found free play in the struggle for a perpetual monopoly of student government offices.

Behind the political rhetoric, however sincerely maintained, lay a tooth-and-claw social competition. The fraternity student with his colorful costume, his sword, and his arrogance was opposed by the brown-shirted legions with their leveling pretensions. The goal of the latter was not social revolution but merely a new power elite which they would dominate. In this ambition, the National Socialist German Student Union epitomized the drive of the parent party as a whole.

But the Nazi appeal clearly extended beyond the socially disadvantaged students. The fraternity leadership was, after all, disturbed by the penetration of the movement into its own preserves. Students from old academic families were becoming involved, too. Hard times were having their impact upon the youth of the upper middle class, even if the older generations remained tied to traditional nationalism.

EIGHT

Planning for the Third Reich:
Student Activities during the Last Years
of the Republic

The story of the rise of the National Socialist Student Union is scarcely edifying. The ambitious, arrogant and intolerant Nazi student leaders hardly conform to the common stereotype of idealistic youth. Yet the Nazis would never have achieved their amazing resonance at the universities in the 1930s if they had not tapped a wellspring of idealism among great numbers of German students. The Nazi sympathizers, for the most part, saw in the movement a hope for national revival.

Even in the violent and hate-filled political climate of the 1930s, when ugly attacks were made on men like Dehn, Nawiasky, and Gumbel, a spirit of self-sacrifice and idealism was not entirely absent from student life. The hatred which so frequently spilled over into attacks on the "enemies" within the nation went hand in hand with a renewed faith in Germany's future and a willingness to dedicate time and effort to the national cause. To be sure, this idealism had been distorted and twisted by the obtuse doctrines of the political Right. But democratic groups had made little or no attempt to capture the imaginations of Germany's student youth; the educational authorities had been content to let things drift, leaving prerevolutionary educational programs intact, and to criticize instead of analyze the growing student affection for the radical Right. The Right, in its turn, was ready with panaceas, programs, and causes which channeled the idealism not only of a militant minority but of that large majority that was concerned about Germany's future and found little to cheer in Germany's present plight. The apathy of many students of the 1920s was giving way in the 1930s, in Germany as elsewhere, to student involvement.

The idealism of the early 1930s, like so much of student politics, took the form of quasi-rebellion from what were held to be the middle-class values common in the older generation. Preoccupation with material things, scarcely an option in the depression years anyway, was to be replaced by dedication to Nation and *Volk*. The representative of the new generation distinguished himself from the individualistic, materialistic old middle class by his commitment to "community service, by personal responsibility." He was not a self-centered egotist nor a representative of a social class, "but a man of his *Volk*. He does not live for himself, but amalgamated in the organic totality."[1]

The old men to be exorcised bear less relationship to the older generation in Germany than to the German image of the English middle class. As we have seen, the new generation was not so much rebelling as attempting to put into practice the rhetorical values of the older generation. In many cases their efforts were indeed aided by governmental authorities.

Two programs in particular fueled the idealistic drives of Germany's students in the last years of the Republic; one military, another social and economic. In paramilitary training programs the students hoped to provide the nation with the prepared military reserves denied Germany by the Versailles Treaty. An extensive program of agricultural service work aimed at restoring agriculture, opening up new areas to agricultural settlement, and providing new channels of communication between Germany's academic youth and its farm population. In spite of the illusions inherent in these activities, they were clearly a departure from the negativism of the past.

After the graduation of World War I veterans from the universities in the early 1920s, paramilitary activities did not arouse serious interest for several years. Late in 1927 the *Stahlhelm, Bund der Frontsoldaten* (Steel Helmet Union of Frontsoldiers) began actively to seek student members.[2] The *Stahlhelm* was nominally an organization of war veterans who had seen action on the front; by May 1926, it had opened its membership to nonveterans.[3] As early as 1923, the *Stahlhelm* had established auxiliary youth groups.[4] Organizing activities at the universities were initiated at the same time as the movement was undergoing an internal transformation which would result in increased participation in the political arena.[5] Organizing efforts lagged until late in 1928, when a large number of local groups were founded. In October of the following year, a national organization under the name *Stahlhelm-Studentenring Langemarck* was announced. At first this separate student organization existed only to handle questions specifically related to the university. The students were integrated in the local *Stahlhelm* groups for all other activities. The student organizations were kept strictly under the thumb of the parent *Stahlhelm*.[6]

The *Stahlhelm*'s chief attraction for students was its militaristic ideology and its paramilitary training program. Military activities centered around a series of "war sport" camps during vacations.[7] After 1928, vacation war sport camps were also arousing increased interest in the *Hochschulring* movement. The *Hochschulring* found the camps an effective answer to the paramilitary training which Student Union members were receiving in the SA. In addition, the new program had reawakened the interest of many fraternities in participating in *Hochschulring* activities. Paramilitary training was proving to have an appeal which transcended political and confessional boundaries.[8]

The *Hochschulring*'s military program was inaugurated in October 1928 at a national meeting at Boitzenburg castle in the Uckermark. A minimum military educational program was defined to include group calisthenics, field exercises, and shooting marksmanship. The national leadership promised to cooperate with local groups in the holding of vacation camps.[9] The overriding aim of this program was announced as the

> striving for the physical means which will give us the possibility to fulfill our foreign policy demands in East Central Europe (*Mitteleuropa*). The participation of *Hochschulring* students in the military movement should also offer the opportunity to convey the ideas of the *Hochschulring* to diverse circles of the German people and give each individual man the opportunity to measure his strength for practical political tasks and to demonstrate if he is in the position to win recognition for himself and for the idea which he represents.[10]

The *Stahlhelm* and the *Hochschulring* soon joined forces in their military training program.[11] In the summer of 1929, the *Ring* held three summer camps with *Stahlhelm* cooperation. The *Stahlhelm* provided military instructors as well as many of the participants.[12] During the following year, fraternity leagues played an active role in recruiting camp students and financing camps. Almost all of the leagues joined a camp committee set up to cooperate with the *Hochschulring* and the *Stahlhelm*.[13] An honorary committee of friends of the military movement, set up to raise funds, included a number of retired officers and *Stahlhelm* leaders.[14]

The camps were intended to provide the experience of community living under strict discipline as well as the rudiments of military training.[15] Camp programs often included political instruction, but chief activities were either directly related to military training or aimed at physical fitness. At a representative camp near Nuremberg in 1930, the students began the day with sports. After-breakfast activities included field exercises, firing with small caliber weapons, or marches. In the afternoon, sports were followed by lectures on military and economic themes.[16]

In 1930, the paramilitary training program was given a boost by the efforts of a *Burschenschaft alte Herr* and decorated war veteran, Otto Schwab. On his own initiative, Schwab called a meeting in Berlin of representatives of the fraternity leagues early in 1931 to establish new guidelines for the military sport program.[17] At this meeting, a new organization, the "Academic-Scholarly Military Office" (*Akademisch-Wissenschaftliches Wehramt* or *AWA*) was founded to coordinate military sport activities throughout the nation.[18] The *Hochschulring* conceded all future programs to the new group. Local units, called "Academic-Scholarly Regional Offices" (*Akademisch-Wissenschaftliche Kreisämter*) were established at almost all universities. In addition to an enlarged camp program, the regional offices began to sponsor weekend exercises during the term.[19] The Academic Military Office issued pass books to individual students in which completion of its diverse programs could be recorded. In this way the fraternities were able to check on their members' participation in war sport activities, which they generally made compulsory.[20]

At a number of universities, student governments also established "military offices" which extended Academic-Scholarly Military Office activities to non-fraternity students.[21] In Würzburg, for example, the two offices were in reality combined. Funds were procured from the student council's budget and from professors' contributions. The University's Institute for Physical Education provided funds, instructors, and equipment.[22] The participants were primarily fraternity students, since only in this way could the training be made compulsory.[23] In December 1932, the student council tried to remedy this by petitioning the Bavarian government as well as the University Senate to require a minimum program of military sport and physical education for admission to state examinations.[24] At the same time the program was extended to include sponsorship of lectures in military science.[25]

Police officials were naturally concerned about the renaissance in student paramilitary exercises. To be sure, they no longer seemed as great a threat to the state as in the early years of the Republic; but they could embarrass Germany's foreign relations, since they skirted violation of the Versailles Treaty. And according to a 1921 law for implementation of the treaty, the judicial authorities had the responsibility to prosecute all treaty violations.[26]

Military sport activities, nevertheless, soon found a friend in the person of General Wilhelm Groener, Minister of the Army in the Brüning cabinet. Groener considered an overly stringent interpretation of the Versailles Treaty in this area to be self-defeating. He questioned whether most of the activities of the students really conflicted with the Treaty. In fact, Groener saw a number of advantages for the government in lending its support to this program. Government aid would prevent the movement from seeking succor on the Right. It would channel the program into areas which would not embarrass Germany abroad and at the same time would promote the physical education of youth and thus aid national defense. For Groener, the use of the hated Treaty of Versailles to prosecute the students was a serious political mistake; instead the government should provide clear guidelines to the student groups as to which activities were permissible and which were not.[27] In a secret report to the cabinet, Groener made a number of proposals for aiding the military sport movement among students and other youth groups. He recommended that existing governmental financial support for physical education programs be channeled into those organizations which carried on military sports. Those groups which adopted government restrictions on these activities would be provided with funds. The army, to be sure, could not aid the program because of the provisions of the Treaty of Versailles; but Groener pointed out that the army strongly favored the physical training of youth.[28]

The Groener report signaled a change in policy by national and state governments in regard to the military sport movement. Private encouragement largely replaced police harassment.[29] However, specific suggestions were only implemented by the succeeding Papen cabinet, under the urging of Interior Minister Freiherr von Gayl. In September 1932, President von Hindenburg, Chancellor von Papen, and Minister von Gayl jointly announced the establishment of a National Committee for the physical fitness of youth (*Reichskuratorium für Jugend-ertüchtigung*) with Gayl as chairman and General Edwin von Stülpnagel as president and chief administrator.[30] The initial budget provided for an expenditure of 1,500,000 Marks, considerably more than had been appropriated for physical education programs in recent years, and eighteen military sport schools were established.[31] Both the *Deutsche Studentenschaft* and the Academic-Scholarly Military Office, now euphemistically called the Academic-Scholarly Work Office (*Akademisches Wissenschaftliches Arbeitsamt*) announced their adherence to the new program and appointed representatives to sit on the board.[32]

Groener's hunch that government support of military sport activities would wean students away from the Nazis was worriedly shared by the National Socialist German Student Union. The active role of the rival *Stahlhelm* in Academic Military Office programs also disturbed the Nazis. The real aim of the military sport program in the Nazis' view was to "involve a large number of German students in 'unpolitical' activities and keep them away from National Socialism."[33] This intention was summed up by an alleged quote from an Interior Ministry official: "We will drive (*bimsen*) these young people until they are too tired in the evening to trouble themselves about politics."[34] When "Papen's reactionary clique" went so far as to establish the National Committee for the Physical Fitness of Youth and openly encouraged war games at the universities, the National Socialists tried to meet the challenge by establishing their own paramilitary organization, the *Studentenbund* (St. B.). All Student Union members were ordered to take six months of training in the SA and then devote two years of service to the student formations before returning to the SA or SS.[35] Special *Studentenbund* groups for cavalry, navy, and flying were also planned.[36]

Although SA leader Röhm announced support for the student paramilitary group, local SA and SS organizations reacted angrily.[37] The students were accused of setting up class organizations and destroying good worker-student relations. Many student SA members altogether refused to participate in the *Studentenbund*. The attempt was a failure, and the *Studentenbund* was quietly dissolved in the early days of the Third Reich.[38] By this time the Student Union was in a position to reap what the "Papen clique" and their friends at the university had sown in the field of military education.

Growing student interest in military education programs in the early 1930s was paralleled by increased attention to the "work-service" (*Arbeitsdienst*) movement. Work service encompassed a number of diverse programs. Since the early 1920s , a number of nationalist groups, notably the *Jungdeutscher Orden* and the *Stahlhelm,* had supported the idea of compulsory work-service in the countryside as a substitute for the military service denied Germany by the Treaty of Versailles. Young men would be taught military discipline while at the same time contributing to national reconstruction through land reclamation, harvest work, flood control, and other labor. A similar plan was suggested by the Center Party leader Matthias Erzberger, who hoped that compulsory work-service would include citizenship education and help reduce juvenile delinquency.[39] A number of youth movement groups favored voluntary work service in work camps but rejected entirely any military emphasis. Instead, a spirit of dedication, cooperation, community living, and self-government reigned in the youth movement camps which were first established in 1925. It was largely through these camps that many students were first acquainted with the idea of voluntary service.[40]

During the post-1929 depression, work service was viewed as a partial solution to the problem of unemployment. In June 1931, the Brüning government introduced an extensive voluntary work program (called *Freiwilliger Arbeitsdienst* or FAD) to be sponsored and funded by the "National Establishment for Employment Aid and Unemployment Insurance" (*Reichsanstalt für Arbeitsvermittlung und Arbeitslosenversicherung*). The government's voluntary work-service program included vocational education as well as employment on public works projects.[41]

Although there were a number of attempts in the 1920s to establish student work-service programs, it was only in the early 1930s that the work-service idea aroused widespread student interest. The 1930 Breslau national student convention issued a demand for immediate introduction of a compulsory work-service year for all nineteen-year-old males. Military sports were to be an important feature of the proposed compulsory camps.[42] Later in the year, voluntary camps were established by the regional *Deutsche Studentenschaft* organization in southwestern Germany.[43] The National Socialist German Student Union also strongly endorsed the idea of a compulsory work-service year.[44] Early in 1931 the *Deutsche Studentenschaft* leadership planned to establish offices for work-service in all regions and to set up a nationally coordinated voluntary program.[45] The *Deutsche Studentenschaft* also joined the *Deutsches Studentenwerk*, the student welfare organization, and the numerous private welfare, youth, and labor organizations in lending their aid to the federal government's voluntary program set up in June 1931. By 1932, large numbers of students were participating in voluntary camps throughout Germany and many of the local student governments had established camps of their own.

The student work camps were designed to fulfill several objectives. They were directed at performing economic tasks which were desperately needed but for which state and private initiative was not available. The students carefully avoided competing with other sections of the economy. By inviting young workers and peasants to the camps, they hoped to build respect between different social classes through common "physical labor" and through comradely "companionship (*Zusammenleben*)."[46] They tried in a small way to put the unemployed into productive work. Finally, they hoped to improve the physical health of Germany's youth.[47]

A particularly active work-service program in Hamburg provides an example of the goals the students hoped to achieve. The Hamburg student council ran six camps in the summer of 1932, with a total of 250 participants. Additional students had been sent to camps organized by welfare and youth groups.[48] The first Hamburg work camp, set up in May, was attended by five students and seventeen unemployed workers. Free room, board, work clothes, and a nominal amount of pocket money were provided to all participants. The aim of the camp was to reclaim swampland for farming. The organizers hoped that the workers involved would use their camp training to enter settlement programs and become farmers.[49]

The National Socialist German Student Union expended considerable effort upon the student work-service program. It hoped that the camps might offer an effective environment for propaganda work among students and workers and that they might also be used for paramilitary training.[50] Since the Student Union controlled many of the student governments which were establishing these programs, they saw more chance of controlling these camps than they had with the military sport camps. In the fall of 1932, Gerhard Krüger instructed all local Union leaders to devote particular effort to the establishment of work-service programs. Each Union chapter appointed an Official for Work Camps who in turn sought the corresponding post in student government. All chapters were directed to insure that a work camp be set up by the student governments and, if possible, that the camps be in National Socialist hands.[51]

The Nazis publicly insisted that voluntary work camps were only a temporary expedient. A compulsory work program for all German youth remained the ultimate goal. Their minimum program called for a mandatory work year for all prospective university students. Such a work year, it was hoped would significantly reduce the numbers of students at the overcrowded universities, an increasing problem because of unemployment among university graduates. At the same time, it would provide a year of ideological education for high school graduates.[52]

In the fall of 1932, the Nazi leaders of the *Deutsche Studentenschaft* began a campaign for the introduction of a work-service year for all high school graduates. In December, serious negotiations with the Reich government commenced.[53] The Schleicher cabinet proved sympathetic but rejected a compulsory program as unworkable under the present circumstances. The Army Ministry in particular hoped that work-service camps might eventually provide the basis for a national militia.[54] In January 1933, the national government offered full support for a voluntary work-service program for high school graduates. The local student governments were delegated responsibility for carrying out this program in cooperation with local commissars for work service. All spring graduates would be given the opportunity to spend four months in work-service programs and an additional month and a half at a military sport camp. The chief thrust of the program, which would also include unemployed workers, would be land reclamation in preparation for settlement in eastern Germany.[55] The *Deutsche Studentenschaft* leadership was chagrined that a compulsory program had been at least temporarily rejected; but they had won an important role in the carrying out of a voluntary program on a much more impressive scale than previously had been possible.

Between 1930 and 1933, the soil had been prepared for a national government which would unite German academic youth under a program of national revival. The Weimar Republic had few remaining defenders, *völkisch* ideology and dictatorship few unregenerate opponents. Thousands of students were anxious to help restore the nation's economy and military power.

It would be a mistake to read too much into the opposition to the National Socialist Student Union among right-wing students in the early 1930s. The ideological gap between the opposition forces and the Nazis was far less significant than personal and political jealousies. The search for authoritarian solutions not only was shared by the Nazis and the traditional Right but had extended well into the Center. The organized Catholic minority, most demonstrably, was moving rapidly to the Right after 1930. In the early 1930s, the *Görres Ring* championed their own national revival, which was to be found neither in the "mechanistic" parliamentarianism of the moderate Left, the class struggle of the far Left, or the paganism and super-nationalism of the far Right. Rather, a revived authoritarianism, founded in Christian principles and dedicated to solving social tensions through experiments in a corporative economy, was suggested. Mussolini and Italian fascism in particular offered a model alternative, clearly acceptable to the Church.[56]

National Socialist rhetoric by 1932 had become common student currency. A typically vacuous position statement announced in September 1932 by the *Cartell Verband*—with its 10,000 student members the largest of the Catholic fraternity leagues—illustrates the penetration of Nazi phraseology into a Catholic stronghold:

> The *Cartell Verband* is dedicated as a German student league to German *Volkstum* which is determined and fashioned as a living unity by ancestry, and living space, by blood and soil, language and custom, by fate and culture. According to our conviction, this German nationality is the fertile soil of the spirit which lives as the expression of the German *Volk* soul and the product of the creative *Volk* spirit in German art, poetry and literature, German morality, German customs and German language, the German conception of law, the German striving for knowledge and science, German values and achievement. This dedication to and membership in the German nationality extends at once to work in the service of the nation and identification with the will of the people, to responsible and obligating consciousness of self, to a living sense of community, to a cultural position, to a spiritual shaping of the personality.[57]

The political weather in which Nazism blossomed in the early 1930s can best be described as idealism distorted by serious intellectual limitations. The students were well aware of depression, unemployment, and the provisions of the Treaty of

Versailles. But the vast majority had been educated to seek solutions which conformed with the vague mythology of *völkisch* prose. One searches in vain for analyses and critiques of Brüning's economic policies, the causes of the depression, or the complexities of international relations in student journals. Politics and economics in the modern sense were understood only superficially. The activist students of the 1930s were animated by a belief in a moral rearmament which skirted politics entirely. Instead, such placebos as physical fitness, national togetherness, return to the soil were expected to restore Germany to prosperity and greatness. National Socialism thrived not only in an atmosphere of middle-class hardship and discontent but in one of ignorance and political näivete. If the supposedly well-educated students were driven by irrational analyses, one can only despair for much of the rest of the population. Certainly the German educational system was not training men and women for citizenship in a modern state.

A student's interest in military sport or labor-service programs did not lead him inexorably into the Nazi camp. But the Student Union's own emphasis on such programs provided the Nazis with a constructive image as part of a general movement of national revival. Although support for National Socialism was far from unanimous, many otherwise skeptical students were ready to reserve judgment and await the achievements of the new government which entered office at the end of January 1933.

NINE

"Battle-Stations" of the Third Reich:
The Students' National Socialist Revolution

In a memo on 19 April 1933, the chief of the *Deutsche Studentenschaft* office of scholarship (*Wissenchaft*), Georg Plötner, summed up the program of the Nazi students for the universities. "The state is conquered," Plötner wrote,

> The universities are not yet [conquered].... When they are institutions of a political state, when they are battle stations [motivated by] the same spirit as this state, when they are centers of the greatest political activity, then no private man in the person of a professor or in the person of a student can find a home there. It is precisely this turnabout against the private man, against the capably educated representative from bourgeois society, the breeding ground of liberalism—precisely in this turnabout that the new German university differentiates itself fundamentally from the "autonomous" educational academies of a liberal republic.[1]

Within a few short months, students who accepted Plötner's program would contribute to the destruction of that eminence and world repute which the achievements of German scholarship and science for over a century had brought to the "autonomous educational academies." Before 1933, the Nazi movement lacked both a program and clear ideological guidelines in its approach to higher education. The Party leadership viewed the universities with distrust and suspicion. The university traditions of academic freedom and pure scholarship ran contrary to the totalitarian aspirations of the Nazi movement; and few professors had been attracted to the Party or its policies before 1933. Germany's new rulers could hardly permit the universities to persist as alien intellectual oases within the nation; a radical transformation of the universities was inevitable. A new scholarship would have to be created to provide grist for the mills of Nazi ideology; a future student generation would have to be indoctrinated and prepared for the future service of state and nation.

A decisive role in destroying the universities' liberal heritage and making them into docile instruments of the Party and state fell to the students. For several years, they had proved receptive to Nazi appeals; now in the Third Reich they would be called upon to prove their mettle by forming an academic fifth column. But the goals of the Nazi movement at the universities did not stop at the creation of controls over scholarship and the redirection of intellectual endeavors. Nazi students would take the lead in restructuring extracurricular life with the aim of producing a new "student type" ideologically prepared and physically trained to meet the new demands for leadership and service.

In the months after the Nazi seizure of power, Germany was transformed from a pluralistic democracy into a totalitarian state. This Nazi goal was achieved largely through bureaucraticization—extending the Nazi Party and state bureaucracies into all areas of society and absorbing existing organizations within a single network. Terror was one weapon in this goal. But for the most part the nation accepted the new order passively.

The students throughout the Weimar Republic had held the idea of hierarchical bureaucratic control close to heart, so it is not surprising that the students of 1933 acquiesced without a struggle in the authoritarian reorganization of student life. Few thought of mourning democracy (although many certainly objected to the quality of the new personnel). Potential little *Führer* existed in abundance. Many of the rest, looking to their future government careers, noisily joined in the action.

The first order of business for the Nazi militants after 31 January 1933 was to finish the job begun in Königsberg the previous summer: the creation of a new system of student government based on the *Führer* principle. At first the political situation was not altogether promising. Opposition groups within the *Deutsche Studentenschaft* had retained the momentum initiated late in 1932, and the National Socialists continued to meet reversals in student elections throughout the month of February.[2] Whereas the activities of left-wing students could be curtailed with threats of violence and police aid, national opposition groups still retained friends in high places.[3]

In order to temper the fears of their fraternity opponents about their future independence, the Nazis in the *Deutsche Studentenschaft* leadership decided to seek a compromise which would preserve their control while providing the fraternities with a seemingly greater voice in student affairs. The new plan envisioned the balancing of the *Führer* principle on the local level with a so-called corporate chamber (*bündische Kammer*) on which the fraternities and other nationalist groups would sit.[4] In February, Hitler had replaced Papen's man Kähler as Reich Commissar of the Prussian Ministry of Culture with his old friend, Bernhard Rust, a former schoolmaster dismissed in 1930 ostensibly for psychological reasons. The *Deutsche Studentenschaft* seized the opportunity to reopen negotiations with this key ministry for a new Prussian student ordinance. In March, they submitted a model student constitution to Rust, incorporating both the *Führer* principle and the chamber of groups. The ministry produced a new student ordinance based on this model. Krüger then persuaded the National

Socialist Minister of the Interior, Wilhelm Frick, to bring pressure on the other state governments to follow the Prussian example. Frick also promised to introduce a new national law which was necessary for the implementation of the membership provisions of the proposed Prussian ordinance.[5]

The new Prussian student law of April 1933 made the *Führer* principle the basis of student government.[6] The *Führer* of each student body was to be appointed by his predecessor with the approval of the *Deutsche Studentenschaft Führer*. He was also given the power to choose all office holders. Unlike the proposed Rostock constitution of the previous fall, however, the new student ordinance provided for a chamber of groups open to representation of all student organizations subject to the sole qualification that they agreed to educate their membership "for amalgamation with the community of the *Volk* through military service training, work service, and physical education."[7] Of course this provision, instead of providing fraternities with a strong voice in student affairs, was to be used as a means of controlling them. A two-thirds majority of the chamber could, with the assent of the two "elders," depose the student *Führer*, an unlikely possibility at best. The powers given the student governments were similar to those provided by the state governments under the Republic and much less generous than the *Deutsche Studentenschaft* had sought. Gerhard Krüger, who would lose his post during the summer, had wanted full student control over discipline, so that the faculties could not interfere with actions against left-wing student dissidents.[8] Instead, students were merely represented on existing faculty disciplinary bodies as well as committees concerned with student economic support and welfare programs. They were put in charge of military sport, work-service, and physical education activities, and they were given an advisory voice on the university senates and faculties when questions arose relating to student affairs. Membership was limited to students of German "ancestry and mother tongue," regardless of citizenship. All students, upon matriculation, would be required to swear that their parents and grandparents were German in order to be admitted to membership.[9] "Non-Aryan" students, excluded from student government, student welfare establishments, and athletics, still found themselves subject to student fees.[10]

A new *Deutsche Studentenschaft* constitution was announced several days later. Like the Prussian Student Ordinance, it provided for an all-powerful *Führer* who appointed national office holders and regional leaders. It also included a League Advisory board, including representatives from the fraternity leagues and other national student organizations.[11]

The new constitution projected the continuation of the greater German coalition, but Austrian and Czech authorities balked at relations between their citizens and an organization with close ties to the Nazi government. The Sudeten German branches were dissolved in May. In Austria, where the Catholics had walked out of the *Deutsche Studentenschaft* in December 1932, an order by the clerical fascist government to ban the rump group remaining came in August 1933. Strict controls over all Austrian student groups were put into effect.[12] During the following year, the *Deutsche Studentenschaft* kept its Austrian connections alive through a so-called Economic office of Reich German University Students (*Wirtschaftsstelle reichsdeutscher Hochschüler*). German students studying in Austria were carefully screened; most were activists willing to proselytize for Nazism. Their activities were closely watched by the Austrian authorities.[13] The *Deutsche Studentenschaft,* whose greater-German union had been the focus of the struggles of the 1920s, now had to be content with the lone foreign outpost of the Technical Institute in the free city of Danzig.

The *Deutsche Studentenschaft* constitution and the state student laws of 1933 were superseded a year later by a constitution bestowed by Interior Minister Frick "at the direction of *Führer* and *Reich* Chancellor Adolf Hitler." The 1934 constitution, written in a period when Nazi power was consolidated and the students' "revolution" was clearly over, severely restricted student powers. Provisions for student participation in university administrations were conspicuously absent. The role of the *Deutsche Studentenschaft* was now defined as insuring "that the students fulfill their duty to university, *Volk,* and state. Above all, [the *Deutsche Studentenschaft*] has the responsibility to educate the students as honorable and militant [*Wehrhaften*] German men ... prepared for the responsibility of selfless service among the *Volk* and in the state...."[14] The chief foci of education were to be work-service and SA work.

Combined student and government initiatives were also applied to the questions of Jewish, Marxist, pacifist, and other politically undesirable students. In March 1933, the *Deutsche Studentenschaft* had recommended that both Jews and Communists be excluded from all student activities and student buildings.[15] The law "against the overenrollment of German schools and universities" of 25 April 1933 limited Jewish students to a quota of 1.5 percent at each university. Only sons of Jewish front-soldiers were exempted. Students sitting on local matriculation commissions were advised by *Deutsche Studentenschaft Führer* Krüger to insure that this quota was viewed as a maximum and that those universities with fewer than 1.5 percent not increase the percentage now.[16] In June and July, under government orders, all Jewish student clubs and fraternities were outlawed.[17]

Communist, Socialist, and pacifist student organizations were forced out of existence during the spring of 1933 through terror and outright prohibition.[18] In June and July, the state governments excluded all students from the universities who in the past year had been "active in a communist sense" whether or not they had been party members.[19] In August, these measures were extended to include all students active in Marxist causes or in "anti-national activity."[20] Student governments cooperated with these expulsions by supplying names to the administrations and keeping a watchful eye out to make sure that the orders were carried out.[21] The numbers expelled for political reasons were not large; by October, ninety-two students had been excluded from Prussian universities; but the expulsions were a distinct warning against any future attempts to revive left-wing organizations. Above and beyond these measures, Republican students of all persuasions, from former members of the Socialist groups to members of the Catholic *Windhorst Bund,* were systematically excluded from privileges such as student loans, scholarships, and tuition exemption, privileges for which members of the SA, SS, and, for a time at least, the *Stahlhelm* were given first consideration.[22]

If the faculties balked at accepting their new role in the Nazi state, they were whipped along by the spontaneous fervor of their students. On 11 February 1933, the National Socialist German Student Union widely circulated a petition among Germany's professors welcoming Adolf Hitler's appointment as chancellor.[23] At the same time, attacks on "antinational" professors, who could no longer count on police protection, proliferated. In mid-February, the *Völkischer Beobachter* gleefully reported that a group of SA students had stormed a building at the State Art School in Berlin, where state examinations were in progress. Three Jewish professors were thrown out on the street and the doors of the "Marxist professors' studio" fastened shut with hinges and nails.[24] But continued outbreaks of this nature soon received the censure of authorities, who preferred to get rid of political opponents with legal weapons. State opposition to the students' initially "spontaneous" revolution soon forced them to reject incendiary approaches.[25]

By March, plans for a more organized campaign against undesirable professors became apparent. In Bavaria, the Student Union compiled a list of eleven professors with a notation about their political beliefs, memberships, and associations.[26] The national Student Union office prepared its own list of undesirable professors.[27] The law for the reorganization of the career civil service of 7 April 1933 permitted the dismissal of all professors who were either "politically undependable" or had Jewish ancestors.[28] The new law did not go far enough for the *Deutsche Studentenschaft* leaders, who, in any case, speedily lent their services to the purge. Local student officers were directed to carefully compile a list of all professors to whom the law might apply: Jews, members of Socialist groups or the *Reichsbanner,* and professors who had criticized "the national *Führer,* the movement of national upheaval, or the front soldiers."[29] In addition, an enumeration of all liberal or pacifist professors was necessary, so that students might organize boycotts of instructors not covered by the law.[30]

The *Deutsche Studentenschaft*'s nationwide boycott campaign was launched early in May. It was directed both against professors not covered by the civil service law and against those whose cases were still pending. In order to avoid a diffuse general boycott, students were advised to concentrate upon several typical representatives whose known racial or political background made them defenseless. Permission for a boycott against a particular professor was necessary from the central organization, which would then widely publicize the action. In addition, the *Deutsche Studentenschaft* announced its own behind-the-scenes efforts to eliminate all Jewish professors exempted from the civil service law by reason of their war service from sitting on examination committees. In this way, a boycott of these professors would be more effective, since no student need fear

to meet them later on his exam committee.[31] At the same time, the local offices
for scholarship were charged with sponsoring lectures which would provide a
suitable alternative for those of boycotted professors.[32]

In carrying through the boycotts, the *Deutsche Studentenschaft* judiciously
opposed the violence and noisy demonstrations which had characterized earlier
actions. For best propaganda effect, the boycotts were made to appear both
spontaneous and peaceful. Strong-arm methods to prevent students from entering
classes were expressly forbidden.[33] In spite of this order, however, there were a
number of cases where SA students were posted at strategic locations to enforce
the boycotts.[34] Everywhere, informal pressure was put upon the students to
participate.

Terror and intimidation do not have to take a violent form. The German
teaching community was well aware that they were being watched, that Nazi
students were carefully noting what they said in their lectures and who their
friends and associates were, and that a regiment of political opportunists waited
in the wings to fill their posts if their loyalty to the new order was questioned.
During the first two years of Nazi rule, an estimated 14.34 percent of all German
university teachers were removed or resigned from their posts, including 11
percent of the full (*ordentliche*) professors. The numbers ranged from 50 percent at the medical academy in Düsseldorf and over 32 percent at the universities
of Berlin and Frankfurt, to only 4 percent at Rostock and 1.6 percent at
Tübingen. Those dismissed included many of Germany's most prominent scientists and scholars, among them five Nobel laureates. Political reliability rather
than scholarly achievement became the chief criterion for replacing these men:
service in the SA, the SS, participation in work-service camps, and the personal
judgments of rectors, now appointed by the state, and National Socialist ministers of Culture.[35]

Considering the tremendous losses to the German academic world sustained in
these purges, the absence of student protest outside of a few isolated instances is
as remarkable as the scandalous spy system organized by the militants. To be
sure, a protesting student would have faced expulsion, but a massive response by
that large body of students whose nationalist sentiments were supposedly girded
with a belief in academic freedom, might have forced the authorities to act with
more hesitation.

Students were ready to carry through the wishes of the new government, even
in those isolated cases where their professors put up some resistance. At the
Darmstadt Technical Institute late in May 1933, Lieser, a Nazi instructor in the
architectural division, had prepared a memo in conjunction with an architectural
student noting the politics and character of the teachers in his division. In addition, he had publicly criticized the national sentiments of the faculty of the
Institute at a student demonstration in memory of Albert Leo Schlageter, martyr
to the French occupation of the Ruhr. When the faculty became aware of this
memo—after the Ministry of Culture had given it to the Rector for comment—
they reacted by withdrawing Lieser's license to teach (*venia legendi*), demanded

his immediate dismissal, and closed the Institute in fear of student reaction. Initially, the Minister of Culture supported this decision. The students, however, proceeded to occupy the Institute until the order to close was withdrawn and resumed the occupation on the following day to demand Lieser's reinstatement. In the meantime, a newly appointed chancellor reconvened the Senate, which under considerable pressure reversed the earlier decision. The students announced their victory with the statement that, "We will never leave a comrade in the lurch who is fighting with us for our goals at the Technical Institute."[36]

The boycott campaign was only a temporary phenomenon. It was part of the first revolutionary stage of National Socialism. After the spring of 1933, the government preferred to use legal means to purge the faculties, and student leaders were quietly told to avoid further outbreaks.[37] Promises to permit student government influence in the appointment and dismissal of professors were also forgotten. Student influence on appointments and dismissals after 1933 was largely through informal channels. Student leaders might make their wishes known to government authorities or have their opinions solicited regarding a particular appointment. The students' interuniversity contacts were probably quite helpful in determining a professor's political reliability. In February 1935, Albert Derichsweiler, then head of the Student Union, was appointed to a university commission set up by the party. Since this commission had to approve new university appointments, the Student Union officers were put to work suggesting new appointments or dismissals or the need for the creation of new university chairs.[38]

After the first flush of Nazi success, there were a number of isolated acts of protest which demonstrated that all students were not in agreement with the changes taking place. There was a sizable protest in Bonn late in 1934 when the eminent theologian Karl Barth was suspended from teaching.[39] And in June 1934, students at the University of Munich risked their careers for a professor of business law named Mittels who had recently arrived from Heidelberg. Mittels, who allegedly peppered his lectures with veiled anti-National Socialist allusions, speedily developed a large following among Munich's law students. After a lecture he was scheduled to deliver on 26 June was canceled, a large group of demonstrating students was forcibly dispersed. During the following days, a number of anonymous posters appeared on the walls of the university. One exhorted the students to consider this challenge: "Are you at the University to be annoyed by student big-wigs or to enter into the inheritance of German scholarship?"[40] A second summed up the problem in a pithy phrase: "In the Third Reich we march—in the Fourth Reich we study."[41] Throughout the month of June, members of the Munich law club (*Juristische Fachschaft*) repeatedly expressed dissatisfaction with the existing government. At one meeting, a speaker in SA uniform had been greeted with whistles and foot-stamping, and his criticism of Austrian Prime Minister Dollfuss had excited general murmurs. At another meeting, the deputy *Gauleiter*, Otto Lippold, was surprised to find the students cheering his allusions to difficulties the new regime had faced. When the

Nazi historian Walter Frank called former Chancellor Heinrich Brüning a "capable parliamentarian," he won prolonged applause from an otherwise silent audience. A speech two weeks later by the president of the Society of German Architects on "Spatial Order and Village Formation in the German Countryside (*Raumordnung und Dorfbildung in der deutschen Landschaft*)" was greeted by continuous laughter.[42] The events in Munich were unique, but they betokened a more silent resistance taking hold among serious students who chose their courses by seeking out those professors who continued to speak the truth and turned increasingly to disciplines like theology and natural science where strict political conformity was not necessary. In the later 1930s, the Freiburg economist Constantin von Dietze reported, a professor who criticized the status quo did not fear so much that spies might be present as that recurrent loud applause might arouse suspicions outside the lecture hall.[43]

In 1933 one student action more than any other focused the attention of the world on Germany and its universities and the barbarism that was consuming the "nation of poets and thinkers." This was the book burnings, the so-called action or struggle against the un-German spirit, in which the works of many of Germany's most renowned authors were thrown into the flames.[44] The precedent for the book burnings was the national convention of the early *Burschenschaften* on 18 October 1817, at which the names of reactionary authors had been consigned to the flames in imitation of Luther's burning of the papal bull three hundred years earlier.

The idea for a campaign against "un-German literature" stemmed from Joseph Goebbels' Ministry for "Popular Enlightenment and Propaganda" (*Volksaufklärung und Propaganda*), established on 13 March 1933.[45] The *Deutsche Studentenschaft* assumed charge of the action early in April. On 6 April, a newly established head office for press and propaganda, under the leadership of Hans Karl Leistritz, announced without further details a four-week campaign to begin 12 April.[46] At the same time, a letter was sent to a large number of nationalist writers, asking for articles for a newsletter in conjunction with the campaign. The limited response to this request was hardly encouraging.[47] On 8 April, a second memo sent to all student governments explained and set forth plans for the action, which the memo justified as a response to the propaganda of world Jewry against the new Germany. During the following four weeks, all students would empty their libraries and those of their acquaintances of un-German works. The student governments would propagandize their campaign with mass meetings, pamphlets, and press reports. Between 26 April and 10 May, the books would be collected in one spot. At 6:00 P.M. on 10 May, bonfires of books would be lit in all German university towns. At each university, a local committee, consisting of the student government *Führer*, three other students, a professor, a member of the "Battle Union for German Culture" (*Kampfbund für Deutsche Kultur*) and a writer, would direct the campaign.[48] On 12 April, the *Deutsche Studentenschaft* announced twelve theses "against the un-German spirit," as a theme of the campaign. During the following week these theses were placarded throughout Germany. They called upon German students to defend the purity of the German language and literature, to reject the Jewish and liberal spirits, and to make the German university into "a stronghold of German *Volkstum* and a battle station [created from] the power of German spirit."[49] The placards included the demand that Jewish works should appear henceforth in "Jewish" languages, and that German works by Jewish authors be designated as translations.[50] On 27 April, an initial blacklist of condemned authors was sent out to the students.[51]

Throughout the second half of April and the early part of May, the *Deutsche Studentenschaft* headquarters in Berlin received reports from all areas of the Reich that the campaign was going smoothly: large numbers of books had been collected, meetings held, and the cooperation of local authorities, the police, and youth groups assured.[52] The carrying out of the action was largely under local direction, and its course varied with the circumstances. Privately owned bookstores and libraries also came under search and seizure. In the atmosphere of 1933, there certainly must have been isolated cases of violence. But the arrival of a threatening group of armed and uniformed students was sufficiently intimidating without the use of force.[53] In Greifswald, all bookstores and lending libraries were requested to bring in their books voluntarily. Those who did so could display a placard reading: "We stand behind the action of the *Deutsche Student-enschaft* 'against the un-German spirit.'" Those who refused faced a boy-cott.[54] In many cases the police themselves assisted in these searches, acting to impound books provisionally, pending new legislation.[55] Occasional student governments did resist. The *Führer* of the *Göttingen* student council and the leader of the action committee criticized the twelve theses because they greatly overemphasized the Jewish danger to German letters.[56] The Hamburg student government was accused in April of openly sabotaging the action because it was said to be "impracticable" in Hamburg.[57] The following day, the *Deutsche Studentenschaft Führer* at Hamburg reported to the regional leader, however, that 1,000 volumes had already been collected from Hamburg libraries with the help of the police.[58]

Resistance to the campaign was not totally absent. An outright refusal to take part in the book burnings came from the universities in Württemberg, where the Student Union state leader, Gerhard Schumann, later a well-known Nazi poet, opposed the action. The Tübingen student government avoided book burnings altogether, whereas Stuttgart refused to hold a torchlight parade.[59] Widespread resistance greeted a sinister order by Georg Plötner, the head of the *Deutsche Studentenschaft* office for scholarship, who presided over the movement to boycott professors. In conjunction with the action against the un-German spirit, Plötner called for the erection of pillories at all universities: "a crude tree trunk, something over the height of a man, in the area of the university. On the pillory we will nail the productions of those that are not of our spirit . . . and we will let these pillories remain for all time, as long as we need them. Today for the writers, tomorrow for the professors."[60] The reaction to this plan was so negative

that Press and Propaganda Chief Leistritz sent a postcard to all student governments canceling it, at least until a more propitious moment.[61] In spite of this
notice, several student governments did erect pillories, without further protest
from the national leadership.

The 10 May festivities in Berlin were broadcast over national radio. The
events in other university towns were carried by regional radio stations.[62] The
Berlin broadcast included both a report of the bonfire activities and an address by
Goebbels to the assembled students.[63] Only a limited number of books were
actually burned, accompanied by ritual incantations:

> *Against* decadence and moral decay, *for* propriety and morality in the family
> and the state: Heinrich Mann, Ernst Glaeser, Erich Kästner . . . . *Against* soul
> disintegrating overestimation of the instinctual life, *for* the nobility of the
> Human soul: Freudian school, *Zeitschrift Imago* . . . . *Against* the literary be-
> trayal of the soldiers of the World War, *for* the education of the people in a
> spirit of preparedness: Erich Maria Remarque . . .[64]

A Bonn newspaper described the day's events in that city. In spite of a
rainstorm, thousands of students marched in a parade led by those in Nazi
uniform followed by the fraternities, "with fluttering flags and clanging of
spurs," the female students, and the "free students." The parade circled around
the "funeral pile" and came to rest in the market square. The student government *Führer* and two professors addressed the crowd. As the books burned, the
assembly sang the *Horst Wessel* song. Among the flags of the fraternities flew a
solitary black, white, and red imperial flag with the superscript "The Saar is
German."[65]

After 10 May, the campaign to purge libraries and bookstores continued with a
"testing week" between 22 and 27 May. The student governments were instructed by a memo of 16 May 1933 to inform bookdealers beforehand that a
search of the stores would take place. Voluntary compliance by the book stores
was necessary.[66] After this final action, suppression of "un-German" literature
was left to the state and police.

The successful campaign against the un-German spirit bears witness to the
large numbers of students who in 1933 could be mobilized to work for the Nazi
movement. In a sense, the campaign marked the closing rather than the opening
of a chapter in German student history. The spontaneous enthusiasm which
characterized the campaign echoed the mass demonstrations of the Weimar Republic. The mass rallies to follow in the Third Reich no longer were based on
student initiative and planning but were merely coordinated with the current
demands of state and party. The Nazi leaders no longer looked with favor upon
independent action but wished for organization and discipline: a student army
which could be trained without fanfare and mobilized when circumstances demanded. Indoctrination, not demonstration, was the core requirement for students in the Third Reich. The new state required scholars who quoted *Mein
Kampf*, not rowdy street fighters.

TEN

The Making of the National Socialist Student:
Student Activities and
Educational Programs, 1933–35

For those students who relished the political struggle and excitement of the last years of the Republic, the reality of the Third Reich must have been a disappointment. The revolutionary fervor of the early months of 1933 was soon stifled by the assertion of bureaucratic controls. Like their counterparts in the paramilitary SA, the radical activists of the National Socialist German Student Union found themselves to be dispensable. The successful post-1933 student leader was a capable organization man. Order, conformity, participation in officially sponsored programs were now demanded of all students.

Extensive extracurricular educational programs mushroomed after the spring of 1933. Their sponsors maintained that the university had not in the past and probably would not in the future provide the necessary political education for the Third Reich. If prospective scholars and teachers were taught not only elements in Nazi ideology but the application of their disciplines to the new society, the universities would be secured. In 1935, Albert Derichsweiler, the Student Union *Führer*, wrote that the Nazi student must consider himself part of a "revolutionary shock troop at the university which bursts the neutral position of the so-called educated, and calls a definite halt to the alienation of German people from nature and from the tasks of history through theories of abstract scientific knowledge."[1]

The universities could not be reformed overnight. The students had to take the lead in a long-range program which would build upon the university heritage while placing it at the service of the new order.[2] The soil had been prepared in part by students of the Weimar Republic. Flourishing military training and work-service programs were already in existence and had only to be co-opted by the Nazis and turned to their indoctrination purposes. The fraternities also were potentially available for Nazi educational programs. By broadening and strengthening activities already long tested, the Nazis might hope to extend their influence throughout the student' population. No student would be permitted to escape the educational net, nor would any be permitted to sit passively while others labored and drilled for the cause of the new Germany.

Since political education, work-service, and military training were hardly new programs, there was no clear division of function among the student groups who had competed in these areas before 1933. The rivalries and administrative chaos which were characteristic of Party and state throughout the Third Reich were reflected in miniature on the student scene. The Student Union, as the student arm of the National Socialist Party, insisted on its claims as the ideological vanguard of the student world. The fraternities and the *Stahlhelm* continued their substantial demands on the time and loyalty of their membership. While the Academic Military Regional Offices sought to control military sport activities, the SA showed increasing interest in taking them over.

Rivalry between the *Deutsche Studentenschaft* and the National Socialist German Student Union was a continuing problem for several years. To be sure, the Student Union had won control over the fortunes of the *Deutsche Studentenschaft* in Graz in 1931. But the leaders of the *Deutsche Studentenschaft*, although theoretically subject to Student Union discipline, refused to take orders from Student Union leaders and took an independent course. The conflict was finally resolved on 5 November 1936 with the establishment of a Reich student leadership (*Reichsstudentenführung*), headed by Gustav Adolf Scheel, which coordinated both organizations. In the spring of 1933, at many local universities, the National Socialist university group *Führer* (*Hochschulgruppenführer*) also held the post of student government *Führer*. The national *Deutsche Studentenschaft* leadership under Gerhard Krüger nevertheless insisted that the student governments continue to play an independent role. The campaign against the un-German spirit was in part an effort by Krüger and his supporters to prove that the *Deutsche Studentenschaft* was a thoroughly Nazi organization and that it had an important part to play in the new university.[3] The Student Union was not immediately informed about the bookburning campaign launched independently by the *Deutsche Studentenschaft*. Only on 11 April 1933, a day before the publication of the twelve theses against the un-German spirit, did an order go out from the Student Union national *Führer* in Munich (Dr. Friedrich Oskar Stäbel) directing the local groups to support the campaign. Stäbel's directive indeed stated that the Student Union groups must not only support the action, "but of course take over the leadership."[4]

In the background of the bookburning action, a power struggle raged between Stäbel and *Deutsche Studentenschaft Führer* Gerhard Krüger. Early in April, Stäbel succeeded in getting a Party order which made the Student Union the exclusive representative of the Party at the universities. Local Student Union leaders would henceforth also serve as officers for University questions in the Party *Gauleitung*. All student party members would have to join the Student Union.[5] On 20 April, the chief of staff of the Party organization, Robert Ley, appointed Stäbel to the newly created post of "Officer for all university and student questions in the party leadership."[6] Stäbel also won the support of Baldur von Schirach, who as Reich Youth leader was at least nominally the head of all youth groups.[7] Prussian Minister of Culture Rust, in his turn, defended the independence of the *Deutsche Studentenschaft* as the state-recognized student organization.[8] On 4 July 1933, Stäbel issued an order to his organization giving Student Union officers control over *Deutsche Studentenschaft* officers at all levels.[9] Krüger issued a counterorder which insisted on continued independence at least until the Party and state should rule otherwise.[10] But Stäbel's official support proved stronger. Unable to prevent interference by the Student Union in student government affairs, Krüger and the two *Deutsche Studentenschaft* elders in the national leadership resigned their posts at the end of August.[11] Frick, the Reich Minister of the Interior, appointed Stäbel to Krüger's post early in September 1933, thus combining the leadership of the two organizations and temporarily ending the conflict.[12] Stäbel also received Krüger's post as the officer for general student affairs in the Reich Ministry of the Interior.[13]

Stäbel's difficulties did not end with his assumption of the personal leadership of both the Student Union and the *Deutsche Studentenschaft*. In the spring of 1934, he had to fight off an attempt by Schirach to make the Student Union a section of the Hitler Youth.[14] In addition, Stäbel, who had completed his own studies in 1928, lacked the personal qualities necessary to command the respect of his more idealistic subordinates. Indeed, Stäbel's corrupt, lavish and tyrannical conduct of his offices was a carbon copy of the self-seeking spirit of the worst of the Party bosses.[15] Corruption extended down to the regional and local levels of both the *Deutsche Studentenschaft* and the Student Union, where large sums of money were used for "administration." Many student leaders were provided with automobiles for personal use. In Berlin, the local Student Union group had seven automobiles. Money, which should have been sent to the national office, was used instead to buy automobiles, to outfit the members with SA and SS uniforms, and to buy instruments for a marching band.[16]

Stäbel's misrule did not continue for long. In May 1934, when Rust achieved his goal of heading the newly established Reich Ministry of Culture, Stäbel resigned his office.[17] Until July, he remained as head of the *Reichsschaft der Studierenden*, a superorganization which included both the *Deutsche Studentenschaft* and the students in the *Fachschulen* (technical and business schools). On 19 July, Rust appointed Andreas Feickert, the head of the *Deutsche Studentenschaft* office for work-service, to the leadership of the *Deutsche Studentenschaft*.[18] At the same time, Rudolf Hess announced that Stäbel had left his Student Union post to take an office in the Party leadership.[19] The Student Union leadership was taken on by Albert Derichsweiler, the western regional leader, and the Student Union and the *Deutsche Studentenschaft* leaderships were once again separated.[20]

The rivalry between the Student Union and the *Deutsche Studentenschaft* was rekindled after Stäbel's fall, since the *Deutsche Studentenschaft* leadership once again attempted to seize the initiative in student affairs.[21] In theory, the *Deutsche*

Studentenschaft remained the representative body of all students, while the Student Union constituted the Nazi elite.[22] In practice, the two organizations continued to spar for control of all aspects of student life.

Control of the student press was a high priority in the effort to enforce ideological conformity. Both the Student Union and the *Deutsche Studentenschaft* sought to win control of this crucial medium. In April 1933, the Student Union leadership instructed their regional subordinates to carry through the coordination of the student press. All editors of student newspapers for the coming semester would be required to show active membership for at least one semester in the Student Union. They were to be appointed by the local Student Union leaders. A National Socialist press service, the "National Socialist Student Correspondence," was set up to insure that all newspapers would have similar coverage on national issues. Local news was also required to have a clear Nazi character. Immediately upon publication, copies of the newspapers were to be sent to both the local Student Union Press offices and the central press office.[23] The order was in some cases only grudgingly complied with. In June, a notice reported that some local newspapers had not yet used the National Socialist Student Correspondence.[24] The actual competence of the Student Union was in question. The local student governments who controlled the student newspapers were responsible to the press and propaganda offices of the *Deutsche Studentenschaft*, which set up its own press service in October 1933.[25]

In spite of the appointment of Oskar Stäbel, already Student Union national *Führer*, to the post of *Deutsche Studentenschaft Führer* in September 1933, competition in press affairs continued. Upon Stäbel's insistence, the Student Union's journal, the *Deutsche Studentenzeitung*, edited by Stäbel's friend Hans Hildebrandt, was made the official newsletter of the *Deutsche Studentenschaft*, and all members were compelled to subscribe.[26] Stäbel and Hildebrandt both profited financially from this move, which engendered much resentment.[27] To strengthen the *Deutsche Studentenzeitung*'s position, Hildebrandt made a concerted effort to monopolize all articles and reports from the Party and associated organizations, attempting to dissuade these organizations from dealing with his competitors.[28] The *Deutsche Student*, which published serious articles by professors and other authorities, was generally acknowledged to be a more interesting and popular paper. The arrangement with the *Deutsche Studentenzeitung* expired with Stäbel's loss of office in July 1934.

The *Deutsche Studentenschaft*'s Press Office extended its influence far beyond the local student newspapers. Through its efforts many other newspapers carried special student sections. It also helped to coordinate nationwide student campaigns. In the fall of 1933, it devoted its efforts to mobilizing student action in the election campaign for the Reichstag and the national plebiscite.[29]

Close watch was kept over the fraternity press which was encouraged to support campaigns organized by the *Deutsche Studentenschaft* press office. In July 1934, the *Deutsche Studentenschaft* established a special information service for the fraternity press. The fraternity leagues were also told to limit public discussion about controversies among them.[30] The following year, the fraternity press, together with the local student press, was united in a special section of the National League of German Journal Publishers (*Reichsverband der Deutschen Zeitschriften-Verleger*) by order of the president of the Reich Press Chamber (*Reichspressekammer*), Nazi press overlord, Max Amann. All periodicals were henceforth to be sent to the student section offices in Munich.[31] While the student press continued to retain a certain diversity relative to local circumstances, or fraternity league leadership, central guidelines enforced a high degree of uniformity.

In organizing student life, the Nazis were able to build upon programs already well established. Military training, work-service, borderland work, political discussions: all had won enthusiastic volunteers before 1933; now continuing participation would be a test of loyalty to the new order. In 1933, financial aid was limited to those students who demonstrated their national feelings in their extracurricular life.[32] During the following years, such demonstrations became increasingly compulsory.

The *Deutsche Studentenschaft* had championed a compulsory work-service program since the Nazis had taken the leadership in July 1931. They regarded the extensive voluntary work-service program adopted by the Schleicher cabinet in January 1933 as a temporary expedient. In June 1933, an order from the *Deutsche Studentenschaft* made participation in work-service programs mandatory for all students in their first four semesters. To insure compliance, students were told that ten weeks of service would be a requirement for registration in the upper semesters beginning with the spring semester of 1934.[33] The *Deutsche Studentenschaft*'s ultimate goal was compulsory long-term service for high school graduates who planned to enter the universities. In 1933, about 10,500 high school graduates voluntarily entered a work service program for six months.[34] In January 1934 the *Deutsche Studentenschaft* requested that the state governments require in future at least six months of work-service for all students before they commenced their studies. In this way, political education might begin before the students even entered the universities. A proper social orientation, consistent with the ideology of the Third Reich, would be formed by sharing work and recreation in a communal setting with the sons of workers and farmers.[35] Compulsory service would also reduce the numbers of students actually entering the universities. An order by Interior Minister Frick, in February 1934, provided state sanction for compulsory service. Henceforth, no student would be allowed to register without evidence that his service had been completed.[36] The *Deutsche Studentenschaft* then announced that all Easter 1934 graduates would be required to enter work-service programs in May, for six months, in order to register in the fall.[37] Compulsory work-service for high school graduates foreshadowed the law of 1 July 1935 which required work-service for all German youth.[38] In the spring of 1935, in the expectation of a national law, all students who had not yet done so were ordered by the *Deutsche Studentenschaft* to spend their summers in work-service camps.[39]

The spirit of self-sacrifice which characterized the pre-1933 work-service programs did continue in the voluntary programs sponsored by the *Deutsche Studentenschaft* for students who had completed their compulsory work-service. Under the rubric "country service" (*Landdienst*), voluntary agricultural work was emphasized: aid to settlement programs in border areas and harvest assistance.[40] The students who participated in "country service" were not always segregated in work camps, but were occasionally able to live in close contact with the farm population. A particularly active program was started in Silesia in 1934. During the summer, two hundred students, including forty girls, spent six weeks in Silesian villages. The students' efforts aimed not only at helping the farmers in their work but at developing the political consciousness of the local population. Winning the peasants' confidence, they were able to aid the organizing work of the Hitler Youth, the German Girls' Club (*Bund deutscher Mädel*) and the SA. The students also came prepared with knowledge of folk customs and traditions which they hoped to encourage and strengthen among the Silesian peasants. Armed with the myth of blood and soil, and fearful of the intrusions of Slavic folklore, they organized folk-singing and folk-dancing festivals in an attempt to reacquaint the villagers with their German heritage.[41]

Compulsory military training, like work-service, continued to be a prime objective of the *Deutsche Studentenschaft* after the Nazi seizure of power. During the spring of 1933, the Academic Work Office (formerly called the Academic Military Office) clung to its central role in the sponsorship of paramilitary programs. The Reich Commisar for the Voluntary Work-Service promised to aid the Academic Work Office by providing labor for the construction of military sport camps.[42]

Before May 1933, the *Stahlhelm* dominated all military sport activities through the Academic Work Office. Although on 26 April the national *Stahlhelm* had put its organization under Hitler's leadership, *Stahlhelm* groups continued to function independently until their dissolution in August 1934.[43] The *Stahlhelm* won numerous recruits in the spring and summer of 1933, particularly among fraternity students, who found it necessary to demonstrate their political reliability in some way but hesitated joining either the SA or the Student Union. Since many of the fraternities began to require membership in an organization providing paramilitary training, the *Stahlhelm* seemed an appropriate substitute for the SA. The Student Union, in spite of many denials, accused the *Stahlhelm* of competing with it and conducting an independent student political effort.[44] At the beginning of May, the *Deutsche Studentenschaft* formally took control of the local Academic Work Offices from the fraternity leagues. Local Military Office leaders were, in future, directly responsible to the student government *Führer*.[45] During the following weeks, *Stahlhelm* leaders were systematically removed from the military offices and replaced by members of the Student Union. The national Academic Work Office, headed by Ernst Moritz, a *Stahlhelm* leader who had joined the Nazi Party in April, remained in existence until July but found its directives ignored by the local offices.[46] The Student Union set up its own military office and appointed Schwab, the founder of the Academic Work Office, as its head with the hope of circumventing the *Deutsche Studentenschaft* and succeeding the *Stahlhelm* as the central control for military sport.[47]

The *Stahlhelm* did not accept eclipse gracefully, but its independence faded quickly.[48] In July, the *Stahlhelm Studentenring* followed the example of the national *Stahlhelm* and submitted to the authority of the Student Union.[49] In September, the Student Union agreed to accept all *Stahlhelm* members who had joined before 30 January 1933, and other members on six months' probation. At the end of this period, in April 1934, the *Stahlhelm Studentenring* was formally dissolved within the Student Union.[50]

With the *Stahlhelm* out of the picture, *Deutsche Studentenschaft* Chief Krüger succeeded in persuading Prussian Minister of Culture Rust to issue an order making physical education, including military exercises, mandatory for all members of the *Deutsche Studentenschaft* in Prussia during their first two semesters.[51] In addition, Rust promised to appoint a military sport teacher to all Prussian universities.[52] The other states quickly followed the Prussian example.[53]

In practice, local student governments often required much more extensive military sport programs than the governmental orders actually envisioned. A report from Hesse in the summer semester of 1933 indicates that mandatory military exercises ranged from six hours a week at the Pedagogical, Music, and Art Institutes in Mainz to thirteen hours a week at the Technical Institute in Darmstadt. Girls were required to take three hours a week of first-aid education.[54] In Braunschweig, where military sport was not yet required, four hundred of the thousand enrolled students participated voluntarily for six hours on Wednesday afternoons and again on Saturday mornings.[55] The government seems to have hesitated to give its sanction to these activities for fear of the effect upon foreign opinion. Nevertheless, an order of the Prussian government on 28 July decreed Wednesday and Saturday afternoons free of classes to encourage military education.[56]

With the decline of the *Stahlhelm,* the burden of leadership of student paramilitary training was taken up by the local SA groups. The SA had actively recruited student members to the point where many fraternities complained that their members were forced to join under the threat that their fraternities would otherwise be banned.[57] In order to save control of the military sport program for the *Deutsche Studentenschaft,* Krüger agreed in July to coordinate his efforts with those of the SA.[58] In fact, the SA soon won exclusive control of all military sport activities. On 9 September 1933, Hitler issued an order for the creation of university SA offices at all universities. Under the terms of a July agreement between Colonel Walther von Reichenau, the chief of the ministerial office in the Ministry of the Army, and Friedrich Wilhelm Krüger, the head of the SA's education office (*Ausbildungswesen*), student military training would have come under Friedrich Wilhelm Krüger's control. Krüger's organization, which was primarily concerned with military education of youth, was in effect a liaison between the army and the SA. If the agreement had been carried out, regular army officers as well as former officers with army connections who were high in Krüger's organization would have provided the army with indirect control over student military training.[59] Instead Röhm announced the establishment of a central SA university office within his own organization. He appointed Schwab as its head and ordered all local SA university offices to accept Schwab's leadership.[60] The army was in this manner more or less excluded from the military training of students, since the SA educational office was relegated to a meaningless supervisory role.[61] Control of student military training was undoubtedly conceived of by the SA leadership as one means to the eventual subordination of the army. Potential reserve officers would be subject to prior SA indoctrination.

Between 25 October and 11 November 1933, Röhm permitted free entry of students into the SA for a probationary period. Once again, separate SA units were set up at the universities.[62] In addition, the SA assumed responsibility for the military education of students who were not members.[63] The following month, Stäbel ordered all fraternities to make membership in the SA, SS, or *Stahlhelm* mandatory.[64] An order of the Ministry of the Interior, accompanying the proclamation of the *Deutsche Studentenschaft* constitution of February 1934, required all members to complete service directed by the SA or SS in order to be permitted further registration.[65] Two months earlier, Stäbel had announced to the *Deutsche Studentenschaft* leaders that in the future the work of all students would be judged not only by their scholarly capacity but by the certificate of good service from the SA.[66]

New military obligations were not always welcomed by the students, although they had their long-awaited chance to defend the fatherland. Frequently overloaded with military exercises several times a week, they sometimes lacked time and energy for their studies. The Prussian Ministry of Culture received a number of complaints from university rectors and deans about excessive SA military office demands upon the time of the students.[67] It was even reported that in some areas students had been hauled out of their classes to participate in SA service.[68] In other cases, students shirked their SA duties when possible and did not come to practice on time.[69] Many successfully avoided SA service altogether, while claiming to university offices that they were fulfilling their obligations.[70] SA stalwarts often expressed annoyance at the un-Nazi political attitudes of many students in the SA.[71] The SA University Office therefore made plans for a program of political education to supplement military training.[72] After the purge of the SA on 30 June and 1 July 1934, however, the SA University Offices were abandoned. Control of military education passed to Friedrich Wilhelm Krüger and the SA Office for Military Education, which in October set up new local university offices.[73] When military conscription was introduced in March 1935, special student military training programs became superfluous, and the SA's military education apparatus was disbanded. For a brief period, then, student military training had become a vehicle for the extension of SA power among the students. The SA organization, however, never won the support of more than a small elite, and the group's eclipse was correspondingly swift and decisive.

Political indoctrination was a key feature of the work-service program and played a minor role in student military training activities. In addition, however, the students found themselves devoting a considerable portion of their time to programs of political and ideological education. The partisans of the Nazi state demanded the minds as well as the hearts of Germany's academic youth. Only then could they consider the universities really reformed and German scholarship be put at the service of new masters.

After May 1933, the educational activities of the *Deutsche Studentenschaft* were coordinated by a head office for political education which supervised four subordinate offices: scholarship (*Wissenschaft*), work-service, military service, and physical education.[74] In practice, both work-service and military service functioned independently. The Office for Scholarship, which directed all educational programs related to the university and its disciplines, was elevated to head office status in October 1934.[75] An Office for Political Education (*Schulung*) took over the task of political indoctrination in the fall of 1933 and was reorganized in February 1934 as the Head Office for Comradeship Education and Folklore Work.[76] The activities of the various educational offices frequently overlapped with each other and with the educational programs of the National Socialist German Student Union.

Under the direction of the Office for Scholarship, all *Deutsche Studentenschaft* members were required to join a disciplinary group (*Fachgruppe*) corresponding to their major field of interest.[77] These groups were united into national societies. The disciplinary societies enabled the *Deutsche Studentenschaft*'s educational arm to reach those students not in the Student Union, the *Stahlhelm*, or the SA.[78] The old leadership of the disciplinary groups was replaced by reliable Student Union members.[79] The initial tasks of the reformed disciplinary societies, as sketched by Georg Plötner, the head of the *Deutsche Studentenschaft* offices for Political Education and Scholarship, were quite extensive. A model constitution, distributed by Plötner in June 1933, included the following tasks:

1a. furthering a customary relationship of scholarly cooperation between student and university teacher.

b. carrying through boycott actions against professors who cannot be teachers at a German, ie., political university.

. . . .

d. cooperation and participation in the selection of students for this university.

e. cooperation and participation in the appointment of university teachers [the veto as goal].

2a. carrying through a curricular reform relative to future professional needs of students.

    b. creating an immediate relationship to professions through day-to-day contacts with *Volk* comrades of all manner of professions who are already professionally active.

    c. political education . . . .[80]

In practice, the activities of the disciplinary societies did not conform with this broad definition. Supplementary educational programs were central to society work. In Würzburg, in 1933, the disciplinary societies each sponsored lecture and discussion sessions. The law students and the economists, for example, explored subjects such as "worker and nation," "the political foundations of the Third Reich," and the "spiritual battle against Marxism." The medical and dental students' program included the "gas war of the future." The language arts (*Philologie*) group discussed *Mein Kampf* and the theme of "worker and nation." All Würzburg disciplinary societies also held discussions about work-service and the problems of the German border areas.[81] The philological societies were instructed in 1934 to concentrate throughout Germany on the "discussion of scholarship from the point of view of National Socialism." The technical disciplinary societies were directed to study how their curriculum might be reformed to fulfill the needs of the nation. Military applications of their knowledge were stressed, as was the relationship of their discipline to economic and social questions.[82] Beginning in 1934, all society leaders met in national study camps for intensive orientation. The camps were also attended by sympathetic professors and men from private life.[83]

    In 1934, the theme of the *Deutsche Studentenschaft*'s academic program was the practical application of knowledge gained at the universities. The local student offices were encouraged to study ways in which students might contribute to economic reconstruction by "the preparation for the carrying through of agricultural planning, the relocation of industry, the creation of a healthy relationship between town and country, the question of unemployment."[84] Student studies were published by the.*Deutsche Studentenschaft* in a series called "The Young Scholarly Front."[85]

    A widely publicized program was sponsored by the universities of Lower Saxony, where students endeavored to fight the image that the universities were ivory towers which taught theory without real applications. Economics students, under this program, studied the economy of the area in an effort to find out how employment might be increased and what household industries the farm population might develop to supplement their incomes. The students also organized an advertising campaign to aid the local handicraft industry.[86] It was certainly programs of this nature which capitalized upon the populist instincts of many students and won them for the Nazi cause.

    The disciplinary groups in most cases proved not to be an efficient medium for political education. In order to insure political conformity, a greater degree of regimentation was necessary. The work-service camps provided a captive audience. During the first summer of the Third Reich, a nationally coordinated educational program was introduced in the student work camps.[87] When work-service was made compulsory for high school graduates the following year, all students received political indoctrination before they entered the university.

The notion that student living units organized along the disciplined model of the work camps might be the solution to the educational problem was widely discussed by student leaders during the summer of 1933.[88] The construction of comradeship houses was formally proposed by the *Deutsche Studentenschaft's* Office for Work-Service in July 1933.[89] In September, Heinz Roosch, previously head of the Göttingen society for work camps, became head of the Office for Political Education and was charged with establishing guidelines for the creation of comradeship houses. Roosch's directives called for the establishment of living units with about thirty men in each. The students would sleep in large barracks and eat in a common dining room. The communal activities of the house would include political education, regular morning physical exercises, discussion of school work in a political context, and social gatherings with SA comrades and workers.[90]

On 29 September 1933, Stäbel met with representatives of the state educational ministries, the leaders of the fraternity leagues, and other interested parties at the Reich Ministry of the Interior, under the sponsorship of State Secretary Pfundtner. The fraternities were reassured at this meeting that they would not be replaced by comradeship houses. Instead, they were encouraged to reorganize their own living units to incorporate the spirit of the comradeship house. A representative of the Prussian Ministry of Culture suggested a goal of 50 to 180 students in comradeship houses at each university. Since the fraternities would supplement this work, the *Deutsche Studentenschaft* houses could be limited to free students.[91]

Initially, the comradeship houses were intended to help organize those students "who in no way are formally tied, whom one can never get hold of either for a plenary meeting or any activity in student government."[92] But early in 1934, steps were taken to insure that all students experience some form of community living. A directive of the Head Office for Political Education, in February 1934, ordered all students to live in such a living unit for their first two or three semesters. They were to choose between two semesters in the comradeship houses set up by student governments or three semesters in the comradeship living units run by the National Socialist German Student Union or the fraternities.[93] In order for a fraternity living unit to receive necessary recognition, its leader was required to spend one semester in the student government's comradeship house. Fraternities which did not maintain recognized comradeship units were threatened with suspension.[94] The comradeship units were further required to offer their facilities for the use of the "Strength through Joy" groups, to invite unemployed workers to share their dining facilities, and to hold several "comradely evenings" with young workers.[95] Educational materials for the first three semesters were sent out from the *Deutsche Studentenschaft* central offices. In addition, new students were required to attend a lecture series to be set up at all universities.[96] During the second and third semesters all students participated in military sports. Students in the upper semesters were to continue their political education in the disciplinary societies.[97]

Female students were provided political education in separate groups, where the role of women in a Nazi society was stressed. The women were encouraged to take first aid courses, a course in protection from gas warfare, and to volunteer their time for service in school infirmaries, cafeterias, and student welfare organizations.[98]

Until November 1934, leadership of the *Deutsche Studentenschaft*'s extracurricular educational program fell to the National Socialist German Student Union, which provided leaders of the comradeship houses and political instructors. After November 1934, the Student Union assumed independent control of all educational activities formerly the province of the *Deutsche Studentenschaft*.[99] All Student Union members participated in an intensive training program which enabled them to lead student educational activities. Beginning in the spring of 1934, Student Union members involved in political instruction were required to attend study camps.[100] Other Student Union members were also strongly encouraged to attend such camps at which the creation of an esprit de corps joined indoctrination as a primary aim.[101]

In November 1934, the Student Union began a nationally coordinated program of education for its membership. Literature and Party materials for discussion were selected by the central organization. Instructors for the student body at large were chosen from the outstanding students in the Student Union course.[102]

By the summer of 1935, the lives of Germany's students had been carefully regimented. Their political education was insured by the extensive program of the National Socialist German Student Union. Throughout Germany, the majority of students were required to spend at least their first three semesters in communal living quarters, where they were the objects of an intense indoctrination campaign. New students received additional orientation during their six months in the work camps. All male students participated in a rudimentary military education program and would now also be subject to universal military training. Women students learned the elements of first aid and protection against chemical warfare. In student disciplinary societies, the Nazi aspects of the university curriculum received central attention. Only the fraternities continued, for the moment, to lead a relatively independent existence, as long as they fulfilled the minimum objectives of student leaders. The colorful student life of the past had been replaced by a dreary uniformity from which there was little escape. For those who absorbed themselves in the work of the Nazi movement, there was ample opportunity for leadership and the satisfaction of participating in the regeneration of the nation. But for many others, disillusionment, fed by resentment at the encroachments upon study time, and annoyance with the petty politicking of the Nazi students most certainly was growing. The goals of the students of the Weimar Republic had at least in part been realized; the programs which they favored—work-service, military training, a university serving nationalist goals—were now flourishing. But the totalitarian aspects of Nazi society which accompanied these programs had been anticipated by very few.

The Nazi revolution in Germany profited at the universities from an enormous reservoir of student good will and anticipation. Whether or not, after the initial months of nationalist fervor, the Nazi government succeeded in retaining student enthusiasm is a matter for speculation. The Nazis could depend upon a substantial student elite which, with government and party backing, could establish a firm grip on student life. Since university enrollments were restricted after 1933, and since matriculation and later success were conditional upon political reliability, political protest required far greater courage than it had under the Weimar Republic. Student organizations independent of Party control, which might have provided a meeting ground for the discontented, were progressively eliminated. But in the last analysis, even thoughtful students may have agreed that there was no viable alternative to the present regime. The Republican system had been tried and had failed. The Nazi movement at least united the nation and had instituted a number of programs which gave hope of ending Germany's economic difficulties and international weakness. If the German university in its traditional form had to be sacrificed to the new sense of national purpose, it was certainly not the only casualty. Who, indeed, could quarrel if the new order demanded a strong personal commitment on the part of every German? Three generations of students had dreamed of a government which would call forth such a commitment. Now that the drums were beating out the muster to arms, could a German patriot fail to heed the call?

ELEVEN

Sabers and Brown Shirts:
The Fraternities and the Third Reich

The student fraternities represented a special problem for the National Socialist university. Their nationalist credentials were unimpeachable. Their unique position in the university community was hallowed by a long tradition stretching back to the eighteenth century. Their appearances in colorful costumes at festive occasions were an inevitable aspect of the university scene. With alumni members sprinkled among the higher circles of the government bureaucracy and to a lesser extent within the Nazi Party, their position seemed difficult to challenge. Loyal members in the far-flung German communities abroad represented a reservoir of potential support for the Nazi government. And the approximately 60 percent of male students in fraternities in 1933 were an important factor in Nazi plans at the university.[1]

In spite of fraternity accommodation to the new era, their continued independence was an increasing source of discomfort for the Nazi militants who found this independence a threat to their own total supremacy. The fraternities also counted enemies among the student rank and file who resented the elitist claims of fraternity life. The nominal coordination of the fraternities in the first months of 1933 was therefore to prove insufficient, and within three years of the Nazi takeover they were destroyed. Their temporary survival was as notable as their demise and illustrates the temporary compromise of the Nazi movement with the forces of the old regime. Once National Socialist control was consolidated, however, and the educated middle class bent to the purposes of the regime, the traditional character of university life could only be regarded as a danger. The future subjugation of the intelligentsia required Nazi monopolization of the students' free time at the universities and the insulation of students from conservative *alte Herren*. The illusion of a classless society fostered by Nazi populism could not tolerate the remaining symbols of aristocratic and intellectual arrogance.

At the outset, the new government made an important concession to the dueling fraternities which demonstrated the support they now had in high places. Late in March, the Bavarian Justice Ministry lifted the ban on the *Mensur*.[2] On 6 April, the Prussian Minister of Justice strongly recommended that the *Mensur* no longer be punished as an illegal duel. "Enjoyment of the Mensur," the Minister concluded in a letter to the Attorney-General which was later published in the press, "springs from the combative spirit which should be strengthened, not confined, in academic young people."[3] The following week, the Prussian Ministry of the Interior ordered the police not to interfere with the *Mensur* if carried out in private.[4] A law of 26 May 1933 made all duels legal where there was no mortal danger.[5]

Notwithstanding this concession, the fraternities soon found that if they were to maintain their strength in the new era they would have to propitiate the new powers. On 21 April 1933, Oskar Stäbel opened the gates for an increased Nazi role in the fraternities, by ordering all student organizations to permit membership in the Nazi Party, the Student Union, or the SA, or face a ban from all academic celebrations. Unofficially at many universities the fraternities were pressured to make membership in a Nazi organization mandatory, and many, fearing for their survival, did just that.[6] Whereas in April the fraternity opposition to the Nazis in the *Deutsche Studentenschaft* was still seeking a champion in Vice Chancellor von Papen, by the beginning of May expressions of loyalty to the Nazi movement were becoming commonplace.[7]

In April, the *Deutsche Wehrschaft*, long a Nazi stronghold, became the first fraternity league to appoint a *"Führer"* with unlimited dictatorial powers. The *Deutsche Wehrschaft* organization was subdivided into *Gaue*, each with a *Gauleiter*, copying the Nazi Party organization. All members were required to participate actively in the SA, the SS, or the Nazi Party.[8] In May, the wave was joined by almost everyone else. The Protestant *Schwarzburgbund* announced early that month that they "avow[ed] their faith in the unique national and social rising of their people; they avow[ed] their faith in the *Führer* of this rising, in Adolf Hitler."[9] On May 6, the Catholic *Cartell Verband* declared its loyalty in a letter to Hitler. "It makes us all the more happy," the letter read, "that a peoples' Chancellor, Adolf Hitler, whom the *Cartell Verband* admires because of his powerful strength of will, stands at the summit of the German national government; and [the *Cartell Verband*] is confident ... that he will lead the German people into better times."[10] The reform *Burschenschaften* announced support, at their convention, "to our *Führer* Adolf Hitler, to the national and social state, to the state that is held aloft by the pillars of blood and soil."[11] The *Deutsche Burschenschaft* convention proudly reported that Hitler had adopted their long-time slogan, "honor, freedom, fatherland."[12] The *Kyffhäuser Verband*, whose slogan, "With God for Kaiser and Reich," had been maintained throughout the life of the Weimar Republic, reinterpreted it in July as "With God for Hitler and German national socialism."[13]

On 20 May, the General German Society of Dueling Fraternities (ADW) met at Goslar to rewrite its constitution. Henceforth all member dueling fraternities were ordered to exclude Jews and Freemasons. The constitution also reinterpreted the dueling code to encompass all Germans: "The German dueling student protects and respects—in his professional and political life as well as in his student life—not only his own honor, but the honor of every German *Volk*-comrade."[14]

The Nazi movement was not, however, to be content with voluntary expressions of support. At the end of May, the party appointed *Deutsche Studentenschaft Führer* Krüger, Student Union *Führer* Stäbel, and Karl-Heinz Hederich, a leading *Burschenschafter,* to organize the Nazification of the fraternities. At the beginning of June, the three issued a directive, with Hitler's approval, for the reconstruction of the fraternity leagues. The *Führer* of each league was to be "a personality whose National Socialist world view is tested and authenticated."[15] All dueling leagues not yet in the ADW were to join it immediately and to adopt the membership provisions of its new constitution. All nondueling leagues were ordered to accept similar strictures.[16] In order to dispel confusion, membership qualifications were subsequently made to conform to the Law for the Reconstruction of the Career Bureaucracy. All students with at least one Jewish grandparent were to be excluded from the fraternities and the alumni groups. Non-Jews with Jewish wives were also excluded, as were all Freemasons.[17] *Alte Herren* who had fought on the front in World War I or in the free corps were exempted from the exclusions, as were those who were too old or sick to have fought in the war and were government officials before 1 August 1914. The fraternities were of course given freedom to adopt more stringent requirements.[18]

The *Führer* principle was adopted by the fraternity leagues with some confusion but little overt protest. The Student Union and the *Deutsche Studentenschaft* exercised a veto over the appointments to the *Führer* posts and insisted that all *Führer* be long-time National Socialists.[19] Although it was not initially required, most fraternities were ordered by their league *Führer* to adopt the *Führer* principle on the local level.[20] The "Aryan" membership requirements aroused some discontent among the *alte Herren* who protested against the consequent disloyalty to long-time fraternity comrades. A circular letter in the *Miltenberger Ring,* one of the smaller leagues, summed up the attitudes of many who found it to be a "heavy burden on the conscience to have to separate themselves from men whose patriotic convictions were indisputable and whose fraternity loyalty was praiseworthy, merely because these fraternity brothers were not of pure Aryan descent."[21] But the burden of the new requirements was softened for many of the older *alte Herren* by the front-soldier exemptions.

In the summer of 1933 it was already patently clear that defiance was impossible. Rumors were rife that fraternities which did not sufficiently demonstrate their enthusiasm for the Nazi regime would be disbanded.[22] Fraternities which were out of favor feared that local student governments would discourage new students from joining them, making continued existence economically difficult.[23] Since competition for the decreasing numbers of new students was intense, few fraternities could afford to alienate the local student leadership. The proposals for "comradeship houses" in the summer of 1933 might well have provided a substitute for the fraternities. Local Nazi student leaders made no secret of their hatred for anything but outright subordination from the fraternities. In Kiel the student government *Führer* went so far as to order all fraternities suspended for eighteen months and their houses put at the disposal of the SA staff. They were ordered to meet only once a week and not to take any new members. They were also to accept the Kiel *Führer* as virtual dictator over all their affairs.[24] The fraternity students simply refused to comply and were eventually supported by Gerhard Krüger, who promised a uniform regulation for student government relations with fraternities.[25]

Under these circumstances it was scarcely an accident that the leagues and their member fraternities responded to the general atmosphere of intimidation by jockeying with each other to prove themselves most loyal to the Nazi movement. The "comradeship house" program, when first suggested during the summer of 1933, was seized upon as one means to demonstrate this loyalty. In July, the *Deutsche Burschenschaft* ordered its local groups to establish living units along military lines for students in their first two semesters by 1 October.[26] In Hamburg, in August, many fraternities had already begun such living arrangements in which intensive political education programs had been organized in cooperation with the local student governments.[27] In the fall of 1933, fraternity "comradely living units" (*Wohnkameradschaften*) for new members proliferated throughout Germany. Those fraternities which did not succeed in constructing officially recognized "comradely living units" faced the prospect of few or no new members.

The Catholic fraternities presented a special problem. The only large group that had rejected the Nazi movement before 1933, they came under especial and continued surveillance. They were to suffer from a particular burden in proving their loyalty to the new order. When at the end of March 1933, the German bishops issued a joint statement ending the restrictions on Catholic participation in the Nazi movement, the Catholic fraternities struggled to prove that their faith was not incompatible with National Socialism. They encouraged their members to join the Student Union, the SA, and the *Stahlhelm*.[28] Their public statements anxiously expressed loyalty to the new government.[29] An acceptable nationalist past was even rediscovered. The brief fraternity membership of Leo Schlageter, martyr to the French occupation of the Ruhr in 1923, provided a new symbol.[30]

The Catholic fraternities were the first student groups to come under pressure to reorganize according to the desires of the Nazi movement. Early in May 1933, representatives for reorganization of Catholic fraternity leagues were appointed by the *Deutsche Studentenschaft*.[31] To insure the Nazification of the Catholic fraternities, the *Deutsche Studentenschaft* demanded the right to approve new national officers, including the editors of league journals.[32] Prominent *alte Herren* were forced out of their posts, among them former Chancellor Marx, who resigned his chairmanship of the alumni committee (*Philisterausschuss*) of the *Kartellverband* (KV).[33]

In July the Catholic fraternity leagues fulfilled the *Deutsche Studentenschaft* directives for Nazification of all fraternities, replacing their democratic organization with the dictatorial *Führer* principle and modeling their membership restrictions on the law for the reconstruction of the career civil service.[34] Many of the Catholic fraternities further demonstrated their National Socialist transformation by ordering all active members to join the Student Union forthwith.[35]

But the accommodation of the Catholic fraternities to the new Germany was not yet complete. On 30 January 1934, Oskar Stäbel, then the *Führer* of both the *Deutsche Studentenschaft* and the Student Union, called the Catholic fraternity leaders together and announced that they would henceforth be required to accept Protestant members.[36] The *Deutsche Studentenschaft* constitution of February 1934 forbade organizations of a confessional nature.[37] The *Cartell Verband* and the enlarged Catholic *Burschenschaften* immediately complied, promising to open their membership rolls to all members of the *Deutsche Studentenschaft*. Both pledged, however, to avoid any measures which might discourage practicing Catholics from remaining in good conscience in their organizations.[38] The *Unitas Verband,* which had a stronger religious orientation, accepted the ruling only under protest. Agreeing to accept religious Protestants whose life styles conformed to their church's moral precepts, *Unitas* insisted on continuing Catholic religious observances while arranging separate services for Protestant members.[39]

At the same time that Stäbel was ordering an end to sectarian fraternities, he offended the Catholic students further by delivering a number of speeches championing the duty of all students to defend their honor with weapons. He insisted that this would be in accord with the Nazi principle: "Honor can only be cleansed with blood."[40] Stäbel even prodded *Cartell Verband Führer* Albert Derichsweiler to join him on a trip to Rome to sound out the possibilities of a change in the ruling.[41]

Although the Catholic fraternities were now willing to accept non-Catholic members, they did not actively recruit them, nor did they have many applicants. They continued to be overwhelmingly Catholic. In spite of Stäbel's original assurances, the ban on confessional organizations was interpreted in many areas to mean that the fraternities could not participate in religious activities of a confessional nature. They were forced for this reason to hold religious observances in private and eschew participation as a group in public Roman Catholic events.[42]

The fraternities' running leap onto the bandwagon of 1933 gave them only a temporary reprieve. There were far too many enemies watching for opportunities to criticize the new recruits. The replacement of fraternity leaders by National Socialists from the rank and file had secured many self-seeking careerists into positions of power. Jockeying with each other for immediate advantage, the new fraternity *Führer* proclaimed their own orthodoxy and derided their rivals. The upshot was a self-destructive competition which made the task of the fraternities' enemies that much easier.[43]

Why did this infighting occur? In part it was certainly the result of personal animosity between the several *Führer* of the competing leagues. Fierce fraternity loyalties played a role. Long-time resentment at the social pretensions of the *Corps,* or deep-seated scorn for the newer leagues or the nonduelers as well as confessional conflicts were also factors in the struggle. Desire for personal advancement on the part of student leaders was evident as was the traditional goal of the fraternities to insure future success for their members.

Between 1933 and 1935, the fraternities congregated into two broad blocks. Those fraternities which had a traditional claim to membership in the "national movement," in particular the *Burschenschaften,* the *Turnerschaften,* and the *Kyffhäuser Verband,* began to take the offensive in the summer of 1933. Their aim was in part to monopolize student offices for their fraternities at the expense of the *Corps* and the Catholics, and to win recognition as the Nazi elite in student life. The *Corps* in particular found themselves under attack as both "liberal" and "reactionary" in the student press and even on the radio.[44] At many universities the *Burschenschaften* were attempting to gain a monopoly of the recognized "comradeship houses." Since the *Burschenschaften* were on the whole comfortably large, they were also in many cases behind the moves to close those fraternities which did not have many active students.[45]

In defense, the fraternity leagues under attack were forced to forge a system of informal alliances in order to adopt a common policy within the *Deutsche Studentenschaft* and the local student organizations.[46] The conflict between the two groups was temporarily smoothed over by the *Deutsche Studentenschaft* constitution of February 1934 which theoretically provided chairman Stäbel with a czarship over the leagues. A new *Deutsche Studentenschaft* office, "Chairman of the Leagues" (*Obmann der Verbände*), was filled in March by Hans Heinrich Lammers, Hitler's State Secretary of the Reichschancellery and *Führer* and *alte Herr* of a minor fraternity league, the *Miltenberger Ring.* Lammers's role was to mediate the quarrel among the fraternities, but in practice he became the central target of the political leagues.

In the eighteen months which followed his appointment, Lammers attempted to weld the fraternities together in a unified group under his leadership. A legalistic bureaucrat rather than a potential dictator, his attempts to conciliate all comers were often frustrated. Because he was chief of the Reichschancellery, all information relating to governmental administration was funneled across his desk. Lammers's potential power has been compared to that of Martin Bormann, the grey eminence who ran the Nazi party chancellery in the last years of the Third Reich. The extent of Lammers's influence as a member of Hitler's inner circle is difficult to calculate. Throughout his months of concern with fraternity affairs, he maintained that his actions expressly conformed with Hitler's wishes, and his correspondence mentions repeated conversations with Hitler on student matters. There is scarcely evidence that the *Führer* had an overwhelming interest in student affairs. It is more likely that Hitler was annoyed by the constant bickering among Lammers, Rust, Feickert, and Schirach about the fraternities to the degree that he finally insisted that Lammers disengage himself from the quarrel. At any rate, Lammers's support did at least give the fraternities a temporary breathing period. Lammers had nothing to gain from his relations with the fraternities, which earned him a number of powerful enemies. He appears to have been motivated only by his belief in the fraternity idea and his loyalties to the benefits of his own student experience.

Lammers faced his first major crisis in the fall of 1934. On 20 September, *Deutsche Studentenschaft Führer* Andreas Feickert announced a new order affecting comradeship education without first consulting Lammers, Derichsweiler, or the other members of the *Deutsche Studentenschaft* steering committee, but with the verbal approval of Minister of Culture Rust. The order required that all new students enter a comradeship house approved by the *Deutsche Studentenschaft*. The comradeship houses were to be provided mainly by the fraternities but coordinated by a local *Führer* for education. The *Deutsche Studentenschaft Führer* and the local *Führer* would also assume direct control of the fraternities together with the right to appoint or dismiss their leaders.[47]

Fraternity circles greeted the new order with consternation and denounced it as illegal. No basis in law existed which could force all students to spend a year in a comradeship house. Feickert's zeal for power over the fraternities threatened their independence and existence. Fraternities which did not set up such houses or lost recognition for lack of numbers or other reasons would be effectively eliminated from the competition for new members. Fraternities with recognized comradeship houses would be forced to take students whom they did not want.[48]

Lammers's response came on 27 September in a telegram to Feickert which read: "The *Führer* and Reichschancellor disapproves of your order of the twentieth of September. You are to suspend the carrying out of your order."[49] The fraternity blocs once again divided over this issue. The "political" leagues announced their qualified support for Feickert. To be sure, their leadership also recognized the dangers to their continued existence in the Feickert plan; however, they thought a satisfactory compromise was possible, and by supporting Feickert they might prove themselves to be orthodox Nazis.[50] Their reservations were carefully expressed in private only. Publicly, their support for Feickert was demonstrated by their signatures on a letter to Minister Rust, agreeing entirely to the 20 September order.[51] As events proved, the "political" leagues lacked the support of many of their member fraternities.[52] Student Union *Führer* Derichsweiler, no friend of the fraternities, strongly objected to Feickert's unilateral initiative.[53] Rust, who had at first aproved Feickert's order, tried to assume a neutral position in the uproar that followed.[54]

At a meeting on 18 October, confronted by Hitler's apparent annoyance as portrayed by Lammers, Derichsweiler's pointed criticisms, and reports that

Rudolf Hess was backing Derichsweiler in behalf of the Party organization, Feickert agreed to suspend his order and negotiate a compromise plan.[55] A week later, Rust told Feickert in the presence of Derichsweiler and other student leaders that he would only support a voluntary program. No fraternity could be forced to set up a comradeship house nor any student forced to join one.[56] In spite of these developments, the student government *Führer* of Marburg, Munich, Jena, and Erlangen, apparently with Feickert's tacit approval, began to carry out the Feickert order.[57] At other universities the leaders moved ahead with voluntary programs.[58] On 10 November, five "political" leagues announced their voluntary acceptance of the Feickert order with a few minor changes.[59] For Lammers and his supporters these developments were still ominous. The establishment of elite fraternities prepared to accept all comers in their comradeship houses would seriously undermine those fraternities who would not or could not follow suit. They were finally saved by Rust's order of 14 November, which transferred all student political educational programs from the *Deutsche Studentenschaft* to the Student Union.[60] Rust most certainly regretted the necessity for this move which transferred important powers from a state-sponsored to a Party-sponsored organization. But his hand had been forced by Derichsweiler's strong Party backing.

The Student Union immediately canceled Feickert's order.[61] The *Deutsche Studentenschaft's* comradeship houses were taken over. Comradeship education would for the present be entirely voluntary.[62] Fraternities were free to set up their own comradely dwelling units; however, the Student Union would not distinguish among the fraternities or direct students to any particular one.[63] If it were true, as more than one fraternity leader suspected, that the fraternities had escaped the *Deutsche Studentenschaft* only to fall prey to the still more ravenous jaws of the Student Union, the danger would at least await the spring thaw.[64]

The furor over the Feickert plan had scarcely quieted when the "political" leagues renewed their offensive, resigning as a group from the General German Dueling Society (ADW) and charging the other leagues with failure to carry through a thorough purge of Jews and Freemasons.[65] The five leagues which had left the ADW pledged to enforce the Nazi Party membership strictures for their fraternities: "Aryan" ancestry of all members and spouses would have to be proved as far back as 1 January, 1800. No exceptions for front soldiers would be permitted.[66]

On 15 December 1934, the five leagues—the *Deutsche Burschenschaft,* the *Verband der Turnerschaften,* the *Deutsche Sängerschaft,* the *Deutsche Wehrschaft,* and the *Naumburger Thing*—joined with the *Akademischer Fliegerring* in a "*Völkisch* Dueling Society" (*Völkischer Waffenring*). In addition to resurrecting the racial issues, the *Völkisch* Dueling Society also discussed the creation of a new *völkisch* concept of honor to challenge the "reactionary" and snobbish honor code which governed the ADW fraternities. Hans Dabelstein, a *Turnerschafter* who proposed the new concept, stated that honor should no longer have any individual reference, but should only be applied in relationship to the community of the *Volk* to which each German belonged. A student would no longer have to suffer a personal insult in order to institute honor proceedings; indeed, any insult to the *Volk* or any member of the *Volk* community was an insult to everyone. All violators of National Socialist laws also insulted the honor of the *Volk*. Since each student was required by conscience to demand satisfaction when encountering breaches to the honor of the *Volk*, and this honor could only be restored by blood, the implications were staggering.[67] But the members of the *Völkisch* Dueling Society seem to have taken the proposal quite seriously.

Early in January, Lammers met this new challenge by organizing a bloc of leagues friendly to him, the Community of Student Leagues or GStV (*Gemeinschaft studentischer Verbände*).[68] The strict conditions for admission to this new bloc reflected a defensive reaction to the attacks of the *Völkisch* Dueling Society. Member leagues would have to give proof that all Freemasons would be excluded. No "non-Aryans" would be permitted in the active student groups. Those leagues which had previously been confessionally limited would have to give proof of their nonsectarian character as well as practice and would have to agree to excise all religious goals. The GStV was further closed to dueling leagues which did not belong to the ADW.[69]

Lammers's ultimate intention was to unite all fraternity leagues under his political leadership. The GStV quickly organized local groups at all universities. The fraternities joining were asked to permit the local GStV organization the exclusive right to order their relations with the universities, the Student Union, other Nazi groups, and all student organizations.[70] The aim of the GStV was not only to coordinate and unify fraternity contacts with the rest of the university community, but to shield them as well from the attacks of their enemies.

Lammers's success was insured by an agreement he reached with Derichsweiler on 12 March 1935, under which both the Nazi Party and the Student Union promised in future to treat the GStV as the sole representative for the fraternity leagues.[71] Derichsweiler also pledged not to interfere in the internal affairs of the fraternities. Lammers, in turn, promised that the members of the GStV would assist the Student Union's educational program.[72] After this agreement had been reached, the dissenting leagues had no choice but to accept Lammers's leadership. At the beginning of May, the *Burschenschaften*, the last holdout, agreed to enter the GStV.[73] The *Kyffhäuser Verband*, which had considered the *Völkisch* Dueling Society reactionary, refused to submit to Lammers who, they claimed, had no intention of "creating National Socialist educational communities."[74]

The political climate in which the GStV was founded was by no means favorable to the fraternities. Increasingly, voices in party circles were raised calling for the destruction of these "feudal" relics. The attacks of the fraternities upon one another were picked up by the Nazi press and turned upon the fraternities as a group. Instances of old-fashioned hijinks were blown out of proportion and contrasted with the lot of millions of unemployed Germans.

The most determined foe of the fraternities was in a good position to challenge their existence seriously: Baldur von Schirach, for four years the leader of the Student Union, was now National Youth *Führer* and the leader of the Hitler Youth. Schirach had neither forgotten nor forgiven the humiliation he had suffered at the hands of the fraternity students in Munich. As his Hitler Youth leaders reached university age, they became an important group in student politics, supplying by 1935, by all accounts, a substantial percentage of the leadership of both the Student Union and the Deutsche Studentenschaft. Since under Schirach's prodding antifraternity propaganda and activities were a frequent phenomenon with the Hitler Youth, more and more students entered the universities with an antifraternity attitude.

An organized campaign by the Hitler Youth against the fraternities achieved national notice in June 1934. A number of articles ridiculing and caricaturing the fraternity students were published in the Hitler Youth press. In a number of university towns the Hitler Youth excluded fraternity members altogether.[75] More serious incidents were reported from Cologne, Königsberg, and Bonn. In Cologne a parade of fraternity students was pelted with flour. In Königsberg the Hitler Youth on a number of occasions paraded in the streets with cartoons and effigies mocking the students. When several students publicly remonstrated, they were set upon and beaten.[76] In Bonn, a monocled *Corps* student was burned in effigy, and there were several reports of attacks on students.[77] At a Hitler Youth assembly attended by several fraternities, a speaker had criticized the wearing of fraternity colors and suggested that the fraternities would soon disappear. Because the fraternity members walked out after this insult, the local student government *Führer* forbade the wearing of colors. The fraternities refused to knuckle under and with the help of Langhoff, the *Deutsche Studentenschaft* leadership managed to force the resignation of the Bonn student *Führer*.[78]

During the following year, the Hitler Youth's antifraternity campaign concentrated on press attacks. *Wille und Macht*, the key journal of the Hitler Youth, greeted the formation of the Community of Student Leagues with an article entitled, "Reactionaries without Brown Varnish."[79] A reprint of this article was distributed to students in Berlin.[80] Reports of speeches by Hitler Youth leaders attacking student fraternities were common.[81] Early in July, Schirach committed himself publicly for the first time to opposition against the fraternities. The Hitler Youth, Schirach announced, were tired of "Heidelberg romanticism." Hitler Youth members would not be permitted to join fraternities. If they had already joined, they would have to resign immediately or face expulsion from the youth group and lose all credit for Hitler Youth service.[82]

Schirach's attitude was widely shared by leaders in the Student Union, the Nazi Party, and the *Deutsche Studentenschaft*. While the student press was open to critics of the fraternities, the fraternities could defend themselves only in their own journals.[83] Throughout the spring and summer of 1935, the attacks grew in number and virulence. The fraternities were accused of "conforming to the view of life of a ruling caste, and embodying since the [age of] humanism an academic community estranged from the *Volk*."[84] Their origins were traced back to feudalism and Freemasonry.[85] Their alleged lackadaisical attitude toward the Nazi movement was said to be that of a "lazy, arrogant, and satisfied bourgeoisie."[86] Even State Secretary Lammers, as the fraternities' champion, was not immune to public criticism. Usually obliquely, but on occasion even with the mention of his name, he was accused of aiding anti-Nazi reaction.[87] The July issue of Julius Streicher's pornographic anti-Semitic *Der Stürmer* published Schirach's order banning Hitler Youth membership in the fraternities and asked slyly, "And what is that gentleman doing, who with the authority of a certain chancellery, a corresponding title on his note paper and a uniform that also brings duties with it, is still today pleading the cause of the Jews, the freemasons, and the servants of the Jews?"[88] When Hitler, upon Lammers's urging, banned the *Stürmer* for three months, Streicher telegraphed Lammers calling him a saboteur of the Third Reich and denounced him with a series of expletives. A formal apology from Streicher, on Lammers's request, did follow several days later.[89]

One incident in particular crystallized the opposition to the fraternities and provided ammunition for a concentrated public attack. On 21 May 1935, Hitler delivered a major foreign policy address over the radio which all Germans were honor-bound to listen to. The members of the *Corps* "Saxo-Borussia" in Heidelberg, one of the most exclusive *Corps* in Germany, left their house during the speech, and witnesses reported that they were publicly drunk and rowdy at a restaurant although Hitler was still speaking. Five days later, members of the same *Corps* loudly speculated at another restaurant about the *Führer*'s eating habits. How did he eat his asparagus, they wondered? These affronts to the *Führer* were quickly punished by the Heidelberg academic discipline committee which suspended the *Corps* for four semesters. One student was expelled and four were reprimanded.[90] The *Kösener SC Verband* and the local GStV quickly acted to exclude the *Corps*.[91] But these actions availed little. The "Saxo-Borussia" affair became public currency in July, unlike earlier similar incidents involving fraternities, and was made the basis for an all-out press assault. Schirach used the incident as justification for his membership ban on the fraternities. Andreas Feickert, at last able partially to revenge his defeat of the previous fall, welcomed Schirach's action and labeled the "Saxo-Borussia" affair merely an obvious sign of the dominant fraternity attitude toward the Nazi movement. Feickert's comments were widely publicized in the party press.[92]

"Saxo-Borussia" had the misfortune of being an aristocratic *Corps* and a member of the *Kösener SC Verband*. The *Burschenschaften* did not hesitate to use the affair for their own anti-*Corps* propaganda mill. The fact that a similar incident involving the *Burschenschaft* "Holzminda" in Göttingen was not widely publicized demonstrated that the *Burschenschaften* had more influence in the press than had the *Corps*.[93] It does not seem to have occurred to the *Burschenschaft* leaders, who were determined to succeed by destroying the *Corps*, that for the majority of Germans and Nazi Party members the subtle distinctions between the *Burschenschaften* and the *Corps* were not readily apparent.

The entrance of the *Deutsche Burschenschaft* into the GStV did not deter them from their independent political path. Less than a week after this event, the Eisenach *Burschenschaft* convention heard *Burschenschaft alte Herr* and Bavarian *Gauleiter* Adolf Wagner exhort them to continue to prove their Nazi mettle. Wagner asserted that the fraternities would go under if they did not become, "on the one hand ideological storm troops of the National Socialist movement . . . on the other hand the educational organ of the potential leadership."[94] He directed the fraternities that wished to follow his program to form "battle societies" at every university.[95]

What Wagner's exhortation meant in practice was soon demonstrated under his watchful eye in Munich. The *Burschenschaften* in the Bavarian capital came to an agreement with the local Student Union which closely resembled the Feickert plan of the previous fall. The individual *Burschenschaften* pledged to "anchor themselves as political education cells within the National Socialist German Student Union."[96] This action was taken against Lammers's command which forbade any political groupings within the local GStV organizations.[97] Although *Deutsche Burschenschaft* boss Glauning had agreed to prevent such local agreements when he brought his league into the GStV, he now pleaded that he could do nothing about the Munich *Burschenschaften* because of the involvement of Wagner and the local party organization.[98]

The March agreement between Lammers and Derichsweiler had mentioned no specific plans for cooperation between the GStV and the Student Union. During the following three months, Derichsweiler showed no sign that he had any intention of setting up guidelines for cooperation. His inaction was as much the product of general incompetence as of personal hostility to the fraternities. Lammers, in his turn, had ordered all local GStV leaders to establish contacts with Student Union groups. In some instances they were able to reach agreement; in others they met with distrust and outright refusal.[99]

Even in those instances where cooperation was achieved, many Student Union leaders in their May and June reports to Derichsweiler complained of a lack of enthusiasm. In Braunschweig, the fraternities were reported to be indifferent. There were no "dependable" comrades in most fraternities to lead the educational program.[100] The *Gau* student *Führer* of Hesse reported that the local fraternity students were either opposed or indifferent to National Socialism.[101] The Student Union leader of upper Bavaria noted that "the majority of students [have no] political instincts and [are] lethargic . . . [which has resulted in a situation] . . . where the entire student body has lost every interest in political life, cultural life and student work."[102] The Würzburg GStV was said to have become the "cloak of reaction," outwardly promising cooperation but "internally they carry on nothing but opposition."[103]

Even in Bonn, where the Nazi student group was controlled by fraternity

students, the head of the GStV, Karl Kracke, was disturbed by the unwillingness
of the fraternities to carry out "somewhat acceptable education."[104] Of thirty-
one Bonn dueling fraternities, sixteen were said to have acceptable programs,
only eight of which were really satisfactory. One Catholic fraternity had invited
the rector from the University of Münster to address them and applauded him
eagerly when he referred to former Chancellor Marx as the greatest postwar
chancellor. Another had included a priest in their program. Many had no educational programs at all.[105]

For the Nazi militants, the fraternities were decidedly uncongenial. They
refused to knuckle under to Nazi leadership, and since the freedom for independent action by the fraternities and the GStV was undefined, the local student
leaders were never certain what actions they could take without incurring Lammers's wrath.[106]

How much Derichsweiler's own attitude toward the fraternities was changed
by these reports is uncertain. As a member of a Catholic fraternity, he had
damaged his relations with his fraternity brothers in the past by his frequently
expressed wish that Catholic students be permitted to duel. When his subordinates in the Student Union publicly criticized the fraternities, Lammers, or the
GStV, he protested privately that he could not control his organization—a
pathetic admission for a Nazi *Führer*, if it were true.[107]

On 22 June 1935, Derichsweiler surprised the fraternities by a unilateral order
for a fraternity education program under the control of the Student Union. Each
fraternity was ordered to announce by 10 July three participants for a study camp
who in turn would be trained to direct the fraternities' educational program for
the fall term. Neither Lammers nor the league leaders had been forewarned of
this action, and they were deliberately excluded from participating in carrying
out the program.[108] The local National Socialist group leaders were given exclusive control of "political and ideological" education within the fraternities. All
alte Herren were expressly forbidden by the order from any participation in the
political education of the active students.[109]

Lammers was taken by surprise by Derichsweiler's announcement.[110] He
immediately called an emergency meeting of fraternity leaders. On 1 July he sent
Derichsweiler a long list of grievances, enumerating the faults of Derichsweiler's
new order and the troubles which had arisen between the Student Union
and the GStV since the March agreement. He formally rejected the order
in the name of the GStV and, pending future negotiations, announced that
the fraternities would not register their members for the proposed study
camps.[111]

Burschenschaft Führer Hans Glauning angrily dissociated himself from
Lammers in a letter sent to Lammers and Derichsweiler.[112] In addition, many
fraternities, under pressure from local National Socialist group leaders, ignored
Lammers's advice and announced registrants for the summer camps.[113] Derichsweiler's response to the letter was that his action had been taken with the

support of the national Party leaders and that he would refer Lammers's complaint to them.[114]

Meanwhile, Lammers had given Hitler his version of the conflict. Hitler did not, however, choose to overrule the order, as Lammers wished, but merely requested that Derichsweiler postpone the deadline for the fraternities to announce their representatives in the summer camps until 25 July.[115] On 15 July, Hitler, Lammers, Hess, Rust, Ley, Adolf Wagner, Gerhard Wagner, Schirach, and Derichsweiler met to discuss the fraternity problem. Lammers reported after the meeting that Hitler was by no means friendly to the fraternities, but he did not favor their destruction, at least for the present. He approved of the GStV and of Lammers's work in it. According to Lammers, Hitler had ordered Derichsweiler to alter his order so that no control over the fraternities by the Student Union would be implied. Political education programs would take place entirely outside of the fraternities, whose relations with the Student Union would be mediated by the GStV. Hitler also opposed the formation of local Nazi blocs of fraternities. He promised Lammers that Schirach's order forbidding Hitler Youth members from joining fraternities would be lifted.[116] Several months later, Lammers revised his report of the conference by noting that Hitler had projected the final end of the fraternities as a "slow death."[117]

Lammers's interpretation of Hitler's attitude was disputed in part by the other parties to the conflict. The official newsletter of the Hitler Youth in August repeated Schirach's order to ban membership in fraternities and despite frequent complaints by Lammers, the order was never rescinded.[118] Derichsweiler repudiated Lammers's report of the conference with Hitler and gave his own version to a meeting of the Student Union leaders early in August.[119] According to Derichsweiler, Hitler had praised the Student Union and said of the fraternities, "They will only remain in existence so that their members can be better supervised."[120] At some universities the fraternities were still under strong pressures to submit official registrants for Derichsweiler's summer study camps.[121] On 8 August Gerhard Wagner, the *Reich* Medical *Führer* and official party representative for student affairs, wrote to Lammers canceling the March agreement between the Student Union and the GStV.[122]

Lammers hoped to use the summer vacation to strengthen the GStV. On 24 July, he requested that all fraternity leagues grant him full powers to represent them along with dictatorial control within the GStV. He requested that those fraternities which had not done so voluntarily should conform their membership to Nazi Party standards by 1 November 1935. Freemasons, in order to remain in their fraternities, would have to formally renounce their Masonic oath, and even then they would be ineligible to hold office. It was essential that this new purge appear entirely voluntary, in order to soften the effect upon foreign opinion and because such voluntary action would visibly demonstrate the strong Nazi sentiments of the fraternity members.[123]

The unity that Lammers sought turned out to be elusive. Glauning refused, in the name of the *Deutsche Burschenschaft*, to grant Lammers the powers he requested over his league. In a letter to Lammers, he criticized the GStV for its past policy which he claimed had made conditions worse for the fraternities.[124] On 23 August, because of Glauning's continued defiance and his open attacks in the pages of the *Burschenschaftliche Blätter* against Lammers and the other fraternity leaders in the GStV, Lammers expelled the *Deutsche Burschenschaft* from his organization.[125] The *Deutsche Burschenschaft* leadership appeared quite pleased and relieved that an open break with Lammers had come at last. "We saw it as especially necessary," the *Burschenschaft* statement on their expulsion self-righteously announced, "to demand a sharp action by all of the leagues to prevent the offenses of a feudal-reactionary minority which is preventing the breakthrough of Socialism into the fraternities."[126]

With his radical flank removed, Lammers was faced with rebellion among the conservatives. Max Blunck, the *Kösener Senioren Convent Führer*, refused to agree with Lammers's instructions to expel all "non-Aryans" from the league by 1 November, unless Adolf Hitler would publicly state that he had no objections to this move.[127] Blunck hoped, if he could not prevent this final purge which was directed primarily at Jewish war veterans, that he might at least mitigate the *alte Herren* agony of conscience in betraying their comrades by making it appear that the government was behind the move. The success of Lammers's plans, however, was conditional on voluntary compliance which would demonstrate that the fraternity leagues were loyally Nazi. Although Lammers pleaded and cajoled, Blunck insisted that Lammers seek a statement on the matter from Hitler. Lammers, his patience worn thin, expelled the *Kösener Verband* on 5 September 1935. The following day, his plans shattered by his inability to control two of the largest and most influential fraternity leagues, Lammers resigned as GStV *Führer*.[128] Withdrawing completely from student politics, he also resigned as Chairman of the Leagues in the *Deutsche Studentenschaft*.

Although Lammers told a meeting of fraternity league leaders still in the GStV on 8 September that they should continue their efforts for unity and support his successor, all those present knew that the organization could not survive without Lammers and voted to disband.[129]

Without Lammers to shield them, the fraternities were at the mercy of their enemies. Schirach, never having lifted his ban on fraternity membership for the Hitler Youth, now moved to enforce it.[130] On 25 September, the SA forbade its members to belong to *Corps* in the *Kösener Verband*. The *Kösener Verband* leadership attempted to extricate its members from a difficult situation by announcing itself dissolved but at the same time ordering all *alte Herren* to carry out by 15 October the membership purge of non-Aryans which Blunck had earlier denied Lammers.[131] This only increased the *Corps* members difficulties. The SA refused to lift its order for any *Corps* until all *Corps* were purged; the old *Kösener Verband* leadership was unable to comply because they could no longer enforce their will on the disbanded organization.[132] Only after all former *Kösener Corps* decided to close down entirely did the SA agree to lift the embarrassing order.[133]

The fate of the fraternities as a whole hinged on the attitude of Derichsweiler. In an interview for the *Völkischer Beobachter*, Derichsweiler had announced that "the time for negotiations and discussions has come to an end because of our decision to present the young student generation with the alternative: National Socialist German Student Union or fraternity, political student or unpolitical philistine."[134]

It was clearly not Derichsweiler's intention to permit the fraternities to survive independently. In private discussions with fraternity leaders, he let it be known that by 1 November all students would have to choose between the Student Union and fraternity membership. The Student Union would run comradeship houses for those students who chose to join them. The fraternities were invited to be the nuclei of these comradeship houses which would then retain the old names and permit their members to participate in the *Mensur*. *Alte Herren* might join in a sponsor circle (*Foerderer Kreis*) for the comradeship houses.[135] Derichsweiler hoped in this manner to win not only the fraternity membership, their houses and property for the use of his organization, but also continued financial support from the *alte Herren*. Fraternities would not be forced to become comradeship groups, but in most cases they would be hard pressed to win new members if they did not cooperate.

The first league to comply with Derichsweiler's extraordinary program for absorbing the fraternities was the *Deutsche Burschenschaft*.[136] On 19 October 1935, about 3,500 *Burschenschaft* students met at the Wartburg for the final Wartburg festival. Announcing the *Burschenschaft*'s merger into the Student Union, Hans Glauning justified this action with the belief that "the essence of the original *Burschenschaften* can now best be realized in the National Socialist German Student Union and this organization is the only form of community that the German student can, with moral justification, unite in today."[137] According to official reports, following Glauning's speech, the *Burschenschaften* "lowered their flag, doffed cap and band and League *Führer* Glauning, with an agitated voice, transferred the flags of the original *Burschenschaften* to the head of the national office of the Student Union, Derichsweiler, who accepted the flags with the pledge always to honor them."[138] In this emotional ceremony, the *Burschenschaften* had won their symbolic, if hollow, victory over the other fraternities. Any hope that a loose *Burschenschaft* organization within the Student Union was possible was quickly dispelled. The Union soon denied any intention of accepting all members of fraternities which had become comradeship groups.[139]

The other leagues were not even to be permitted to enter the Student Union as a unit—the decision and application would have to be made by individual fraternities. Such application was by no means assured of success, since the Union intended to remain a comparatively small elite organization.[140] And without doubt, the *alte Herren* strongly resented what was clearly an unconcealed grab for the fraternities' property.[141] Nevertheless, most of the fraternity leagues had little choice but to disband and permit the active students in the individual fraternities to make the decisions which could well affect their future prospects. Of these, some disbanded, others reached agreement with the Student Union, while some attempted to maintain a precarious independent existence. Early in November, the fraternities were excluded, by order of the Ministry of Culture, from uniformed participation at university convocations.[142] In December, Derichsweiler ordered all Student Union members to leave the remaining fraternities by 15 January 1936.[143] Early in 1936, fraternity students were physically attacked on a number of occasions by Hitler Youth and *Jungvolk* at the University of Jena.[144] The fraternities' freedom of movement was increasingly circumscribed. In Marburg, in April, they were forbidden to hold their traditional songfests in the *Marktplatz*. Early in May, they were forbidden to wear their colors at their own commemoration festival (*Stiftungsfest*) on pain of expulsion from the university.[145] On 15 May 1936, Rudolf Hess forbade members of any Nazi Party organization to belong to fraternities.[146]

Presented with the unconcealed enmity of Nazi Party and state, the old dueling fraternities disappeared. One Catholic fraternity league, "Unitas," managed to survive until July 1938 when the National Student *Führer* succeeded in gaining a police order disbanding all Catholic student fraternities and *alte Herren* groups.[147]

The survival of the fraternities for almost three years after the Nazi seizure of power is more surprising than their slow death. The loyalty of thousands of *alte Herren*, many in positions of prestige and power, was perhaps the major reason that they were able to continue for so long. The Nazi student leaders were never united in their attitudes to the fraternities; some believed that they could be made effective tools of the Nazi movement, while others saw the fraternities as the chief focus of student anti-Nazi opposition. At first, Stäbel, Feickert, Derichsweiler, and many local student leaders, lacking sufficient funds to include all students in their indoctrination programs, attempted to force the fraternities to accept their domination of educational programs within the fraternities and to put fraternity facilities at their disposal. Many of the fraternities were willing to accept these demands as long as they did not infringe on their independence and their right to select their own members; other fraternities verbally complied but dragged their feet; a third group sought political advantage by acceding to all demands. Lammers, emerging as the champion of the fraternities, defended the position of the first group. When he failed to unite the leagues behind him and withdrew from student affairs under Hitler's prodding, Derichsweiler had the field to himself. In a bold move he sought to destroy the fraternities, while appropriating much of their property. The new comradeship groups, Derichsweiler hoped, would provide a united cadre for his organization.

Derichsweiler's hunch that many of the fraternity students would seize upon this for political advantage, while hoping to retain at least a measure of their old style of life, was borne out by the actions of the *Burschenschaften*. But as

Lammers, a loyal National Socialist as well as loyal *alte Herr,* put it, "friendship is not the same as comradeship."[148] In the regimentation of the Student Union, the traditional character and values of the German student fraternities had no more prospect of survival than the democratic ideas of the early *Burschenschaften.* Honor, as well as freedom, had been sacrificed for Fatherland.

The German fraternities had a long tradition of political activism and dissent. Most fraternity students had made no secret of their distaste for the Weimar Republic, and many a young man who between 1918 and 1933 had sought companionship in a *Burschenschaft* or a *Corps* probably acquired a sympathy for right-wing politics which he had not had before he went to the university. But the fraternities hardly constituted a real threat to the Nazi government, whose pronouncements they accepted docilely and with little sign of resentment.

The demise of the fraternities illustrates the ironies involved in the fall of the old Germany. The fraternities had long been nationalistic and authoritarian; duty and discipline were two of their prime principles. Their ultimate aim had long been to "train servants for the nation." During the Weimar years most fraternities had, through the medium of the *Hochschulring,* explicitly supported the ideal of an organic, hierarchical society which the Nazis claimed at last to have implemented. Since the seizure of power, fraternity leaders had scurried to cooperate with Nazi demands.

The German student in the fraternities was willing to bend to authority but also liked his beer. When the Nazis figuratively took away his beer, he was at a loss to understand how it had happened. But his career meant more to him than his beer. Where earlier the student joined a fraternity to insure his future in government or the professions, he now joined a Nazi organization.

The evidence indicates that the overwhelming majority of fraternity members acquiesced passively in the coordination and the subsequent destruction of the fraternities. The will to resist came largely from the *alte Herren* who maintained an ideological commitment to the fraternity tradition. Many of the students found the Nazi arguments against the fraternities to be convincing. Fewer students joined and those that did found themselves to be on the defensive. The very ambiguity of this defense made the fraternities vulnerable.

There was no rational political reason for the demise of the fraternities. They were destroyed because Nazi zealots could not bear any organization they could not control. They were attacked because their social exclusiveness no longer conformed to the prevailing ethic. They were despised as relics of the old imperial Germany which had no place in a revolutionary Nazi commonwealth. They were suspect because they offered an alternative, however innocuous, to the new norm of student militance. They were feared because they presented a possible meeting ground for the new opposition to the police state, the silent opposition of apathy.

The end, when it came, scarcely reflects favorably on the German fraternity system. The traditional virtues which the fraternities claimed to inculcate—courage, honor, self-discipline—were trampled in the race to conform. Lifelong comrades were sacrificed to the new Aryan code. The opportunism and careerism that had long been unspoken fraternity values now patently governed the conduct of the fraternity league *Führer,* whose unprincipled attacks upon each other certainly hastened the inevitable climax. Fritz Hilgenstock's threat, in the spring of 1933, that the fraternities which had not feared to protest against a Republican regime might be called upon to fight the National Socialists too if the latter restricted student freedom, was founded in illusion. The fraternity students clearly lacked the will, the courage, and the unity to carry on such a battle.

TWELVE

Conclusion

The destruction of the fraternities in the winter of 1935 and 1936 completed the odyssey of the German student from reaction to fascism. The National Socialist students shared many beliefs with the students of the previous decade, but these beliefs had been tempered by a profound psychological transformation. The fraternity student of the early 1920s, even if he larded his political vocabulary with *völkisch* metaphors, maintained a subconscious point of reference in prewar society; he sought to return to a situation where hierarchy, tradition, and political and social stability promised him membership in an educated elite. The restoration of nationalist faith in Germany, he hoped, would wean the German people from their liberal, democratic, or Marxist errors and make possible a return of the Empire, transformed into an idealized but still recognizable form.

For the student of the 1930s, National Socialism offered a world view which confronted the problems of modern life directly. National Socialism was a mass movement in an age when only a mass movement could be successful. It had all the appeal of revolutionary Jacobinism in that it promised not a return to the past but an advance into the future. It would create a republic of virtue that would topple the temples of reaction and root out the prophets of socialist revolution. It would create unity at home and victory abroad.

The transition from the elite consciousness of the Wilhelmine students to the militant egalitarianism of the National Socialist students is of fundamental significance for understanding the Weimar Republic and the rise of a totalitarian system in Germany after 1933. The broad National Socialist appeal to students was plain before the onset of world depression. Nazi success in student organizations preceded the Party's national electoral success by several years.

The nostalgia of the middle classes for Imperial society was a natural reaction to their difficulties in the 1920s. But many of their sons and daughters who came of age in the late 1920s and early 1930s did not share this nostalgia for a past they could not remember. They accepted the egalitarianism established by the Weimar constitution and confirmed by an economic crisis which had blurred the distinctions between bourgeois and worker. They objected to the Weimar Republic not because it had destroyed an idyllic past, but because it was unable to cope with the present. They were receptive to a vision of a new, more united state, supported by all Germans and bringing forth the sense of dedication and commitment the Weimar Republic lacked. Their vision was not entirely new: *völkisch* ideology had developed in the old Empire in response to the tensions which underlay Imperial society. But National Socialism appealed to the new generation because it severed the ties between *völkisch* thought and political reaction.

The National Socialist revolution was possible because so many young people had turned their backs on the past, not only upon democratic government, but upon traditional Germany. The divide which separated the student generation of the immediate postwar period from that of the 1930s was manifest in their attitude toward the university. The students of the early 1920s, in spite of their nationalist bellicosity, were defenders of the university community of students and scholars and the humanist tradition. The National Socialist students were determined to topple the barriers which separated the university from the world outside and to make the university subservient to their movement and its goals. Not a self-governing commonwealth, but a dictatorship was the prescription of the defenders of the *Führer* principle. Academic freedom, faculty-student trust, the bonds of fraternity, even Germany's intellectual heritage—all were casualties to a youth contemptuous of tradition.

The victory of the National Socialists over the traditional Right at the universities was in part a question of organization. The National Socialist Student Union was a political group able to use political methods effectively. New conservative groups whose major purpose was discussion were not as at home on the field of political action. For the fraternities, politics was largely a peripheral matter. The Student Union members were full-time propagandists. In addition, they benefited from the dynamic of a mass political movement outside of the universities.

At the same time, the Student Union was a student movement distinct from the parent party, with an autonomous organization. It was in a position to develop a program tailored to the university setting, attuned to student sensibilities and with emphasis upon those issues which concerned students most. It represented the signal success of the Nazi policy of auxiliary organizations, a policy copied from German Social Democracy.

The Nazi attractions undoubtedly included their support of specific programs to put *völkisch* aims into effect, notably restrictions on Jews. The Nazis' most compelling plank at the universities appeared, however, to be their stress upon an egalitarian program. The Nazi courtship of workers of the hand and the brain, their attack on the old class system, the visible uniformity of the brown shirts themselves, all had unique appeal which transcended mere *völkisch* platitudes about the *Volk* community. The Young Conservatives continued to unite *völkisch* ideals with elite programs. The Nazis, using similar phrases, nevertheless represented a more realistic approach to modern mass society. Not unlike Socialism, National Socialism appeared to harness the energy of the millions who were the key to the politics of the future and to the resurrection of Germany as a world power. And unlike Social Democracy, the Nazis won support from all classes.[1] The ideological appeal of National Socialism to students was, it is logical to conclude, based in part on its relevance to the mass age. Since the movement promised social change, a democratic image, and security for the professional middle class, it presented more realizable goals than reaction or Young Conservatism. The similarities between the Nazi program and those of other groups on the nationalist Right, nevertheless, helped to disarm many would-be rivals.

Traditional conservatives, whose strongholds were the fraternities, viewed the Nazis as a section of the nationalist movement which they could not afford to alienate. Like their professors, who demonstrated a deep well of understanding for what they rationalized as the misguided idealism of the Nazi students at the universities, they preferred to seek out their enemies on the Left. All were to experience a moment of truth in the excesses of the spring of 1933, but the traditionalists remained unable to confront National Socialism head on. In the fraternities these men had to fight an internal as well as an external foe, and indeed the enemy within themselves. They were alternately attracted and repelled by the National Socialist program and could not construct a defense against it. The defenders of fraternity life suffered a crisis of confidence; uncertain about their own values, they were afraid to distance themselves from National Socialism. They therefore permitted their independence to be eaten away until they were destroyed. The revolution could not be satisfied with vocal expressions of loyalty; this upheaval demanded souls.

The National Socialists won out not only against the traditionalist Right but the democratic Center and Left. In the struggle for the hearts of student youth, the Republic came in a weak third. The Republic suffered from its own internal divisions. Its leaders failed to provide it with a unifying faith and a sense of national purpose which might have attracted young people to its banner. It offered no program of national reconstruction which would have involved students in planning for the future. The Republic lacked inspirational leaders who might have appealed directly to the young. Only Gustav Stresemann, the great German foreign minister, did not conform to the image of the Republican politician tied to the wishes of narrow interest groups; and Stresemann was the sole statesman of the Center or Left who developed a student following. The National Socialist Party was unique in that it offered strong and compelling leadership.

The unique dynamism of the Nazi movement effectively engaged thousands of students, radicalized them, and created an effective weapon for the takeover of the universities. Their victory was one aspect of a profound crisis in German middle class culture and the widespread receptivity to fascist nostrums which appeared to offer solutions to it. The Nazi appeal to students does not surprise, since the Party did well among those same social groups which provided the bulk of the student community. Student politics in the Weimar Republic were distinguished from middle class politics only in their youthful fervor which speeded the drift to radical solutions.

The problems of the university illustrate the inability of traditional institutions to respond creatively to the crisis of the middle class. To the extent that is is possible to discuss university ideology, the German universities were profoundly antimodern. The university fostered romanticism and escapism by promoting its concerns above society's concerns, by elevating culture and tradition above practical affairs. The university culture of the 1920s was barely opened to new influences, continuing to try to do well what it had done well in a less complicated age. Moreover, the nonpartisan nationalism that much of the professoriate paraded faintly masked an undercurrent of hostility to democratic institutions and a nostalgic sympathy for prewar hierarchical government. Overall, the university milieu subtly encouraged an anti-Weimar mood among its charges.

Ironically, the democraticization of the university community under government pressure tended to foster radical student politics. With official encouragement, the student councils set up after the war were designed to provide a student vote in university governance unprecedented anywhere. Yet the councils were never able to fulfill this promise, because of the premature foundation of a national student organization and of the introduction of proportional representation, which favored political electioneering. Local student politics were speedily dominated by national politics, and the students were lost as potential spearhead of university reform. The politicization of the student movement was fostered by the professoriate who, while opposed to the expansion of the student role in the academic realm, were sympathetic to the hundred-year-old tradition of student nationalism.

The rapid enrollment rise in the Weimar Republic testified to the continued attraction of the university image and the assumption that university education still conferred social status. Yet status also required professional positions, and there were not enough of these to meet the increased demand. "Trained unemployability," in Schumpeter's phrase, was the product of a university which failed to expand its role while serving increasing student numbers. Yet, since the universities defined their purpose almost exclusively as the advancement of knowledge, they refused to set limits upon the number of students entering their professional programs. The consequent crisis in professional employment helped to radicalize students and graduates alike.

While the middle classes eagerly sought higher education, the lack of mobility within German society served effectively to bar workers' children from the universities. Workers were cut off from the university culture, just as they were excluded from middle-class social and cultural institutions generally. The workers' spokesmen were cut off as well. Marxist professors as well as Socialist supporters were few, although the Marxist parties consistently attracted the allegiance of 40 percent of the German voters. In effect, a large part of the country was unknown, misunderstood, and dismissed as alien by the university community.

Nevertheless, the Marxist "problem" could not safely be ignored. Indeed, the long flirtation of German intellectuals with romantic ideologies which began during the Napoleonic wars was an attempt to create an integrated political society in a fragmented nation, an attempt which preceded the rise of the socialist movement. The romantic ideals of German nationhood rooted in a *Volk* community were beliefs which attempted to counter the serious class, confessional, and regional divisions within the German nation. The failure of the liberal movement to win mass support predisposed many intellectuals either to *völkisch* politics or to support of an undemocratic hierarchical state ruled by "experts." The success of a Marxist Socialist movement before the war tended to reinforce the class divisions within the country and frustrated the pretensions of intellectuals and middle class politicians to exercise the leadership role they believed their due. The increasing fragmentation of the middle class with the rise of interest group politics had similar effects.

Students, because of their temporary release from societal concerns, share with intellectuals the ability to transcend interest group politics and to concentrate upon larger issues of national purpose. Yet the transcendence of parochiality all too often results in the transcendence of reality. The *völkisch* movement provided an integrative ideology which promised to overcome both the class struggle and the disintegration of middle class political life in the parliamentary system. National issues such as the Treaty of Versailles, German rearmament, and pan-Germanism provided grounds for broad popular consensus, but social issues proved less amenable to nationalist rhetoric. Moreover, the political climate of the Weimar period discouraged the discussion of domestic issues in concrete terms. Accustomed to a government run largely by bureaucratic fiat, the Weimar public had little understanding of economic and social policy when this policy transcended their diverse petty interests. The limited political sophistication of the voting public contributed to the proliferation of political parties committed to narrowly defined programs. The students shared the general political immaturity, since their civic education was virtually nonexistent and their university studies contemptuously ignored contemporary problems. Viewed naively from the students' outside vantage, the politics of petty interest appeared a fault of the parliamentary system rather than of a politically backward community. The national issues, which seemed poorly handled by feuding politicians, were necessarily the means of bringing the public together under a more unified, political system.

National Socialism was the first genuinely integrative movement in modern German history, the first party with apparent appeal to almost all levels of society. Benefiting from the deterioration of the economic position of the middle class, the Nazis were able to organize a new anticapitalist coalition of unemployed workers, salaried employees, and small businessmen. Much of the

Nazi success was founded on their ability to combine a contradictory but easily understood social reforming program with rabid nationalism. While the Party did not attract large numbers of working class voters, it made every effort to include workers in its appeal. Too, the Nazis had the drive and the nerve to destroy the Marxist movement in Germany and coordinate the workers through force into the national community.

The National Socialists were able to appeal to students on two grounds. Not only did they offer the attraction of an integrative, unifying movement, but they appeared to promise a solution to the job crisis which threatened students directly. Anti-Semitism reinforced both appeals by blaming national disintegration on the Jews and blaming the professional job crisis on Jewish competition. On the positive side, programs like the labor service brought students together with other social groups in an attempt to revive the national economy.

Since the Nazis offered a unique way out of the crisis they won apologists and supporters among almost all groups of students: Catholics, Protestants, and non-believers, fraternity and free, dueling and nondueling, men and women, wealthy and impoverished. Much of the Nazi strength was among the hitherto unorganized free students, the greater part of whom were the children of the proletarianized middle classes. It was this group that burst upon the universities of the Weimar Republic in unprecedented numbers as a result of both educational reforms and economic conditions. It was this group that expected the university to provide them not only with an escape from proletarianization but a path for social advancement. Ostracized by the socially secure and increasingly aware that their professional futures were in doubt, these students were susceptible to political adventurism. Marxism, with its promise of a workers' state and a classless society, offered little to inspire them. After all, they expected the Third Reich to provide them with an equal opportunity to achieve professional and economic success and status. Political commitment would become the chief criterion for advancement. The appeal of National Socialist ideology to students was all the greater for its clever rationalization and channeling of social resentment and personal ambition.

The Nazis also met with some success in recruiting the offspring of the elite who still provided a substantial proportion of university students. The realities of war, inflation, and depression affected the young more deeply than the older generation, radicalized them, democratized them, made them see their parents' tenacious hold upon the attitudes of lost affluence as a charade. They too were ready for a change.

At other times, in other places, this mood would have aided left-wing political movements as it has in the contemporary German Federal Republic. In part the fault lay with the left-wing parties with their militant hostility to bourgeois Germany and their anti-intellectual image. More important, perhaps, was the mutual hostility between Socialists and government bureaucracy which persisted even after the 1918 revolution. Almost half of the Weimar students came from civil service homes. The majority hoped for civil service jobs. Side by side with hostility toward the Republic, their identification with the state remained a reality.

Many capitalists supported the Nazis to maintain the capitalist system. But many more Germans and certainly many students had more interest in maintaining the traditionalist hierarchical bureaucratic system in which they had a stake. The Socialists and Communists were the chief critics of this system, and they seemed to threaten the students' future status and security. The Nazis, on the other hand, promised economic revival, social peace, and an expanded bureaucracy purged only of Jews and political dissidents. Many students therefore saw no reason for opposing the Nazis and good reason to remain passive as insurance in case of a Nazi victory. Many others undoubtedly were hopeful of career benefits should the Nazis win.

We have noted the relative scarcity of workers and businessmen's sons at the Weimar universities and the relative preponderance of youth from small business, crafts, and most notably white collar and government employee backgrounds. The contribution of small businessmen to Nazism and other fascist movements is proverbial. The contribution of the salaried middle class has been less thoroughly documented, although the social and economic position of this group was clearly at stake in the interwar period. In Germany, an unusual proportion of both professionals and the salaried middle class were state employees. Professionals like teachers and doctors were given civil service standing and considered themselves government servants. Once the German civil service had been liberal; now much of it had become antiliberal. The Wilhelmine state which had provided them with economic security and social standing was more congenial to them than the Weimar Republic. Their children, who made up the largest group of university students, similarly rejected Weimar. Some joined the Nazis, some supported them, most of the rest remained favorably disposed but passive.[2]

This disposition of the children of the old civil service–professional elite who would soon become the new elite helps to explain not only the smooth grasp by the Nazis of the wheels of power, but the relative success of their government until the debacle of the war. There were a lot of young people around quite willing to contribute to this success. Hans Zehrer, editor of the influential right-wing journal *Die Tat* argued in the early 1930s that the academics had turned to the Right, with the middle class as a whole, because the Weimar Republic had undermined their social status. Young "academics" undoubtedly sensed this loss of status only indirectly and partially. Their politics wavered between the old elitism nurtured by their parents and the university system, and the new populism which appeared to conform to twentieth century reality. National Socialism, for some, solved the problem. Here they could join the elite of a new and popular movement.

The flimsy coalition which the Nazis were able to create had little long-term cohesiveness. The unity the Nazis appeared to offer was molded from impossible promises and barely concealed the underlying resentment of the Nazi minions themselves. The universities were to suffer at an early stage, since their traditional goals scarcely conformed with those of the Third Reich and the patrician tone of the university establishment angered the declassé Party leaders. Overenrollment was cheaply solved with the expulsion of Jews and with compulsory labor service. The requirement of political conformity from students and professors alike quite intentionally devalued the universities' research and educational functions.

The militant minority, whose ranks swelled after January 1933 with opportunists and careerists, strove to turn the universities into National Socialist academies devoted to producing future toadying bureaucrats. Once the "revolutionary" stage was over the militants could prove their mettle only by prodding the masses of students. While state and party directives defined the Nazi university objectives, student initiative carried the process a great deal further. More than most groups, the university students were compelled to participate in Nazi-directed activities and were closely watched for signs of deviance.

The superficiality of student support for the Nazis became clear quite early. After the initial enthusiasm of the takeover months, the nationalist coalition fell apart. While student organizations accepted the initial stages of coordination without protest, Nazi attempts to gain complete control of student life met resistance. But the attempts by Catholics and Protestants, fraternity men and scholars, to go on living as usual were frustrated. Within the Nazi student movement, the radical group motivated by social resentment prevailed over those less militant who were prepared to accept some degree of religious and social pluralism. With firm party backing, the militants were able to counter the nominal Nazis within the state bureaucracy who attempted to protect traditional student organizations and limit Nazi control over student lives. By 1936, regimentation was complete.

The student generation of the 1920s and 1930s contributed to the destruction of the Weimar Republic and the rise of the Third Reich. Yet, beyond a hard core of militants, the students were anvil rather than hammer of the Nazi movement. Germany's new masters used the heirs of the old elite for their own ends. Supporters of the new order enjoyed short-run benefits. But the cost of submergence within an anti-intellectual and brutally intolerant regime was the moral and cultural destruction of the German *Bildungsbürgertum* and all that it affirmed and denied.

NOTES

Introduction

1. See, e.g., Karl Dietrich Bracher, *Die Auflösung der Weimarer Republik,* dritte Auflage (Villingen/Schwarzwald: Ring-Verlag, 1955), pp. 146–49.

2. See especially Lewis S. Feuer, *The Conflict of Generations* (New York/London: Basic Books, 1969). Feuer's comparative study tends to stress the psychologically aberrant character of student militants. He attempts to place student revolt in the narrow framework of Oedipal rebellion and insists that student movements take on an extra irrational quality because of their origins in psychological conflict.

3. See, e.g., Kenneth Keniston, *Youth and Dissent* (New York: Harcourt Brace Jovanovich, Inc., 1971); F. Musgrove, *Youth and the Social Order* (London: Routledge & Kegan Paul, 1964); Jürgen Habermas, *Toward a Rational Society: Student Protest, Science and Politics,* trans. Jeremy J. Shapiro (Boston: Beacon Press, 1970); Seymour Martin Lipset, "Introduction: Students and Politics in Comparative Perspective," in *Students in Revolt,* Seymour Martin Lipset and Philip G. Altbach, eds., (Boston: Beacon Press, 1969).

4. Erik H. Erikson, *Childhood and Society* (New York: W. W. Norton and Co., 2nd edition, 1963), pp. 263–64.

5. Peter Loewenberg, "The Psychohistorical Origins of the Nazi Youth Cohort," *American Historical Review,* 76, 5 (December 1971): 1457–1502.

6. See, e.g., Adolf Leisen, "Die Ausbreitung des völkischen Gedankens in der Studentenschaft der Weimarer Republik" unpublished dissertation (Heidelberg, 1964); and especially Jürgen Schwarz, *Studenten in der Weimarer Republik: Die deutsche Studentenschaft in der Zeit von 1918 bis 1923 und Ihre Stellung zur Politik* (Berlin: Duncker and Humblot, 1971). Schwarz's analysis is valuable for the period covered, particularly his discussion of student living conditions. His approach, however, emphasizes the impact of ideology to an unnecessary degree, and his attempt to break up the years he covers into categorical periods is artificial. The impact of right-wing ideology upon twentieth century Germany generally is discussed by Kurt Sontheimer, *Anti-demokratisches Denken in der Weimarer Republik* (Munich: Nymphenburger Verlagshandlung, 1962); Klemens von Klemperer, *Germany's New Conservatism: Its History and Dilemma in the Twentieth Century* (Princeton: Princeton University Press, 1957); and in somewhat exaggerated

fashion by George L. Mosse, *The Crisis of German Ideology: Intellectual Origins of the Third Reich* (New York: Grosset and Dunlap, 1964).

7. See the fine analysis in Fritz Ringer, *The Decline of the German Mandarins: The German Academic Community, 1890–1933* (Cambridge: Harvard University Press, 1969).

8. This is true in the German Federal Republic as well. See Habermas, *Rational Society*, p. 3.

9. See Wolfgang Kreutzberger, *Studenten und Politik, 1918–1933: Der Fall Freiburg im Breisgau* (Göttingen: Vandenhoeck and Ruprecht, 1972), pp. 12–13. Kreutzberger counterposes a neo-Marxist analysis which associates the students with a general middle-class revolt.

10. Mosse, *Crisis of German Ideology,* for example.

11. See, e.g., Hans Peter Bleuel and Ernst Klinnert, *Deutsche Studenten auf dem Weg ins Dritten Reich* (Gütersloh: Sigbert Mohn, 1967).

12. See Barrington Moore, *Social Origins of Dictatorship and Democracy* (Boston: Beacon, 1967), pp. 435–42; also Ralf Dahrendorf, *Society and Democracy in Germany* (Garden City: Doubleday-Anchor, 1967) and James J. Sheehan, "Conflict and Cohesion among German Elites in the Nineteenth Century," in *Modern European Social History,* Robert J. Bezucha, ed. (Lexington/Toronto/London: D.C. Heath, 1972), pp. 3–27.

13. See Gustav Stolper, Kurt Häuser, and Knut Borchart, *The German Economy, 1870 to the Present* (New York: Harcourt Brace and World, 1967) for a survey of the economic history of the Weimar Republic and its social effects.

14. Habermas, *Rational Society*, p. 29; also see Allesandro Cavelli/Alberto Martinelli, "Ein theoretischer Rahmen zur vergleichende Analyse der Studentenrevolte," in Klaus R. Allerbech and Leopold Rosenmayr, *Aufstand der Jugend* (Munich: Jeventa Verlag, 1971).

15. Pearl S. Buck, *How It Happens: Talk about the German People, 1914–33*, with *Erna von Pustau* (New York: John Day, 1947), p. 146.

16. Ibid., pp. 141–42.

Chapter One

1. See especially Fritz Blättner, "Gymnasium und Universität," *Studium Generale* (Berlin, Göttingen, Heidelberg: Spring Verlag, 1963), pp. 304–5; Frederic Lilge, *The Abuse of Learning: The Failure of the German University* (New York: MacMillan, 1948), pp. 16–17. Also Helmut Schelsky, *Einsamkeit und Freiheit: Idee und Gestalt der deutschen Universität und Ihrer Reformen* (Reinbek bei Hamburg: Rowohlt, 1963), 151.

2. See Wolfgang Zapf, *Wandlungen der deutschen Elite: Ein Zirkulationsmodell deutscher Führungsgruppen 1919–1961* (Munich: R. Piper, 1965), pp. 49–50.

3. For the social background of German student unrest in the first half of the nineteenth century see Konrad H. Jarausch, "The Sources of German Student Unrest, 1815–1848" in Lawrence Stone, ed., *The University in Society,* Volume 2 (Princeton: Princeton University Press, 1974).

4. See for example, F. Solger, "Die Statistik des Hochschulverbandes über den akademischen Nachwuchs," in *Mitteilungen des Verbandes der deutschen Hochschulen* (hereafter cited as MdVddH), 11, 1/2 (February 1931): 2–11; Hans Heinrich Borcherdt, "Das Nichtordinarien Problem an den deutschen Hochschulen," *MdVddH* 11, 3/4 (March 1931): 32–36. Alexander Busch's *Die Geschichte des Privatdozenten* (Stuttgart: Ferdinand Enke Verlag, 1959) is the best study in the field but somewhat weak on the Weimar Republic.

5. See Joseph Ben David, "The Growth of the Professions and the Class System," in Richard Bendix and Seymour Martin Lipset, *Class, Status, and Power* (New York: The Free Press, 1966), p. 466.

6. In 1929—79,245 students were asked about their career goals (see *Vierteljahrshefte zur Statistik des deutschen Reichs*, 38, 1929, Ergänzungsheft I, p. IE26). The careers most commonly mentioned were:

teachers at secondary schools	20,365
doctors	10,408
private industry and business	8,317
government administration	7,405
lawyers (Rechtsanwalt)	6,201
pastors	5,254
judges (Richter)	4,420
dentists	4,420
free professions (including writers, editors, politicians, musicians, actors, etc.)	2,083

7. See for example the resolution of the corporation of German Universities in 1920, *MdVddH*, Sonderheft, July 1920, p. 76; *Das Akademische Deutschland*, 3, p. 258; *MdVddH*, XI, 3/4 (March 1931), pp. 30–31. By 1929 the states of Saxony, Thuringia, Hamburg, Braunschweig, Anhalt and Lippe required 3 years of university study for public school teachers. Hesse required 2 years. In Prussia separate pedagogical academies were set up because Carl Becker did not think (to his regret) that the Prussian universities were equipped to educate the public school teachers in citizenship. See Geh. Rat. Prof. Dr. Brandi, "Bericht des Schulausschusses," *MdVddH* 9, 3/4 (April 1929): 89 and Gertrud Bäumer, *Deutsche Schulpolitik* (Karlsruhe: G. Braun, 1928), pp. 217–18, pp. 103–4, et passim.

8. W. Richter, "Finanznot und Universitäten," *MdVddH* 12, 5/6 (June 1932): 74–75.

9. Dr. Brandi, "Reichsreform und Hochschulen," *MdVddH* 9, 3/4 (April 1929): 109.

10. Brigitte Schroeder-Gudehus, "The Argument for the Self-Government and Public Support of Science in Weimar Germany," *Minerva* 10, 4 (October 1972): 544, and Kurt Zierold, *Forschungsförderungen in drei Epochen* (Wiesbaden: Franz Steiner Verlag, 1968), p. 69 et passim.

11. Even the Reichstag's generosity seems limited. Compare the 59.2 million R.M. given the society between 1924 and 1933 with the cost of the Prussian Staatsoper (30 Million R.M.) and the Pergamon Museum (40 million). See Zierold, p. 36.

12. Zierold, *Forschungsförderungen*, pp. 29–33.

13. Foreign donors were more consistent backers, supplying between 10 and 15 percent. Between 1923 and 1933, the Rockefeller foundation contributed $500,000. See Schroeder-Gudehus, *Support of Science in Weimar Germany*, p. 542.

14. At Cologne, a Kuratorium was headed by Mayor Konrad Adenauer until 1933; see Willehad Paul Eckert, *Kleine Geschichte der Universität Köln* (Cologne: J. P. Bachem, 1961), p. 167. See also "Eingabe an die Bürgerschaft der Freien und Hansestadt Hamburg betr. das Hamburgische Hochschulgesetz," *MdVddH* 1, 7 (1 April 1921): 73–80.

15. *Das Akademische Deutschland* (Berlin: Weller, 1930, 1931), 1:126.

16. Wilhelm Katner, ed., *Die Universität zu Köln, 1919–69* (Berlin: Länderdienst Verlag, 1969), p. 55.

17. Eckert, *Geschichte der Universität Köln*, p. 192.

18. Quotation is from Rudolf Smend, "Hochschule und Parteien," *Das Akademische Deutschland*, 3, p. 153. See also Hans Peter Bleuel, *Deutschlands Bekenner: Professoren zwischen Kaiserreich und Diktatur* (Munich: Scherz Verlag, 1968). There was a plan in the Prussian Landtag in 1920 to turn some of the universities into schools for training

workers who aspired to the bureaucracy, but it was probably never seriously considered (see *MdVddH* 1, 1 [1 October 1920]: 32).

19. A short-lived exception was the Socialist-Communist coalition in Thuringia in 1924 which attempted to establish and staff a new pedagogical division at the University of Jena and systematically overruled faculty nominations in other fields. See *MdVddH* 4, 1 (March 1924): 2–8, and 4, 2 (May 1924): 26–27.

20. Haenisch briefly shared his office with Adolf Hoffman of the USPD, who had no impact on the universities.

21. "Aus dem neuen Kulturministerium: Ein offener Brief an Professor Saenger von Konrad Haenisch," *Die Neue Rundschau* 30 (Bd. I, 1919): 17–27. The Prussian Ministry, with 12 of 23 universities, 4 of 10 Technical Institutes and its large professional staff, was unquestionably the dominant voice in higher education. The other states tended to follow Prussian initiatives.

22. Becker served as State Secretary of the Prussian Ministry of Culture between April 1919 and March 1921 and from November 1921 to February 1925 and as Minister of Culture from March to November 1921 and from February 1925 until January 1931.

23. See Kurt Düwell, "Staat und Wissenschaft in der Weimarer Epoche, Zur Kulturpolitik des Ministers C. H. Becker," *Historische Zeitschrift*, Beiheft 1, 1971, especially p. 47.

24. See e.g., *MdVddH* S.H. (July 1920): 56–57.

25. For model statutes, see Werner Richter and Hans Peters, *Die Statuten der Preussischen Universitäten und Technischen Hochschulen* (Berlin: privately printed, 1929).

26. Helmut Schelsky, *Einsamkeit und Freiheit* (Reinbek bei Hamburg: Rowohlt, 1963), pp. 164–68; Erich Wende, *C. H. Becker: Mensch und Politiker* (Stuttgart: Deutsche Verlagsanstalt, 1959), pp. 115–19.

27. See especially *MdVddH* 11, 9/10 (November 1931): 100–2. Also Dr. Brandi, "Reichsreform und Hochschulen," *MdVddH* 10, 7/8 (October 1930) and *MdVddH* 10, 9/10 (December 1930): 15.

28. Gustav Radbruch, in *Die Deutschen Universitäten und der Heutige Staat* by Wilhelm Kahl, Friedrich Meinecke, Gustav Radbruch (Tübingen: J. C. B. Mohr, 1926), p. 33.

29. Wende, *C. H. Becker*, pp. 102–3.

30. Ibid., p. 102.

31. Heinz Radke, "Hochschule und Akademiker in ihren Beziehungen zur öffentlichen Meinungsbildung," unpublished dissertation (Munich 1957), p. 170. Radke cites a number of examples. For a systematic investigation of the political views of the professors of this period see Fritz Franz Klaus Ringer, "The German Universities and the Crisis of Learning, 1918–32," unpublished dissertation (Harvard, September 1960).

32. Theodor Eschenburg, "Aus dem Universitätsleben vor 1933," *Deutsches Geistesleben und Nationalsozialismus*, Andreas Flitner, ed. (Tübingen: Rainer Wunderlich Verlag, 1965), pp. 40–41.

33. Ibid., pp. 35–36.

34. Ibid., pp. 34–35.

35. Ibid., p. 35.

36. Ernst Lemmer, *Manches war doch anders: Erinnerung eines deutschen Demokraten* (Frankfurt/Main: Verlag Heinrich Scheffler, 1968), pp. 60–61.

37. See, e.g., Kurt Sontheimer, "Die Haltung der deutschen Universitäten zur Weimarer Republik," *Universitätstage 1966: Nationalsozialismus und die Deutsche Universität* (Berlin: Walter de Gruyter and Co., 1966), p. 31.

38. Fritz K. Ringer, *The Decline of the German Mandarins: The German Academic Community, 1890–1933* (Cambridge: Harvard University Press, 1969), p. 446.

Chapter Two

1. James E. Russell, *German Higher Schools* (New York: Longmans, Green, 1899), p. 90.

2. W. Lexis, *A General View of the History and Organization of Public Education in the German Empire,* trans. G. J. Tamson (Berlin: A. Asher, 1904), p. 62. According to Ssymank (Friedrich Karl Alfred Schulze and Paul William Ssymank, *Das Deutsche Studententum von den ältesten Zeiten bis zum Weltkriege* [Leipzig: Voigtländers, 1910, p. 423.]) some states also maintained the monopoly of the *Gymnasien* for pre-law studies.

3. Schulze and Ssymank, *Das Deutsche Studententum,* p. 426; *Deutsche Hochschulstatistik* (Berlin: Struppe & Winckler), Summer Semester 1928, Winter Semester 1928/29.

4. Students entering the secondary schools had to pass an examination and were also expected to be free of contagious diseases.

5. For a statistical breakdown see Michael S. Steinberg, "Sabres, books, and brown shirts: The radicalization of the German students, 1918–35," unpublished dissertation (Johns Hopkins University, 1971), pp. 74–75.

6. *Deutsche Hochschulstatistik,* Summer 1928.

7. Ibid.; *Preussische Hochschulstatistik* (Berlin: Verlag Reimar Hobbing), Winter Semester 1924/25. The percentage of students actually coming from working class homes was probably larger than the official statistics indicate because of the reluctance of some to indicate that their homes were on the bottom of the social scale.

8. Ibid.

9. For a detailed study of these changes see *The Reorganization of Education in Prussia,* Issac Kandel and Thomas Alexander, trans. (New York: Bureau of Publications, Teachers College, Columbia 1927).

10. *Deutsche Hochschulstatistik,* Summer 1928

11. Ibid. Alternate routes to the university were more significant in the states of Saxony, Württemberg, Thuringia, and Hamburg than they were in the rest of Germany.

12. According to an investigation by G. Pröbsting, the percentage of all ten-year-olds in Prussia enrolled in the sixth class of secondary schools almost doubled between 1910 and 1928. He gives the following percentages: 1910, 8.9; 1919, 11.4; 1920, 11.4; 1921, 11.6; 1922, 12.0; 1923, 13.0; 1924, 14.2; 1925, 16.0; 1926, 16.6; 1927, 16.4; 1928, 17.6. See Wilhelm Schlink and Hans Sikorski, "Die Berufsaussichten der Akademiker," *Das Akademische Deutschland,* 3 (Berlin: C. A. Weller, 1930–31): pp. 175–192.

13. In the summer semester of 1919, there were already 12,964 enrolled students in Berlin, 8,250 in Munich, 6,557 in Bonn, and 5,798 in Leipzig. There were three universities with between 4,000 and 5,000 students (Göttingen, Münster, Breslau), six with between 3,000 and 4,000 students (Marburg, Frankfurt, Freiburg, Halle, Tübingen, Heidelberg), five with between 2,000 and 3,000 students (Jena, Würzburg, Giessen, Königsberg, Greifswald) and five with fewer than 2,000 students (Rostock, Kiel, and Erlangen and the new universities of Hamburg and Cologne). Figures are from *Burschenschaftliche Blätter,* 21 November 1919.

14. Rudolf Frahn, *Ruheloses Leben* (Düsseldorf: Peter Diedrichs Verlag, 1949), p. 33.

15. Ibid., p. 35.

16. Theodor Geiger, *Die soziale Schichtung des deutschen Volkes* (Stuttgart, 1932). Geiger includes the university-educated professionals (p. 98) who, however, are more properly identified with the elite in spite of their economic problems in this period. In general the professionals were either self-employed or highly ranked within the civil service.

17. Jenö Kurucz, *Struktur und Funktion der Intelligenz während der Weimarer Republik* (Cologne: Grote, 1967), p. 107.

18. Jürgen Kocka, *Klassengesellschaft im Krieg 1914–1918* (Göttingen: Vandenhoeck & Ruprecht, 1973), p. 82.

19. Speech delivered by Dr. Otto Friedländer to a meeting of the Verband Sozialistischer Studentengruppen Deutschlands und Österreichs in Berlin in 1929, Deutsches Zentralarchiv, Abteilung Merseburg, Preussisches Ministerium für Kunst, Wissenschaft und Volksbildung (hereafter cited as Merseburg, K, W & V), Rep. 76, Va 1, Titel XII, nr. 25, Bd. V, items 190–206.

20. Michael H. Kater, "Krisis des Frauenstudiums in der Weimarer Republik," *VSWG* 59, 2 (1972): 213–16.

21. Ibid.: 224–25.

22. *Niedersächsische Hochschulzeitung,* August 5, 1920, pp. 1–2, Merseburg, K, W & V, Rep. 76, Va, Sekt. 1, Titel XII, nr. 38, items 9–11.

23. F. Kolbe, "Der Lebensraum des deutschen Akademikers," *Academia* (15 October 1932), pp. 160–64.

24. *Akademische Turnbundsblätter,* November 1924. Students in Germany are ordinarily expected to complete programs of independent study during vacations.

25. During the summer vacation of 1922—26,803 students reported working: 6,026 reported doing hand work in factories, 3,347 reported forestry or agricultural work and 1,107 reported peat or mine work (ibid.).

26. Erich Kästner from "Meine sonnige Jugend (1946/48)" in *Kästner für Erwachsene* (Frankfurt/Main: S. Fischer Verlag, 1966), pp. 527–28.

27. Michael H. Kater, "The Work Student: A Socio-Economic Phenomenon of Early Weimar Germany," *Journal of Contemporary History* 10, 1 (January 1975): 75.

28. Jürgen Schwarz, *Studenten in der Weimarer Republik: Die Deutsche Studentenschaft in der Zeit von 1918 bis 1923 und Ihre Stellung zur Politik* (Berlin: Duncker and Humblot, 1971), pp. 81–82.

29. Kater, "work student," p. 84.

30. *Das Akademische Deutschland,* 3, p. 345. *Deutsche Hochschulstatistik,* Winter semester 1929/30, p. 28. For the 1929/30 winter semester, 6.3 percent of Prussian students reported working during semester, 12.3 percent during the vacation. The figures for Bavaria were 4.9 percent and 11.2 percent respectively, for Saxony 8.6 percent and 12.4 percent, for Württemberg 1.1 percent and 15.2 percent. To these must be added the unknown but large number who sought employment unsuccessfully. See also Kater, "work student," pp. 87–88, and Schwarz, pp. 72–73.

31. Michael H. Kater, *Studentenschaft und Rechtsradikalismus in Deutschland 1918–1933* (Hamburg: Hoffmann und Campe, 1975), pp. 77–80.

32. Schulze and Ssymanck, p. 195.

33. The first of these, the *Gesamtverband alte Korpsphilister,* was founded in 1888 (See Schulze and Ssymanck, p. 437).

34. Former fraternity students played important political roles particularly in the Center Party, and the liberal and right-wing parties. For example, in the Reichstag of 1925 at least 88 of 472 deputies were former fraternity members. Of these 27 were in the German National Peoples Party, 19 in the German Peoples Party, 21 in the Center Party, and 9 in the German Democratic Party. (See *Schwarzburg,* 1 January 1925, pp. 25–26). The Reichstag elected in 1928 also included at least 88 former fraternity members (See *Bayerische Hochschulzeitung,* 25 April 1929, p. 4). Many prominent politicians of the Republic retained an active interest in the fraternities.

35. In 1920, for example, the *Deutsche Burschenschaft* set up a special employment office. Similar offices were also set up in Austria and locally in Berlin and southeastern Germany (*Handbuch für den deutschen Burschenschafter,* ed. Hermann Haupt, third

edition [Berlin: Verlag der Burschenschaftlichen Blätter, 1925], pp. 177–82); for the Kösener SC Verband see *Deutsche Corpszeitung*, September 1924, p. 121.

36. Schulze and Ssymank, p. 348.

37. Quoted in Hans Heigert, "Romantik und Idealismus, und die Staatsmystik in deutschen Bürgertum," unpublished dissertation (Heidelberg, 1949), p. 232.

38. *Die Schwarzburg*, 2 February 1920, pp. 61–63; Anton Baak, "Grundlagen Entwicklung und Wesen der Organisation der Deutschen Studentenschaft," unpublished dissertation (Münster i.W., 1927), pp. 17–18.

39. *Die Schwarzburg*, 2 February 1920, pp. 38–39.

40. Ziegler, *Der Deutscher Student*, p. 109.

41. *Die Schwarzburg*, May 1926, pp. 113–15. Even those students who rejected the duel on religious grounds were often accused of cowardice.

42. Mohammed Rassem, "Der Student als Ritter: Eine Skizze nach Eichendorff," *Studium Generale*, 16, Nr. 5 (1963): p. 275.

43. Ziegler, p. 110.

44. Radke, p. 232n.

45. Schulze and Ssymank, pp. 446–47.

46. Friedrich Ernst v. Schwerin, "Die Entstehung der Vereine Deutscher Studenten in der anti-semitischen Bewegung," *Beiträge VDSt zur Geschichte des Kyffhäuser Verbandes der Vereine Deutscher Studenten*, Wolfgang Stahlberg, ed. (Berlin, Charlottenburg: Bernard & Graefe, 1931), pp. 15–16.

47. Friedrich Naumann was eventually persuaded to resign from the Kyffhäuser Verband after several years of controversy over his political activities, particularly his support of Social Democratic candidates in run-off elections for the Reichstag. A strong group among the active students supported Naumann's programs, but the pressures of conservative *alte Herren* proved more potent (Robert Oswald, "Unsere Auseinandersetzung mit der Parteipolitik," *Beiträge VDSt zur Geschichte . . .*, Stahlberg, ed., pp. 81–127).

48. The percentage of Jewish students reached a high point in Germany in the late nineteenth century: 9.32 percent of all Prussian students studying in Prussian universities were of the Jewish faith in 1895. Fifty percent of the Prussian Jewish students studied medicine, constituting 19.92 percent of all Prussian medical students. The Jews constituted only 1.14 percent of the total population of Prussia in that year (See Arthur Ruppin, "Die Sozialen Verhältnisse der Juden in Preussen und Deutschland," *Jahrbücher für Nationalökonomie und Statistik*, Series 3, 23:375, 779). In contrast, according to 1928 statistics, only 4.69 percent of the Prussian university students were of Jewish faith in that year. The percentage of medical students who were Jewish had declined to 8 percent (*Deutsche Hochschulstatistik*, summer 1928). The absolute number of Jewish students did not rise markedly after the turn of the century.

49. The Kyffhäuser Verband was greatly influenced by Adolf Stöcker's Christian Social movement in this area.

50. "Pro-Patria," *Deutsche Corpszeitung*, 10 December 1920/January 1921, pp. 190–93.

51. Baden State Ministry to Prussian State Ministry, Merseburg, K, W & V, Rep 76, Va 1, Titel XII, Nr. 11, Bd. IV, item 5.

52. Copy for the archives, Merseburg, K, W & V, Rep. 76, Va, 1, Titel XII, Nr. 11, Bd. IV, item 31.

53. "Richtlinien für den Abwehrkampf," *V. C. Rundschau*, April 1926, p. 9.

54. Ibid.

55. Karl Massman, "Die 34. Verbandstagung der Vereine Deutscher Studenten," *Akademische Blätter*, 1 September 1919, pp. 132–33.

56. Wolfgang Zorn, "Die politische Entwicklung des deutschen Studententums 1918–31," *Darstellungen und Quellen zur Geschichte der deutschen Einheitsbewegung*

im neunzehnten und zwanzigsten Jahrhundert (Heidelberg: Carl Winter, 1965), 5:230–33.
"Politische Richtlinien der Burschenschaft," *Burschenschaftliche Blätter*, 23 December
1918.

57. Quoted in *Akademische Blätter*, 16 July 1919, pp. 83–84; Bleuel and Klinnert,
Deutsche Studenten . . ., pp. 57–58.

58. Merseburg, K, W, & V, Rep. 76, Va, 2, Titel XIII, Nr. 16, Bd. II, item 79;
"Bericht über die Teilnahme der Deutschen Studentenschaft an den Beisetzungsfeier-
lichkeiten für die Kaiserin," April 1921, Bundesarchiv, Abteilung Frankfurt, records of
the Deutsche Studentenschaft (hereafter cited as Frankfurt, DSt.), Bd. 84.

59. See, e.g., "Politisierung des Wingolfs," *Wingolfs Blätter*, 28 February 1919;
Zorn, "Die politische . . .," *Darstellungen und Quellen . . .*, pp. 234–35; Johannes Fuchs,
"Die politisierung des deutschen Waffenstudententums," *Deutsche Hochschulzeitung*,
13 December 1919, pp. 1–2.

60. See, e.g., Harald Laeuen, ed., *Volk und Hochschule: Neue Folge des
Burschenschaftlichen Handbuches für Politik* (Frankfurt: H. L. Brönners Druckerei und
Verlag, 1927); Wilhelm Berensmann, Wolfgang Stahlberg and Friedrich Koepp, eds.,
Deutsche Politik: Ein Völkisches Handbuch (Frankfurt: Englert und Schlosser, 1926);
Hermann Seidenstücker, "Gedanken über die Erziehungsaufgabe der Korporationen in
unserer Zeit," *Akademische Turnbundsblätter*, November 1926, pp. 225–29.

61. *Schwarzburg*, March 1922, pp. 26–32.

62. Edgar Stelzner, "Ehren und Ehrenschutz," *Das Akademische Deutschland* 2: pp.
45–54.

63. Walther Schulz, "Die Deutsche Studentenschaft," *Wirken und Werke innerhalb der
deutschen Studenschaft*, Hans Sikorski, ed. (Marburg: Schriftleitung der "Akademischen Blätter," 1925), p. 21.

64. "Aus anderen Verbänden," *Deutsche Corpszeitung*, April 1926, pp. 26–27.

65. Fritz Loewens, "Jungdeutsche Studenten," *Jungdeutsche Stimmen*, 31 January
1920, p. 62.

66. "Die Deutsche-Akademische Gildenschaft an alle Jungdeutschen Wandervögel,"
Jungdeutsche Stimmen, November 1920; A. Jeegel, "Akademische Gilden und Geistes-
verwandtes: besonders aus dem Bereich des Wandervogels," *Schwarzburg*, April 1921,
pp. 9–12.

67. In August 1919, the Deutsche Burschenschaft announced union with Austrian
Burschenschaften ("Burschentag in Eisenach," II, *Burschenschaftliche Blätter*, 19 September 1919, pp. 121–23); on 20 September, all Austrian Corps which had not previously
done so joined the Kösener Verband ("Anschluss der österreichischen Korps und den
Kösener SC," *Burschenschaftliche Blätter*, 10 October 1919, pp. 22–23).

68. Friedrich Karl Alfred Schulze and Paul Ssymank, *Das deutsche Studententum . . . .*,
p. 341; *Handbuch für den Deutschen Burschenschafter* (Berlin: Verlag der DB, 1932), p.
257.

69. Brunhild Mayfarth geb. Ruprecht, "Die Stellung der Studentenschaft besonders
der Mitteldeutschen Universitäten zu politischen und sozialen Fragen von 1848 bis
1918," unpublished dissertation (Jena, 1957), p. 139; "Stellung des A.D.B. zur Judenfrage," *Der Wehrschafter*, 1 January 1921, p. 10; *Handbuch für den Deutschen
Burschenschafter*, p. 257; Oskar F. Scheuer, *Burschenschaft und Judenfrage* (Berlin,
1927), p. 53.

70. *Die Burschenschaft Alemannia zu Bonn und ihre Vorläufer: Geschichte einer
deutschen Burschenschaft am Rhein*, vol. 2: 1890–1924 (Bonn, 1925), pp. 426–28;
Deutsche Zeitung, 18 August 1920.

71. "Die 35. Verbandstagung der Vereine Deutscher Studenten," *Akademische Blätter*, September 1920, pp. 125–27; "Nach der V.T. 1921," ibid., pp. 145–48.

72. Albert Wolff, "Waffenstudententag 1920," *Deutsche Corpszeitung*, 10 December 1920, pp. 185–88.
73. "Der Kongress 1921," *Deutsche Corpszeitung*, 5 June 1921, pp. 61–63.
74. "Der Kösener Kongress 1923," *Deutsche Corpszeitung*, June 1923, pp. 39–43.
75. *Das Akademische Deutschland* 2:665.
76. Compiled from membership figures in Bleuel and Klinnert, *Deutsche Studenten . . .*, p. 261.
77. *Deutsche Corpszeitung*, September 1924, pp. 128–29; Erwin Willmann, "Die Krise im RSC 1929/30" in *Das Akademische Deutschland* 2:298.
78. For a more detailed survey of the political position of the fraternity leagues in this period, see Steinberg, "Sabres, Books, and Brown Shirts," pp. 168–92.

Chapter Three

1. Wolfgang Zorn, "Die politische Entwicklung des deutschen Studententums 1918–31," *Darstellungen und Quellen zur Geschichte der deutschen Einheitsbewegung im neunzehnten und zwanzigsten Jahrhundert* (Heidelberg: Carl Winter, 1965), 5: 236–37; Gerhard Schmidt, "Akademische Wehr," *Hochschulstimmen*, 2 October 1919.
2. Zorn, "Die politische . . .," p. 238.
3. Merseburg, K, W & V, Rep. 76, Va, XII, Nr. 35, Bd. I, item 101; Zorn, "Die politische . . .," p. 239.
4. See e.g., *Berliner Tageblatt*, 27 April 1920, Merseburg K, W & V, Rep. 76, Va, 2, Titel XII, Nr. 16, item 48.
5. *Akademische Blätter*, 1/16 June 1920, p. 47; Hans Schröder, "Zur politischen Geschichte der Ernst Moritz Arndt-Universität Greifswald," *Festschrift zur 500-Jahrfeier der Universität Greifswald* (Greifswald, 1956), pp. 137–39.
6. See file in archives of the University of Marburg, 1954/16, III, K17; also Ernst Lemmer, MdR., "Das Drama von Mechterstädt: Erinnerungen aus dem Kapp Putsch," *Casseler Tageblatt*, 23 March 1930; Wilhelm Meyer, "Mit dem V.D. St. Marburg in Thüringen," *Akademische Blätter*, 16 July 1920, pp. 89–90.
7. "Die Verwilderung unserer politischen Sitten," *National-Zeitung-8 Uhr Morgenblatt*, 8 July 1920, Marburg, 1954/16, III, K17.
8. Marburg archive, 1950/9, item 224; Marburg archive, 1954/16, Akten III, K17, item 5 & item 29.
9. Zorn, "Die politische . . .," p. 261; *Deutsche Corpszeitung*, June 1920, pp. 73–74.
10. See, e.g., Merseburg, K, W, & V, Rep. 76, Va, 1, Titel XVIII, Nr. 9, Bd. XL, items 195–200 and 203, and Rep. 77, Titel 4043, Nr. 52, Bd. 1, item 11; also Hans Jürgen Kuron, "Freikorps und Bund Oberland," unpublished dissertation (Erlangen, 1960), p. 81; Gerhard Fliess, "Bürgerliche Studentenbewegung in Dienste des deutschen Imperialismus und Militarismus," *Wissenschaftliche Zeitschrift der Friedrich Schiller Universität Jena*, Gesellschafts- und Sprachwissenschaftliche Reihe, 1966, p. 296; and R. G. L. Waite, *Vanguard of Nazism: The Free Corps Movement in Postwar Germany 1918–1923* (Cambridge: Harvard University Press, 1952), p. 242.
11. *Burschenschaftliche Blätter*, 24 May 1919, pp. 39–40; "Die Uttenruthia Ohrdrusensis: Verbindung und Politik," *Schwarzburg*, 1 July 1926, pp. 171–77.
12. Zorn, "Die Politische . . .," p. 245.
13. Ibid., pp. 261, 279; Carl Schramm to General State Commissar von Kahr, 20. Oct, 1923, Schramm correspondence, NSDAP Hauptarchiv, Hoover library microfilm, reel 53, folder 1268.

14. Hans Ochsenius, "Die Studentenschaft der Hansischen Universität zu Hamburg bis 1939 unter besonderer Berücksichtigung der gesamten studentischen Entwicklung im Altreich," unpublished dissertation (Hamburg, 1941), p. 32; Universitätsbibliothek Würzburg, records of Nationalsozialistischer deutscher Studentenbund (hereafter cited as Würzburg, NSDStB) 21-alpha 474.

15. Zorn, "Die politische...," p. 280; Ernst Deuerlein, ed., *Der Hitler-Putsch: Bayerische Dokumente zum 9. November 1923* (Stuttgart: Deutsche Verlags-Anstalt, 1962), document 113, report of the assembly in the university on 12 Nov. 1923, pp. 257–58; ibid., report of the situation of the government of Upper Bavaria, Minn 73696, p. 357, note 191.

16. See for example, Karl Heinrich Keck, "Ein Bund der Frontsoldaten an deutsche Hochschulen," *Akademische Blätter*, 1 May 1919.

17. Günther Ehrenthal, Die deutschen Jugendbünde (Berlin Zentral-Verlag, 1929), pp. 66–67; Zorn, "Die politische...;" *Jungdeutsche Stimmen*, December 1920, pp. 450–55.

18. H. O. Wagner, "Der Deutsche Hochschulring," in Hans Sikorski, *Wirken und Werke innerhalb der deutschen Studentenschaft* (Marburg: Schriftleitung der 'Akademischen Blätter,' 1925), p. 42.

19. Ibid.

20. Karl H. Erb, "Deutscher Hochschulring," *Burschenschaftliche Blätter*, 3 September 1920, pp. 96–97.

21. *Allgemeiner Deutscher Waffenring*, Taschenbuch 1925, p. 16, captured documents T81, roll 256, folder 253-d/147.

22. Josef Eugen Held, "Der Deutsche Hochschulring und die katholische Studentenschaft," *Süddeutsche Akademische Stimmen*, 22 June 1921.

23. "Das junge Deutschland," *Schwarzburg*, February/March 1921, p. 13; "Um die deutsche Volksgemeinschaft," *Süddeutsche Akademische Stimmen*, 13 April 1921.

24. *Deutscher Hochschulring Nachrichtenblatt*, February/March 1921, pp. 18–19.

25. Constantin Schoening, "Der Deutsche Hochschulring: Tätigkeitsbericht und Organisation," ms., 1922, Merseburg, K, W & V, Rep. 76, Va, 1, Titel XII, Nr. 39, items 60–62.

26. For the Young Conservatives see Kurt Sontheimer, *Antidemokratisches Denken in der Weimarer Republik* (Munich: Nymphenburger Verlagshandlung, 1962); Klemens von Klemperer, *Germany's New Conservatism* (Princeton: Princeton University Press, 1957); Armin Mohler, *Die Konservative Revolution in Deutschland, 1918–32* (Stuttgart: Friedrich Vorwerk Verlag, 1950).

27. Edmund Forschbach, "Wehrhafter Student und politischer Soldat," *Academia*, 15 September 1933. Arthur Moeller van den Bruck, author of *Das Dritte Reich* and advocate of a German Socialism, was a leading Young Conservative thinker.

28. Friedrich Koepp, "Politische Erziehung," *Akademischer Blätter*. December 1921; Hans Joachim Schwierskott, *Arthur Moeller van den Bruck und der revolutionäre Nationalismus in der Weimarer Republik* (Göttingen, Berlin, Frankfurt: Musterschmidt Verlag, 1962), pp. 62–63.

29. "Hochschule für nationale Politik," *Jung-Akademischer Pressedienst*, 6 November 1922.

30. Ibid.; Hans Gerber & Kurt Erichson, "Innere Arbeit im Hochschulring," *Deutscher Hochschulring Nachrichtenblatt*, June 1921; Gerhard Bergmann, "Akademische Bewegungen," *Das Akademische Deutschland*, Doeberl, Michael, et al., eds., (Berlin: C. A. Weller, 1930–31), p. 82; Gerhard Klopfer, "Die völkische Akademiker Bewegung," *VC Verband der Turnerschaften-Taschenbuch* (Charlottenburg: Selbstverlag des VC, 1927), pp. 299–300.

31. Paul Engfer, memo to the executive committee of the DHR, 23 March 1924, Würzburg, NSDStB, 554-alpha 453.

32. Edgar Stelzner, "Hochschulfragen und Studentenpolitik," *Burschenschaftliches Handbuch für Politik* (Leipzig: Verlag von Fr. Wilhelm Grunow, 1920), pp. 77–78.

33. Josef Eugen Held, "Der Deutsche Hochschulring und die Katholische Studentenschaft," *Süddeutsche Akädemische Stimmen*, 22 June 1921; Dr. Constantin Schöning, report on the activities and the organization of the Hochschulring, 1922, Universitäts-Bibliothek Würzburg, records of the Deutsche Studentenschaft (hereafter cited as Würzburg, DSt.), 1*00-theta 166.

34. Jürgen Bachmann, "Der Deutsche Hochschulring und seine Aufgaben," *Die Hochschulgemeinschaft*, 1 February 1924; Walter Schulz, speech at delegate assembly of DHR from Oct. 22–28, 1925, Merseburg, Innern, Titel 4043, Nr. 52, Bd. 1, item 109; Erich v. Lölhöffel, "Der aristokratische Gedanke im Hochschulring," *Süddeutsche Akademische Stimmen*, 19 February 1921.

35. Christian Seiler, "Soziale Arbeit und Deutscher Hochschulring," *Deutsche Akademische Stimmen*, 19 February 1921.

36. Otto de la Chevallerie, "Aus der praktischen Arbeit in der Studentenschaft," *Jungdeutsche Stimmen*, December 1920.

37. Edgar Stelzner, "Die Idee des Hochschulrings," *Deutsche Akademische Stimmen*, 19 February 1921; H. O. Wagner, "Der Deutsche Hochschulring," in Sikorski, *Wirken und Werke . . .*, p. 49.

38. Jürgen Bachmann, "Der Deutsche Hochschulring . . ."; Stelzner, "Die Idee . . . ."

39. "Leitgedanken für den Deutschen Hochschulring und die Hochschulringe Deutscher Art, herausgestellt auf der Marienburger Führertagung vom 11.–15. Mai 1924, Würzburg, NSDStB, 554-alpha 453.

40. Paul Müller, "Grenz-und Auslandsdeutschtum im ADB," *Burschenschaftliche Wege*, October 1925, pp. 97–102; "36. Wartburgfest des Wingolfs," *Deutsche Akademische Rundschau*, 15 July 1926, p. 9; P. H. Wideburg, "Wie können wir Grenzlandarbeit treiben," *VC Verband der Turnerschaften-Taschenbuch*, pp. 317–19.

41. DHR Chancellory, circular letter, 17 July 1924, Würzburg, NSDStB, 554-alpha 453.

42. See Steinberg, dissertation, pp. 290–94.

43. DHR, circular letter, 3 December 1923, Würzburg, NSDStB, 554-alpha 453.

44. DHR, circular letter, 15 February 1924, ibid.

45. DHR, circular letter, 22 February 1924, ibid.

46. Ibid.

47. DHR chancellory, circular letter, 14 November 1923, ibid.

48. *Jung-Akademischer Pressedienst*, 23 November 1923.

49. Jürgen Bachmann, "Deutsche Jugend und deutscher Lebenskampf," ibid.

50. Aenania to Erich Müller, 9 February 1924, Würzburg, NSDStB, 554-alpha 453.

51. Adolf Leisen, "Die Ausbreitung des Völkischen Gedankens in der Studentenschaft der Weimarer Republik" unpublished dissertation, (Heidelberg, 1964),pp. 70–71.

52. "Görres Ring," pamphlet, p. 1, Merseburg, K, W, & V, Va, 1, Titel XII, Nr. 24, Bd. II, items 275–84.

53. "Gründung eines Görres Rings," *Schwarzburg*, July 1926, p. 189; "Die Erziehung zur Pflege deutschen Volkstums im Cartell-Verband der Katholischen Studenten-Verbindungen," *Deutsche Akademische Rundschau*, 1 December 1926, pp. 2–3; H. G. Suermann, "CV Versammlung, 1926," *Deutsche Akademische Rundschau*, 15 October 1926, pp. 6–7.

54. Minister of the Interior to Minister of Culture, 11 February 1925, Merseburg, K, W & V, Rep. 76, Va, 1, Titel XII, Nr. 42, Bd. I, item 45; DHR Chancellory, circular letter, 22 February 1924, Würzburg, NSDStB, 554-alpha 453.

55. *Der Student*, 15 May 1925.

56. DHR Chancellory, circular letter, 22 February 1924, Würzburg, NSDStB, 554-

alpha 453; Leadership meeting of the German völkisch student movement, Merseburg, K, W & V, Rep. 76, Va, 1, Titel XII, Nr. 42, Bd. I, item 43.

57. Hans Lutz, "Weg und Ziel der Deutschvölkischen Studentenbewegung," *Der Student,* Easter 1925, pp. 2–4; "Geistige und Körperliche Wehrhaftmachung," Merseburg, K, W & V, Rep. 76, Va, 1, Titel XII, Nr. 42, Bd. I, item 43.

58. Hans Lutz, "Weg und Ziel ...," pp. 2–4; Leadership meeting of the German völkisch student movement, op. cit.

59. *Hochschulgemeinschaft,* 15 June 1924.

60. Hans Lutz, "Weg und Ziel ...," pp. 2–4.

61. For a discussion of the later career of the Hochschulring, see Steinberg, dissertation, Chapter 6.

Chapter Four

1. Friedrich Georg Jünger, *Grüne Zweige: Ein Errinnerungsbuch* (Munich: Carl Hanser Verlag, 1951), p. 222.

2. See e.g., F. Holzwarth, "Der Würzburger Studententag," *Süddeutsche Akademische Zeitung,* 28 April 1921, p. 2.

3. "Tagungsbericht des Ersten Allgemeinen Studententages Deutscher Hochschulen in Würzburg," captured documents (Burschenschaft, Germania, Marburg/Lahn), T81, roll 257, 5047564-760.

4. Ibid.

5. The traditional view of this action has been that this formula was adopted to satisfy Austrian demands (cf. Zorn, "Politische ...," p. 250; Walther Schulz, "Die Deutsche Studentenschaft," *Wirken und Werke innerhalb der deutschen Studentenschaft,* Hans Sikorski, ed. [Marburg/Lahn: Schriftleitung der "Akademischen Blätter," 1925] pp. 15–16; Anton Baak, "Grundlagen, Entwicklung und Wesen der Organisation der Deutschen Studentenschaft," unpublished dissertation [Münster, 1927], p. 44). In view of the meager representation of the Austrians at Würzburg, however, and the uncertainty regarding the creation of student self-government in Austria, it appears that many of the Reich Germans were quite eager to "compromise" with the Austrians.

6. Memorandum of C. H. Becker, 16 October 1920, Merseburg, K, W & V, Rep. 76, Va, 1, Titel XVIII, Nr. 16, Band I. Student dues were first collected in Prussia under this provision in the 1920/21 Winter-Semester.

7. Baak, pp. 45–46; also Merseburg, K, W & V, Rep. 76, Va, 1, Titel XVIII, Nr. 16, Bd. I, items 115–131; Zorn, "Politische ...," p. 266. Thuringia recognized the Jena student government on 23 August. Hesse issued an ordinance on 8 December, Württemberg on 13 January, Hamburg on 4 February, and Bavaria on 16 January.

8. Adolf Leisen, "Die Ausbreitung des völkischen Gedankens in der Studentenschaft der Weimarer Republik," unpublished dissertation (Heidelberg, 1964), pp. 45–46.

9. Baak, *Grundlagen ...,* pp. 46–47; *Niedersächsiche Hochschulzeitung,* 5 August 1920, pp. 1–6; "Die Beschlüsse des zweiten ordentlichen Studententages," *Nachrichtenblatt der Deutschen Studentenschaft,* 17 August 1920.

10. "Die Beschlüsse des zweiten ordentlichen Studententages," op. cit.

11. In the 1926 Bonn student convention, 28 of 139 delegates were Austrian or Bohemian.

12. For a detailed account of the constitutional struggle see Steinberg, dissertation, pp. 223–44.

13. "Amtlicher Bericht des Presseausschusses des Würzburger Studententages," Merseburg, K, W & V, Rep. 76, Va, 1, Titel XVIII, Nr. 16, Band I, Nr. 517–18.

14. Baak, "Grundlagen ...," pp. 56–57; Merseburg, K, W & V, Rep. 76, Va, 1, Titel XVIII, Nr. 16, Band I, item 627.

15. Ibid., Band II, item 299.

16. Ibid., item 215. The journal was sponsored jointly by the Bavarian, Berlin, and Austrian Kreise. Racist articles were usually Viennese in origin.

17. For a detailed study of the Lessing affair, see Steinberg, dissertation, Chapter 7. See also A. Messer, *Der Fall Lessing* (Bielefeld: Witter, 1926) and Kurt Hiller, *Köpfe und Tröpfe* (Hamburg/Stuttgart: Rowohlt, 1950), pp. 301ff.

18. R. Schilling, "Der 9. (8.) Deutsche Studententag in Bonn," *Schwarzburg,* September 1926, pp. 241–46; "Der deutsche Studententage," *Deutsche Akademische Rundschau,* 15 August 1926, pp. 2–3; Report of the ninth German national student convention in Bonn, 31 July–5 August 1926, Merseburg, K, W & V, Rep. 76, Va, I, Titel XII, Bd. I, Nr. 38.

19. Otto Eckart to Prussian Ministry of Culture, 21 September 1926, Merseburg, K, W & V, Rep. 76, Va, I, Titel XII, Nr. 38, Bd. I, items 293–95; Johannes Höber, "Der Studententag 1926 in Bonn am Rhein," *Republikanische Hochschulzeitung,* 1926, pp. 1–22; "Der deutsche Studententag: sein Verlauf und seine Ergebnisse," *Deutsche Akademische Rundschau,* 15 August 1926, p. 1.

20. For a detailed discussion of the convention, see Steinberg, dissertation, pp. 395–405.

21. "Studentische Verfassung in Baden," *Vossische Zeitung,* Merseburg, K, W & V, Rep. 76, Va, 1, Titel XVIII, Nr. 16, Bd. 3; Minutes of the second regional meeting in Stuttgart of the 1925/26 winter semester on 22 and 23 February, Frankfurt, DSt., Band 79; *Akademische Mitteilung,* 16 December 1925, Frankfurt, DSt. Bd. 126.; DSt. exec. board to regional office VI of the DSt., Frankfurt, DSt., Bd. 79. See also correspondence between executive board and Heidelberg student government, January–May 1926, Frankfurt, DSt., Bd. 126.

22. Merseburg, K, W & V, Rep. 76, Va, 1, Titel XVIII, Nr. 16, Bd. 3, item 136.

23. "'Der Streit' um das Preussische Studentenrecht," pamphlet, University of Marburg archive, Acc. 1950/9, item 645.

24. Becker to rectors and curators, 19 April 1926, Merseburg, K, W & V, Rep. 76, Va, 1, Titel IX, Nr. 2, Bd. 1, item 10.

25. "Die Antwort des Preussischen Kultusministers in Sachen des Kopfbeitrages für die Deutsche Studentenschaft," *Deutsche Akademische Rundschau,* 1 August 1926, pp. 4–5.

26. "'Der Streit' um das Preussische Studentenrecht," op. cit.

27. Report of the council meeting of the Bonn student government of 13 December 1926, Frankfurt, DSt., Bd. 93; Report of the second reading of the constitutional amendment in accordance with the instructions of the Prussian Ministry of Culture, Frankfurt, DSt., Bd. 93.

28. Report of the meeting of the cultural committee of the Prussian Landtag, 9 December 1926, Marburg, 1950/9, item 645.

29. Wende, *Carl Becker,* pp. 258–59; Memo of the DSt. exec. board regarding the order of the Prussian Ministry of Culture of 24 December 1926, Frankfurt, DSt., Bd. 2; "Um die Preussische Studentenschaft," *Deutsche Akademische Rundschau,* 1 January 1927, pp. 8–9.

30. "Studentenvater," *Kladderadatsch,* as cited in J.A.P. *Informationsblatt,* 5 January 1927. A second cartoon appeared on 16 January.

31. "Das alte und neue Studentenrecht," Marburg, Acc. 1950/9, item 645.

32. Ibid. The deadline was later moved forward until 30 November in a meeting between Becker and the rectors. See, "Um die akademische Freiheit," *Deutsche Akademische Rundschau,* 1 December 1927, pp. 4–5.

33. Ibid.

34. Schmadel to Regional Office IV of the DSt., 16 September 1927, Frankfurt, DSt., Bd. 77.

35. DSt. exec. board, circular letter, 30 September 1927, Frankfurt, DSt., Bd. 9. Guidelines for the reorganization of the Deutsche Studentenschaft after 1 October 1927, suggested by region 3, Frankfurt, DSt., Bd. 76.

36. Report of the eleventh German student convention in Danzig, 1928, Merseburg, K, W & V, Rep. 76, Va, 1, Titel XII, Nr. 38, Bd. II, items 20–21.

37. *Nachrichtenblatt der Deutschen Studentenschaft,* 25 November 1927, pp. 239–41, Marburg, Acc. 1950/9.

38. "Um die akademische Freiheit: Die Deutsche Studentenschaft gegen Dr. Beckers Zwang," *Deutsche Akademische Rundschau,* 1 November 1927, pp. 10–11.

39. Report of H. Seidel on the central committee meeting of 22 and 23 October in Jena, Frankfurt, DSt., Bd. 77.

40. DSt. exec. board, circular letter, 25 October 1927, Frankfurt, DSt., Bd. 3.

41. "Die Einheitsfront der studentischen Verbände," *Jung-Akademischer Pressedienst,* 5 November 1927, p. 3.

42. Minutes of the central committee meeting in Goslar, 9 December 1927, Frankfurt, DSt., Bd. 9.

43. "Kundgebung der deutschen Studentenschaft," *Burschenschaftliche Wege,* December 1927, p. 111.

44. Merseburg, K, W & V, Rep. 76. Va, 1, Titel XVIII, Bd. 4.

45. Letter of Kurt Corbach, Cologne, 27 November 1927, Frankfurt, DSt., Bd. 78.

46. In Aachen forty-one percent of the students voted: 360 voting "yes" and 21 voting "no." See Merseburg, K, W & V, Rep. 76, Va, 1, Titel XVIII, Nr. 16, Bd. V, Nr. 41.

47. Minutes of the regional meeting of region IV of the DSt. in Hirschberg i. Schlesien from Nov. 25–27, 1927, Frankfurt, DSt., Bd. 77.

48. "Tagung der Preussischen Studentenschaften in Goslar," *Deutsche Akademische Rundschau,* 1 January 1928, p. 5.

49. Prussian Landtag, session 322, 7 December 1927, Frankfurt, DSt., Bd. 203.

50. Prussian Minister of Culture to the university rectors, 6 December 1927, Marburg, 1950/9, item 645.

Chapter Five

1. For student paramilitary activities in the early 1920s, see Steinberg, dissertation, chapter 5.

2. Hans Ochsenius, "Die Studentenschaft der Hansischen Universität zu Hamburg bis 1939 unter besonderer Berücksichtigung der gesamten studentischen Entwicklung im Altreich," unpublished dissertation (Hamburg, 1941), p. 32; Universitätsbibliothek Würzburg, records of the Nationalsozialistischer deutscher Studentenbund (hereafter cited as Würzburg, NSDStB) 21-alpha 474.

3. Röhm, *Geschichte eines Hochverräters,* p. 264, as cited by R. G. L. Waite, *Vanguard of Nazism: The Free Corps movement in postwar Germany 1918–1923* (Cambridge: Harvard University Press, 1952), p. 209.

4. See, e.g., "An alle deutschen Studenten," *Völkischer Beobachter,* 27 July 1926.

5. Würzburg, NSDStB, 8-alpha 464.

6. Captured documents (*Reichsstudentenführung*), T81, roll 236, 5020954.

7. Hoover, *NSDAP Hauptarchiv,* 34A, 1796; "Nationalsozialistischer Studentenkampf," *Völkischer Beobachter,* 8 July 1926; statement of approval, 16 July 1937, Würzburg, NSDStB, 17-alpha 471.

8. *Nationalsozialistische Hochschulbriefe,* 15 December 1926.

9. Winter Semester 1925/26, Würzburg, NSDStB, 14-alpha 469.

10. Würzburg, NSDStB, 17-alpha 471.

11. Kater (*Studentenschaft*..., p. 112) notes that at Jena, 27 percent of the Union members were work-students in the 1928 summer semester, contrasting with only 5.7 percent of the general student body.

12. Announcement, 20 February 1926, Hoover, *NSDAP Hauptarchiv*, 88, folder 1839; PND Nr. 541, PND Nr. 545, ibid; *Völkischer Beobachter*, 22 November 1927, ibid.

13. Haupt to NSDAP leadership, 13 January 1928, Würzburg, NSDStB, 7-alpha 463; Tempel to NSDAP leadership, division organization, 8 February 1928, NSDStB, 17-alpha 471.

14. "An alle deutschen Studenten," *Völkischer Beobachter*, 27 July 1927, Hoover, NSDAP Hauptarchiv, 34A 1796.

15. Arthur von Behr to editor of the *Deutsche Zeitung*, 4 October 1927, Würzburg, NSDStB, 1-alpha 459.

16. NSDAP treasury to Wilhelm Tempel, 4 October 1927, captured documents, T81, roll 236, 5020633.

17. Baldur von Schirach, *Ich glaubte an Hitler* (Hamburg: Mosaik Verlag, 1967), pp. 18–34.

18. Ibid., pp. 56–58.

19. Letter to Georg Rettig, 21 June 1928, Würzburg, NSDStB, 14-alpha 469.

20. Schirach to Rettig, no date, Würzburg, NSDStB, 20-alpha 473; in his autobiography, Schirach claimed that he even had to pay for office supplies and postage out of his own pocket. (Schirach, *Ich glaubte an Hitler*, p. 59).

21. Hess to the local groups of the NSDStB, 11 July 1928, Würzburg, NSDStB, 9-alpha 465. This is the only reference to an attempt to expel Schirach. Hess claims in the letter that Hitler personally rescinded the order.

22. Tempel to the NSDAP leadership, 5 February 1928, Würzburg, NSDStB, 7-alpha 463.

23. Ibid.; Manuscript entitled "for publication in the *Völkischer Beobachter*," 6 February 1928, Würzburg, NSDStB, 7-alpha 463.

24. Report of NSDStB group in Kiel, September 1928, Würzburg, NSDStB 7-alpha 463.

25. Tempel to Hitler, 8 June 1928, Würzburg, NSDStB, 14-alpha 469; 28 March 1928, Würzburg, NSDStB, 17-alpha 471. Tempel publicly announced in June that his resignation was for scholastic reasons; however, he had tried to resign in March because of lack of Party support.

26. Rudolf Hess to NSDStB groups, 11 July 1928, Würzburg, NSDStB, 9-alpha 465. Schirach's testimony at the Nuremberg proceedings (International Military Tribunal, *Trial of the Major War Criminals*, vol. 14 [German], 23 May 1946, p. 409), that he was personally the choice of a majority of leaders, appears to be without foundation. His subsequent assertion, that he was chosen by Hitler after a meeting of leaders (*Ich glaubte an Hitler*, p. 58), also does not conform with the documents which indicate that the Party's first choice was Haupt, who refused the position.

27. Schirach faced a number of local revolts against his authority. Many Student Union members, who were also enrolled in the SA, became involved in Walter Stennes's (the leader of the East German SA) attack against Hitler's authority in the spring of 1931. After a purge of the ringleaders of this attempted coup a number of Student Union groups attempted to withdraw once again and seek the protection of local Party organizations. Schirach claims, in his autobiography, that the continuing dissent was fanned by Otto Strasser's agents who hoped to increase support for Strasser's movement among the students. After a large number of expulsions, including the entire group at the University of Erlangen, Schirach was able to restore his authority. See Körber to Hildenbrandt, 25 April 1931, Würzburg, NSDStB, 2-alpha 460; NSDStB regional leader VII to leaders in

Region VII, 7 March 1931, Würzburg, Würzburg student records, IV 31; Schirach to Karl Georg Schäfer, 7 May 1931, Würzburg, NSDStB, 1-alpha 459; Bertold Jakob to Schirach, 27 January 1930, Würzburg, NSDStB, 1-alpha 459; Wilhelm Neumann to NSDStB leadership, 28 January 1930, ibid.; Schirach, *Ich glaubte an Hitler,* p. 89.

28. See Dietrich Orlow, *The History of the Nazi Party 1919–1933* (Pittsburgh: U. of Pittsburgh Press, 1969), p. 149.

29. Cited by Kreutzberger, p. 111.

30. See Kater *Studentenschaft...,* pp. 125–26 and table 10, p. 217. Kater's social categories, however, are too broad to adequately describe the Würzburg group. In any case, statistics relating to students' fathers' professions in the light of the social upheaval of the 1920s present serious difficulties in interpretation.

31. Schirach to W. C. Meyer, 14 June 1930, Würzburg, NSDStB, 5-alpha 461. These aims were subsequently incorporated in local group constitutions. See, e.g., constitution of NSDStB group to Friedberg i. H., 14 November 1930, Würzburg, NSDStB, 4-alpha 39; constitution of NSDStB Berlin, 15 April 1930, Würzburg, NSDStB, 1-alpha 459.

32. Schirach to W. C. Meyer, 14 June 1930, Würzburg, NSDStB, 5-alpha 461. These aims were subsequently incorporated in local group constitutions. See, e.g., constitution of NSDStB group in Friedberg i.H., 14 November 1930, Würzburg, NSDStB, 4-alpha 39; constitution of NSDStB Berlin, 15 April 1930, Würzburg, NSDStB, 1-alpha 459.

33. Schirach to W. C. Meyer, 14 June 1930, Würzburg NSDStB, 5-alpha 461.

34. Constitution of the Kiel NSDStB, Würzburg NSDStB, 7-alpha 463.

35. Captured documents (Reichsstudentenführung) T81, roll 236, 5020938.

36. NSDStB leadership, circular letter of educational leader, April 1931, Würzburg, NSDStB-alpha 469.

37. See, e.g., *Bayerische Hochschulzeitung,* 26 January 1928, Hoover, NSDAP Hauptarchiv, reel 88, 1839; Report of work during summer semester, 1928, 28 July 1928, Würzburg NSDStB 6-alpha 472; Königsberg NSDStB to NSDStB leadership, 15 August 1928, Würzburg, NSDStB 7-alpha 463; Wolfram Schütz to NSDStB leadership, 17 May 1929, Würzburg NSDStB, 4-alpha 39.

38. Placard in Munich Police records; clipping from *Völkischer Beobachter,* 22 January 1931, Hoover NSDAP Hauptarchiv, reel 88, folder 1839. The *Münchener Post* reported that Weber had previously accepted an invitation to participate in a discussion with Feder before the University's Political Science Association (*Staatswissenschaftliche Fachschaft*) and had therefore declined the NSDStB invitation several days earlier. See clipping in Hoover, NSDAP Hauptarchiv, reel 88, folder 1839.

39. Activity Report of the Kiel NSDStB, Winter Semester 1929/30, Würzburg, NSDStB, 7-alpha 463; *Völkischer Beobachter,* clipping 1930, Hoover, NSDAP Hauptarchiv, reel 88, folder 1839; Report of the work of the NSDStB group in Breslau, 24 May 1927, Würzburg, NSDStB, 2-alpha 460.

40. *Bayerische Hochschulzeitung,* 26 January 1928, Hoover, NSDAP Hauptarchiv, reel 88, 1839.

41. Activity report of NSDStB, Kiel, Winter Semester, 1929–30, Würzburg, NSDStB, 7-alpha 463.

42. Paul Steigleider to NSDStB leadership, 15 July 1929, Würzburg, NSDStB 2-alpha 460.

43. NSDStB-Breslau, report on the Winter Semester of 1927/28, 6 March 1928, Würzburg, NSDStB, 2-alpha 460.

44. "Themen für die Arbeitsgruppen des NSDStB, SS. 1931," Würzburg, NSDStB, 7-alpha 463.

45. Von Leers to Merzdorf, 24 October 1932, Würzburg, NSDStB, 15-alpha 470.

46. NSDStB-Göttingen to NSDStB leadership, 12 June 1929, Würzburg, NSDStB 4-alpha 39.

47. April 1931, Würzburg, NSDStB, 14-alpha 469.

48. NSDStB leadership, circular letter, 24 September 1931, Würzburg, Hamburg student records, alpha 512.

49. Draft of a letter by the national leader of education, Würzburg, NSDStB, 15-alpha 470.

50. Report of the National leader for education, 15 October 1932, Würzburg, NSDStB 15-alpha 470.

51. Reel 88, folder 1839, "Was sind wir und was wollen wir?" Hoover, NSDAP Hauptarchiv. The leaflet was also published in *Junge Revolutionär*, the Student Union journal, in July 1927.

52. "Leitgedanken in den Fragen der Hochschulreform," *Die Bewegung*, 27 January 1931.

53. "Hochschulreform und Wissenschaft," manuscript by Andreas Feickert, Würzburg, DSt. 1*06-theta 340.

54. Hans Glauning, "Verbindungsstudent und Nationalsozialismus," *Nationalsozialistische Hochschulbriefe*, 15 December 1926.

55. Paul Steigleider (Bonn) to NSDStB leadership, 5 July 1929, Würzburg, NSDStB 2-alpha 460; NSDStB-Königsberg to NSDStB leadership, 15 August 1928, Würzburg, NSDStB, 7-alpha 463; "Von der alten zur neuen Front: Adolf Hitler vor dem Münchener Studenten," *Völkischer Beobachter*, 22 November 1928, Hoover, NSDAP Hauptarchiv, reel 88, folder 1839; Horst Bernhardi, "Die Göttinger Burschenschaft 1933 bis 1945," *Quellen zur Geschichte der deutschen Einheitsbewegung in neunzenten jahrhundert* (Heidelberg: Carl Winter Universitätsverlag, 1957), pp. 207–8.

56. NSDStB-Hannover to Gerhard Krüger, list of trustworthy men, 1932, Würzburg, NSDStB A128-alpha 64; Klitzing (NSDStB Göttingen), to NSDStB national leadership, 1 February 1929, Würzburg, NSDStB 4-alpha 39; Stäbel (NSDStB-Karlsruhe) to NSDStB leadership, 25 April 1930, Würzburg, NSDStB 6-alpha 462.

57. Prince Hubertus zu Löwenstein, *Towards the Further Shore* (London: Victor Gollancz Ltd., 1968), p. 59.

58. Kurt Krüger, "Die Erneuerung der studentischen Verbindungen durch den Nationalsozialismus," *Akademischer Beobachter*, December 1929.

59. Christian Zinsser to Tempel, 22 June 1928, Würzburg NSDStB, 1-alpha 459.

60. Police report, 5 August 1929, Merseburg, Innern, Rep. 77, Titel 4043, Nr. 266, item 70; "Zur Aufklärung," *Der Wehrschafter*, June 1929, pp. 53–54.

61. E. Strömsdörfer to NSDStB, 24 July 1929, Würzburg NSDStB 19-alpha 479.

62. Schirach to Strömsdörfer, 7 December 1929; Strömsdörfer to Schirach, 18 January 1930; Results of the discussions between NSDStB and DW, 12 January 1930, Würzburg, NSDStB 19-alpha 472; Circular letter to NSDStB group leaders, 26 February 1930, circular letter, 20 January 1930, Würzburg, NSDStB 14-alpha 469.

63. Schirach to Joachim Glatzer, 21 February 1930, Schirach to Glatzer, 14 April 1930, Schirach to Glatzer, 8 May 1930, Würzburg, NSDStB 19-alpha 472.

64. "Gründung einer Nationalsozialistischen Deutschen Studentenschaft," 1 March 1930, Hoover, NSDAP Hauptarchiv, Reel 20, item 376.

65. Schirach to Georg Schumann, 23 May 1930, Würzburg, NSDStB, 11-alpha 467; Schirach to Werner Kleen, 9 May 1930, Würzburg, NSDStB 6-alpha 462; Schirach to Kinckebusch, 18 June 1930, NSDStB 1-alpha 459.

66. Gerhard Wobith, "Um die Zukunft der Studentenschaft," *Akademische Blätter*, 15 September 1931, pp. 154–56; Oswald Morenz, "Die Sendung des Nationalsozialismus im

Lichte der deutschen Not,'' *Akademische Blätter,* 15 September 1930, pp. 152–54; Turnerschaft political committee, 16 December 1931, Würzburg, NSDStB 19-alpha 479.

67. Werner Zintarra, ''Nationalsozialismus und Waffenstudententum,'' *Burschenschaftliche Blätter,* January 1931.

68. Walter Werner Reich, ''Nationalsozialismus und Waffenstudententum,'' *Burschenschaftliche Blätter,* May 1931, pp. 188–90; Erhard Pohlandt, ''Burschenschaft als Bewegung,'' ibid., May 1931, pp. 201–2; Walter Eckel, ''Politik und Partei,'' ibid., May 1931, pp. 202–3; Werner Zintarra, Um die Stellung der Korporationen zum Nationalsozialismus,'' ibid., May 1931, pp. 210–11; Friedel Schmitz, ''Nationalsozialismus und Waffenstudententum,'' ibid., June 1931, pp. 236–37; Otto Bickel, ''Was will der Nat.-Soz. Deutsche Studentenbund?'' ibid., June 1931, p. 237. Friedel Schmitz, ''Nationalsozialismus und Waffenstudententum,'' ibid., April 1931; Hans Lude, ''Burschenschaft und Nationalsozialismus,'' ibid., August/September 1931, pp. 284–85.

69. Hans Glauning, ''Burschenschaft und Nationalsozialismus,'' *Burschenschaftliche Blätter,* August/September 1931, pp. 282–84.

70. Schirach, *Ich glaubte an Hitler,* pp. 127–37.

71. See chapter 2.

72. NSDStB Stuttgart to NSDStB leadership, 1 December 1930, Würzburg, NSDStB 11-alpha 467; *Burschenschaftliche Wege,* May 1931, pp. 6–7.

73. Würzburg, NSDStB, 19-alpha 472.

74. Ibid.

75. Gerhard Schröder to Walter Lienau, 5 June 1931; Lienau to Schröder, 10 June 1931, Würzburg, NSDStB, 19-alpha 479.

76. Chapter 7.

77. Schröder to Lienau, 2 July 1931, Schröder to Hilgenstock, Kersten, Teutloff, Kunze, Kuhnke, Teigeler, Heinricht and Lienau, 18 May 1931, Würzburg, NSDStB 19-alpha 472; Report of the negotiations with the KSCV about the honor agreement, 10 October 1931, Würzburg, DSt., 1*04, C3; Minutes of the negotiations between NSDStB and HKSCV, 10 October 1931, New draft of the Erfurt agreement, 4 November 1931, circular letter of the political committee of the Turnerschaften, 16 December 1931, Würzburg, NSDStB 19-alpha 479; Gerhard Krüger, circular letter, 18 December 1931, Würzburg, Hamburg student records, alpha 510; Hans Börner to Schirach, 30 November 1931, captured documents (Krüger correspondence), T81, roll 259, 5051080-85.

78. Würzburg NSDStB Führer to Adolf Hitler, 17 April 1930, Würzburg student records, IV3.

79. *Academia,* 15 January 1931, p. 273.

80. Dr. P. Erhard Schlund O.F.M. Vc, ''Die Religion in Programm u. Praxis der Nationalsozialist. Deutsch. Arbeiterpartei,'' *Academia,* 15 July 1930, pp. 53–56.

81. Dr. P. Erhard Schlund, ''Richtigstellungen,'' *Academia,* 15 February 1931, pp. 291–93.

82. ''Vorortsübergabe und Gesamtausschuss-sitzung in München,'' *Academia,* 15 March 1932; ''CV und Nationalsozialismus,'' *Academia,* 15 April 1932, p. 333; ''Aus den Beschlüssen der 61. C.V. Versammlung,'' *Academia,* 15 September 1932, pp. 136–37; Hans Müller, *Katholische Kirche und Nationalsozialismus* (Munich: Nymphenburger Verlagshandlung, 1963), p. 42.

83. Hildebrandt to Krüger, 9 August 1932, Würzburg, DSt. 1*04, C16.

Chapter Six

1. Werner Klose, *Generation im Gleichschritt* (Oldenburg and Hamburg: Gerhard Stalling Verlag, 1964), p. 16.

2. Letter to national leadership, November 1927, Würzburg, NSDStB, 17-alpha 471; Business leader of the NSDStB to Hans-Joachim Wendenburg, 6 March 1930, NSDStB, 5-alpha 461; report of the NSDStB group in Kiel, Winter Semester 1929/30, Würzburg, NSDStB, 7-alpha 463; Rühle to Walter Funk, 9 October 1932, captured documents (*Reichsstudentenführung,*) T81 roll 236, 5020648-49; Bündesführer, circular letter No. 26, Würzburg, Würzburg student records, IV9; Report of the Officer for University Politics for the month of August, 3 September 1932, Würzburg, DSt., 1*02 C2.

3. Entrance declaration for NSDStB, Berlin, 1926, Würzburg, NSDStB 1-alpha 459; Schirach to Georg Scherdin, 12 January 1928, NSDStB 1-alpha 459; constitution of the NSDStB, Würzburg, NSDStB, 14 alpha 469.

4. See above, Chapter 5.

5. See Kater, *Studentenschaft . . .,* pp. 173–85.

6. Würzburg, NSDStB, 4-alpha 39.

7. Schirach to Hildebrandt, 12 January 1931, Würzburg, NSDStB, 2-alpha 460.

8. Records of Reich Ministry of the Interior, Hoover, NSDStB Hauptarchiv, Reel 34A, folder 1796; NSDStB Hannover, 30 May 1930, Würzburg, NSDStB, 5-alpha 461.

9. NSDStB Cologne, circular letter, 29 June 1929, Merseburg, K, W & V, Rep. 76, Va, 1, Titel XII, Nr. 25, Bd. V, item 137.

10. See Kater, *Studentenschaft . . .,* p. 186.

11. Ibid., pp. 186–93.

12. NSDStB Cologne, circular letter, 26 June 1929, op. cit. Party posts most commonly held by students in 1929 were party speaker (thirty-five), press officer (sixteen), and local group secretary (eighteen).

13. NSDStB leadership to NSDStB Darmstadt, 30 November 1929, captured documents (Reichsstudentenführung), T81, roll 236, 5020636.

14. Captured documents (Reichsstudentenführung), T81, roll 239, 5024772.

15. Membership situation of the NSDStB, 1 September 1932–1 March 1933, Würzburg, 17-alpha 671.

16. For a general summary of student council elections, see Adolf Leisen, "Die Ausbreitung des völkischen Gedankens in der Studentenschaft der Weimarer Republik," unpublished dissertation (Heidelberg, 1964), appendix 2, pp. 280–94.

17. Ibid., p. 280; also Prussian Interior Minister to Prussian Minister of Culture, 6 August 1930, Merseburg, K, W & V, Rep. 76, Va, 1, Titel XII, Nr. 42, Bd. 1, item 135.

18. Report of election committee, Würzburg, Würzburg student records, IV X5; *DSt. Nachrichtenblatt,* 1 May 1928, p. 278; *Der Jungdeutsche,* 26 February 1930; "Sieg der Berliner Studentenwahl," *Berliner Lokalanzeiger,* 7 July 1929, Merseburg, Innern, Rep. 77, Titel 4043, Nr. 260, item 95; "Halle Kammerwahl," Frankfurt, DSt., Bd. 121; Ludwig Franz, "Der Politische Kampf an den Münchener Hochschulen von 1929–1933," unpublished dissertation (Munich, 1949), p. 58; Kurt Hirche, "Der Faschismus der Studentenschaft," *Die Hilfe,* 31 January 1931, pp. 105–109; "Die Braunen Bataillone auf den Hochschulen," *Westdeutscher Beobachter,* 9 July 1931, Würzburg, NSDStB, 21-alpha 474.

19. "Adolf Hitler an die deutsche Studentenschaft," *Völkischer Beobachter,* 4 July 1930, Hoover, NSDAP Hauptarchiv, Reel 88, Folder 1839; "Röhm und Wagner vor Münchens Studenten," *Völkischer Beobachter,* 21 November 1930, ibid.; Puls to NSDStB Reichsleitung, 8 January 1932, Würzburg, NSDStB, 11-alpha 459; Engelken to Krüger, 20 January 1933, captured documents (Reichsstudentenführung), T81, roll 259, 5051117; Schirach to Horst Munske, Würzburg, 7-alpha 463; NSDStB Giessen to NSDStB Würzburg, NSDStB, 4-alpha 39; Bericht über die Astawahlen an der Universität Berlin, captured documents (Reichsstudentenführung), T81, roll 259, 5051294.

20. Knoth to NSDStB, Heurt (July) 2, 1929, Würzburg, NSDStB, 11-alpha 467; *Geschichte der Universität Jena: Festgabe zum vierhundertjährigen Universitätsjubiläum,*

Vol I (Jena: Fischer Verlag, 1958), p. 603; Zingenbein (Kiel) to Schirach, 22 February 1929, NSDStB, 7-alpha 463.

21. Reich leadership, circular letter, 17 January 1929, Würzburg, NSDStB, 14-alpha 469; Glauning to Reuss (Hamburg), 29 January 1928, NSDStB 5-alpha 461.

22. Gerhard Krüger, Officer for university politics, circular letter, 18 December 1931, Würzburg, Hamburg student records, alpha 510; Nolte (Marburg) to DSt. executive board, no date, Frankfurt, Bd. 78.

23. 12 February 1930, Würzburg, NSDStB, 11-alpha 467; Blumel to Stäbel, 30 November 1932, NSDStB, 65-alpha 604.

24. Order regarding the relationship between National Socialist representatives in the DSt. organization and the offices of the NSDStB, 1 September 1931, Würzburg, Würzburg student records, IV 31.

25. Captured documents (Reichsstudentenführung), T81, roll 259, 5051194.

26. NSDStB Business Führer to Dr. v. Renteln (NSDStB Berlin), 21 January 1929, Würzburg, NSDStB 1-alpha 459.

27. H. D. A. Greifswald, declaration, 5 May 1930, Frankfurt, DSt., Bd. 120; Activity Report of the NSDStB group in Kiel, winter semester 1929/30, 28 February 1930, Würzburg, NSDStB, 7-alpha 463.

28. NSDStB Munich to Johann Ludwig v. Eichborn (NSDStB, Breslau), 2 July 1929, Würzburg, NSDStB, 2-alpha 460; Johann Eichborn to NSDStB leadership, 28 June 1929, ibid.

29. NSDStB, Munich to Johann Ludwig v. Eichborn (NSDStB, Breslau), 2 July 1929, Würzburg, NSDStB, 2-alpha 460; Karl Königstein (Greifswald) to Schirach, 6 June 1930, Würzburg, NSDStB, 2-alpha 460.

30. Activity report of NSDStB group, Kiel, winter semester, 1929/30, 29 February 1930, Würzburg, NSDStB, 7-alpha 463; Ilg to v. Kunsberg, 7 March 1931, Würzburg, Würzburg student reports, IV3; Hildebrandt (Bonn) to Schirach, 28 February 1932, Würzburg, NSDStB, 2-alpha 460; H.v. Foldersahm to Schirach, 12 February 1930, Würzburg, NSDStB, 6-alpha 462.

31. Würzburg student records IV X5.

32. Haselmayer to Schirach, 30 March 1931, Würzburg, NSDStB, 5-alpha 461.

33. "Was sind wir und was wollen wir?" (1927), Hoover, NSDAP Hauptarchiv, reel 88, folder 1839.

34. Lenz (Bonn) to NSDStB leadership, 5 July 1929, Würzburg, NSDStB, 2-alpha 460; Paul Steiglider to NSDStB leadership, 13 July 1929, ibid.

35. *Deutsche Hochschulstatistik*, Sommerhalbjahr 1928.

36. Nabersberg (NSDStB Berlin) to DSt. executive board, 22 January 1929, Würzburg, NSDStB 1-alpha 459.

37. von Renteln (NSDStB Berlin) to Schirach, 7 February 1929, Würzburg, NSDStB, 1-alpha 459.

38. Press office of the Erlangen student government, 1 February 1929, Frankfurt, DSt., Bd. 111; Declaration of the student government of the University of Erlangen, 25 April 1929, ibid.

39. NSDStB leadership, circular letter, 10 February 1929, Würzburg, NSDStB, 14-alpha 469.

40. Ibid.

41. Unidentified clipping dated 21 June 1929, Würzburg, NSDStB, 10-alpha 466; Hans Wittmann (Giessen) to NSDStB leadership, 10 July 1927, Würzburg, NSDStB 4-alpha 39; Albrecht Götz von Olenhusen "Die 'Nichtarischen': Zur nationalsozialistischen Rassenpolitik 1933–45, *"Vierteljahrshefte für Zeitgeschichte,* April 1966, pp. 166–67.

42. "Karlsruhe Studentenschaft und Numerus Clausus, oder deutscher Studentenmut," manuscript dated 12 June 1929, Würzburg, NSDStB, 6-alpha 462; Emil Hesselmann, 13

June 1929, Würzburg, NSDStB 6-alpha 462; NSDStB-Tübingen to NSDStB leadership, 18 Heuert (July) 1929, Würzburg, NSDStB, 11-alpha 467.

43. DSt. Halle to DSt. executive board, 19 August 1930, Frankfurt, DSt., Bd. 121; Circular letter, 3 July 1929, Frankfurt, DSt., Bd. 4.

44. "Bericht über den vom 20.-24.7.1929 in Hannover stattgefundenen Studententag," 31 July 1929, Merseburg, K, W & V, Rep. 76, Va, 1, Titel XVIII, Nr. 16, Bd. 7, items 296–300.

45. Minutes of the Central Committee of the DSt., on 7 and 8 February 1931, Würzburg, DSt., 1*01-theta 251.

46. Schirach to NSDStB Munich, 15 January 1929, Würzburg, NSDStB, 10-alpha 466.

47. Schirach to Ferdinand Bohlmann, 27 February 1930, Schirach to Bohlmann, 25 February 1930, statement of Rector Planitz and university council Graven, 17 February 1930, Würzburg, NSDStB, 7-alpha 463.

48. Bodo Danert to Hamburg NSDStB, 30 June 1931; Heinrichsdorf to Danert, 6 July 1931 and 8 July 1931, Würzburg, Hamburg student records, alpha 523.

49. von Renteln to Schirach, 7 March 1928, Würzburg, NSDStB, 1-alpha 459; report about the events of the last four weeks in Braunschweig, 16 January 1931, Frankfurt DSt., Bd. 96; Reich Ministry of the Interior report, Hoover, NSDAP Hauptarchiv 2068, reel 34A, folder 1769 IAN 2100 m./30 8; Ludwig Franz, *Politische Kampf...*, pp. 26–27; Merseburg, K, W & V, Rep. 76, Va, 1, Titel XII, Nr. 42, Bd. 1, item 322.

50. *Angriff*, 29 November 1929, p. 6, Würzburg, NSDStB, 1-alpha 459.

51. "Professoren und Studenten in einer Front!" *Der Student: D.A.R.*, July 1929, p. 8.

52. Oswalt v. Nostiz, "Die Berliner Vorgänge," *Der Student: D.A.R.*, July 1929, pp. 7–8; Selection from the report of the Police President in Berlin, 5 July 1929. Merseburg, Innern, Rep. 77, Titel 4043, Nr. 260, items 149–50; "Burschen Heraus," *Burschenschaftliche Wege*, August 1929.

53. "Burschen Heraus," *Burschenschaftliche Wege*, August 1929.

54. Entrance of the police into the University of Berlin, 12 November 1929, regional leader X of the DSt. to Fregattenkapitan Götting, 4 October 1930, Frankfurt, DSt., Bd. 84; Merseburg, Innern, Rep. 77, Titel 4043, Nr. 260, items 151–52.

55. Even the July events did not produce complete student support of the Berlin students. A plenary meeting of the University of Jena student body voted down a resolution for a mass demonstration protesting the actions of the Berlin police. The Nazis and the Stahlhelm had to organize their own demonstration. See Schimmel (NSDStB Jena) to NSDStB leadership, 5 July 1929, Würzburg, NSDStB, 6-alpha 462.

56. M. Vogel to DSt. executive board and Regions VIII and X, Frankfurt, DSt., Bd. 73.

57. DSt. executive board, 27 November 1929, Frankfurt, DSt, Bd. 5.

58. E. F. Peiper, NSDStB Halle, 11 July 1930, Würzburg, NSDStB, 5-alpha 461.

59. Reich Ministry of the Interior, Hoover, NSDAP Hauptarchiv, 2068, reel 34A, folder 1769, IAN 2100 m/30.8.

60. Ludwig Franz, *Politische Kampf...*, pp. 108–10; *Münchener Post*, 15/16 November 1930.

61. *Geschichte der Universität Jena...*, p. 605.

62. Hoover, NSDAP Hauptarchiv, reel 53, folder 1264 (Schirach correspondence); Herbert Fuhrmann, "Protest gegen Versailles," *Deutsche Studenten-Zeitung*, 22 November 1934, p. 7; Baldur von Schirach, *Ich glaubte an Hitler* (Hamburg: Mosaik Verlag, 1967), pp. 95–96.

63. Kleine Anfrage Nr. 862, Merseburg Innern, Rep. 77, Titel 4043, Nr. 260, item 124.

64. *Sozialdemokratische Partei-Korrespondenz*, April 1929, pp. 159–60.

65. Ilg to NSDStB group Freiburg, 1 July 1931, Würzburg, Würzburg student records IV3.

66. Reich Minister of the Interior, Hoover, NSDAP Hauptarchiv, 2068, reel 34A, folder 1769, IAN 2100, m/30.8; NSDStB, Kiel to the NSDStB leadership, 17 October 1930, Würzburg, NSDStB, 7-alpha 463.

67. Entrance of the Police into the university and university buildings, Order of the Ministry of the Interior of 28 November 1930, Merseburg, K, W & V, Rep. 76, Va, 1, Titel XII, Nr. 42, Bd. 1, item 210; *Kreuzzeitung*, 4 December 1930, ibid., item 184.

68. "Entschliessung der Hochschulrektoren," *Deutsche Allgemeine Zeitung*, 2 December 1930, Merseburg, K, W & V, Rep. 76, Va, 1, Titel XII, Nr. 42, Bd. 1, item 180.

69. *Völkischer Beobachter*, 2 July 1931, Merseburg, Innern, Rep. 77, Titel 4043, Nr. 260, item 223.

70. Bavarian State Ministry for Instruction and Culture to Prussian Minister of Culture, 4 October 1930, Merseburg, K, W & V, Rep. 76, Va, 1, Titel XII, Nr. 42, Bd. I, item 322.

71. Grimme to rectors and senates of Prussian universities, 2 July 1931, Merseburg, K, W & V, Rep. 76, Va, 1, Titel XII, Nr. 42, Bd. 1, items 235–36.

72. Documents and newspaper clippings relating to the Nawiasky affair have been assembled by Franz, *Politische Kampf . . .*, pp. 75–98; Nawiasky distributed a pamphlet in August 1931 retelling his version of the incident: Hans Nawiasky, *Die Münchener Universitätskrawalle* (Munich, 1931). A discussion also appears in Leisen, *Die Ausbreitung des völkischen Gedankens . . .*, pp. 164–66.

73. Nawiasky, *Die Münchener Universitätskrawalle*, p. 2.

74. Franz, *Politische Kampf . . .*, pp. 75–77.

75. Franz, *Politische Kampf . . .*, pp. 77–79; captured documents (Reichsstudentenführung), T81, roll 259, 5051461.

76. Franz, *Politische Kampf . . .*, pp. 80–81.

77. Nawiasky, *Die Münchener Universitätskrawalle*, p. 10.

78. Franz, *Politische Kampf . . .*, p. 81.

79. Nawiasky, *Die Münchener Universitätskrawalle*, p. 11.

80. Franz, *Politische Kampf . . .*, pp. 82–84; captured documents (Gerhard Krüger correspondence), T81, roll 259, 5051461.

81. Franz, *Politische Kampf . . .*, pp. 85–86.

82. Franz, *Politische Kampf . . .*, p. 87.

83. Ibid., p. 88.

84. Ibid., pp. 97–98.

85. See full account in Steinberg, pp. 545–63. See also Werner Prokoph, "Die politische Seite des Falles Dehn'—Zum Faschisierungsprozess an der Universität Halle-Wittenberg in den Jahren 1931 bis 1933," *Festschrift anlässlich des 150. Jahrestages der Vereinigung der Universitäten Wittenberg und Halle, Wissenschaftliche Zeitschrift der Martin-Luther-Universität Halle-Wittenberg. Gesellschafts- und Sprachwissenschaftliche Reihe*, XVI, 2/3 (1967); DSt. position on the Dehn case, captured documents (Gerhard Krüger correspondence), T81, roll 259, 5051107-10; "Der Fall Dehn 2. Teil: 'Der Kampf um D. Dehn,'" Würzburg, 1*07-theta 371. Dehn left Halle under pressure on a two-semester leave in the fall of 1932. His name was on the first list of sixteen professors suspended in April 1933 under the "Law for the Reconstruction of the Career Civil Service."

86. See Steinberg, pp. 563–66.

87. Report by W. Kadehose and Matthaeas, Würzburg, NSDStB, 23-alpha 474; NSDStB Breslau to G. Krüger, 21 November 1932, captured documents (Krüger correspondence) T81, roll 259, 5051354-55; Report of the visit of Reichskommissar Professor

Kaehler in relation to the Cohn case, 21 November 1932, Würzburg, DSt. 1*07-theta 370; Gerhard Krüger to Walther Schlötter, 28 November 1932, ibid.; Leisen, "Die Ausbreitung...," pp. 166–67; *Breslauer Neueste Nachrichten*, 1 February 1933, Wurzburg, NSDStB, 21-alpha 474.

88. NSDStB Leipzig to Gerhard Krüger, Würzburg, NSDStB A128-alpha 64.

89. Fritz Hilgenstock, "Die Deutsche Studentenschaft, studentische Verbände und Nationalsozialistischer Studentenbund," *Burschenschaftliche Blätter*, January 1932, Würzburg NSDStB, 19-alpha 479; DSt. exec. board to DSt. of Halle-Wittenberg, 16 November 1931, Frankfurt, DSt., Bd. 121.

90. *Geschichte der Universität Jena...*, p. 605

91. 12 November 1930, Würzburg, NSDStB, A128-alpha 64; *Burschenscahftliche Blätter*, June 1930, p. 220.

92. "Abschluss des Deutschen Studententages," *Breslauer Zeitung*, 30 July 1930, Merseburg, K, W & V, Rep. 76, Va, 1, Titel XII, Abt. Nr. 38, Bd. 2.

93. *Sudetendeutsche Akademische Zeitung*, 15 August 1930, pp. 1–9; *Deutscher Akademiker Zeitung*, 15 August 1930, pp. 1–4.

94. As cited in Helmut Kuhn, "Die Deutsche Universität am Vorabend der Machtergreifung," *Zeitschrift für Politik* 13 (3, 1966): 243–44.

Chapter Seven

1. Würzburg, DSt., 1*03-theta 254.

2. Free Student Government, Breslau to DSt. Exec. board, 28 April 1928, Frankfurt, DSt., Bd. 97.

3. Report of the negotiations at the extraordinary Germany university conference at Berlin, 18 April 1928, Merseburg, K, W & V, Rep. 76, Va, 1, Titel XVIII, Nr. 16, Bd. VI, item 381; Dr. Woelker, Saxon Ministry of Education to Dr. M. Kloss, Merseburg, K, W & V, Rep. 76, Va, 1, Titel XVIII, Nr. 16, Bd. VI, Nr. 38; Report of the regional meeting in Darmstadt, 19 June 1928, Frankfurt, DSt., Bd. 79.

4. Merseburg, K, W & V, Rep. 76, Va, 1, Titel XVIII, Nr. 16, Bd. 7, items 147–49; "Bayern und die Deutsche Studentenschaft," *Nachrichtenblatt der Deutschen Studentenschaft*, May 1929, p. 13; Richter (Prussian Ministry of Culture) to Müller (Bavarian Ministry of Education and Culture), 30 March 1929, Merseburg, K, W & V, Rep. 76, Va, 1, Titel XVIII, Nr. 16, Bd. 7, item 52; Goldenberger to Becker, 27 March 1929, Becker to Goldenberger, 11 April 1929, Merseburg, K, W & V, Rep. 76, Va, 1, Titel XVIII, Nr. 16, Bd. 7, Items 57–58.

5. Merseburg, K, W & V, Rep. 76, Va, 1, Titel XVIII, Nr. 16, Bd. 7, items 145–46.

6. The position of the student government of the University of Munich regarding the petition of the *Freie Hochschulgruppe* and other organizations to the Bavarian Ministry of Education and Culture, 1 June 1929, Würzburg, NSDStB, 10-alpha 466.

7. Report of the negotiations at the German university conference on 17 and 18 September 1929, Merseburg, K, W & V, Rep. 76, Va, Sekt. 1, Titel XVIII, Nr. 16, Bd. 7, item 379.

8. Bavarian Ministry for Education and Culture to Senate Curators, 7 November 1929, Merseburg, K, W & V, Rep. 76, Va 1, Titel XVIII, Nr. 16, Bd. 7, item 333.

9. Wolfgang Zorn, "Die politische Entwicklung des deutschen Studententums, 1918–31," *Darstellungen und Quellen zur Geschichte der deutschen Einheitsbewegung im neunzehnten und zwanzigsten Jahrhundert*, Vol 5 (Heidelberg: Carl Winter-Universitätsverlag, 1965), p. 301.

10. Bavarian State Ministry for Education and Culture to Senates, 12 February 1930, Merseburg, K, W & V, Rep. 76, Va, 1, Titel XVIII, Nr. 16, Bd. 8, item 4; Württemberg

Ministry to universities, ibid., item 7; Konrad Welte (DSt. Bavaria) to Erich Hoffmann (DSt. Chairman), 13 January 1930, Frankfurt, DSt., Bd. 80.

11. Report of the negotiations of the region VII delegation with Minister Goldenberger, Frankfurt, DSt., Bd. 80.

12. Lienau to DSt. exec. board, 10 November 1931, Frankfurt, DSt., Bd. 80.

13. The situation in Hamburg up until 15 May 1929—report, Frankfurt, DSt., Bd. 122; Hamburg student chairman to H. H. Schulz (DSt. Chairman), 9 December 1930, Würzburg, NSDStB, 5-alpha 461.

14. Activities report of the Hamburg student government for winter semester 1928/29 and summer semester 1929, Frankfurt, DSt., Bd. 122; Kersten, DSt. exec. board to Ernest Möller, 16 November 1928, Frankfurt, DSt., Bd. 122; Hamburg student chairman to H. H. Schulz, 9 December 1930, Würzburg, NSDStB, 5-alpha 461.

15. A. Bachmann to DSt. exec. board, 15 May 1930, DSt., Bd. 122; Heinrichsdorff to DSt. exec. board, 28 November 1931, ibid.; student council minutes, 3 June 1932, Würzburg, Hamburg student records, alpha 514.

16. "Mitteilung des Ministeriums für Volksbildung an das Rektorat der Universität Leipzig zur Deutschen Studentenschaft," 9 December 1928, Würzburg, NSDStB, 8-alpha 464; Report of NSDStB Dresden, Winter Semester, 1929–30, Würzburg, NSDStB, 20-alpha 473; Döring (Leipzig) to NSDStB leadership, 16 December 1928, Würzburg, NSDStB 8-alpha 464; Döring to NSDStB leadership, 16 November 1928, ibid.; Hermann Neumann to Walter Schmadel, 11 January 1929, Frankfurt, DSt., Bd. 77; Report of the assembly in Dresden, 26 February 1930, ibid., Bd. 105; excerpt from the minutes of the Dresden student council meeting of 3 February 1930, ibid.

17. Report about the negotiations of the German university conference in Herrenchiemsee on 22 and 23 September 1930, Merseburg, K, W & V, Rep. 76, Va, 1, Titel XVIII, Nr. 16, Bd. 8, items 121–22.

18. Frankfurt, DSt., Bd. 126; Exec. board of DSt. to members of central committee, 26 March 1930, Frankfurt, DSt. Bd. 10.

19. Freiheitliche Studentenschaften an der Universität und Technischen Hochschule Berlin to Becker, 30 January 1928, Merseburg, K, W & V, Rep. 76, Va, 1, Titel XII, Nr. 25, Bd. V, item 12; Berliner Tageblatt, 6 February 1938, ibid., item 15.

20. Exec. board of Deutscher Studentenverband to Becker, 15 December 1938, Merseburg, K, W & V, Rep. 76, Va, 1, Titel XVIII, Nr. 16, Bd. 7, items 35–38.

21. Prussian Min. of Culture to Prussian State Bank (Seehandlung), 27 June 1930, Merseburg, K, W & V, Rep. 76, Va, 1, Titel XII, Nr. 25, Bd. V, item 301; Görres Ring to Becker, Merseburg, K, W & V, Rep. 76, Va, 1, Titel XII, Nr. 24, Bd. II, item 274; Minister of Culture to Prussian State Bank, 25 July 1938, ibid., 286; Minister of Culture to Prussian State Bank, 7 August 1929, ibid., item 293; Minister of Culture to Prussian State Bank, 22 May 1929, Merseburg, K, W & V, Rep. 76, Va, 1, Titel XII, Nr. 25, Bd. V, item 103; Minister of Culture to Prussian State Bank, 1 July 1928, ibid. item 117.

22. Prussian Minister of Culture to Prussian Minister of the Interior, 24 April 1930, Merseburg, Innern, Rep. 77, Titel 4043, Nr. 260, item 142.

23. The only important exceptions were two of the four major Catholic leagues, the Kartellverband and Unitas, both of which refused to join in the united statement drawn up at the meeting. See DSt. exec. board, circular letter 16 February 1928, Frankfurt, DSt., Bd. 3; "Die studentischen Einzelgruppen für die DSt.," Deutsche Akademische Rundschau, 15 March 1928, pp. 7–8.

24. Regional Office I of DSt. to DSt. exec. Board, 13 March 1928, Frankfurt, DSt., Bd. 731; "Von den deutschen Hochschulen," Deutsche Akademische Rundschau, 1/15 May 1938.

25. Report of the meeting of the student fraternity leagues on 11 November 1928 in Berlin, Frankfurt, DSt., Bd. 4.

26. DSt. exec. bd. circular letter, 2 December 1929, Frankfurt, DSt., Bd. 194; Franz Schramm (Deutsche Sängerschaft) to DSt. exec. board, 11 February 1929, Frankfurt, DSt., Bd. 188; DSt. exec. board to Franz Schramm, 5 December 1928, ibid.; minutes of the central committee meeting of 20 and 21 June 1931, Frankfurt DSt., Bd. 11.

27. Gerhard Krüger to Reichstag deputy Mutschmann, 16 December 1931, Würzburg, NSDStB, 23-alpha 475; Wolf Bartosch (Vienna Technical Institute) to DSt. exec. board, 7 May 1928, Frankfurt, DSt., Bd. 81.

28. Minutes of the negotiations at the regular regional meeting of DSt. region I on 8–10 June 1928 in Königsberg, Frankfurt, DSt., Bd. 73; speech by Walter Schmadel in Danzig, "Zum Verfassungskampf der Deutschen Studentenschaft," Merseburg, K, W & V, Rep. 76, Va, 1, Titel XVIII, Nr. 16, Bd. VI, items 436–448.

29. See appendix to minutes of the regional meeting in Darmstadt on 21–22 May 1927, Frankfurt, DSt., Bd. 79 for a typical program.

30. DSt. exec. bd. circular letter, 4 November 1929, Frankfurt, DSt., Bd. 5; "Sonderbericht vom 13. Deutschen Studententag," *Sudetendeutsche Akademische Zeitung*, 15 August 1930.

31. DSt. exec. bd., circular letter, 5 May 1931, appendix 4, Frankfurt, DSt., Bd. 5.

32. DSt. exec. bd., circular letter, 18 October 1928, Frankfurt, DSt., Bd. 68.

33. DSt. exec. bd., circular letter, 1 June 1928, Frankfurt, DSt., Bd. 226.

34. Report of the demonstration against the war-guilt-lie, 28 June 1928, Frankfurt, DSt., Bd. 118; Deutscher Studentenverband to Becker, 15 December 1928, Merseburg, K, W & V, Rep. 76, Va, 1, Titel XVIII, Nr. 16, Bd. 7, items 35–38.

35. Preliminary papers for the twelfth German Student Convention in Hannover in 1929, Frankfurt, DSt., Bd. 4.

36. Ibid.

37. Circular letter to all NSDStB group leaders and representatives of the NSDStB to the Student Convention in Hannover, Würzburg, NSDStB, 14-alpha 469.

38. "Verlauf des Deutschen Studententages," *Der Student: Deutsche Akademische Rundschau*, early August 1929, pp. 4–8.

39. Schmadel to German Youth organizations, 28 June 1929, Frankfurt, DSt., Bd. 226; DSt. exec. bd. to signers of petition, no date, ibid.

40. Report of the police president on the German student convention in Hannover between 20 and 24 July 1929, 31 July 1929, Merseburg, K, W & V, Rep. 76, Va, 1, Titel XVIII, Nr. 16, Bd. 7, items 296–300; *Der Student: Deutsche Akademische Rundschau*, early August 1929, pp. 4–8.

41. Circular letter to all NSDStB group leaders and NSDStB representatives at the Hannover student convention, no date, Würzburg, NSDStB, 14-alpha 469.

42. DSt. exec. bd., circular letter, 30 October 1929, Frankfurt, DSt., Bd. 10; Free student government of the University of Greifswald to the DSt. exec. bd., 5 November 1929, Frankfurt, DSt., Bd. 120.

43. DSt. exec. bd., circular letter, 4 November 1929, Frankfurt, DSt., Bd. 5; DSt. exec. bd., report about the central committee meeting on 23 and 24 November in Berlin, 27 November 1929, Frankfurt, DSt., Bd. 10.

44. Lienau to DSt. exec. bd., Frankfurt, DSt., Bd. 80.

45. Friedrich Glombowski, "Kritische Bemerkungen zum 13. Studententag in Breslau," *Hallische Universitätszeitung*, 1 November 1930, Frankfurt, DSt., Bd. 11.

46. Minutes of the central committee meeting of 12, 13, and 14 December 1930, Würzburg, DSt., 1*01-theta 251; regional leader III to DSt. exec. board, student governments of Region III, et. al, 27 January 1931, Frankfurt, DSt., Bd. 76.

47. Statement of 12 March 1931, Würzburg, Hamburg student records, alpha 510.

48. "Studentenschaft unterstützt Volksbegehren," *Saale Zeitung*, clipping in Merseburg, K, W & V, Rep. 76, Va, 1, Titel XII, Nr. 42, Bd. I, item 209.

49. "Mitteilungsblatt für nationalsozialistische Vertreter in den Körperschaften der 'Deutschen Studentenschaft,' " Würzburg, NSDStB, 14-alpha 469.

50. Minutes of the central committee meeting of 16 July 1931, Frankfurt, DSt., Bd. 11.

51. Schirach to Graz NSDStB group, 29 May 1931, Würzburg, NSDStB, 4-alpha 39.

52. Report to Dr. Richter of the Prussian Ministry of Culture, 4 August 1931, Merseburg, K, W & V, Rep. 76, Va, 1, Titel XII, Nr. 38, Bd. 12, items 197–98.

53. *DSt. Akademische Correspondenz,* 21 July 1931, Merseburg, K, W & V, Rep. 76, Va, 1, Titel XII, Nr. 38, Bd. 12, items 191–92.

54. Ibid., item 194.

55. Ernst Mauke, "Der 14, Grazer Deutsche Studententag," *Burschenschaftliche Wege,* August 1931.

56. Office for Political Education of the DSt., circular letter, 19 November 1931, Würzburg, DSt., 1*50-theta 11.

57. DSt. Office for Political Education, circular letter, 22 February 1932, Würzburg, DSt., 1*50-theta 11.

58. DSt. Office for Political Education, circular letter, 2 January 1932, Würzburg, DSt., 1*50-theta 11.

59. Georg Schwarting (NSDStB group leader in Hannover) to Krüger, 17 December 1931, Würzburg, NSDStB a128-alpha 64.

60. *Geschichte der Universität Jena,* p. 598; Wigand (Hamburg Univ. rector) to Hamburg student council, 2 August 1932, Würzburg, Hamburg student records, alpha 516.

61. Stahlhelm university group and German National Student Union of Königsberg, 26 January 1932, Frankfurt, DSt., Bd. 216; Stahlhelm national office to DSt. exec. board, 3 February 1932, ibid.; Gerhard Krüger and Hans Gierlichs to Aschoff, 6 February 1932, ibid.

62. Berlin Police president to Minister of the Interior, 3 February 1932, Merseburg, Innern, Rep. 77, Titel 4043, Nr. 260, item 230.

63. DSt. Office for Political Education, circular letter, 10 March 1932, Würzburg, DSt., 1*50-theta 11; "Der Kampf der deutschen Jugend um ihren Lebensraum," Frankfurt, DSt., Bd. 78.

64. February 20, 1930, Würzburg, NSDStB, 23-alpha 475.

65. Correction of the Deutsche Burschenschaft to the minutes of the meeting of fraternity leagues on 7 May 1932, Frankfurt, DSt., Bd. 71.

66. Fritz Hilgenstock to the Burschenschaften, October 1931, Würzburg, DSt., 1*04 theta 311; Appendix to the circular letter of the student fraternity league service of 31 May 1932, Frankfurt, DSt., Bd. 13.

67. Correction of the Deutsche Burschenschaft to the minutes of the meeting of fraternity leagues on 7 May 1932, Frankfurt, DSt., Bd. 71.

68. Fritz Hilgenstock, "Die Deutsche Studentenschaft, Studentische Verbände und Nationalsozialistischer Studentenbund," *Burschenschaftliche Blätter,* January 1932.

69. DSt. exec. board, circular letter to the fraternity leagues , 9 March 1932, Frankfurt, DSt., Bd. 6.

70. Ellersiek (Regional leader, DSt. region VII) to DSt. exec. board, 5 March 1932, Frankfurt, DSt., Bd. 80; Gerhard Krüger to Ellersiek, 7 March 1932, ibid., regional leadership, DSt. region V, circular letter, 23 March 1932, ibid.; region VII, circular letter, 29 April 1932, Frankfurt, DSt., Bd. 80; DSt. exec. board, circular letter, 14 April 1932, Frankfurt, DSt., Bd. 6.

71. L. Retlau (Pseudonym for W. Lienau), "Der Pfahl im Fleisch," *Sturmfahne*, typed copy, Würzburg, DSt., 1*02, C.
72. Stäbel to Schirach, 15 November 1931, Würzburg, NSDStB, 19-alpha 479.
73. Lienau to Schirach, 16 November 1931, Würzburg, NSDStB, alpha 479-19; Börner (Halle) to Schirach, 30 November 1931, Würzburg, NSDStB, 5-alpha 461; Schirach to Börner, 15 December 1931, ibid.
74. Gerd Rühle to Baldur von Schirach, 13 January 1932, Würzburg, NSDStB, 19-alpha 479; Fritz Hilgenstock, "Die Deutsche Studentenschaft, studentische Verbände und Nationalsozialistischer Studentenbund," *Burschenschaftliche Blätter*, January 1932.
75. Captured documents (Reichsstudentenführung), T81, roll 236, 5020830.
76. Gerhard Krüger to fraternities, no date, Hamburg student records, alpha 510; Prof. Kloss, chairman of the financial advisory board of the DSt. to Gerhard Krüger, 5 February 1932, Würzburg, DSt. 1*02, C1.
77. Report of resignations, 5 April 1932, Merseburg, K, W & V, Rep. 76, Va, 1, Titel XVIII, Bd. VIII, Nr. 16, items 264–69; Kraak, Hilgenstock, Welte and Gierlichs to DSt. exec. Board, 20 March 1932, Frankfurt, DSt., Bd. 71.
78. NSDStB Reich business leader to Karl Pechartscheck, 27 March 1932, Würzburg, NSDStB, 5-alpha 461; DSt. exec. board, circular letter, A33 1931/32, 18 April 1932, Würzburg, DSt., 1*02, C1.
79. Statement of Gierlichs, Kraak, Schulz, Welte, 13 April 1932, Würzburg, DSt., 1*04-theta 307, Krüger to NSDStB regional leaders of the DSt. and the local groups, circular letter Nr. 15, Würzburg, DSt., 1*02, C2.
80. NSDStB Reich leadership to regional leaders, group leaders, National Socialist regional leaders in the DSt., and agents in the fraternity leagues, 10 May 1932, Frankfurt, DSt., Bd. 13.
81. Appendix to circular letter of the Student Fraternity League Service, 21 May 1932, Frankfurt, DSt., Bd. 13; "Deutsche Burschenschaft und hochschulpolitische Lage," *Burschenschaftliche Blätter*, 9 June 1932, pp. 201–2.
82. Frankfurt, DSt., Bd. 203.
83. NSDStB Reich leadership, Officer for university politics, circular letter, 9 June 1932, Würzburg, DSt., 1*02 C1; Dr. Kurt Valentin, "Der Königsberger Studententag," *Burschenschaftliche Wege*, Septermber 1932, pp. 13–14.
84. "15. Deutscher Studententag zu Königsberg, 16. 7. 32," *DSt. Akademische Correspondenz, Sonderkorrespondenz* Nr. 3, Merseburg, K, W & V, Rep. 76, Va, 1, Titel XII, Nr. 38, Bd. 12, items 209ff.
85. Ibid.
86. Ibid.
87. Ibid.
88. Study group, circular letter, 18 October 1932, Frankfurt, DSt., Bd. 26; DSt. exec. board, 6 October 1932, Würzburg, DSt., 1*04-theta 311.
89. Gerhard Krüger to Gregor Strasser, 22 November 1932, Würzburg, NSDStB, 23-alpha 475.
90. Ruth Carlsen, "Der Kampf um die Verfassung der Rostocker Studentenschaft 1932/33," *Wissenschaftliche Zeitschrift der Universität Rostock, Gesellschafts-und-Sprachwissenschaftliche Reihe*, 1964, p. 259. Carlsen's essay is a detailed study of the controversy over the proposed Rostock constitution.
91. University-political study group, 24 November 1932, Frankfurt, DSt., Bd. 26.
92. Carlsen, "Der Kampf ...," pp. 261–63; poster announcing referendum, Frankfurt, DSt., Bd. 74; 23 November 1932, Würzburg, NSDStB, A128-alpha 64.

93. Carlsen, "Der Kampf . . .," p. 260.
94. Carlsen, "Der Kampf . . .," p. 263; Schickert to Gerhard Krüger, 23 December 1932, Frankfurt, DSt., Bd. 76.
95. Werner Ruhberg, NSDStB Rostock to Krüger, 13 January 1933, Würzburg, NSDStB, A128-alpha 64.
96. Würzburg, NSDStB, A128-alpha 64.
97. Leaflet, January 1933, Würzburg, NSDStB, A128-alpha 64.
98. "Dr. Goebbels vor den Studenten," *Angriff*, 30 January 1933, Würzburg, NSDStB, 12-alpha 467.
99. Carlsen, "Der Kampf . . .," p. 266.
100. Ibid., p. 267.
101. Statement of student council in Jena, Frankfurt, DSt., Bd. 126; Preliminary statement of the program of Jena fraternity election list for the 1933 student council elections, *Geschichte der Universität Jena,* p. 649.
102. University-political study group of student fraternity leagues, circular letter, 12 December 1932, Frankfurt, DSt., Bd. 26.
103. University-political study group, circular letter, 22 February 1933, Frankfurt, DSt., Bd. 26.
104. University-political study group, circular letter, 24 November 1932, Frankfurt, DSt., Bd. 26.
105. Halle rector to Reich Kommissar of the Prussian Ministry of Culture, 11 January 1933, Merseburg, K, W & V, Rep. 76, Va, 1, Titel XVIII, Nr. 16, Bd. IX, item 108–21; Draft of a model constitution for the student governments, ibid., items 84–94; Reich Kommissar of the Prussian Ministry of Culture Kahler to University-political study group, 28 January 1933, ibid., item 130.
106. Gerhard Krüger to Rudolf Hess, 31 January 1933, Würzburg, DSt., 1*02, C2, 31 January 1933.
107. Report by Gerhard Krüger, September 1932, Würzburg, DSt., 1*02, C2; DSt. executive board, circular letter, 11 December 1932, Würzburg, DSt., 1*01-gamma 1933.
108. NSDStB, circular letter of the univ. supervisor, 10 January 1933, Würzburg, DSt., 1*02 C2.
109. DSt. exec. Bd. to Hilgenstock, 21 December 1932, Würzburg, DSt., 1*04-theta 311; Ulrich Kersten to Krüger, ibid., 9 January 1933; DSt. exec. Bd. to student fraternity leagues, 18 January 1933, ibid.; Lothar Grosse to Gerhard Krüger, 23 January 1933, Würzburg, DSt., 1*04-theta 311; Kersten to the fraternity leagues, 27 January 1933, ibid.
110. Coordinating committee of student fraternity leagues (Mittelstelle studentischer Verbände), circular letter, 13 December 1932, Würzburg, NSDStB, alpha 472.
111. Gerhard Krüger, report for the month of December 1932, 11 January 1933, Würzburg, DSt., 1*02, C2.
112. Klaus Schickert and Hans Werdauer to members of the student law committee of the student fraternity leagues, no date, Würzburg, DSt., 1*04-theta 311.
113. University-political study group, circular letter, 22 February 1933, Frankfurt, DSt., Bd. 26.

Chapter Eight

1. E. Günther Gründel, *Die Sendung der Jungen Generation* (Munich : C. H. Beck, 1933), p. 331.
2. Report of Prussian Interior Ministry, 4 January 1931, Merseburg, K, W & V, Rep. 76, Va, 1, Titel XII, Nr. 42, Bd. 1, items 195–96.

3. B. H. Berghahn, *Der Stahlhelm Bund der Frontsoldaten* (Düsseldorf: Droste Verlag, 1966), p. 100.
4. Ibid., p. 33.
5. Ibid., pp. 105–7.
6. Report of Prussian Minister of the Interior, 4 January 1931, Merseburg, K, W & V, Rep. 76, Va, 1, Titel XII, Nr. 42, Bd. 1, Items 195–96.
7. "Stahlhelm-Studententagung," *Der Student*, 15 June 1929, pp. 10–11; Report of the police president, 14 January 1930, Merseburg, K, W & V, Rep. 76, Va, 1, Titel XII, Nr. 42, Bd. 1, item 81.
8. "Die Arbeit dem Deutschen Hochschulrings 1929–30," DSt. Würzburg, 1*00-theta 166.
9. The regular conference of the German Hochschulring, 25–28 October 1928, Würzburg, NSDStB 554-alpha 453.
10. Conference at the Boitzenburg Castle, 25–28 October 1928, police report, 10 April 1929, Merseburg, Innern, Rep. 77, Titel 4042, Nr. 52, Bd. 1, item 139.
11. Hofmeier (NSDStB, Köthen) to NSDStB leadership, 1 November 1929, Würzburg, NSDStB, 8-alpha 464.
12. Prussian Minister of the Interior to Prussian Minister for Science, Art, and Popular Education, 29 October 1929, Merseburg, K, W & V, Rep. 76, Va, 1, Titel XII, Nr. 39, items 186–87.
13. The Work of the German Hochschulring, 1929/1930, Würzburg, DSt. 1*00-theta 166.
14. The Work of the German Hochschulring, 1929/1930, Würzburg, DSt. 1*00-theta 166.
15. Prussian Minister of Interior to the Prussian Minister for Science, Art, and Popular Education, 29 October 1929, Merseburg, K, W & V, Rep. 76, Va, 1, Titel XII, Nr. 39, items 186–87.
16. Police director of Nuremberg-Fürth, 22 September 1930, Hoover, NSDStB Hauptarchiv, Reel 34 A, folder 1796; "Military movement in the radical right student movement," Report of the Reich Minister of the Interior to Prussian Minister for Science, Art, and Popular Education, 29 October 1929, Merseburg, Rep. 76, Va, 1, Titel XII, Nr. 39, items 186–87.
17. Otto Schwab to fraternity leagues, 10 February 1931, Würzburg, DSt., 1*05 C4.
18. Otto Schwab to the fraternity leagues and the Academic Military Offices, 18 May 1931, Würzburg, DSt. 1*05 C4; minutes of the meeting of the fraternity leagues at the VDI house about the question of military work, 18 February 1931, ibid.
19. Hans-Joachim Düning, *Der SA-Student im Kampf um die Hochschule (1925–35)* (Weimar: Verlag Hermann Böhlaus Nachfolger, 1936), pp. 91–92.
20. Minutes of the regular Weinheimer Senioren Convent convention on 9 and 10 May 1932 and the joint meeting of the WSC with the Weinheimer Verband Alter Corpsstudenten on 9 and 10 May 1932, Frankfurt, DSt., Bd. 199.
21. October 24, 1932, Würzburg, Hamburg student records, alpha 522; 5 December 1932, Würzburg, Würzburg student records, IV3.
22. Report of the Military Office leader, 5 December 1932, Würzburg, Würzburg student records, IV3; 15 November 1932, Würzburg, Würzburg student records, IV16.
23. Report of the Military Office leader, 5 December 1932, Würzburg, Würzburg student records, IV3.
24. Student council secretary's report about the council meeting of 13 December 1932, 14 December 1932, Würzburg, Würzburg student records IV5.
25. Ibid.
26. Report of the government president of Wiesbaden, 9 April 1930, Merseburg,

Innern, Rep. 77, Titel 4043, Nr. 52, Bd. 1; 22 July 1930, Merseburg, K, W & V, Rep. 76, Va, 1, Titel XVIII, Nr. 16, Bd. VIII, items 85–91.

27. Groener to Chancellor Brüning, 1 August 1930, Bundesarchiv Koblenz R43 II/519 Reichskanzlei Akten betreffend Jugendertüchtigung, Zug. 3, Bd. 1, 18–20, item 18; Groener to Brüning, October 1930, ibid., 2V-6r, items 2–6.

28. Bundesarchiv Koblenz R43II/519 Reichskanzlei Akten betreffend Jugender- tüchtigung Zug 3, Bd. 1, 100 V-100R, items 50–69.

29. Report about the military-political education conference of the Deutsche Student- enschaft in Potsdam, June 1931, 7 July 1931, Würzburg, Hamburg student records, alpha 516.

30. Clipping, "Erlass des Reichspräsidenten über die Körperliche Ertüchtigung der Jugend," Wolffs Telegraphisches Büro, 14 September 1932, Bundesarchiv Koblenz, R43II/519 Reichskanzlei Akten betreffend Jugendertüchtigung, Zug 3, Bd. 1, 50V-69, item 100.

31. Francis L. Carsten, *The Reichswehr and Politics 1918–33*, (Oxford: Clarendon Press, 1966), pp. 354–55.

32. Minutes of the AWA leadership meeting in Berlin on 3 December 1932, Würzburg, DSt., 1*05 C4; Krüger to Oberregierungsrat Dr. Erbe, Reich Ministry of the Interior, captured documents, T81, roll 243, 5029357.

33. NSDStB Bundesleitung, St. B, order 4, 26 October 1932, Würzburg, Würzburg student records, IV 9.

34. NSDStB Bundesleitung, 17th memo of the Union's university supervisor, ibid.

35. Bundesführer Rühle to group leaders, 31 October 1932, Würzburg, NSDStB, 65-alpha 604; NSDStB. Bundesführer, Studentenbund order no. 4, 20 October 1932, Hoover, NSDAP Hauptarchiv, reel 34 A, folder 1796.

36. Studentenbund Order No. 2, 12 October 1932, Würzburg, Würzburg student records IV9.

37. Clipping, Gerd Rühle, "Nationalsozialistische Studentenbataillone?" *Völkischer Beobachter*, 23–24 October 1932, Hoover NSDAP Hauptarchiv, reel 34A, folder 1796.

38. Linde to Walter Schlüter, 18 November 1932, Würzburg, Würzburg student records, IV3; Linde to Hans Hildebrandt, 11 November 1932, ibid.; Linde to Kunsberg, 4 November 1932, ibid.; Report of Hellmut Merzdorf and Kurt Wagner, Leipzig, 25 Feb- ruary 1933, Würzburg, NSDStB A128-alpha 64.

39. Wolfgang Benz, "Vom freiwilligen Arbeitsdienst zur Arbeitsdienstpflicht," *Vier- teljahrshefte für Zeitgeschichte*, October 1968, pp. 317–21.

40. Ibid., p. 321.

41. Wolfgang Benz, "Vom freiwilligen Arbeitsdienst zur Arbeitsdienstpflicht," *Vier- teljahrshefte für Zeitgeschichte*, October 1968, p. 324.

42. Schulz to Prussian Ministry of Culture, Merseburg, K, W & V, Rep. 76, Va, 1, Titel 12, Abt. 38, Bd. XII, item 143; DSt, executive board, memo to the student govern- ments, appendix no. 6, 5 May 1931, Frankfurt, DSt., Bd. V.

43. Regional Office VI of the Deutsche Studentenschaft to Deutsche Studentenschaft executive board, 18 December 1930, Frankfurt, DSt., Bd. 79; Minutes of the negotiations at the regular regional meeting of region VI of the Deutsche Studentenschaft in Karlsruhe, 29–30 November 1930, ibid.

44. "Leitgedanken an den Fragen der Hochschulreform," *Die Bewegung*, 27 January 1931.

45. "Der 14. Deutsche Studententag," *Deutsche Akademische Zeitung*, 25 July 1931; DSt. executive board, memo to the members of the central committee, 7 March 1931, Würzburg, DSt. 1*01-theta 251.

46. Regional Office VII report on regional conference, 5–6 December 1931, Frankfurt,

DSt. Bd. 80; DSt. executive board circular letter, 27 January 1932, Würzburg, DSt. 1*70-gamma 305.

47. DSt. executive board circular letter, 27 January 1932, Würzburg, DSt. 1*70-gamma 305.

48. Wolf Müller to DSt. Office for Work Service, Würzburg, Hamburg student records, alpha 515.

49. Voluntary work service office of the Hamburg student government, Würzburg, DSt. 1*70-gamma 305.

50. Das Werkjahr für Abiturienten,'' lecture by Andreas Feickert, Würzburg, Hamburg student records, alpha 646.

51. NSDStB Bundesleitung, circular letter 19 of the University Supervisor, 31 October 1932, Würzburg, DSt. 1*02 C2.

52. Regional meeting of DSt. region VII in Erlangen, report on the lecture, "Arbeitsdienst und Werkjahr," by Andreas Feickert, 3 December 1932, Frankfurt, DSt. Bd. 80.

53. DSt. executive board, circular letter to student governments, 11 December 1932, Frankfurt, DSt., Bd. 227.

54. Report by Gerhard Krüger, January 1933, Würzburg, DSt. 1*05 C4.

55. Akademische Korrespondenz, 10 February 1933, Frankfurt, DSt., Bd. 227; "Freiwillige Meldung zum Werkhalbjahr 1933," Frankfurt, DSt., Bd. 203.

56. Ludwig Illig, "Die Herbsttagung des Görresrings," Academia, 15 January 1931, pp. 267–69.

57. "Die Beschlüsse der 61. CV. Versammlung," Academia, 15 September 1932, p. 138.

Chapter Nine

1. DSt. Führer, appendix to circular letter of 19 April 1933, Frankfurt, DSt., Bd. 7.

2. DSt. Akademische Korrespondenz, 10 March 1933, pp. 5–7; Heinrichsdorff, Hamburg to DSt. exec. board, 11 February 1933, Frankfurt, DSt., Bd. 122; Proske, U. Bonn Kurator to Prussian Minister of Culture, 8 February 1933, Merseburg, K, W & V, Rep. 76, Va, 1, Titel XVIII, Nr. 16, Bd. IX, item 135.

3. Hebeler, NSDStB, Berlin-Charlottenburg, 9 March 1933, captured documents (Gerhard Krüger correspondence), T81, roll 259, 5051201-07.

4. G. Krüger to Herbert Walendy (NSDStB, Jena), 16 February 1933, Würzburg, NSDStB, A128-alpha 64.

5. DSt. exec. board to Frick, 4 April 1933, Würzburg, DSt. 1*02 C2; Frick to educational administrators of the states, 11 April 1933, captured documents (NSDStB) T81, roll 260, 5051493.

6. DSt. exec board to A. Schiller, 7 April 1933, Frankfurt, DSt., Bd. 188.

7. Prussian student ordinance, April 1933, captured documents (NSDStB), roll 260, 5051497-503.

8. Krüger, circular letter, 28 February 1933, Würzburg, Hamburg student records, alpha 527.

9. Prussian Student Ordinance, April 1933, captured documents (NSDStB), T81, roll 260, 5051497-503.

10. Haupt (Prussian Ministry of Culture) to U. of Breslau Kurator, 29 May 1933, Merseburg, K, W & V, Rep. 76, Va, 1, Titel XVIII, Nr. 16, Bd. IX, item 204.

11. Constitution of the Deutsche Studentenschaft, April 1933, captured documents (Gemeinschaft Studentischer Verbände), T81, roll 81, 92467-69.

12. Merseburg, K, W & V, Rep. 76, Va, 1, Titel XVIII, Nr. 16, Bd. IX, item 272.

13. Austrian office of the DSt. to Andreas Feickert, 19 September 1934, Würzburg, DSt. 1*34-gamma 156.

14. DSt. constitution, captured documents (Miltenberger Ring), T81, roll 78, 90013-16.

15. Minutes of the DSt. central committee meeting on March 21 and 22, 1933, Frankfurt, DSt., Bd. 226.

16. DSt. Führer, circular letter, 11 May 1933, Würzburg, DSt., 1*01-gamma 2.

17. Prussian Minister of Culture to Prussian Rectors, 23 June 1933, Merseburg, K, W & V, Rep. 76, Va, 1, Titel XII, Nr. 42, Bd. 1, item 363.

18. Thuringian Minister of Education to Rector, University of Jena, 5 April 1933, Merseburg, K, W & V, Rep. 76, Va, 1, Titel XII, Nr. 42, Bd. 1, item 347; Niemann to Academic Club for the study of the new Russia, 10 April 1933, Würzburg, Hamburg, alpha 523.

19. Prussia, 29 June 1933, Merseburg, K, W & V, Rep. 76, Va, 1, Titel XII, Nr. 42, Bd. 1, item 367; Bavaria, 13 July 1933, ibid., item 384; Hamburg, 14 July 1933, ibid., item 385; Saxony, 24 July 1933, ibid., item 387.

20. Prussian Minister of Culture to universities, 14 October 1933, Merseburg, K, W & V, Rep. 76, Va, 1, Titel XII, Nr. 42, Bd. 1, item 457.

21. DSt. Führer, circular letter, 13 June 1933, Würzburg, DSt., 1*01-gamma 2.

22. Karl Blume to Führer of student gov't in Münster, captured documents (Reichsstudentenführer NSDStB), T81, roll 244, 5031105; Rust to Prussian rectors, 22 April 1933, Merseburg, K, W & V, Rep. 76, Va, 1, Titel XII, Nr. 35, Bd. 3, item 187.

23. NSDStB national leadership, 11 February 1933, Würzburg, NSDStB, 76-alpha 604.

24. "Studenten-Selbsthilfe gegen roten Terror," *Völkischer Beobachter*, 18/19 February 1933, Hoover, NSDAP Hauptarchiv, reel 34A, folder 1496.

25. NSDStB Regional Führer Donat (Region VIII), circular letter 6, Würzburg, NSDStB, A135-alpha 69.

26. Donat, circular letter 5, Würzburg, NSDStB, A135-alpha 69; Würzburg, DSt., 1*07-theta 32.

27. NSDStB national leadership, directive 2 of the Officer for Press and Propaganda, Würzburg, Hamburg student records, alpha 527.

28. Karl Dietrich Bracher, Wolfgang Sauer, Bernhard Schulz, *Die Nationalsozialistische Machtergreifung* (Cologne: Westdeutscherverlag, 1960), pp. 497–98.

29. DSt. Führer, circular letter, 19 April 1933, Würzburg DSt., 1*01-gamma 37.

30. Ibid.

31. DSt. Führer, circular letter, A35/1932-33, Würzburg, DSt. 1*01-gamma 37.

32. "Tasks of the Office for Science," appendix to circular letter of 5 May 1933, Würzburg, DSt., 1*01-gamma 37.

33. Walcher to NSDStB regional leadership in Karlsruhe, 25 April 1933, Würzburg, NSDStB, 104-alpha 48; Wolfgang Kunkel, "Der Professor im Dritten Reich," *Die deutsche Universität im Dritten Reich* (Munich: R. Piper and Co., 1966), pp. 122–23.

34. DSt. Office for Science to DSt. Führer, 10 May 1933, Würzburg, DSt. 1*07-theta 321; G. Krüger and Georg Plötner to Forest (Tharandt), 11 July 1933, Würzburg, DSt., 1*03-alpha 47; Haupt to Krüger, 14 June 1933, Würzburg, DSt. 1*07-theta 321.

35. Bracher et al., *Machtergreifung*, p. 322.

36. Friedrich Walcher, report of the events at Darmstadt Technical Institute, Würzburg, NSDStB, 104-alpha 48; Hackert to Stäbel, 2 June 1933, Würzburg, DSt., 1*03-theta 355.

37. Regional Führer of central German NSDStB to Minister President Manfred von Killinger, 12 August 1933, captured documents (NSDStB), T81, roll 239, 5024403.

38. NSDStB circular letter, 2 March 1935, captured documents (NSDStB) T81, roll 237-5021789-91

39. See Würzburg, DSt. 1*07-theta 321.

40. Merseburg, K, W & V, Rep. 76, Va, 1, Titel XVIII, Nr. 16, Bd. X, items 135–39.

41. Ibid.

42. Ibid.

43. Hans Maier, "Nationalsozialistische Hochschulpolitik," *Die deutsche Universität im Dritten Reich* (Munich: R. Piper and Co., 1966) p. 94.

44. The "action against the un-German Spirit" is the subject of an excellent study by Hans Wolfgang Strätz, "Die Studentische 'Aktion wider den undeutschen Geist' im Frühjahr 1933," *Vierteljahrshefte für Zeitgeschichte*, October 1968, pp. 347–72.

45. Ibid., p. 348.

46. Ibid., p. 350; Head Office for Press and Propaganda of DSt., circular letter 1, Würzburg, DSt., 1*21.

47. 6 April 1933, Würzburg, DSt., 1*24, no. 282.

48. DSt. Office for Press and Propaganda to student gov'ts, Würzburg, DSt., 1*21.

49. "12 Thesen wider den undeutschen Geist," ibid.

50. Ibid.

51. Office for Enlightenment and Publicity (formerly press and propaganda), 27 April 1930, Würzburg, DSt. 1*21, Nr. 140.

52. *DSt. Akademische Korrespondenz*, 24 April 1933, captured documents (Provenance unknown), T81, 243, 5029514; Battle committee of the Technical Institute in Braunschweig to Office for Propaganda and publicity [*sic*], 26 April 1933, Würzburg, DSt. 1*21; "Plan über die Durchführung der Aktion der Deutschen Studentenschaft in Berlin," ibid.; Erlangen Student gov't to Office for Enlightenment and publicity, 6 April 1933, ibid.; Student gov't of U. Breslau to DSt. Office for Press and Propaganda, 29 April 1933, ibid.; "Für das Deutsche in der Kultur; Eine Kundgebung der Studentenschaft," *Bayerische Staatszeitung*, 6 May 1933.

53. Student government of the University of Breslau to the DSt. Office for Press and Propaganda, 28 April 1933, Würzburg, DSt. 1*21.

54. Student government of University of Greifswald to Office for Enlightenment and Publicity, 17 May 1933, ibid.

55. von Eichborn (Halle) to DSt. Office for Press and Propaganda, 5 May 1933, ibid.; Leistritz to Breslau student Führer, 6 May 1933, ibid.; Hamburg student gov't to Regional Führer II, 20 April 1933, Würzburg, DSt., 1*24, No. 181; Strätz, "Die Studentische ...," pp. 365–67.

56. DSt. Göttingen to Leistritz, 24 April 1933, Würzburg, DSt., 1*21.

57. Letter to DSt. regional leader II, Reinhold Schulze, 19 April 1933, Frankfurt, DSt., Bd. 74.

58. Hamburg student gov't to regional leader II, 20 April 1933, Würzburg, DSt. 1*24, No. 181.

59. Strätz, "Die Studentische ...," p. 359; Appendix 2 to circular letter A*33/1932/33, 19 April 1933, Frankfurt, DSt., Bd. 7.

60. Strätz, "Die Studentische ...," p. 356.

61. Leistritz to student gov'ts. Würzburg, DSt. 1*01, gamma 37.

62. Because the *Deutsche Studentenschft* had failed to comply with Goebbels's regulations regarding preparations for reportage, the radio refused to carry reports from other localities. See Student government of the University of Munich to DSt. Office for Enlightenment and radio, 24 May 1933, Würzburg, DSt., 1*24, no. 232; Leistritz to Silesian Radio, West German Radio, Bavarian Radio, 20 and 21 April 1933, Würzburg, DSt. 1*21.

63. Deutschlandsender GMBH Berlin to Leistritz, 9 May 1933, Würzburg, DSt., I*21.
64. DSt. Office for Enlightenment and Publicity to student gov'ts, 9 May 1933, Würzburg, DSt. I*21.
65. "Flamme empor!: Die Bonner Studenten-Kundgebung ...Wider den Undeutschen Geist," *General-Anzeiger für Bonn und Umgegend,* Würzburg, DSt., I*21.
66. DSt. Head Office for Enlightenment and Publicity, circular letter, 16 May 1933, Würzburg, DSt., I*21, Nr. 29.

Chapter Ten

1. Albert Derichsweiler, "Student der Bewegung," *Volk im Werden,* March 1935, p. 83.
2. Ibid.
3. Strätz, "Die Studentische...," pp. 352–53.
4. NSDStB leadership, order of 11 April 1933, Würzburg, NSDStB, alpha 475-23.
5. Order of Party Organization leader, 4 April 1933, ibid.
6. Captured documents (Reichsstudentenführung NSDStB), T81, roll 260, 5051713.
7. Rust to Frick, 13 July 1933, Bundesarchiv, Abteilung Frankfurt, records of Obmann der Verbände (hereafter cited as Frankfurt, OdV,) 13 July 1933.
8. Ibid.
9. Order no. 10 of NSDStB national Führer, 4 July 1933, Würzburg, NSDStB 50-alpha 5.
10. Krüger to Herbert Hahn, 22 July 1933, Würzburg, DSt. 1*03-theta 355.
11. Hans Weidauer to State Police Office in Münster, 4 September 1933, captured documents (Reichsstudentenführung, 1933), T81, roll 259, 5050184-85; Hans Weidauer to Theodor Blahut, 23 August 1933, ibid., 5050260-64.
12. *Die Deutsche Studentenschaft: Nachrichtendienst,* 9 October 1933, captured documents, T81, roll 243, 5029435.
13. *Academia,* October/November 1933, p. 174.
14. Archival memo, 23 April 1934, Frankfurt, OdV, Bd. 12; Plan of the Reich Youth Führer for the reconstruction of the NSDStB, ibid.; archival memo, 24 April 1934, ibid.
15. See Würzburg, DSt. 1*02-theta 414, and 1*03-theta 414, and Frankfurt, OdV. Bd. 7 and Bd. 3.
16. Archival memo, 10 July 1934, Frankfurt, OdV., Bd. 3; Stäbel to Rust, 20 June 1934, Würzburg, DSt., 1*02-theta 414.
17. Archival notice, Merseburg, K, W & V, Rep. 76, Va, 1, Titel XVIII, Nr. 16, Bd. X, items 2–3.
18. Deutsche Nachrichtenbüro, 19 July 1934, captured documents, T81, roll 261, 5053112.
19. Captured documents (Reichsstudentenführungs-Archiv of NSDStB), T81, roll 236, 5020640.
20. The shakeup in student leadership coincided with the bloody purge of the SA on 30 June and 1 July 1934. Although Stäbel was a member of the SA, he had had continual trouble with the SA leadership since his appointment as *Deutsche Studentenschaft Führer.* The evidence that the student shakeup had anything to do with the SA purge is merely circumstantial—the SA University Offices were dissolved on 20 July, immediately after Stäbel's withdrawal from student affairs. See Würzburg, DSt. 1*05 C5; captured documents (Reichsstudentenführungs-Archiv of NSDStB), T81, roll 236, 5020640; Merseburg, K, W & V, Rep. 76, Va, 1, Titel XVIII, Nr. 16, Bd. X, item 17.
21. For a further discussion of this rivalry, see Steinberg, pp. 751–54.
22. After Stäbel's fall the Student Union was integrated with the Party organization on

all levels, and membership was reduced to Party members and members of the Student Union before 20 January 1933. Hess defined the reformed Student Union as a "spiritual SS." See Ernst Maker, "Organisation des NSD-Studentenbundes der NSDAP," *Deutsche Studentenzeitung,* 22 November 1934; "Verordnungsblatt der Reichsleitung der Nationalsozialistischen Deutschen Arbeiterpartei," August 1934, captured documents (Miltenberger Ring), T81, roll 76, 87122; "Studentenbund eingegliedert," July 1934, Würzburg, DSt., 1*05, C5; Rudolf Hess, deputy Führer to the NSDStB Führer, 24 July 1934, Würzburg, NSDStB, 17-alpha 471; NSDStB Reichsführer, circular letter, 28 September 1934, captured documents (NSDStB), T81, roll 237, 5021915-22.

23. Stäbel and Hans Hildebrandt (Press Office leader), Special order of NSDStB, 50-alpha 5.

24. Order to all NSDStB Press Officers, 27 June 1933, ibid.

25. DSt. Office for Enlightenment and Publicity, circular letter, F3 1933/34, Würzburg, DSt., 1*01-gamma 53.

26. NSDStB Reich leadership, Office of Press and Propaganda, Press Order No. 1, 27 October 1933, captured documents (NSDStB), T81, roll 237, 5021995-96.

27. "Gründe für die Einstellung der *Deutschen Studentenzeitung* als amtliches Organ der Reichsschaft und der DSt.," Würzburg, DSt., 1*02-theta 414.

28. Hildenbrandt to Oskar Krüger, 12 June 1934, Würzburg, NSDStB, 67-alpha 18.

29. DSt. Office for Enlightenment and Publicity, circular letter, 18 October 1933, Würzburg, DSt., 1*03-gamma 53.

30. DSt. Office for Enlightenment and Publicity, 18 August 1934, captured documents (Miltenberger Ring), T81, roll 76, 88162-65.

31. *Gemeinschaft Studentischer Verbände Nachrichtendienst,* captured documents (Gemeinschaft Studentischer Verbände-Cologne), T81, roll 77, 89235-36; Reichsverband der deutschen Zeitschriftenverleger e.v. Fachgruppe Studentenzeitschriften to GStV., 16 May 1934, captured documents (GStV) T81, roll 261, 5052870; Office of the NSDStB, for Press and Propaganda, 20 May 1935, captured documents (NSDStB), T81, roll 237, 5021974.

32. Hans Schlömer, "Die Ära der Gleichschaltung," *Deutsches Studentenwerk Festschrift,* 1961, p. 72.

33. DSt. Office for Work Service, circular letter, 8 December 1933, Würzburg, DSt., 1*01-gamma 64.

34. Otto B. Roegele, "Student im Dritten Reich," *Die Deutsche Universität im Dritten Reich* (Munich: R. Piper and Co., 1966), p. 153.

35. Head Office for political education to Reich Interior Ministry, 19 June 1934, Würzburg, DSt., 1*50-theta 395.

36. Reich Minister of the Interior, 23 February 1934, Würzburg, DSt., 1*02-theta 414.

37. 23 February 1934, Merseburg, K, W & V, Rep. 76, Va, 1, Titel XII, Nr. 35, Bd. III, item 346.

38. Wolfgang Benz, "Von freiwilligen Arbeitsdienst zur Arbeitsdienstpflicht," *Vierteljahrshefte für Zeitgeschichte,* October 1968, p. 343.

39. DSt. Pressedienst, Sonderdienst, Nachrichtendienst, 12 February 1935, captured documents (Miltenberger Ring), T81 roll 76, 87141.

40. DSt. Office for Work Service, Office for Border Work, circular letter, 21 June 1934, Würzburg, DSt., 1*33-gamma 120.

41. George Weber, "Studentischer Landdienst in Schlesien," *Nationalsozialistische Schlesische Hochschulzeitung,* 15 November 1934, pp. 3–5.

42. Academic Work Office to regional offices, 20 March 1933, Würzburg, DSt., 1*05, C4.

43. Volker R. Berghahn, *Der Stahlhelm: Bund der Frontsoldaten 1918–1935*. (Düsseldorf: Droste Verlag, 1966), pp. 260–74.

44. Stahlhelm Studentenring "Langemarck" Student Office, 12 May 1933, captured documents (C. V. Franco-Ratia Würzburg), T81, roll 242, 5027951; NSDStB, Würzburg to fraternities, 19 May 1931, ibid., 5027940.

45. DSt. head office for political education, office for military work to student government Führer, 2 May 1933, Würzburg, DSt., 1805, C4.

46. Academic Military Office to the military sport teachers at the universities, no date, Würzburg, DSt., 1*05, C4; Academic Military Office to DSt. Führer, 21 July 1933, ibid.

47. Stäbel to NSDStB regional leaders and university group Führer, 2 May 1933, Würzburg, DSt., 1*05, C4.

48. Stahlhelm national office, 24 May 1933, Merseburg, K, W & V, Rep. 76, Va, 1, Titel XVIII, Nr. 16, Bd. IX, items 205–8.

49. Würzburg, NSDStB, 65-alpha 604.

50. Statement by Stäbel and Kiekebusch, 22 September 1933, captured documents (Reichsstudentenführungs-Archiv of NSDStB), T81, roll 236, 5020671.

51. Archival memo, discussion in the Ministry of Culture, 27–28 April 1933, Würzburg, DSt., 1*05, C4; DSt. Office for Political Education, Office for Military Work to Military Office leaders, 2 May 1933, Würzburg, Würzburg student records IV16.

52. Head of Office for Military Service to Gerhard Krüger, 29 April 1933, captured documents (Reichsstudentenführung 1933), T81, roll 259, 5050057.

53. Würzburg, Würzburg student records, IV16.

54. Report of NSDStB, Darmstadt, Würzburg, DSt., 1*05, C5.

55. Report of the work of the Braunschweig student gov't, Würzburg, DSt., 1*03-theta 253.

56. Prussian Minister of Culture, 28 July 1933, Würzburg, DSt., I*05, C3.

57. Leonensia Heidelberg report for Winter Semester 1933/34, captured documents (Miltenberger Ring), T81, roll 76, 88087; Vereinigung der Alt-Herren Vereine, Tübinger Korporationen, 17 August 1933, captured documents (GStV), T81, roll 79, 91061-98; Stahlhelm National Office, 24 May 1933, Merseburg, K, W & V, Rep. 76, Va, 1, Titel XVIII, Nr. 16, Bd. IX, items 205–8.

58. DSt. Führer, circular letter 7 July 1933, Würzburg, DSt., 1*05, C4; Gerhard Krüger to Friedrich Wilhelm Krüger, 28 July 1933, ibid.

59. Karl Bracher, et al, *Die Nationalsozialistische Machtergreifung*, pp. 893–95; for SA-army relations see Herman Mau, "Die zweite Revolution"—der 30 Juni 1934, *VJZG*, I 2 (April 1953), pp. 119–37.

60. 9 September 1933, captured documents (Miltenberger Ring), T81, roll 81, 72719.

61. Karl Bracher, et al, *Die Nationalsozialistische Machtergreifung*, p. 895.

62. SA Führer, 16 October 1933, Würzburg, DSt., 1*05, C5.

63. Order by Adolf Hitler, 9 September 1933, ibid.

64. DSt. circular letter, 4 October 1933, ibid.; NS. Gemeinschaft Corpsstudentischer Verbände, captured documents (Miltenberger Ring), T81, roll 78, 90192.

65. *Trial of the Major War Criminals before the International Military Tribunal* (Nuremberg, 1948), vol. 42 (English): 422–23.

66. Führer meeting in Salem, December 1933, Würzburg, DSt., 1*02-theta 387.

67. Memo of the Prussian Minister of Culture, 16 March 1934, Merseburg, K, W & V, Rep. 76, Va, 1, Titel XII, Nr. 35, Bd. III, item 403; memo of the Führer of the Reich SA University Office, 16 April 1934, ibid., item 404.

68. Archival notice, Frankfurt, OdV, Bd. 7, 20 October 1934.

69. Merseburg, K, W & V, Rep. 76, Va, 1, Titel XII, Nr. 35, Bd. III, item 521.

70. DSt. Reich Führer, circular letter, 18 April 1934, Würzburg, DSt., 1*01-gamma 51.

71. "Denkschrift zur Lage der Deutschen Hochschule," memo by Bennecke, 11 June 1934, Merseburg, K, W & V, Rep. 76, Va, 1, Titel XII, Nr. 35, Bd. II, item 524.

72. Ibid.

73. Chief of SA Office of Miltary Education to SA-University Offices, 10 October 1934, Würzburg, DSt., 1*05, C5; NSDStB Reich Führer, circular letter, 28 September 1934, captured documents (NSDStB), T81, roll 237, 5021815-22; SA Office of Military Education, 16 October 1934, Frankfurt, OdV, Bd. 8.

74. "Grundzüge der Arbeit des Hauptamtes für politische Erziehung der Deutschen Studentenschaft," May 1933, Würzburg, DSt., 1*06-theta 346.

75. Order of Andreas Feickert, winter semester 1934-35, Würzburg, DSt., 1*00-gamma 67.

76. DSt. Reich Führer, circular letter, 15 February 1934, Würzburg, DSt. 1*01-gamma 51.

77. DSt. Head Office for Political Education, Office for Scholarship, circular letter, 18 October 1933, Würzburg, DSt. 1*01-gamma 2.

78. Student government of the University of Göttingen, semester report of the Office for Scholarship, summer semester 1933, 15 July 1933, Würzburg, DSt., 1*00-gamma 254; "Die Politische Schulung in der Würzburger Studentenschaft," Würzburg, Würzburg student records IV27.

79. Fritz Cornelius (Göttingen) to the DSt. Office for Scholarship, 1 June 1933, Würzburg, DSt., 1*00-gamma 254.

80. "Satzungen Aufbau und Aufgaben der Fachschaften und Fachgruppen der DSt.," Appendix 1 of circular letter A58/1932–33, Würzburg, DSt., 1*01-gamma 2.

81. Education plan for the disciplinary groups and other educational groups, Würzburg, summer semester 1933, Würzburg, Würzburg student records, IV27.

82. DSt. Office for Scholarship, Reich Disciplinary group "Technik," circular letter, 3 May 1934, Würzburg, DSt., 1*22-gamma 90.

83. Meeting of the Disciplinary groups in Resau, 16–17 June 1934, Würzburg, DSt., 1*10-gamma 278; Catholic Theological Reich Disciplinary Society, circular letter, 10 August 1934, ibid.

84. Instructions of the Head Office for Scholarship for the Winter Semester 1934/35, Würzburg, NSDStB, 52-alpha 7.

85. Ibid.

86. Karl Dittmann, "Studentenarbeit in der Landschaft," DSt. Wissen und Dienst, Gilbhard 3, 1935, pp. 5–7, captured documents (Lammers records), T81, roll 261, 5052865-67.

87. 10 May 1933 order, Würzburg, DSt. 1*01-gamma 37.

88. Heinz Roosch to Feickert, Würzburg, DSt. 1*50-gamma 220; Hans Georg Petrusch, "Denkschrift für die Errichtung und Einrichtung eines Studentenwohnhauses," 25 July 1933, Merseburg, K, W & V, Rep. 76, Va, 1, Titel XII, Nr. 43, Bd. 1, item 10.

89. Office for Work Service, circular letter, 21 July 1933, Würzburg, DSt., 1*01-gamma 2.

90. Heinz Roosch, "Das studentische Kameradschaftshaus," September 1933, captured documents (Studentenschaft an der Universität Würzburg), T81, roll 242, 5028062-64.

91. Minutes of the meeting in the Reich Ministry of the Interior on 29 September 1933 concerning the construction of Comradeship houses, captured documents (Miltenberger Ring), T81, roll 78, 89912-22.

92. Führer meeting, Salem, December 1933, Würzburg, DSt., 1*02-theta 387.

93. DSt. Head Office for Political Education, circular letter, 24 February 1934, Würzburg, DSt. 1*50-theta 17.

94. DSt. circular letter, 23 January 1934, U. of Würzburg, Studentenschaft, captured documents, T81, roll 242, 5028410-11.

95. DSt. Head Office for Political Education, requirements for official recognition of comradely living units, February 1934, ibid., frame 5028412.

96. First Reich Education Plan, Summer semester 1934, Würzburg, NSDStB, 15-alpha 470.

97. Office for Scholarship, February 1934, Würzburg, DSt., 1*02-theta 590.

98. Regional leadership of region II of the NSDStB Office for female students to the NSDStB female group leaders of region II, captured documents (NSDStB), T81, roll 237, 5022125.

99. See below, chapter 11.

100. NSDStB Educational Officer, circular letter RSchl. a/34, Würzburg, NSDStB, 55-alpha 10.

101. Gerhard Mähner, "Die politische Erziehungsarbeit in den Schulungslagern des NSD Studentenbundes," *Volk im Werden,* March 1935, pp. 93–99; Hermann Eder, "'Wir zieh'n an einem Strick . . .' Brief aus dem Schulungslager," *Deutsche Studentenzeitung,* 22 November 1934, p. 3.

102. Reich education plan, 1 November 1934–30 April 1935, captured documents (Reichsstudentenführung, 1933–36), T81, roll 258, 5049490-95.

Chapter Eleven

1. For the reasoning behind this 60 percent figure, see Steinberg, pp. 797–99.

2. "Strafverfolgung der Mensur hört auf," *Burschenschaftliche Blätter,* April 1933, p. 159.

3. Prussian Minister of Justice to the Attorney General, 6 April 1933, Merseburg, K, W & V, Rep. 76, Va, 1, Titel XII, Nr. 11, Bd. V, item 105.

4. Prussian Minister of the Interior to the governmental presidents, the police president in Berlin and the Office of the secret police, 13 June 1933, Merseburg, K, W & V, Rep. 76, Va, 1, Titel XII, Nr. 11, Bd. IV, item 109.

5. 19 June 1933, Merseburg, K, W & V, Rep. 76, Va, 1, Titel XII, Nr. 11, Bd. IV, item 111.

6. Student office of the Stahlhelm-Studentenring Langemarck, captured documents (NSDStB), T81, roll 259, 5051452-53; Heinz Kiekebusch, memo, 24 May 1933, Merseburg, K, W & V, Rep. 76, Va, 1, Titel XVIII, Nr. 16, Bd. IX, items 205–208.

7. Karl Heinz Hederich to Stäbel, 20 June 1933, captured documents (NSDStB Reichsführung), T81, roll 239, 5024618-20; Krüger to Gille, 13 April 1933, captured documents (NSDStB), T81, roll 259, 5051312-13.

8. Deutsche Wehrschaft Führer, circular letter, 21 April 1933, Würzburg, DSt., 1*04 C15.

9. Karl Kühlmann, leader of the Office for University Politics of the Schwarzburgbund, 9 May 1933, Würzburg, DSt. 1*04 C15.

10. "Kundgebungen," *Academia,* 15 May 1933, pp. 3–4.

11. "Zum 50. Bundestag in Frankenhausen," *Burschenschaftliche Wege,* May 1933.

12. "Burschentag 1933," *Burschenschaftliche Blätter,* June 1933, p. 229.

13. "Das erste Kyffhäuserfest im neuen Reich," *Akademische Blätter,* August 1933, pp. 129–32. The text reads, "nationalen Sozialismus."

14. Report of the meeting of the extraordinary dueling students convention on 20 May 1933 in Goslar, captured documents (Miltenberger Ring), T81, roll 81, 92480-84; constitution of 20 May 1933, Würzburg, NSDStB, 19-alpha 472.

15. *Telegraphen-Union Nachdienst,* 3 June 1933, p. 3, Würzburg, DSt., 1*04, theta 311.

16. Ibid.

17. Lammers to ADW, 29 June 1933, captured documents (GStV), T81, roll 81, 92552-56.

18. Lammers to ADW, 30 June 1933, ibid., 92557.

19. Memo, 23 June 1933, captured documents (DSt., Amt für Wissenschaft), T81, roll 239, 5024611.

20. Circular letter of CV Führer, 9 July 1933, captured documents (C. V. Franco-Ratia, Würzburg), T81, roll 242, 5028040-41; draft of a circular letter of the Miltenberger Ring Führer to the member groups, captured documents (Miltenberger Ring), T81, 92580-83; speech of the Führer of the Schwarzburgbund, Dr. W. Behne, "Die Aufgaben deutscher Studentenschaft," 28 July 1933, Würzburg, DSt., 1*04 C6.

21. Daeschner and Stahlberg to fraternity brothers in Karlsruhensia, captured documents (Miltenberger Ring), T81, roll 77, 88472-73.

22. Hans Lammers, circular letter, 18 September 1933, captured documents (Miltenberger Ring), T81, roll 78, 89892 95.

23. Hamburg student government, circular letter to the fraternities in Hamburg, 15 August 1933, Würzburg, Hamburg student records, alpha 517.

24. Hans Ewoh't to Dr. Meinshausen, 14 July 1933, Würzburg, DSt., 1*04, theta 314; Kiel dueling fraternities to the Reich Minister of the Interior, the NSDStB Führer, the ADW central office, the DSt. Führer, 14 July 1933, ibid.

25. Krüger to student government Führer at Kiel, 19 July 1933, Würzburg, DSt., 1*04, theta 314.

26. Horst Bernhardi, "Die Göttinger Burschenschaft 1933 bis 1945," vol. 1 in *Darstellungen und Quellen zur Geschichte der deutschen Einheitsbewegung im neunzehnten und zwanzigsten Jahrhundert* (Heidelberg: Carl Winter Universitätsverlag, 1937), p. 211.

27. Hamburg student government, circular letter to the fraternities in Hamburg, 15 August 1933, Würzburg, Hamburg student records, alpha 517.

28. Statement of Aenania-Munich, 1 May 1933, Würzburg, DSt., 1*04, C16; order of KV in regard to military sport, May 1933, ibid.

29. Rheno-Palatia, Breslau to central office of the CV, May 1933, captured documents (C. V. Franco-Ratia Würzburg), T81, roll 242, 5027903; "Kundgebungen," *Academia,* 15 May 1933, pp. 3–4; Hans Müller, *Katholische Kirche und Nationalsozialismus: Dokumente von 1930–1935* (Munich: Nymphenburger Verlag, 1963), document 55, p. 30.

30. Captured documents (C. V. Franco-Ratia Würzburg), T81, roll 242, 5027875.

31. NSDStB group in Tübingen, 2 May 1933, Würzburg, DSt., 1*04 C16; Archiv der Deutschen Studentenschaft, file 227, ibid.; Konrad Welte to Gerhard Krüger, 15 May 1933, captured documents (NSDStB Reichsführung), T81, roll 239, 5024770-71.

32. Minutes of meeting between Gerhard Krüger and Konrad Welte, Würzburg, DSt., 1*04 C16; Krüger to Welte, 12 May 1933, ibid.

33. May 1933, Würzburg, DSt., 1*04 C16.

34. CV Führer, circular letter, 11 July 1933, captured documents (C. V. Franco-Ratia, Würzburg), T81, roll 242, 5028027-28; CV Führer, circular letter, 19 July 1933, ibid., 5020840-41; letter of KV Führer, 22 July 1933, Würzburg, DSt., 1*04 C16.

35. CV circular letter, August 1933, captured documents (Studentenschaft an der Universität Würzburg), T81, roll 242, 5028049; "Vom Führer des CV," *Academia,* 15 September 1933, p. 145.

36. Langhoff, circular letter, February 1934, captured documents, (Miltenberger Ring), T81, roll 88, 89992-93.

37. *Unitas Verband,* circular letter, 10 February 1934, Würzburg, DSt., 1*04 C7.

38. "Erklärung," *Academia,* March /April 1934, p. 283.

39. Unitas Verband Führer Karl Erbprinz zu Löwenstein, circular letter, 21 February 1934, Würzburg, DSt., 1*04, C7; *Academia*, March/April 1934, p. 316.

40. Interview with Dr. Stäbel for the "Ring," 2 May 1934, Würzburg, DSt. Akten, 1*02-gamma 10; clipping, Albert Derichsweiler, "Meine Stellung zur Satisfaktion," *Academia*, NSDStB 17-alpha 471.

41. Hans Schlömer, "Vor 25 Jahren: Die Auflösung der Korporationsverbände 1935," *Unitas*, November 1960, p. 210.

42. Fritz Nonhoff to Albert Derichsweiler, 20 July 1934, captured documents (GStV), T81, roll 262, 5053786; Schenk to Derichsweiler, monthly report, June 1935, Würzburg, NSDStB A109-alpha 53; Schenk to Derichsweiler, 23 July 1935, Würzburg, NSDStB A106-alpha 50.

43. This struggle is discussed in more detail in Steinberg, pp. 826–900.

44. Günther Kraaz to Thomalla, 21 October 1933, captured documents (Miltenberger Ring), T81, roll 78, 90205.

45. Kraatz to Lammers, 13 September 1933, captured documents (Miltenberger Ring), T81, roll 81, 92711-13.

46. Miltenberger Ring Führer, circular letter, 23 September 1933, captured documents (Miltenberger Ring), T81, roll 78, 89898-901; Miltenberger Ring Führer, circular letter, 1 November 1933, ibid., 89941-45.

47. Order of 20 September 1934, Würzburg, NSDStB, 52-alpha 7.

48. Position of the Kösener SC Verband to the order of the Reichsführer of the DSt. of 20 September 1934, Merseburg, K, W & V, Rep. 76, Va, 1, Titel XII, Nr. 43, Bd. 1, items 160–70.

49. Lammers to Feickert, 27 September 1934, Frankfurt, OdV, Bd. 4.

50. Schwab to Lammers, 4 October 1934, Frankfurt, DSt., Bd. 4.

51. Archival memo, 18 October 1934, Frankfurt, OdV., Bd. 7. The leagues were the Deutsche Burschenschaft, the Deutsche Gildenschaft, the Deutsche Wehrschaft, Kyffhäuser Verband, Schwarzburgbund, Sondershäuser Verband and the Verband der Turnerschaften.

52. Archival memo, 4 October 1934, ibid.

53. Albert Derichsweiler, "Stellung zur Verfügung Feickerts," 1 October 1934, ibid.; NSDStB Führer, 10 October 1934, captured documents (NSDStB), T81, roll 237, 5021813.

54. Archival memo, 25 October 1934, Frankfurt, OdV., Bd. 8.

55. Minutes of the meeting of the leagues on 8 October 1934, Frankfurt, OdV., Bd. 7.

56. Reichsminister Rust über das Kameradschaftshaus," captured documents (Miltenberger Ring), T81, roll 76, 88231; Lohr to Pohlausen, 7 November 1934, Merseburg, K, W & V, Rep. 76, Va, 1, Titel XII, Nr. 43, Bd. 1, item 204.

57. Corps Thuringia to Lammers, 28 October 1934, Frankfurt, OdV., Bd. 8; Blunck to Lammers, 29 October 1934, ibid.

58. Breslau student Führer to DSt., 3 November 1934, Merseburg, K, W & V, Rep. 76, Va, 1, Titel XII, Nr. 43, Bd. 1, item 265; ibid., 5 November 1934, item 264.

59. DSt. Führer, circular letter, 10 November 1934, Würzburg, DSt., 1*01-gamma 51.

60. NSDStB Reichsführung, circular letter, 16 November 1934, captured documents (NSDStB), T81, roll 237, 5021803-05.

61. NSDStB Reichsführung, 20 November 1934, captured documents (Miltenberger Ring), T81, roll 78, 90055.

62. NSDStB Office for Political Education, 26 November 1934, captured documents (NSDStB), T81, roll 237, 5021920-23.

63. Ibid.

64. Langhoff to Nordmann, 18 November 1934, Frankfurt, OdV, Bd. 10.

65. "Wahrheit und Recht: Zum Austritt der D.B. aus dem ADW," 29 November

1934, ibid., 87480-86; *Mitteilungen der Deutschen Wehrschaft*, Gilbhard, Nebelung, 1934, Frankfurt, OdV, Bd. 11; "Konflikt in der Studentenschaft," *Kreuz-Zeitung*, 6 November 1934.

66. Results of the proceedings of the court of honor in the case of the Deutsche Burschenschaft: Schwab vs. Arnecke, 21, 22, and 27 February 1935, captured documents (Miltenberger Ring), T81, roll 78, 90355-56; also "Wahrheit und Recht," op. cit.

67. "Blut und Ehre!" *Der Student im Dritten Reich: Beiblatt des Niederdeutschen Beobachters*, 6 April 1935, captured documents (GStV), T81, roll 77, 88845; Hans Dabelstein, "Revolutioniert den Ehrbegriff," *Pflug und Schwert*, February 1935.

68. 12 January 1935, captured documents (Miltenberger Ring), T81, roll 76, 87113; league meeting on 12 January 1932, ibid., roll 80, 92098-99.

69. GStV, 23 April 1935, captured documents (Studentenschaft an der Universität Würzburg), T81, roll 242, 5028311.

70. Witthauer, circular letter, 10 April 1935, captured documents (GStV), T81, roll 78, 90481-82.

71. GStV, 12 March 1935, captured documents (C.V. Franco-Ratia, Würzburg), T81, roll 242, 5028342; text of agreement between the NSDStB and the GStV, captured documents (GStV, Cologne), T81, roll 77, 89256; *GStV Nachrichtendienst*, 23 March 1935, ibid., roll 77, 89573.

72. CV Mitteilungen, May 1935, captured documents (C. V. Franco-Ratia, Würzburg), T 81, roll 242, 5028324.

73. Minutes of the committee of the GStV, captured documents (GStV), T81, roll 78, 90762-66; 1 May 1935, ibid., roll 78, 90867; declaration of the Deutsche Burschenschaft, 1 May 1935, ibid., roll 79, 90876.

74. "Unser Standpunkt zur politischen Lage," *Akademische Blätter*, May 1935, captured documents (GStV Berlin), T81, roll 78, 90553-54.

75. Short report about the attacks on students at the German universities, summer 1934, Frankfurt, OdV., Bd. 12; Rector Wolf, Kiel to students, Merseburg, K, W & V, Rep. 76, Va, 1, Titel XII, Nr. 35, Bd. III, item 446; Rector Wolf to Gauleiter Lohse and Oberbürgermeister, 26 June 1934, ibid., item 443.

76. Short report about the attacks on students at the German universities, summer 1934, Frankfurt, OdV, Bd. 12; Emil Popp, *Zur Geschichte des Königsberger Studententums, 1900–1945* (Würzburg: Holzner Verlag, 1955), p. 167.

77. Report on the incidents between the Hitler Youth and the Bonn *Waffenring*, June 1934, Frankfurt, OdV., Bd. 12.

78. "Neuer Studentenführer," *Kölnische Zeitung*, 19 June 1934, captured documents (Miltenberger Ring), T81, roll 261, 5053056; "Bonner Studenten legen Farben ab," *Reichs-Jugendpressedienst Nachrichtendienst*, 15 June 1934, p. 2, Würzburg, DSt., 1*10-gamma 278; Zaeringer to Lammers, 4 July 1934, OdV., Bd. 12.

79. "Reaktionäre ohne braune Tünche," *Wille und Macht*, copy printed on 4 March 1935, captured documents (GStV), T81, roll 81, 92431-32.

80. Zaeringer to GStV, 3 March 1935, captured documents (GStV), T81, roll 77, 89028-29.

81. Alte Münstersche Landsmannschaft to GStV Führer, Münster, 11 April 1935, captured documents (GStV), T81, roll 78, 90515; G. Kraaz to Dr. Nordmann, 29 June 1935, ibid., roll 78, 90543.

82. "H. J. muss aus den studentischen Korporationen austreten," *Lokal Anzeiger*, 7 July 1935, captured documents, (GStV), T81, roll 262, 5053758; "H. J. oder Verbindung: Ein Wichtiger Befehl des Reichsjugendführers," *Der Führer*, 6 July 1935, ibid., roll 77, 88568.

83. GStV Cologne, 28 May 1935, captured documents (GStV), T81, roll 79, 91414-15.

84. Helmut Freudenberg April 1935, Würzburg, NSDStB, 55-alpha 210.

85. Landsmannschaft Führer to GStV, captured documents (GStV), T81, roll 79, 90905.

86. Gau Halle/Merseburg NSDStB, monthly report, May 1935, Würzburg, NSDStB, A109-alpha 53.

87. V. Obenitz to GStV., 25 April 1935, Bundesarchiv, Abteilung Frankfurt, records of Gemeinschaft studentischer Verbände (hereafter cited as Frankfurt, GStV), Bd. 34; Lammers to Himmler, 13 June 1935, ibid.

88. "Die Hitlerjugend gibt die rechte Antwort," *Der Stürmer*, July 1935, Frankfurt, GStV, Bd. 38.

89. Meeting of GStV on 24 July 1935 in Berlin, captured documents (GStV), T81, roll 79, 91109-39.

90. "Das Heidelberger Urteil: Saxo-Borussia auf vier Semester suspendiert," *Deutsche Corpszeitung*, June 1935, pp. 1117-1119, captured documents (Kösener SC Verband), T81, roll 248, 5036986-87; *Berliner Börsenzeitung*, 5 July 1935, captured documents (GStV), T81, roll 242, 5053728.

91. 20 July 1935, captured documents (Kösener SC Verband), T81, roll 48, 5036129; K. Werner to GStV, captured documents (GStV), roll 82, 93676.

92. *Völkischer Beobachter, Süddeutsche Ausgabe*, 18 July 1935, captured documents (GStV), T81, roll 262, 5053734; clipping, Andreas Feickert, "Klarheit in der Studentenschaft," *Heidelberger Neueste Nachrichten-Heidelberger Anzeiger*, captured documents (Miltenberger Ring), T81, roll 77, 88577-79; *Sonder-Pressedienst*, July 1935, captured documents (NSDAP Reichsleitung Abtlg. f.d. Kult. Frieden), T81, roll 242, 5027798-800.

93. G. Kraaz to Dr. Nordmann, 6 July 1935, Frankfurt, GStV, Bd. 41.

94. "Vom Verband zur Kampftruppe: Gauleiter Wagner über die Aufgabe des Korporationsstudententums," *Rheinisch-Westfälische Zeitung*, Frankfurt, GStV, Bd. 41.

95. "Letzter Appell an das Korporationsstudententum," *Burschenschaftliche Blätter*, May 1935, pp. 200–2.

96. "NS-Studentenbund und Korporationen," *Völkischer Beobachter*, 6 June 1935, Würzburg, NSDStB, Nr. 19-alpha 472; "Kampfgemeinschaft der Student," *Fränkische Tages Zeitung*, 7 June 1935, captured documents (Miltenberger Ring), T81, roll 261, 5053639.

97. Oskar Haug to Dr. Witthauer, 2 June 1935, captured documents (GStV), T81, roll 78, 90425; Lammers to Glauning, 4 June 1935, ibid., 90415-16.

98. Hans Glauning to Lammers, 14 June 1935, Frankfurt, GStV, Bd. 57.

99. Captured documents (GStV), T81, roll 78, 90740, roll 79, 91341–43, 51–52, 72–75, 86, roll 77, 89143–44, 89088–89, 93, 97, 98, 89118.

100. NSDStB Gauleitung, Süd-Hannover-Braunschweig to Derichsweiler, 31 May 1935, Würzburg, NSDStB, A109-alpha 53.

101. NSDAP Gauleitung Kurhessen, Gau student Führer to Derichsweiler, 4 June 1935, ibid.

102. Gau Munich-Upper Bavaria student Führer to Derichsweiler, 6 June 1935, ibid.

103. R. Schenk to NSDStB, 4 May 1935, Würzburg, NSDStB, A106-alpha 50.

104. Karl Kracke report to GStV Berlin, captured documents (Miltenberger Ring), T81, roll 82, 93717-19

105. Ibid.

106. Correspondence regarding Munich controversy, April–June 1935, captured documents, (BStV), T81, roll 78, 90449, 51, 77, 43, 41–42, 35–36, 39–40, 15–16, 21–22, 25–27.

107. Meeting of the GStV on 22 June 1935, Corpshaus Saxo-Borussia, captured documents (GStV), T81, roll 79, 91195.

108. "Korporationen an der Wende," *Berliner Tageblatt*, 9 July 1935, captured documents (GStV), T81, roll 242, 5053737.

109. Lammers to Derichsweiler, 1 July 1935, Frankfurt, GStV, Bd. 38.

110. Meeting of the GStV, 22 June 1935, Corpshaus Saxo-Borussia, captured documents (GStV), roll 79, 91194-211.

111. Lammers to Derichsweiler, 1 July 1935, Frankfurt, GStV, Bd. 38; GStV Circular letter, 9 July 1935, captured documents (C.V. Franco-Ratia, Würzburg), T81, roll 242, 5028380-84.

112. Glauning to Lammers, 3 July 1935, captured documents (GStV), T81, roll 79, 90856-58.

113. "Die Entscheidung der fränkische Korporationen zu den Richtlinien des NS-Studentenbundes," 14 July 1935, captured documents (Miltenberger Ring), T81, roll 82, 93491.

114. Derichsweiler to Lammers, 4 July 1935, Frankfurt, GStV, Bd. 40.

115. *Hannover Kurier*, 12 July 1935, captured documents (GStV), T81, roll 262, 5053768; NSDStB, circular letter, 16 July 1935, captured documents (NSDStB), T81, roll 237, 5021747; "Die Meldefrist für Korporationen verlängert," *Völkischer Beobachter*, captured documents (GStV), T81, roll 262, 5053800; Lammers to Derichsweiler, 10 July 1935, Frankfurt, GStV, Bd. 40.

116. Meeting of GStV, 24 July 1935, captured documents (GStV), T81, roll 79, 91109-39; Hans Lammers circular letter, 25 July 1935, captured documents (Kösener SC Verband), T81, roll 248, 5036120.

117. Meeting in the Landwehrkasino, 19 October 1935, captured documents (Miltenberger Ring), T81, roll 76, 87684.

118. Typed copy from the *Führerblätter der Hitler-Jugend*, August 1935, Frankfurt, GStV, Bd. 35.

119. Meeting of members of the steering committee of the GStV, 23 August 1935, captured documents (GStV), T81, roll 78, 90751-56.

120. NSDStB monthly report, July 1935, dated 5 August 1935, captured documents (NSDStB Reichsführung), T81, roll 237, 5022594-97.

121. Archival notice, 2 August 1935, Frankfurt, GStV, Bd. 44.

122. Vogelsang, circular letter, 27 July 1935, captured documents (GStV), T81, roll 77, 88813-15.

123. Meeting of the GStV on 24 July 1934, ibid., roll 79, 91103-39.

124. Meeting of the GStV in Berlin on 24 July 1935, captured documents (GStV), T81, roll 79, 911039; Hans Glauning to Lammers, 31 July 1935, ibid., roll 261, 5053312-17.

125. Lammers to GStV steering committee, league Führer and local GStV leaders, 26 August 1935, ibid., roll 77, 89216-22; minutes of the meeting of the GStV steering committee on 23 August 1935, ibid., roll 78, 90751-56.

126. Declaration of the Deutsche Burschenschaft, captured documents (Miltenberger Ring), T81, roll 78, 89720-22.

127. Meeting of the League Führer of the GStV on 8 September 1935, Frankfurt, GStV, Bd. 18; "Kurzer Rückblick über die Vorgänge innerhalb des deutschen Korporationsstudententums in den letzten Monaten," captured documents (Miltenberger Ring), T81, roll 78, 89727-33; "Kösener SC. weigert sich Arier-paragraph durchzuführen," *Die Hitler Jugend*, 14 September 1935, captured documents (GStV), T81, roll 262, 5053865.

128. GStV, circular letter, 6 September 1935, captured documents (Miltenberger Ring), T81, roll 76, 87514-15.

129. Meeting of the league Führer of the GStV on 8 September 1935, Frankfurt, GStV, Bd. 18.

130. "Baldur von Schirach in Heidelberg," *Frankfurter Zeitung*, 1 October 1935, captured documents (Kösener SC Verband), T81, roll 247, 5035777.

131. Press office of the KSCV, 1 October 1935, captured documents (Kösener SC Verband), T81, roll 247, 5035843; *Burschenschaftliche Blätter*, October 1935, p. 9, captured documents (Miltenberger Ring), T81, roll 76, 87884.

132. Kösener SC Verband Abwicklungsstelle, 24 October 1935, captured documents (Kösener SC Verband), T81, roll 248, 5036042-43.

133. Dr. R. Lepsius to the Chief of Staff of the SA, 21 October 1935, captured documents (Kösener SC Verband), T81, roll 248, 5036037; Dr. R. Lepsius, 25 October 1935, ibid., 5036030.

134. CV Führer, 14 October 1935, captured documents (Studentenschaft an der Universität Würzburg), T81, roll 242, 5028372.

135. KSCV Abwicklungsstelle, circular letter, 17 October 1935, captured documents (Kösener SC Verband), T81, roll 248, 5036048-49; KSCV Abwicklungsstelle, circular letter, 14 November 1935, ibid.; directive of the head of the NSDStB, no date, Würzburg, NSDStB, A107-alpha 51.

136. Order of Derichsweiler, captured documents (NSDStB), T81, roll 237, 5021723-25.

137. *Deutsches Nachrichtenbüro*, October 1935.

138. *Burschenschaftliche Blätter*, October 1935, pp. 1–4.

139. Gerhard Wagner, "Umbruch studentischer Lebensformen," *Völkischer Beobachter*, 3 November 1935, as quoted in *Miltenberger Ring Zeitung*, October–December 1935, pp. 3–6.

140. Ibid.; *Wissen und Dienst*, 2 November 1935.

141. Meeting of the Miltenberger Ring officers, 19 October 1935, captured documents (Miltenberger Ring), T81, roll 76, 87513-665.

142. Reich and Prussian Minister for Science, Education and Popular Education, 7 November 1935, Marburg, 1954/16 III E.1; Rust, circular letter, 7 November 1935, Würzburg, DSt., 1*02-gamma 6.

143. "Nachrichten: Studentenbund und Korporationen," *Wissen und Dienst*, 11 December 1935, captured documents (NSDAP Reichsleitung, Abtlg. für d. Kult. Frieden), T81, roll 242, 5027717.

144. *Geschichte der Universität Jena*, p. 659.

145. Marburg, 1954/16, IIIE.1, item 9, 2 May 1936; item 10, 29 April 1936; item 13, 25 May 1936.

146. Reichsstudentenführung, circular letter, 15 March 1936, captured documents (Reichsstudentenführungsarchiv), T81, roll 236, 5020962.

147. Hans Schlömer, "Vor 25. Jahren: Die Auflösung der Korporationsverbände 1935," *Unitas*, November 1960, pp. 209–13.

148. Transcript of the speech of Lammers on 19 October 1935 in Berlin, captured documents (Miltenberger Ring), T81, roll 76, 87700-15.

Chapter Twelve

1. See especially David Schoenbaum, *Hitler's Social Revolution* (Garden City, N.Y.: Doubleday and Co., 1966).

2. William Sheridan Allen's Study of a German town [*The Nazi Seizure of Power* (New York: Quadrangle, 1965)] with a large civil service population also indicates the Nazi appeal to state employees.

BIBLIOGRAPHICAL ESSAY

The documentary sources for the history of the students in the Weimar Republic are extensive. Beginning in the late 1930s, the archives of the *Deutsche Studentenschaft*, the *Nationalsozialistische Deutsche Studentenbund*, and the fraternity leagues were assembled at Würzburg. The records of the NSDStB and those for the *Deutsche Studentenschaft* for the period after 1933 are still housed in the library of the University of Würzburg. The pre-1933 *Deutsche Studentenschaft* records have been transferred to the *Bundesarchiv, Aussenstelle*, Frankfurt/ Main. The fraternity archives were returned to the leagues after the war and were unavailable for this study. (The *Deutsche Burschenschaft* papers are housed in the Frankfurt archive, but the *Deutsche Burschenschaft* controls access to them.) The university library in Würzburg also holds records of Würzburg and Hamburg student activities. Records of the *Gemeinschaft Studentischer Verbände* and of the *Obmann der Verbände* are available at the Frankfurt archive. I also made extensive use of the documentary holdings of the University of Marburg library relating to student affairs and of the records of the Prussian Ministries of Culture and the Interior which are housed in the *Deutsches Zentralarchiv, Abteilung* 2, Merseburg (German Democratic Republic). The Ministry of Culture archives were invaluable for the study of governmental policy toward students. The records of the Ministry of the Interior included reports about the activities of radical student groups.

The documents captured by the American army at the end of World War II and microfilmed at Alexandria included a large amount of diverse material relating to student affairs. These records are catalogued in the *Guides to German Records microfilmed at Alexandria, Virginia* (Washington: The National Archives, National Archives and Records Service, General Services Administration, 1958–). Student records are listed in Guide No. 3, *Records of the National Socialist German Labor Party* (1958), Guide No. 20, *Records of the National Socialist*

German Labor Party (Part 2) (1960), and Guide No. 35, *Records of the National Socialist German Labor Party* (1962). Of particular value were additional records of the NSDStB, the *Gemeinschaft Studentischer Verbände*, the Hans Lammers papers, and the records of a number of fraternities and fraternity leagues. The *NSDAP Hauptarchiv*, microfilmed by the Hoover Institution in Stanford, California, includes material relating to Nazi student activities in Munich in the period between 1925 and 1933. I also made use of the records of the *Reichskuratorium für Jugendertüchtigung* at the *Bundesarchiv* in Coblenz.

The *Institut für Hochschulkunde* in Würzburg contains an extensive collection of student periodicals and books on student affairs. I found a number of student journals to be of particular use: the *Cartell Verband*'s *Academia;* the *Kyffhäuser Verband*'s *Akademische Blätter;* the NSDStB's *Akademischer Beobachter* and *Die Bewegung;* the *Deutsche Burschenschaft*'s *Burschenschaftliche Blätter;* the *Allgemeine Deutsche Burschenbund*'s *Burschenschaftliche Wege;* the independent *Deutsche Akademische Rundschau* (merged with *Der Student* in 1926); the *Hochschulring*'s *Deutsche Akademische Stimmen* and *Jungakademische Pressedienst;* the *Schwarzburgbund*'s *Die Schwarzburg;* and *Der Stahlhelmstudent.*

A number of works published in the period between 1918 and 1935 were indispensable as references. The four-volume *Das akademische Deutschland* (Berlin: C. A. Weller Verlag, 1930–31), edited by Michael Doeberl, Otto Scheel, Wilhelm Schlink, Hans Sperl, Eduard Spranger, Hans Bitter, and Paul Frank, provides an overview of the German universities, their history, the state of the academic disciplines, and student life. Exhaustive statistical analyses of the student population were published each term in Prussia (*Preussische Hochschulstatistik* [Berlin: Verlag Reimar-Hobbing, 1924–28]) and after 1928 for Germany as a whole (*Deutsche Hochschulstatistik* [Berlin: Verlag Struppe und Winckler, 1928–35]). An interesting analysis of these statistics is provided by Robert Michels, *Umschichtungen in den herrschenden Klassen nach dem Kriege* (Stuttgart, Berlin: W. Kohlhammer, 1934). Hans Sikorski, ed., *Wirken und Werke innerhalb der deutschen Studentenschaft* (Marburg: Schriftleitung der Akademischen Blätter, 1925) is the *Deutsche Studentenschaft*'s semiofficial guide to student life. Many of the fraternity leagues issued handbooks which included discussions of political and academic questions as well as guides to fraternity life. Among the official student histories are Wilhelm Hagen, *Der Burschenschaftliche Gedanke* (Jena: Eugen Diederichs, 1917); Wilhelm Fabricius, *Geschichte und Chronik des Kösener SC Verbandes,* 3rd edition (Frankfurt am Main: Verlag der Deutschen Corpszeitung, 1921); Wilhelm Fabricius, *Die Deutschen Corps* (Frankfurt am Main: Verlag der Corpszeitung, 1926); anonymous, *Die Burschenschaft Alemannia zu Bonn und ihre Vorläufer: Geschichte einer deutschen Burschenschaft am Rhein,* vol. 2, 1890–1924 (Bonn: privately printed, 1925); Walther Schulz, *Der Deutsche Hochschulring: Grundlagen, Geschichte, und Ziel* (Halle: Verlag von Max Niemeyer, 1921); Wolfgang Stahlberg, ed., *Beiträge zur Geschichte des Kyffhäuser Verbandes der Vereine Deutscher Studenten* (Berlin-Charlottenburg: Bernard und Graefe,

1931); and Dr. Hans-Joachim Düning, *Der SA Student im Kampf um die Hochschule (1925–35)* (Weimar: Verlag Hermann Böhlaus, 1936).

For the development of the German universities in the nineteenth century, Friedrich Paulsen, *Die deutschen Universitäten und das Universitätsstudium* (Berlin: A. Asher, 1902) is still an invaluable reference. The origins and ideals of the modern German university are discussed by Helmut Schelsky, *Einsamkeit und Freiheit: Idee und Gestalt der deutschen Universität und ihrer Reformen* (Reinbek bei Hamburg: Rowohlt Taschenbuch Verlag, 1963); Otto Rühle, *Idee und Gestalt der Universität* (Berlin: VEB Deutscher Verlag der Wissenschaften, 1966); and René König, *Vom Wesen der deutschen Universität* (Berlin: Verlag die Runde, 1935). Abraham Flexner, *Universities: American, English, German* (New York, London, Toronto: Oxford University Press, 1930) offers a somewhat uncritical American view of the German universities. German secondary schools are described in detail by James E. Russell, *German Higher Schools: The History, Organization and Methods of Secondary Education in Germany* (New York, London, Bombay: Longmans, Green, and Co., 1899); and W. Lexis, *A General View of the History and Organization of Public Education in the German Empire,* translated by G. J. Tamson (Berlin: A. Asher and Co., 1904), which provides statistics. Educational reforms in the Weimar Republic are treated favorably by Thomas Alexander and Beryl Parker, *The New Education in the German Republic* (New York: John Day, c. 1929). Carl Heinrich Becker is the subject of a biography by his close friend and associate Erich Wende, *C. H. Becker: Mensch und Politiker* (Stuttgart: Deutsche Verlags-Anstalt, 1959), which suffers from a lack of documentation. Three official university histories which touch on the political situation in the 1920s and 1930s have been published in the German Democratic Republic: Ernst Engelberg, ed., *Karl-Marx-Universität Leipzig 1409–1905; Beiträge zur Universitätsgeschichte,* 2 vols. (Leipzig: Verlag Enzyklopädie, 1959); *Geschichte der Universität Jena: Festgabe zum vierhundertjährigen Universitätsjubiläum* (Jena: Gustav Fischer Verlag, 1958); and Hans Schröder, "Zur politischen Geschichte der Ernst Moritz Arndt-Universität Greifswald," *Festschrift zur 500-Jahrfeier der Universität Greifswald 17. 10. 1956,* 2 vols. (Greifswald: Ernst Moritz Arndt-Universität Greifswald, 1956).

The political role of German professors has aroused considerable interest in recent years. Fritz Ringer, *The Decline of the German Mandarins: the German academic community 1890–1933* (Cambridge: Harvard University Press, 1969) is a thoughtful study of the development of German academic thought in the second Empire and the Weimar Republic. The same author's "The German Universities and the Crisis of Learning, 1918–32," unpublished dissertation (Harvard, 1960) documents the predominance of right-wing political sentiment among professors. Friedrich Lilge, *The Abuse of Learning: The Failure of the German University* (New York: Macmillan, 1948) is a provocative book-length essay which focuses on a number of German intellectuals of the nineteenth and twentieth centuries. Alexander Busch, *Die Geschichte des Privatdozenten*

(Stuttgart: Ferdinand Enke Verlag, 1959) is useful for its statistical information on the social origins of university instructors. The political attitudes of German professors during World War I are treated in Klaus Schwabe, "Zur politischen Haltung der deutschen Professoren im Ersten Weltkrieg," *Historische Zeitschrift* 193 (1961): 601–634, and, by the same author, *Wissenschaft und Kriegsmoral; die deutschen Hochschullehrer und die politischen Grundfragen des Ersten Weltkrieges* (Göttingen: Musterschmidt, 1969). Wilhelm Kahl, Friedrich Meinecke, and Gustav Radbruch, discussed the rightist political trend of the universities at a conference of moderate professors in Weimar in April 1926, and their speeches were published as *Die Deutschen Universitäten und der heutige Staat* (Tübingen: J. C. B. Mohr/Paul Siebeck, 1926). Three recent university lecture series have resulted in essay collections on the universities in the Weimar Republic and the Third Reich: *Die Deutsche Universität im Dritten Reich: Eine Vortragsreihe der Universität München* (Munich: R. Piper and Co., 1966); Andreas Flitner, ed., *Deutsche Geistesleben und Nationalsozialismus: Eine Vortragsreihe der Universität Tübingen* (Tübingen: Rainer Wunderlich Verlag, 1965); and *Universitätstage 1966: Nationalsozialismus und die Deutsche Universität* (Berlin: Walter de Gruyter and Co., 1966).

A great deal of literature has been devoted to studies of German students. Friedrich Karl Alfred Schulze and Paul Ssymank, *Das Deutsche Studententum von den ältesten Zeiten bis zur Gegenwart 1931* (Munich: Verlag für Hochschulkunde, 1932) is an exhaustive and entertaining account of German student history. Werner Klose, *Freiheit Schreibt auf Eure Fahnen: 800 Jahre deutsche Studenten* (Oldenburg: Gerhard Stalling Verlag, 1967) is a briefer treatment with greater emphasis upon politics. Wilhelm Bruchmüller, "Das deutsche Studententum von seinen Anfängen bis zur Gegenwart," in *Aus Natur und Geisteswelt: Sammlung wissenschaftlicher verständlicher Darstellungen,* vol. 477 (Leipzig and Berlin: B. G. Teubner, 1922), is less useful. The character of traditional student life is revealed in Theobald Ziegler, *Der deutsche Student,* 11th and 12th revised editions (Berlin and Leipzig: G. J. Goschen'sche Verlagsbuchhandlung, 1912); William Howitt, *The Student Life of Germany* (London: Longmans, Brown, Green, and Longmans, 1841); Hans Heigert, "Romantik und Idealismus, und die Staatsmystik im deutschen Bürgertum: Eine soziologisch-politische Studie über die studentische Bewegung im vergangenen Jahrhundert," unpublished dissertation (Heidelberg, 1949); Bernard Oudin, *Les Corporations Allemandes d'étudiants* (Paris: R. Pichon et R. Durand-Auzias, 1962); and Gordon Bolitho, *The Other Germany* (New York: D. Appleton Century, 1934), the student diary of an Englishman enrolled in the exclusive *Corps* Saxo-Borussia in Heidelberg. Lutz E. Finke's journalistic assault on the contemporary fraternities, *Gestatte mir Hochachtungsschluck: Bundesdeutschlands Korporierte Elite* (Hamburg: Rütten und Loening, 1963) is entertaining but inaccurate and poorly documented.

There is no thorough treatment of the political activities of German students between 1870 and 1918. Brunhild Mayfarth, "Die Stellung der Studentenschaft besonders der Mitteldeutschen Universitäten zu politischen und sozialen Fragen von 1848 bis 1918," unpublished dissertation (Jena, 1957) is limited in approach but nevertheless valuable. The political activities of German students during the Weimar Republic have attracted more attention. Wolfgang Zorn has chronicled the period between 1918 and 1931, concentrating upon the history of the *Deutsche Studentenschaft*, in "Die Politische Entwicklung des deutschen Studententums 1918–31," *Darstellungen und Quellen zur Geschichte der deutschen Einheitsbewegung im neunzehnten und zwanzigsten Jahrhundert*, 5:223–307 (Heidelberg: Carl Winter Universitätsverlag, 1965); and "Die politische Entwicklung des deutschen Studententums, 1924–31," *Ein Leben aus Freier Mitte: Beiträge zur Geschichtsforschung: Festschrift für Prof. Dr. Ulrich Noack* (Göttingen, Berlin, Frankfurt, Zürich: Musterschmidt Verlag, 1963), pp. 296–330. Zorn discusses the problem of student political activity more broadly in "Student Politics in the Weimar Republic," *Journal of Contemporary History* 5, no. 1 (1970): 128–43. Adolf Leisen, "Die Ausbreitung des völkischen Gedankens in der Studentenschaft der Weimarer Republik," unpublished dissertation (Heidelberg, 1964) is valuable for the early period, although his analysis of *völkisch* thought is stronger than his documentation of its spread among the students. Hans Peter Bleuel and Ernst Klinnert, *Deutsche Studenten auf dem Weg ins Dritte Reich* (Gütersloh: Sigbert Mohn, 1967) is a polemical work based almost exclusively upon the periodicals of the *Institut für Hochschulkunde*. Although one-sided, it contains much interesting material. The East German viewpoint is represented by Gerhard Fliess, "Über die Rolle der bürgerlichen Studentenbewegung in der Zeit der Weimarer Republik," *Wissenschaftliche Zeitschrift der Friedrich-Schiller-Universität Jena, Gesellschafts- und Sprachwissenschaftliche Reihe*, 16, no. 2 (1966), whose tortuous logic attempts to prove complicity between the student movement and the interests of the capitalist ruling class. The development of the *Deutsche Studentenschaft* is discussed in legalistic detail by Anton Baak, "Grundlagen, Entwicklung, und Wesen der Organisation der Deutschen Studentenschaft," unpublished dissertation (Münster, 1927), and Hellmut Volkmann, *Die Deutsche Studentenschaft in ihrer Entwicklung seit 1919* (Leipzig: Verlag Quelle und Meyer, 1925). Hermann Gödde, "Die Anfänge der Studentischen Selbstverwaltung mit besonderer Berücksichtigung der Münchener Verhältnisse," unpublished dissertation (Nuremberg, 1951), is most useful for the student social movement and economic aid programs. Manfred Laubig, "Die Studentische Selbstverwaltung in Deutschland: Geschichte ihrer Ideen und Institutionen," unpublished dissertation (Tübingen, 1955), based primarily on published sources, discusses the development and organizational structure of student self-governing institutions. Thomas Nipperdey, "Die deutsche Studentenschaft in den ersten Jahren der Weimarer Republik," *Kulturverwaltung der zwanziger Jahre: Alte Dokumente und neue Beiträge* (Stuttgart: W. Kohlhammer Verlag, c. 1961), pp. 19–48, is a thoughtful essay. The *Deutsche Studentenschaft* in Prussia after 1927 is the subject of Gerhard Bergmann's article, "Die freien preussischen Studentenschaften nach 1927," *Der Convent*, September (1963), pp. 193–202. Two other brief general accounts are Hans Schlömer, "Studentenschaft und Weimarer Republik," *Unitas* 94, no. 12 (December 1954): 11–15; and *ibid.* 95, no. 1 (January 1955): 11–16. See also Harry Pross's chapter devoted to students in *Vor und Nach Hitler: Zur deutschen Sozialpathologie* (Olten and Freiburg im Breisgau: Walter-Verlag, 1962). Jürgen Schwarz's monograph, *Studenten in der Weimarer Republik: Die deutsche Studentenschaft in der Zeit von 1918 bis 1923 und ihre Stellung zur Politik* (Berlin: Duncker and Humblot, 1971) is particularly valuable for the developments in the *Deutsche Studentenschaft* and for its statistical discussion of German students during the early Weimar Republic. Michael H. Kater's *Studentenschaft und Rechtsradikalismus in Deutschland, 1918–1933* (Hamburg: Hoffmann and Kampe, 1975) offers a valuable analysis of student social conditions and of National Socialism during the Weimar period. Wolfgang Kreutzberger's study of the students at the University of Freiburg *(Studenten und Politik, 1918–1933: Der Fall Freiburg im Breisgau* [Göttingen: Vandenhoeck and Ruprecht, 1972]) adopts a neo-Marxist approach which incorporates suggestive comparisons with contemporary student movements. Anselm Faust's unpublished dissertation about the National Socialist German Student Union between 1929 and 1933 ("Der Nationalsozialistische Deutsche Studentenbund: Studenten und Nationalsozialismus in der Weimarer Republik," Düsseldorf: 1973) was unavailable to this author. The problems of the women students are discussed by Michael H. Kater, "Krisis des Frauenstudiums in der Weimarer Republik," *Vierteljahrschrift für Sozial- und Wirtschaftsgeschichte* 59, no. 2 (1972): 207–55.

There are several useful studies of student affairs at individual universities. J. H. Mitgau, *Studentische Demokratie: Beiträge zur Neueren Geschichte der Heidelberger Studentenschaft* (Heidelberg: J. Horning, 1927) attempts to analyze why student democracy failed at Heidelberg. Emil Popp, "Zur Geschichte des Königsberger Studentums, 1900–1945," Beihefte zum Jahrbuch der Albertus-Universität Königsberg/Pr. (Würzburg: Holzner Verlag, 1955) is a nationalist account based primarily on published sources and somewhat inaccurate. Ludwig Franz, "Der politische Kampf an den Münchener Hochschulen von 1929–1933 im Spiegel der Presse," unpublished dissertation (Munich, 1949) is based entirely upon newspapers and early accounts of events. Franz's extensive quotations from newspapers and speeches are nevertheless a useful source, particularly for the Nawiasky affair. The Dehn affair is retold in detail by Werner Prokoph, "Die politische Seite des 'Falles Dehn': Zum Faschisierungsprozess an der Universität Halle-Wittenberg in den Jahren 1931 bis 1933," *Martin-Luther-Universität Halle-Wittenberg, 1817 bis 1967: Festschrift anlässlich des 150. Jahrestages der Vereinigung der Universitäten Wittenberg und Halle, Wissenschaftliche Zeitschrift der Martin-Luther-Universität Halle-Wittenberg, Gesellschafts- und Sprachwissenschaftliche* Reihe 16, nos. 2 and 3 (1967): 249–72. Hans Ochsenius, "Die Studentenschaft der Hansischen Universität zu Hamburg bis 1939 unter besonderer Berücksichtigung der gesamten studentischen Entwicklung im Altreich," unpublished dissertation (Hamburg 1941) reflects the politics of the date at which it was written and is most valuable for its history of the NSDStB after 1933. The Rostock constitution controversy is explored in Ruth Carlsen, "Der Kampf um die Verfassung der Rostocker Studentenschaft 1932/33," *Wissenschaftliche Zeitschrift der Universität Rostock, Gesellschafts- und Sprachwissenschaftliche Reihe* 13, nos. 2 and 3 (1964): 251–69. Student politics at the Technical Institute in Braunschweig are treated by Ernst-August Roloff, *Bürgertum und Nationalsozialismus: Braunschweig's Weg ins Dritte Reich, 1930–33* (Hanover: Verlag für Literatur und Zeitgeschichte, 1961).

Many other student-related subjects have also interested historians. Among such works are Georg Heer, "Geschichte der Deutschen Burschenschaft," part 4, *Quellen und Darstellungen zur Geschichte der Burschenschaft und der deutschen Einheitsbewegung*, vol. 16 (Heidelberg: Carl Winter's Universitätsbuchhandlung, 1939); Horst Bernhardi, "Die Göttinger Burschenschaft 1933 bis 1945," *Darstellungen und Quellen zur Geschichte der deutschen Einheitsbewegung im neunzehnten und zwanzigsten Jahrhundert* (Heidelberg: Carl Winter Universitätsverlag, 1957); *Deutsches Studentenwerk: Festschrift zum vierzigjährigen Bestehen 1921–1961* (Bonn: Deutsches Studentenwerk, 1961); Albrecht Götz von Olenhusen, "Die 'Nichtarischen' Studenten an den Deutschen Hochschulen: Zur nationalsozialistischen Rassenpolitik, 1933–45," *Vierteljahrshefte für Zeitgeschichte* 14, no. 2 (April 1966): 175–206; Hans Schlömer, "Die Auflösung der Korporationsverbände," *Unitas* 100, no. 11 (November 1960): 200–13; and Hans Wolfgang Strätz, "Die studentische Aktion wider den undeutschen Geist im Frühjahr 1933," *Vierteljahrshefte für Zeitgeschichte* 16, no. 4 (October 1968): 347–72. For Austrian student affairs, Erich Witzmann, "Der Anteil der Wiener Waffenstudentischen Verbindungen an der völkischen und politischen Entwicklung, 1918–38," unpublished dissertation (Vienna, 1940) is a detailed guide. The German students in Prague during the 1920s and 1930s are discussed at length by Wolfram von Wolmar, *Prag und das Reich: 600 Jahre Kampf deutscher Studenten* (Dresden: Franz Müller, 1943). Anti-Semitism is explored in the student community by George L. Mosse, "Die deutsche Rechte und die Juden," in Werner E. Mosse, *Entscheidungsjahr 1932: Zur Judenfrage in der Endphase der Weimarer Republik* (Tübingen: J. C. B. Mohr/ Paul Siebeck, 1965); Oskar F. Scheuer, *Burschenschaft und Judenfrage: Der Rassenantisemitismus in der deutschen Studentenschaft* (Berlin, Vienna: Verlag Berlin-Wien, 1927); and for the period before 1918 by Peter Pulzer, *The Rise of Political Anti-Semitism in Germany and Austria* (New York, London, Sydney: John Wiley and Sons, 1964). The work-service program is discussed by Frieda Wunderlich, *Farm Labor in Germany 1810–1945* (Princeton: Princeton University Press, 1961); and Wolfgang Benz, "Vom freiwilligen Arbeitsdienst zur Arbeitsdienstpflicht," *Vierteljahrshefte für Zeitgeschichte* 16, no. 4 (October 1968): 317–46.

The literature relating to the history of the Weimar Republic is vast. The best survey is Erich Eyck, *A History of the Weimar Republic*, 2 vols., translated by H. P. Hanson and R. G. L. Waite (Cambridge and Oxford: Oxford University

Press, 1962 and 1964). Mention should also be made of Arthur Rosenberg, *History of the German Republic* (London: Methuen, 1936); and *Der Weg in die Diktatur, 1918 bis 1933* (Munich: R. Piper, 1963), a collection of thoughtful essays by contemporary German historians. For the last years of the Republic and the Nazi takeover, the indispensable guides are Karl Dietrich Bracher, *Die Auflösung der Weimarer Republik* (Villingen: Ring Verlag, 1964) and Karl Dietrich Bracher, Wolfgang Sauer, Gerhard Schulz, *Die nationalsozialistische Machtergreifung* (Cologne and Opladen: Westdeutscher Verlag, 1960). Two suggestive works which touch on the social background are Karl Mannheim, *Man and Society in an Age of Reconstruction: Studies in Modern Social Structure* (London: K. Paul, Trench, Trubner and Co., 1940); and Ralf Dahrendorf, *Gesellschaft und Demokratie in Deutschland* (Munich: R. Piper and Co., 1965).

The Youth Movement is best studied in Walter Z. Laqueur, *Young Germany* (New York: Basic Books, 1962); and Felix Raabe, *Die bündische Jugend* (Stuttgart; Brentanoverlag, 1961). A catalogue of Youth Movement groups is included in Günther Ehrenthal, *Die deutschen Jugendbünde: Ein Handbuch ihrer Organisation und ihrer Bestrebungen* (Berlin: Zentral–Verlag, 1929). The best book on the subject of the free corps is Robert G. L. Waite, *Vanguard of Nazism: The Free Corps Movement in Post-war Germany* (Cambridge: Harvard University Press, 1952). The *Stahlhelm* and the *Jungdeutsche Orden* have been treated in two detailed monographs: V. R. Berghahn, *Der Stahlhelm: Bund der Frontsoldaten* (Düsseldorf: Droste, 1966); and Klaus Hornung, *Der Jungdeutsche Orden* (Düsseldorf: Droste, 1958).

German right-wing thought has aroused considerable interest. George L. Mosse, *The Crisis of German Ideology* (New York: Grosset and Dunlap, 1964) is a flawed but nevertheless helpful introduction to *völkisch* thought. Armin Mohler, *Die Konservative Revolution in Deutschland, 1918–1936* (Stuttgart: Friedrich Vorwerk Verlag, 1950) is a detailed guide to the right wing in the German Republic. The Young Conservatives are best studied in Kurt Sontheimer, *Antidemokratisches Denken in der Weimarer Republik* (Munich: Nymphenburger Verlag, 1962); and Klemens von Klemperer, *Germany's New Conservatism* (Princeton: Princeton University Press, 1957). Arthur Moeller van den Bruck and his circle are discussed in Hans-Joachim Schwierskott, *Arthur Moeller van den Bruck und der revolutionäre Nationalismus in der Weimarer Republik* (Göttingen, Berlin, Frankfurt: Musterschmidt Verlag, 1962); and Fritz Stern, *The Politics of Cultural Despair* (Berkeley: University of California Press, 1961).

Finally, three recent studies of student politics should be mentioned. Seymour Martin Lipset, ed., *Student Politics* (New York, London: Basic Books, 1967) and Seymour Martin Lipset and Phillip G. Altbach, eds., *Students in Revolt* (Boston: Beacon, 1970) include several suggestive essays. Lewis Feuer, *The Conflict of Generations* (New York, London: Basic Books, 1969) is subjective and excessively psychoanalytical, but provocative.

INDEX

233